**75TH
ART DIRECTORS
ANNUAL**

Editor
Antje Lenthe-Arcia

Hall of Fame Editor
Myrna Davis

Design Format
Cara Galowitz

Production/Graphic Design
Jane Dekrone

Production Liaison
Fiona L'Estrange

Copy Editor
Jennifer Knox White

Jacket Design
Jacqueline Thaw, Kirshenbaum Bond & Partners

Exhibition Director
Luis De Jesus

Published and distributed by
RotoVision SA
7 rue du Bugnon
1299 Crans
Switzerland

RotoVision SA Sales Office
Sheridan House
112/116A Western Road
Hove, West Sussex BN3 1DD
England
Tel: +44 1273 72 72 68
Fax: +44 1273 72 72 69

The Art Directors Club, Inc.
250 Park Avenue South,
New York, New York 10003-1402,
U.S.A.

RotoVision SA ISBN: *2-88046-274-6*
Watson Guptill ISBN: 0-8230-6550-2

Distribution in the United States by
Watson Guptill Publications
1515 Broadway,
New York, New York 10036,
U.S.A.

Production and color separation in Singapore by
Provision Pte Ltd
Tel: (65) 334-7720
Fax: (65) 334-7721

Printed in Singapore

TABLE OF CONTENTS

Pro bono.

Everyone talks about the lack of time in our lives. We have work, we have chores, we have family obligations. We never seem to have enough time for ourselves.

And yet every year the Art Directors Club asks the busiest people in our business to give up what remains of their free time, to come to New York and to work long hours at judging this exhibition—their only reward being an unpretentious listing as one of the year's judges.

And every year, remarkably, they come, and they work diligently.

There is something special, something exceptional, about being a part of this almost century-old tradition of choosing the best work of the year. That work, as preserved in this Annual, becomes the historical record of our chosen vocation, the source and reference used by curators and historians. These judges assemble the pieces.

We owe them our gratitude for their assiduous service: they have performed jury duty for the profession we love.

—Carl Fischer
President, The Art Directors Club

HALL OF FAME

HALL OF FAME MEMBERS

1972

M. F. Agha
Lester Beall
Alexey Brodovitch
A. M. Cassandre
René Clark
Robert Gage
William Golden
Paul Rand

1973

Charles Coiner
Paul Smith
Jack Tinker

1974

Will Burtin
Leo Lionni

1975

Gordon Aymar
Herbert Bayer
Cipes Pineles Burtin
Heyworth Campbell
Alexander Liberman
L. Moholy-Nagy

1976

E. McKnight Kauffer
Herbert Matter

1977

Saul Bass
Herb Lubalin
Bradbury Thompson

1978

Thomas M. Cleland
Lou Dorfsman
Allen Hurlburt
George Lois

1979

W. A. Dwiggins
George Giusti
Milton Glaser
Helmut Krone
Willem Sandberg
Ladislav Sutnar
Jan Tschichold

1980

Gene Federico
Otto Storch
Henry Wolf

1981

Lucian Bernhard
Ivan Chermayeff
Gyorgy Kepes
George Krikorian
William Taubin

1982

Richard Avedon
Amil Gargano
Jerome Snyder
Massimo Vignelli

1983

Aaron Burns
Seymour Chwast
Steve Frankfurt

1984

Charles Eames
Wallace Elton
Sam Scali
Louis Silverstein

1985

Art Kane
Len Sirowitz
Charles Tudor

1986

Walt Disney
Roy Grace
Alvin Lustig
Arthur Paul

1987

Willy Fleckhaus
Shigeo Fukuda
Steve Horn
Tony Palladino

1988

Ben Shahn
Bert Steinhauser
Mike Tesch

1989

Rudolph deHarak
Raymond Loewy

1990

Lee Clow
Reba Sochis
Frank Zachary

1991

Bea Feitler
Bob Gill
Bob Giraldi
Richard Hess

1992

Eiko Ishioka
Rick Levine
Onofrio Paccione
Gordon Parks

1993

Leo Burnett
Yusaku Kamekura
Robert Wilvers
Howard Zieff

1994

Alan Fletcher
Norman Rockwell
Rochelle Udell
Andy Warhol

1995

Robert Brownjohn
Paul Davis
Roy Kuhlman
Jay Maisel

1996

Bill McCaffery
Erik Nitsche
Arnold Varga
Fred Woodward

Induction into the Art Directors Hall of Fame is the most prestigious award our profession can bestow. The inductees are chosen by a Hall of Fame Selection Committee elected by our club membership.

Those of you who have never had the honor of serving on this committee might be curious as to how it goes about choosing the laureates. It isn't easy. Imagine R. O. Blechman, Lou Dorfsman, Carl Fischer, Milton Glaser, George Lois, Ruth Lubell, Paul Rand, Richard Wilde, Henry Wolf, and myself all in the same room at the same time. Now imagine us agreeing on something. Anything. The task is surmountable only because the members of the committee have come to the meeting prepared. They have the names of people they want to champion, and they have brought samples of their work to show us. David Epstein wrote us a letter recommending someone he felt was deserving. We invite David to the meeting to lobby his cause. He does an effective job. As the nominees' achievements are discussed, the decisions begin to crystallize. Arnold Varga, Bill McCaffery, Erik Nitsche, and Fred Woodward are chosen. In addition, it is decided to give a Special Educator's Award to Steven Heller.

A sincere thank you to my committee members, and congratulations to our newest Hall of Fame laureates.

—Ed Brodsky
Chairperson, Hall of Fame Selection Committee

Bill McCaffery's plan after graduating from the University of Pennsylvania and the Philadelphia College of Art in 1958 was not to embark on an illustrious career in advertising, but to go to New York and spend his time creating art, designing, and playing the saxophone.

He was happily free-lancing as an illustrator for Esquire and as a designer for McGraw-Hill and Harper & Row, and working on myriad other projects, when he was offered an illustration job at Grey Advertising. Looking over the assignment, he ventured to comment on what he thought was wrong with it. Instead of an argument, he was given the opportunity to redesign the entire ad; the next thing he knew, he was a full-time art director.

This beginning typifies the career McCaffery went on to have. A Renaissance man, he does whatever needs to be done, and does it right. His colleague Rudolph deHarak says of Bill, "When there isn't the time, or sometimes when the solution to the problem is too personal to relate to others, he might write the copy himself, take the photograph, design the ad, or execute the finished art."

The newest art director at Grey, McCaffery had no book and no practical experience but plenty of ideas. When handed a job order containing copy and a rough sketch from a copywriter with whom he'd spent no time, he inquired if this were proper procedure. Upon hearing it was, he headed upstairs to the executive suite to explain that the best way to foster the creative process was to bring the copywriter and art director together. The rest is history.

After making his mark as an art director, McCaffery moved to McCann-Marschalk, and then, at the tender age of 27, he joined the agency that would become deGarmo, McCaffery. Eventually, he was invited to try out the corporate world as vice-president and creative head of Norton Simon, Inc. "When I joined Norton Simon, I thought I knew just about everything there was to know about advertising," McCaffery says. But here, reviewing all the advertising for this multibillion-dollar corporation, he learned what it was like to be the client sitting on the other side of the presentation board. With this new knowledge under his belt, McCaffery moved on to Revlon, where, as usual, he started a trend: the first cosmetics campaign to be fashioned around the idea of location as lifestyle was McCaffery's for Ultima II's Bordeaux collection. McCaffery's campaign created such a sensation that department stores expanded on the theme, decorating everything from their windows to inside the entire store.

After leaving Revlon, McCaffery started his own agency, which eventually merged and became McCaffery & Ratner. Here, he made use of the understanding of both sides of the advertising world he had gained from his previous experiences: "When a client hires an agency," he says, "he's really taking on a partner. They both should have the willingness to grow together, to trust one another."

McCaffery has lived much of his life outside of advertising, hanging out with artists and designers such as Andy Warhol, Larry Rivers, Shelia McCaffery, R. O. Blechman, and Robert Motherwell and musicians like Chico Hamilton and Ben Webster. His mind is always working on some creative, informative concept. "He thinks very quickly and ahead of what he is talking about," observes deHarak. In his correspondence with Richard Wurman between 1967 and 1971, McCaffery worked on ideas to make flying time more entertaining. He proposed a series of destination films highlighting major cities around the world, to convey "the way people are in their own habitat . . . the cities we visit are people, not just monuments, museums, and restaurants." This correspondence resulted in the film City/2 ("city over two"), which was shown at the Philadelphia

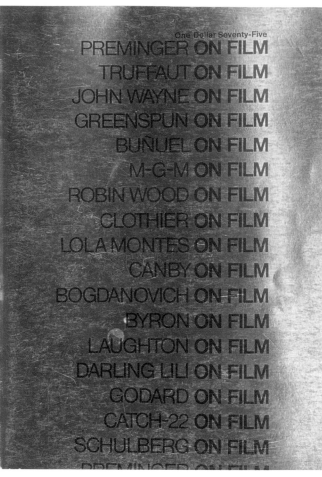

It was six in the morning when we left our hotel. That would be early enough anywhere, but in a sensible country like Ireland it might just as well have been in the middle of the night. Everybody was still asleep. We hadn't wanted to get anyone out of their beds, so the night before we had decided to have breakfast along the way.

It was a fine morning as we drove along the coast road. As they say in that part of Ireland, "It was so clear you could nearly see New York."

It wasn't until an hour or so later, coming into a tiny village, that we met our first traveler of the day; a boy wheeling a bicycle, a big grin on his face.

When we asked him where we could buy ourselves some breakfast he said, "Well, you could go all the way down to the cafe in the village, only it's not open. Or you could come up to my mother's. She runs a guest house. It's just a bit up the road."

If it was that near we thought, we'd leave the car and walk. So off we set, with him smiling away, pushing the bike.

He was still smiling a mile or so later when we followed him through two whitewashed gateposts, along a path through a field and up to a farmhouse door. As he said, it was a bit up the road.

His mother opened the door. "Good morning." she said. We asked her about breakfast. "Of course." she said. "Won't you come in?"

The breakfast that followed was a breakfast we should all have once in our lives. Fat little Irish farm sausages. Bacon that tasted the way bacon did before they started rearing pigs in factories. A loaf of sweet-tasting soda bread as big as a curling stone. Tea strong enough to bend a teaspoon. Eggs and scones and good farm butter, honey, and freshly-made jam.

The cost was three shillings and sixpence. In our language, fifty cents.

It was worth the walk.

IRELAND IRISH TOURIST BOARD

Museum of Art in conjunction with an exhibit of the same name. The 12-minute film records the city from sunrise to sunset, or, as McCaffery describes it, "a day in the life of the city—on, above, and below."

Even if a city is more than just its restaurants, McCaffery knows the importance of those restaurants nonetheless. He has designed the decor, graphics, and advertising for some of the best places to eat in New York, including the Rainbow Room and Rainbow Grill, Gallagher's 33, and L'Etoile. His campaign for Windows on the World, "Confessions of a Jaded New Yorker," which depicted the downtown skyline as a Rorschach inkblot, put the restaurant's name on everyone's lips.

In 1972, McCaffery created the Art Directors Club exhibit Making New York Understandable, in which ADC members and other designers, writers, filmmakers, architects, and planners contributed a variety of materials—including models, photos, films, books, and maps—related to McCaffery's idea: "The decay of the city increases as it becomes less understandable to its citizens," he explained.

Other of McCaffery's high-profile projects include the IMAX film An American Adventure, with Dennis Weaver, which McCaffery wrote and directed; and the award-winning critical magazine On Film, which he founded, designed, and edited. His published books include How to Watch a Parade (Harper) and Noses Are for Roses (McGraw-Hill).

McCaffery's greatness as a visual communicator, deHarak has observed, "lies in his ability to weave his words and images into a broad tapestry of ideas that speaks out with force and continuity to mass audiences." After almost 40 years of experience in advertising, McCaffrey hasn't been seduced by the onslaught of mechanical gadgetry available today. To him, quality work still comes from pure thought. He says, "Advertising changes only in terms of the tools we use to execute it. The essential challenge is still the same: to solve a marketing problem starting with a blank piece of paper and, eventually, an idea that no one has had before."

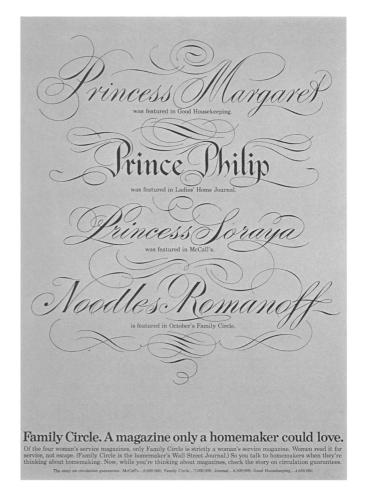

The genius of Erik Nitsche encompasses virtually the entire sphere of visual communications. "I would put him on the top-ten list of the best 20th-century designers in the world," said Michael Aron, graphic artist and professor at the Parsons School of Design. Nitsche's prodigious and globe-straddling career, spanning nearly 60 years, has included art direction, book design, typography, illustration, photography, film, signage, exhibits, packaging, industrial design, corporate design, and advertising.

If Nitsche's name is unfamiliar to some who pride themselves on being knowledgeable about the history of graphic design, this can only be attributed to Nitsche's reluctance to court publicity and to his belief that his work should speak for itself. In an essay about the designer in the late 1950s, P. K. Thomajan wrote, "Self-effacement, {Nitsche} finds, keeps the blighting shadow of the ego out of one's work."

Born in Lausanne, Switzerland, in 1908, Nitsche studied at the Collège Classique of Lausanne and the Kunstgewerbeschule in Munich, and is fluent in French, German, and English. In the early 1930s, he designed covers for such avant-garde publications as Simplicissimus, Jugend, and Der Querschnitt, a multilingual cultural journal that inspired an American publication, Ricochet. Emigrating to the United States in 1934, Nitsche headed for Hollywood, then a small town, quickly developing friendships with such creative professionals as composer Frederic Holländer, Marlene Dietrich, and MGM special-effects director Slavko Vorkapich. In 1936, Nitsche moved to New York, where he began producing illustrations and covers for many major American magazines, including Life, Look, Harpers Bazaar, Town and Country, Fortune, House and Garden, and Vanity Fair.

Keeping a hand in the cinema, Nitsche was responsible for developing memorable advertising and promotional campaigns for Twentieth Century Fox's All About Eve and No Way Out, and The Egg and I, The Imposter, and others for Universal. In the late 1940s, Nitsche created a stunning newspaper campaign for Ohrbach's that gave the off-price New York department store unexpected uptown cachet. He designed subway posters for the New York Transit Authority, redesigned the corporate image for Filene's of Boston, produced catalogues and over 200 classical-album covers for Decca Records, and won a gold medal from the Art Directors Club for his engaging ad campaign in The New Yorker for the Broadway production of The Respectful Prostitute. Any disappointment he felt about not having attended the Bauhaus was assuaged when he heard that László Moholy-Nagy had asked, "Who is this guy doing the Bauhaus in New York?"

Around 1945, Nitsche moved to Pound Ridge, New York, and began commuting between the city and the country. In 1947, he followed Herbert Bayer as art director and vice-president in charge of design at Dorland International in New York, a cosmopolitan advertising agency with branches in several major European cities. But after two successful years there and a brief stint as art director of Mademoiselle, he realized that conventional office life was not for him. Acquiring an old Victorian mansion in Ridgefield, Connecticut, Nitsche updated it with "thrusting terraces, cantilevered porches," and a Plexiglas rooftop bubble over a high-gabled studio where he could work. He became a consultant to Standard Oil of New Jersey, designing books, brochures, and international advertising, as well as taking on special projects. He also became a design and type consultant to New York's Museum of Modern Art, and designed a series of award-winning advertisements for Container Corporation of America.

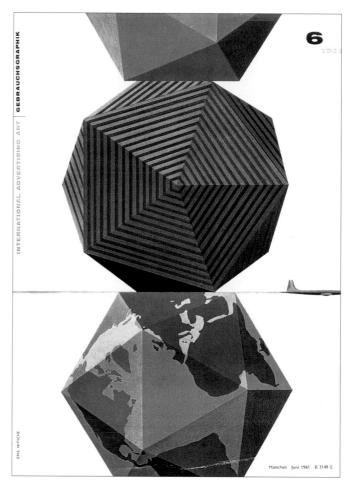

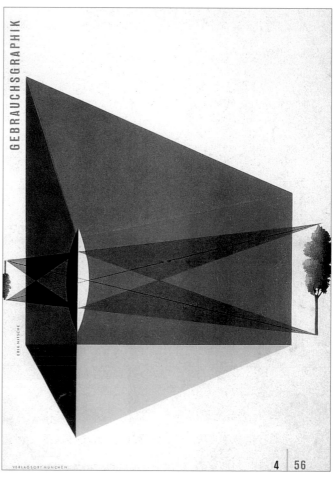

It is evident in all mankind that reason is a peculiar property of our nature, which distinguishes us from the brute animals, as sense constitutes the difference between them and things inanimate. For whereas some are born fools and idiots, that defect obscures not the general goodness of GOD.

John Calvin on man's reason

(Institutes of the Christian Religion, 1535)

Artist: ERIK NITSCHE

CONTAINER CORPORATION OF AMERICA

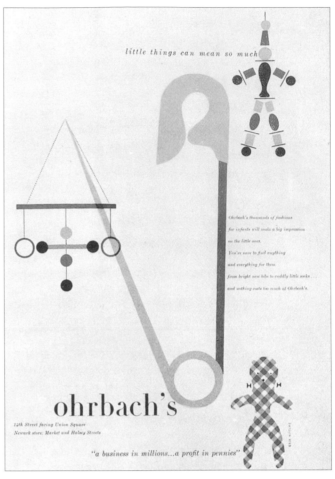

little things can mean so much

Ohrbach's thousands of fashions for infants will make a big impression on the little ones. You're sure to feel anything and everything for them from bright new bibs to cuddly little socks... and nothing costs too much at Ohrbach's.

ohrbach's

14th Street facing Union Square
Newark store: Market and Halsey Streets

"a business in millions...a profit in pennies"

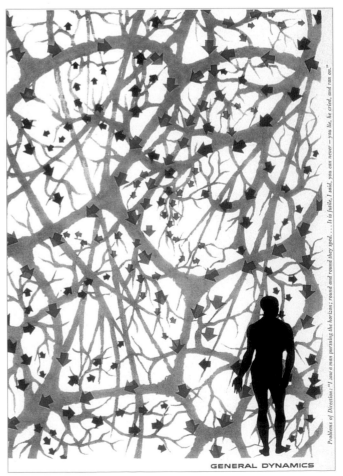

GENERAL DYNAMICS

Problems of Direction: "I am a man pursuing the horizon; round and round they sped. . . . It is futile, I said, you can never — you lie, he cried, and ran on."

Nitsche's historic relationship with General Dynamics began in 1953, when he started working on the General Dynamics account while at Gotham Advertising, a small Madison Avenue agency. Both Nitsche and General Dynamics president John Jay Hopkins felt constrained by the customary agency situation, however. The company was expanding rapidly, gearing itself for both defense and civilian needs, and in the spring of 1955, Hopkins summoned Nitsche to create, with only a few months' notice, an exhibit for the International Conference on the Peaceful Uses of Atomic Energy in Geneva. Nitsche had to create an exhibit that would do justice to the company without revealing anything specific, as its work on the first atomic submarine, the Nautilus, was still secret. Nitsche met the challenge, designing an exquisite lithographic series of six symbolic "Atoms for Peace" posters, each in a different language. Printed in Switzerland, they had an impact around the world. Appointed art director of General Dynamics, Nitsche went on to design two more series of posters, in 1958 and 1960, as well as the company's corporate image, its annual reports and advertising, and, ultimately, a 420-page book of its corporate history, Dynamic America, which was published by Doubleday. The book's dense and richly imagined layout was so inspirational to publication designer Walter Bernard when he arrived in New York about the time it appeared that he would later acknowledge it as "the single most important influence on my work."

"I'm working with fantasy," Nitsche told an interviewer, "with an idealistic image of the future, in which we are more or less involved." The image, he explained, must above all be clearly stated. "I do not want to be obscure. You know, one might easily get carried away by the science-fiction temptation of this subject matter. What I am concerned to do is establish it with a certain classicism. I would hate to have to apologize for a design, to have people puzzle and ask, 'What is it?'"

Nitsche, who describes himself and his wife Renate as "nomads," moved back to Geneva in the early 1960s. There, after founding ENI (Erik Nitsche International), S.A., he designed and researched the 12-volume Science and Technology, of which over two million copies were printed worldwide, and then the 20-volume A History of Music, which was published in three languages. From 1965 to 1980, Nitsche lived in Paris, working on special projects for Hachette, including researching and designing the vast L'Epopée Mondiale d'un Siècle, a five-volume encyclopedia about the last 100 years, with over 2,000 color illustrations; he also painstakingly created the Info-card and Info-map systems, which are as yet unproduced. Nitsche spent the next decade and more in Munich, designing postage stamps for the German Ministry of Communications, and at the same time creating more than 300 Philatelic First Day Covers for the Unicover Corporation in Cheyenne, Wyoming. He returned to the United States in 1996.

In commenting on Nitsche's book design, Steven Heller could be summing up the designer's entire body of work and the strengths that reveal themselves throughout when he says, "There is a simplicity and elegance . . . that brings together a lot of complex information and allows it to be absorbed without being reduced. . . . Much of his work prefigures what is happening today—conceits of layering, a marriage of abstract and real." But even when organizing great masses of material, Heller notes, "Nitsche leaves nothing cold. He is a complete humanist."

Arnold Varga approached advertising as a personal art form. In spite of the fact that he had almost no serious art training and conducted almost all of his professional life within a few miles of his hometown, McKeesport, Pennsylvania, Varga gained international recognition and was honored with eleven gold medals from the Art Directors Club of New York. Photographer Duane Michals, a childhood friend, says with some wonder, "He worked in this little steel town, without any real nurturing, and he bloomed into a major talent. He made it happen on his own energy." Unknown to most, a further obstacle that Varga had to overcome was near blindness in one eye and poor vision in the other.

The second of three sons, Varga was born to Hungarian immigrants who had little schooling. His father, Sigmund Wargo (Varga adopted the spelling closest to the original pronunciation of "Wargo" for his professional name), worked in the local steel mill, but he died when Arnold was ten years old. His mother, Julia, had artistic leanings, expressing them in the decoration of her home and encouragement of her children. Robert, Arnold's elder brother by four years, was the designated family artist, though he earned his living at the mill until he was killed in an accident there at 24. Varga first drew attention from his grade-school teachers when, at the age of 12, he executed a clay bust of Abraham Lincoln. This led the McKeesport Optimist Club to sponsor him for Saturday art instruction at the Carnegie Institute of Technology (now Carnegie-Mellon University). Varga also attended summer art sessions there, as the only child in the class. "I was the big joke of the department," he once commented. In 1945, following his graduation from McKeesport High School, where he somehow flunked art, Varga took a six-month course at the Art Institute of Pittsburgh. These experiences are the sum of his formal art education.

At 18, Varga began free-lancing for Cox's department store in McKeesport. He went in one afternoon to show some drawings to the owner, Robert Cox, and was sent home with an armful of black dresses to sketch for the next day's newspaper ads. (Varga pressed his younger brother, Art, into service as his model for this job.) He would also walk into local shoe stores, usually coming out with some illustration assignments. Commuting to Pittsburgh, Arnold started as a messenger for the Joseph Horne Company, but quickly worked his way into its advertising department. By the early 1950s, the Sterling Linder Davis store lured him to Cleveland, Ohio, 150 miles from home, to head their advertising department. Devoted to his mother, Arnold returned home in 1953 when the Korean War drew Art into the army. There, he was invited to join the Pittsburgh branch of Ketchum, MacLeod & Grove, Inc., as creative art supervisor, working on various national accounts, among them Alcoa, Talon Zipper, and Rubbermaid. Varga later moved to BBDO in Pittsburgh, where he did ads for U.S. Steel.

In 1959, the National Society of Art Directors named Varga Art Director of the Year, having previously bestowed its "golden T-square" on such greats as Saul Bass, Charles Coiner, Walt Disney, Leo Lionni, and Bradbury Thompson. That same year, the Pittsburgh Jaycees chose him as Man of the Year in Art, and Varga's work was featured in a solo exhibition at the Carnegie Institute of Fine Arts, the first time commercial ads were shown there. He was also represented in a show at the Museum of Modern Art in New York.

During the late 1950s, Varga began doing some remarkable free-lance work for several department stores, including Horne, Cox's, John Wanamaker, and Highbee's, frequently collaborating with

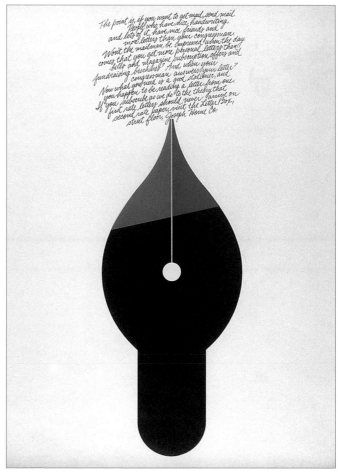

art direction

THE MAGAZINE OF CREATIVE ADVERTISING   JANUARY, 1960 $1.

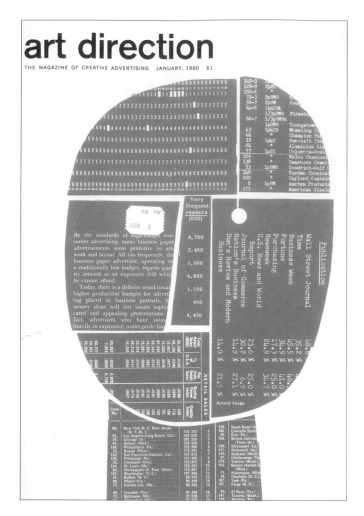

GO AHEAD! HAVE YOURSELF A COLOR FLING. COX'S DID. AND IT WAS FUN...COLLECTING

SPRING FASHIONS FOR YOU THAT WILL SEND YOUR SPIRITS SOARING! SOFT PINKS AND

SHOCKING PINKS! SERENE BLUES, EXCITING BLUES! COOL GREENS, DANGEROUS GREENS!

THEY'RE ALL HERE IN THE MOST PROVOCATIVE COLOR DRAMA COX'S HAS EVER STAGED.

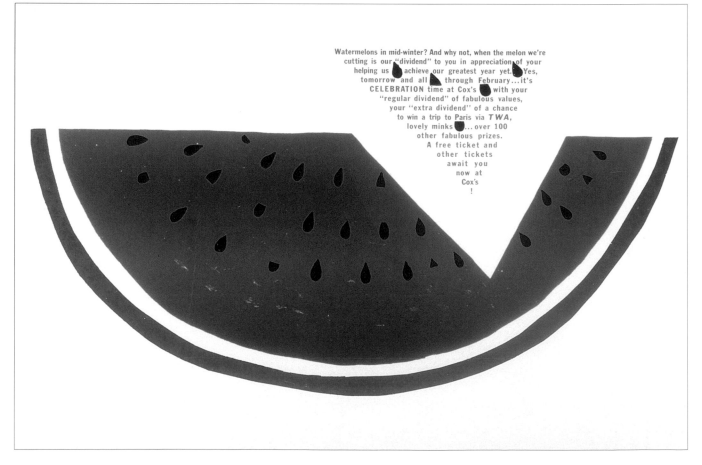

Watermelons in mid-winter? And why not, when the melon we're
cutting is our "dividend" to you in appreciation of your
helping us achieve our greatest year yet. Yes,
tomorrow and all through February...it's
CELEBRATION time at Cox's with your
"regular dividend" of fabulous values,
your "extra dividend" of a chance
to win a trip to Paris via *TWA*,
lovely minks...over 100
other fabulous prizes.
A free ticket and
other tickets
await you
now at
Cox's
!

copywriter Alan Van Dine, whom he knew from BBDO. Van Dine describes Varga's unusual process: "It was completely backwards. Arnold would say 'I want to do a watermelon.' Or 'a baby carriage.' He once wanted to do a box of matches. . . . My job was to come up with something lively to connect the visual. We didn't know at that point which client was going to see it." Sometimes Varga would go into seclusion and Van Dine wouldn't hear from him for a long time. "Then I'd find an envelope of sketches at my door for me to respond to. If I couldn't respond, I'm sure he'd have found another writer." Their distinctive ads, which were not at all about selling merchandise, appealed to these stores' sophisticated customers. "A lot of the ads were very funny, and some were really paintings," Van Dine says. "I would try to write something very trenchant and stay out of the way of it."

In 1967, in response to an assignment to create Horne's annual Christmas newspaper ad, Varga created a caricature of Scrooge that so captured the public imagination, the store was compelled to reprint it for sale as posters, postcards, and Christmas cards. He also designed greeting cards for the American Artist Group, many of which continue to sell. "His work seems to persist in the memory," observes Milton Glaser, marveling at how clearly he can remember Varga's "impeccably rendered and beautiful" images. "One of the main tests of these things is their durability, and they are still very fresh, very innovative."

Darwin Bahm, the designer's New York agent in the late 1960s and early 1970s, said that Varga would turn down big money in favor of a job that paid practically nothing if he thought that he could do something with it. When the Wargo family moved to Pleasant Hills, a suburb of Pittsburgh, Arnold ran a one-man agency from home, doing projects for Kodak, John Wanamaker, Sterling Drug, and other mainstream clients until retiring in the late 1970s. He continued to look after his mother until her death at 93. Varga died in 1994.

Glaser notes that Arnold Varga remained singularly obsessed by his chosen field. The philosophy of this modest, big-boned man never varied from the answer he gave to an interviewer who asked him, at the height of his career, what set him apart from so many other artists who did not achieve his success. Varga chose to describe, in typical understatement, what he thought made an advertisement good: "It's informative. It's honest. It doesn't hurt the eye when you look at it."

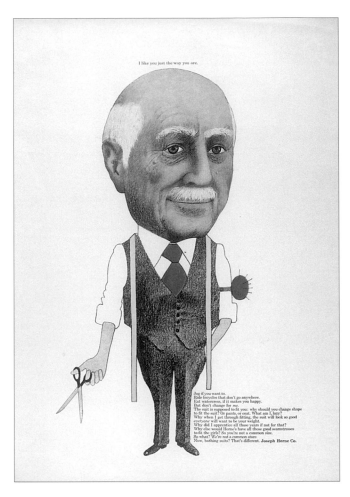

Haunted by the ghost of Christmas presents? Brighten your spirits at Horne's.

A select group of magazine editors, designers, and other denizens of publishing's late hours will remember Fred Woodward this way: sitting in his darkened office, staring silently at the raw materials of his trade—an image, a headline—and waiting. Andie Zellman, an editor who worked with him in the early 1980s at Westward *magazine, described the state as "Fred's art trance." Robert Wallace, senior story editor of* Primetime Live *and former executive editor of* Rolling Stone *for seven years, calls Woodward's creative process "a world where Everests become 'A's and innertubes become 'O's and maybe only John Coltrane and Ornette Coleman can really understand what he's trying to do." To those who've observed him at work, he appears to be, in the words of Leonard Cohen, "waiting for the miracle," the inspiration that will produce a page architecture that unites font, photography, design, and journalism into a creation more powerful and sublime than each of its parts.*

As the art director of Rolling Stone, *Woodward has, in nine years, on a twice-monthly deadline, compiled a body of work that has redefined the possibilities of editorial design. In the process, he has driven himself to become, in the estimation of Paul Davis, "one of the best magazine art directors of all time." Woodward's* Rolling Stone *has garnered more awards than any other magazine in the U.S. and has hastened his entrance into the Art Directors Hall of Fame as the youngest inductee to date.*

Woodward's arrival at the Fifth Avenue offices of Rolling Stone *in 1987 was the natural culmination of a life journey begun in Noxapater, Mississippi (pop. 500), in 1953. As a student at Noxapater High (where he made all-conference quarterback), he found himself attracted to graphic design before he'd ever heard the term. Music provided the gateway. At 17, he was mesmerized by the cover of Crosby, Stills, Nash & Young's* Déju Vu. *"Gold-leaf type, the cover embossed like leather, a tip-on picture—the materials were so rich, I was fascinated," Woodward says. During high school, he likewise took note of a three-year-old music magazine based in San Francisco and spent hours copying his first name in the psychedelic style of the logo. At Mississippi State University and later Memphis State, Woodward switched majors from journalism to physical education to political science before settling on the graphic arts. He had taken only two courses in his new major when he landed his first job at Jack Atkinson's design studio on Goodbar street in Memphis. The pay was $40 a week, the hours were grueling, but the chief client was the new regional magazine,* Memphis. *"I remember asking Jack what an art director did," says Woodward, "and a week later I was one. They felt so bad about what they were paying me that they put me on the masthead." At 23, he began a four-year stint as the art director at* Memphis, *working on intuition and youthful energy, taking as his paragon the* Rolling Stone *of Mike Salisbury, Tony Lane, and Roger Black. In 1980, he moved to Dallas's* D *magazine and then to* Westward, *the Sunday supplement of the Dallas* Times-Herald, *where the staff consisted of two editors and Woodward, who was just beginning to trust his trances.*

Woodward enjoyed total control at Westward, *but he was also convinced that "nobody was looking at it." To get feedback from his peers, he entered the Art Directors Club competition for the first time in 1982. The results stunned him; so much of his work was accepted that he had to take out a small business loan to pay the hanging fees. In 1983, he joined* Texas Monthly. *The circulation was bigger, the platform more visible, and his work started to regularly attract national attention. Here, he began relationships with some of the greatest illustrators and photographers in the country.*

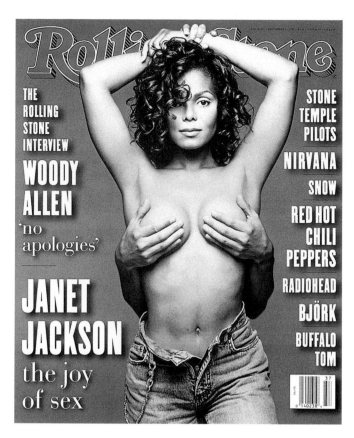

Men are in crisis,
whereas he is not.
He does not know
the meaning of
"crisis." Or perhaps

MR. BIG SHOT

he does, but he
pretends otherwise.
He is Austrian,
after all, and some

By Bill Zehme

PHOTOGRAPH BY HERB RITTS

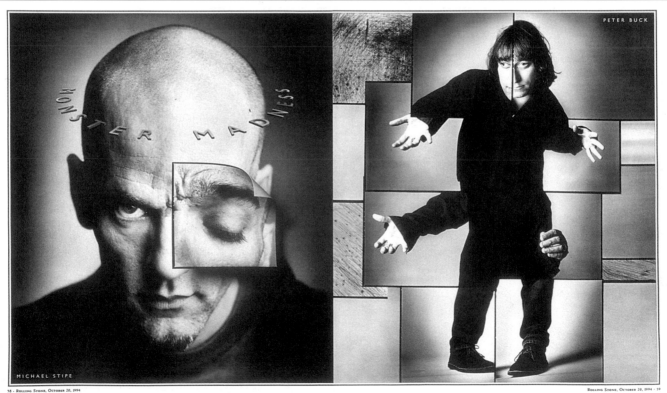

MONSTER MADNESS

MICHAEL STIPE

PETER BUCK

Four years later, Woodward moved to Rolling Stone. When he started, the magazine was counting down to a special 20th-anniversary issue. He and his new staff took to the archives to conduct a blitzkrieg retrospective of the magazine's design history. "I was scared to death," he says. "I wanted to do work that measured up to that 20-year legacy." In his effort to "reconnect Rolling Stone to the roots of the magazine that I loved and waited for every two weeks," Woodward reinstated the Oxford rule framing all editorial, an element that had been tossed aside in an effort to modernize the magazine. "It turned out to be incredibly liberating," he says. "I felt that whatever I did, if I did it inside that border, it was Rolling Stone." According to Steven Heller, Woodward's career can be traced to the lineage that begins with Alexey Brodovitch and continues through Henry Wolf, both of whom expressed admiration for innovation grounded in tradition. "What's great about Fred's work is that it's essentially classically based," says Arthur Hochstein, Time's art director. "It assumes that the written word is something that's valuable.

At Rolling Stone, text has great value, but it's not too sacred to have fun with, as Woodward's quirky type experiments prove. Says Robert Wallace, "Fred's work draws on older and deeper Eastern traditions that are rooted in ideography and nonlinear logic." And, according to Milton Glaser, "the invention and high energy that he brought to the job at the beginning has never flagged. One might truthfully say that Rolling Stone is better now than it has ever been." Perhaps the ultimate tribute can only come from the esteem of a mentor. "I guess we all make mistakes, thinking that our way is the only way to go," says Henry Wolf. "I was guilty of this where it concerned my work as an art director. Along came Fred Woodward with Rolling Stone. That's when I realized there was something new that was good." Jann S. Wenner, chairman of Wenner Media and the editor and publisher of Rolling Stone, last year appointed Woodward the first and only creative director of the company. In this capacity, Fred oversees the visual articulation of Rolling Stone, US, and Men's Journal, as well as the company's other projects, including books and new media. "Fred is truly a visionary in the field of magazine art direction," says Wenner. "He's a creative force whose energy, skill, and talents continue to amaze and astonish me. After close to ten years, his creative DNA has become an integral part of the Rolling Stone spirit."

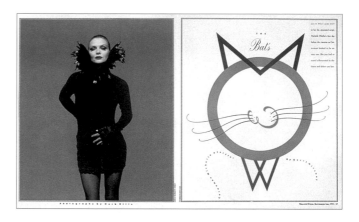

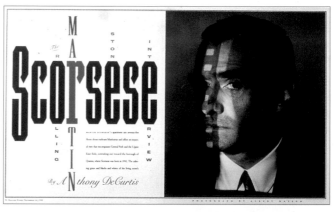

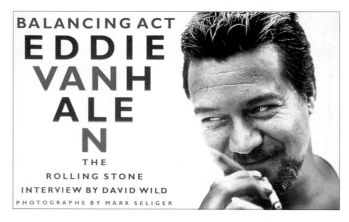

Steven Heller has carved out an impressive career as the foremost authority in the United States on the history of graphic design. A practicing educator, art director, and designer, he is an assiduous writer, the author of numerous magazine articles and many books. Fred Woodward has called him "a force of nature."

At the age of 17, Heller was art directing The New York Free Press, *and over the next six years he worked for* Interview, Rock, Screw, Mobster Times, *the Irish Arts Center, and* Evergreen Review. *At 24, Heller was introduced to the art department of* The New York Times, *where he became art director of the Op-Ed page and then of* The New York Times Book Review. *Today, he is a senior art director for special projects and art director of* The Book Review, *as well as serving as editor of the* American Institute of Graphic Arts Journal of Graphic Design *and instructor in the Master of Fine Arts in Illustration program at the School of Visual Arts.*

Heller has authored, co-authored, or edited over 50 books on the past and present of graphic design and illustration. Among the many topics he has addressed are graphic wit, graphic anger, "borrowed" design, covers and jackets, posters, food packaging, and typography. With Seymour Chwast, he authored Graphic Style: From Victorian to Post-Modern (Harry N. Abrams). He has been published by A & W Press, Harry N. Abrams, Allworth Press, Chronicle Books, Hyperion, Alfred A. Knopf, Penguin, St. Martins Press, Van Nostrand Reinhold, Viking Kestrel, and Watson Guptill, among many others. He is a co-editor of the first anthology of graphic-design criticism, Looking Closer: Critical Writings on Graphic Design (Allworth Press), and its sequel, Looking Closer II. Heller has written the introduction and afterwords for well over a dozen art and graphic-design books. He is a contributing editor to Print, ID, and U&lc, and frequently writes articles for numerous other design magazines.

Heller's talent as a curator has been seen in gallery exhibitions such as The Art of Simplicissimus, Art Against War, The Malik Verlag, and Typographic Treasures: W. A. Dwiggins. He is a three-time recipient of the National Endowment for the Arts Design Grant for research into the lives and works of W. A. Dwiggins and Lucian Bernhard.

Heller is currently the director for How We Learn What We Learn, a 1997 design-education conference hosted by the School of Visual Arts, and is designing the curriculum for The Designer as Author, a School of Visual Arts Master of Fine Arts in Graphic Design program. He is also working on a visual history of the teenager, entitled Teenage Confidential (Chronicle Books), and a collection of essays on the meaning of design, Design Literacy (Allworth Press).

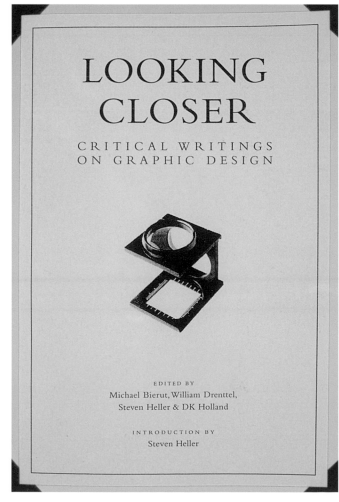

The Art Directors Club is proud to present Calvin Klein with the 1996 Management Award for his ongoing commitment, over more than two decades, to elegance in design and his recognition of its relationship to performance in clothing, packaging, advertising and graphics, housewares and interiors.

Born in 1942 in New York City, Calvin Klein taught himself to draw and sew as a child. After graduating from the New York High School of Art and Design, he attended the Fashion Institute of Technology, graduating in 1962. His first job was an apprenticeship at a Seventh Avenue coat and suit house, where he worked during the day, creating his own portfolio in the evenings and on weekends. In 1968, he started his own label in partnership with a childhood friend, Barry Schwartz. Since he launched his first ready-to-wear collection for women, Calvin Klein's name has become synonymous with modernity in fashion.

Mr. Klein quickly earned recognition from the fashion world. In 1973, he was the youngest designer ever to win the Coty Award, and he went on to win it again in 1974 and 1975. The Council of Fashion Designers of America named Calvin Klein outstanding designer of the year in both womenswear and menswear in 1993; he is the first designer ever to receive both distinctions concurrently.

Recipients

1954
Columbia Broadcasting
*   Company*
Ford Motor Company
Time Inc.

1955
General Foods Corp.
Lord & Taylor
Vogue

1956
Chrysler Motors Corp.
Eastman Kodak Co.
Look Magazine

1957
Hallmark Cards, Inc.
RCA
Reader's Digest

1958
Harper's Bazaar
Union Carbide Corp.
U.S. Information Agency

1959
Condé Nast Publications
IBM Corporation
Johnson & Johnson

1960
General Dynamics
West Virginia Pulp & Paper
*   Company*

1961
Abbott Laboratories
Alcoa
Alfred A. Knopf, Inc.
American Heritage Publishing
*   Co., Inc.*

1962
Macy's New York
Papert, Koenig, Lois, Inc.
Weyerhaeuser Company

1963
Container Corporation of
*   America*

1964
Corning Glass Works

1968
Whitney Museum of
*   American Art*

1970
RCA Corporation

1977
Exxon Corporation
Polaroid

1978
Atlantic Richfield Co.

1979
Mobil Corporation

1980
Volkswagen of America, Inc.

1982
Governor of New York
*   Hon. Hugh L. Carey*

1983
The New York Times Company

1984
Herman Miller Inc.

1985
Federal Express

1986
Pepsi-Cola Company

1987
IBM Corporation

1988
Apple Computer, Inc.

1989
Nike

1990
BMW Motors of America

1991
Absolut

1992
Rolling Stone Magazine

1993
The Gap

1994
Benetton

1995
MTV: Music Television

1996
Calvin Klein

The choice of sculptor Paul Manship (1885–1966) to design the Art Directors Club's first award medal in 1920 underscored a commitment to the ideal of art. Manship, who created the statue of Prometheus for Rockefeller Plaza, had a strong personal style, with elements of both the realist academy and the wildly experimental avant-garde. His medallion for the Art Directors Club depicts Apollo, god of the sun and leader of the Muses, flying on Pegasus, symbol of inspiration. The Muses are represented by the strings of Apollo's lyre.

The Manship medallion has been in continuous use since it was designed. After Gene Federico's handsome solid-cube design began to be used as an award in the 1970s, the Manship medallion served mainly as the President's and Management Medals. It seems fitting that this historic medal has been restored to its principal purpose in celebration of the 75th Annual Awards.

JUDGES

Advertising

Dean Stefanides *(Chairperson)*
Hampel/Stefanides
New York

Simon Bowden
Hill, Holliday, Connors, Cosmopulos, Inc.
Boston

Bryan Burlison
New York

Larry Cadman
New York

Pat Epstein
Lowe & Partners/SMS
New York

Larry Hampel
Hampel/Stefanides
New York

Donald Helme
The Helme Partnership
Dublin, Ireland

Harry Jacobs
The Martin Agency
Richmond, Virginia

Mike Lescarbeau
Fallon McElligott
Minneapolis

Tom Lichtenheld
Fallon McElligott
Minneapolis

John Malecki
Anderson & Lembke
New York

Jack Mariucci
Marlboro, New Jersey

Tom Miller
Goldsmith/Jeffrey
New York

Toshiaki Nozue
Dentsu Inc.
Tokyo, Japan

Jim Perretti
Perretti Productions
New York

Robert Reitzfeld
Beaver Reitzfeld
New York

John Russo
Pedone & Partners Advertising Inc.
New York

Steve Skibba
Skibba & Partners
New York

Frank Schneider
Düsseldorf, Germany

Eddie Van Bloem
Goldsmith/Jeffrey
New York

Tracy Wong
WONGDOODY
Seattle

Graphic Design

Stephen Doyle *(Chairperson)*
Drenttel Doyle Partners
New York

Tony Arefin
I.D. Magazine
New York

Steff Geissbuhler
Chermayeff & Geismar
New York

Marc Gobé
Desgrippes Gobé & Associates
New York

Laurie Haycock Makela
Walker Art Center
Minneapolis

Takenobu Igarashi
Igarashi Studio
Tokyo, Japan

Galie Jean-Louis
Anchorage Daily News
Anchorage

Doug Lloyd
Lloyd + Co.
New York

Rebeca Mendez
South Pasadena

Paul Sahre
Design Office of Paul Sahre
Baltimore

Paula Scher
Pentagram Design
New York

Erik Spiekermann
MetaDesign
Berlin, Germany

Gael Towey
Martha Stewart Living
New York

Todd Waterbury
Wieden & Kennedy
Portland, Oregon

New Media

Rochelle Udell *(Chairperson)*
Condé Nast Publications
Self Magazine
New York

Michael Grossman
Meigher Communications
New York

Brian Loube
R/GA Interactive
New York

Javier Romero
Javier Romero Design Group
New York

Robert Stein
The Voyager Company
New York

Nam Szeto
I-0 360° Design
New York

The 1995 One Show judging: six days and five nights in Barbados.

The 1995 Andy Award judging: seven days and six nights in Rome.

The 1995 Art Directors Show judging: five days and five nights on 20th Street.

As you can see, this year's judges deserve a tremendous amount of credit. Not just for lending their time and critical eyes, but just for showing up.

No, we didn't have the most glamorous surroundings. And still, we managed to assemble a group of some of the most respected names in the business. A group that plodded their way through the most entries in the history of the Art Directors Club awards. (In fact, we received more than twice as many entries this year as were received for the awards last year.)

And, I'm proud to say, we've given out fewer awards than in previous years—making the Art Directors Show one of the toughest shows around to win a medal in.

Thanks again to one of the most "hard-ass" group of judges ever assembled. The ones without the tan lines.

—Dean Stefanides

What delights me is this: I watched 14 judges rifle through more than 6,500 entries, and come up smiling…wondering at the surprise of an installation in Los Angeles, admiring the printing, the paper, and the patience that go into a book, wincing at the precision and sharpness of a film's opening credits. Let the design debate rage — it is a superficial one. What I witnessed was that specificity and invention, as palpable as a heartbeat, the surrender to an idea that is bigger than graphics — that was what drew the admiration of the judges.

—Stephen Doyle

New media is in a formative stage. This allows for enormous creativity.

There are no rules, only the demand for clarity and connection.

—Rochelle Udell

ADVERTISING

GOLD+SILVER MEDALISTS

Gold Medalist/U.S.A.

CAMPAIGN
Cargo Space, Cornering Lights, Lease,
Folding Mirrors
ART DIRECTOR *Todd Grant*
CREATIVE DIRECTORS *Michael Mazza,*
Rich Silverstein
COPYWRITER *Bo Coyner*
PHOTOGRAPHER *Gil Smith*
PRODUCER *Suzee Barrabee*
AGENCY *Goodby Silverstein & Partners*
CLIENT *Isuzu Motors*

ADDITIONAL AWARDS

Gold Medalist
NEWSPAPER, CONSUMER, LESS THAN A FULL PAGE
Cargo Space

Distinctive Merit
NEWSPAPER, CONSUMER, LESS THAN A FULL PAGE
Cornering Lights

Distinctive Merit
NEWSPAPER, CONSUMER, LESS THAN A FULL PAGE
Folding Mirrors

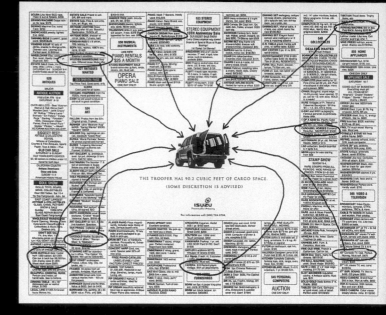

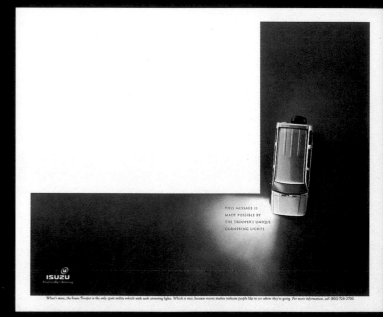

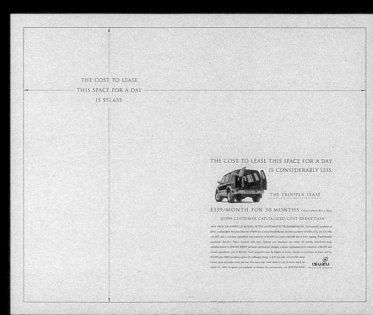

Gold Medalist/England

CAMPAIGN
48,000 Churches, Mother and Son, Your Lo...
ART DIRECTOR *Gary Marshall*
CREATIVE DIRECTORS *Paul Marshall,*
Gary Marshall
COPYWRITER *Paul Marshall*
DESIGNER *Gary Marshall*
PHOTOGRAPHER *Richard Avedon*
AGENCY *Bean MC*
CLIENT *Hennell of Bond Street*

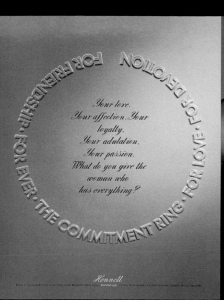

Silver Medalist/U.S.A.

CAMPAIGN
Snowboard, VW Bug, Bike
ART DIRECTOR *Mike Sheen*
CREATIVE DIRECTOR *David Ayriss*
COPYWRITER *John Heinsma*
PHOTOGRAPHER *Mark Hooper*
AGENCY *Cole & Weber*
CLIENT *The Oregonian*

Two hours on the mountain.

Six weeks in traction.

Three days in The Oregonian.

An ad that costs around three dollars a day. A paper that reaches well over a million people each week. A check that goes a long way towards easing the pain. **The Classifieds. 221-8000. Consider it sold.**

Eight hours on the road.

Twelve years in the driveway.

Five days in The Oregonian.

An ad that costs around three dollars a day. A paper that reaches well over a million people each week. A down payment on a car that'll run for more than a day. **The Classifieds. 221-8000. Consider it sold.**

Three hours in the saddle.

Five years in the closet.

Two days in The Oregonian.

An ad that costs about three dollars a day. A paper that reaches well over a million people each week. An empty closet where a closet full of guilt used to be. **The Classifieds. 221-8000. Consider it sold.**

**Bringen Sie
Ihre Eier
doch nach Hause,
wie Sie wollen.
Viel Vergnügen,
Ihre
Papierhersteller.**

Verpackungen aus Papier, Karton und Pappe sind praktisch und notwendig. Sie bestehen fast immer aus Altpapier, können mehrfach verwendet und leicht recycelt werden. Auf dem Gebiet umweltschonender Produktionsverfahren gehören die Papierhersteller übrigens weltweit zur Spitze. Wenn Sie Fragen haben oder mehr Informationen wünschen, rufen Sie uns an: 01 30/83 73 53.

Die Frankfurter Allgemeine empfiehlt: Sammeln Sie Altpapier.

**Schreiben Sie
Ihre Einkaufsliste
doch, worauf Sie
wollen.
Viel Vergnügen,
Ihre
Papierhersteller.**

Papier ist der älteste und wichtigste Informationsträger, den es gibt. Es ist sehr umweltverträglich, denn Papier läßt sich leicht wiederverwerten. Der Recyclingkreislauf funktioniert nur unter regelmäßiger Zufuhr von frischen Fasern. Diese werden aus den Holzresten der Sägewerke gewonnen oder stammen aus dem Holz, das bei der nachhaltigen Bewirtschaftung der Wälder – zum Beispiel bei der Durchforstung – anfällt. Wenn Sie Fragen haben oder mehr Informationen wünschen, rufen Sie uns an: 01 30/83 73 53.

Die Frankfurter Allgemeine empfiehlt: Gehen Sie sorgsam mit Papier um.

**Suchen Sie
sich Ihr
Lieblingsgericht
doch nach der
Form der Dosen aus.
Viel Vergnügen,
Ihre
Papierhersteller.**

Etiketten und Banderolen aus Papier sind informativ und notwendig. Außerdem sind sie sehr umweltverträglich, denn sie lassen sich wiederverwerten. Der Recyclingkreislauf funktioniert nur unter regelmäßiger Zufuhr von frischen Fasern. Diese werden aus den Holzresten der Sägewerke gewonnen oder stammen aus dem Holz, das bei der nachhaltigen Bewirtschaftung der Wälder – zum Beispiel bei der Durchforstung – anfällt. Wenn Sie Fragen haben oder mehr Informationen wünschen, rufen Sie uns an: 01 30/83 73 53.

Die Frankfurter Allgemeine empfiehlt: Gehen Sie sorgsam mit Papier um.

**Sie können
beim Frühstück
natürlich auch
den Kaffeesatz lesen.
Viel Vergnügen,
Ihre
Papierhersteller.**

Zeitungen informieren, unterhalten und sind äußerst umweltverträglich. Ihr Papier besteht häufig sogar zu 100% Altpapier und kann bis zu fünfmal wiederverwertet werden. Die für den Recyclingkreislauf benötigten Frischfasern werden aus den Holzresten der Sägewerke gewonnen oder stammen aus dem Holz, das bei der nachhaltigen Bewirtschaftung der Wälder – zum Beispiel bei der Durchforstung – anfällt. Wenn Sie Fragen haben oder mehr Informationen wünschen, rufen Sie uns an: 01 30/83 73 53.

Die Frankfurter Allgemeine empfiehlt: Sammeln Sie Altpapier.

**Schneuzen Sie
sich doch einfach in
die Finger.
Viel Vergnügen,
Ihre
Papierhersteller.**

Papiertaschentücher sind hygienisch und praktisch. Es gibt sie mit bis zu 100% Altpapieranteil. Auch die Sorten aus reinem Zellstoff sind absolut umweltverträglich. Diese frischen Fasern werden aus den Holzresten der Sägewerke gewonnen oder stammen aus dem Holz, das bei der nachhaltigen Bewirtschaftung der Wälder – zum Beispiel bei der Durchforstung – anfällt. Wenn Sie Fragen haben oder mehr Informationen wünschen, rufen Sie uns an: 01 30/83 73 53.

Die Frankfurter Allgemeine empfiehlt: Gehen Sie sorgsam mit Papier um.

Silver Medalist/Germany

CAMPAIGN
Paper Image Campaign
ART DIRECTOR *Andreas Geyer*
CREATIVE DIRECTORS *Werner Knopf,*
Christian Traut
COPYWRITERS *Dörte Spengler, Dagmar König*
PHOTOGRAPHER *Stuart Redler*
AGENCY *KNSK, BBDO WA GmbH*
CLIENT *Verband Deutscher Papierhersteller*
Initiative Umwelt und Papier

いよいよ開幕プロ野球

セ・リーグ公式戦全日程

プロ野球はパ・リーグが4月1日から、セ・リーグは7日から公式戦が開幕する。開幕日がずれるのは10年ぶり。パの開幕戦は西武―ダイエー、近鉄―日本ハム、オリックス―ロッテ、セは巨人―ヤクルト、中日―阪神、広島―横浜のナイターで幕をあける。パは4日からナイターに入る。

⚾ パ・リーグは4月1日
⚾ セ・リーグは7日から

パ・リーグ公式戦全日程

この新聞、読み終わったら、水でぬらして、野菜の保存にお使いください。

おいしく保存して
おいしく食べよう。
ちゃんと、ちゃんと。
AJINOMOTO.

プロ野球 公式戦全日程

WHAT THE HECK IS A WONGDOODY?

A SMALL ASEXUAL MARSUPIAL

B REALLY IMPORTANT PART TO HOMEMADE NUCLEAR DEVICE

C LAOTIAN CHEESE SNACK

D ILL-NAMED AD AGENCY

For the unsure, simply call Pat Doody at 206.624.5325. By chance, Mr. Doody runs an ill-named ad agency considered by many to be one of the best creative shops in the Northwest. This is evidenced by their work for companies like the Seattle SuperSonics, Walt Disney, Helly-Hansen, K2 Skis, KIRO, Miami Heat, Partnership for a Drug-Free America and Oberto Sausage Company.

WONGDOODY
a k a
JUAN DUTY
a k a
WANGDOODLE
a k a
DONGWOODY
a k a
WONG DONG SILVER.

(OUR NAME ALONE REEKS OF CREDIBILITY.)

"Hello, is this Mr. WONGDOODY? Haha! I'm just calling to tell you ... haha ...that I'm giving you my...hahaha...the 200 gazillion dollar Pepsi account!!! You're an ad agency, aren't you? Hahahaha!!!"

Above, an actual sampling of what we've been called. But mainly, we've been called one of the Northwest's hottest creative shops for our award-winning work for such companies as the Seattle SuperSonics, K2 Skis, Skippers Fish & Chips, Walt Disney Co., Partnership for a Drug-Free America and Oberto Turkey Jerky. If you're looking for unparalleled creative and strategic marketing expertise right here in the Northwest, call Pat Doody at 206.624.5325. Betcha this never happened to Leo Burnett.

WONGDOODY.
OUR EXPERIENCE READS LIKE
A CORPORATE WHO'S WHO.
YET, OUR NAME READS LIKE
A MAJOR GASTRIC TRAUMA.

[*The resumé*]

ALASKA AIRLINES
ALDUS
AMERICAN EXPRESS
CAMPBELL'S SOUP CO.
CBS TELEVISION
DURACELL BATTERIES
E.F. HUTTON
FIRST INTERSTATE BANK
FOUR SEASONS HOTELS
GENERAL FOODS
HERSHEY CHOCOLATE CO.
HOUSE OF SEAGRAM'S
INFINITI AUTOMOTIVE
JBL AUDIO
THE NBA
OWENS-CORNING
PEPSI INTERNATIONAL
PROCTOR & GAMBLE
RICHARDSON-VICKS
ROYAL VIKING CRUISE LINE
TIME, INC.
THE UNITED WAY

[*The digestive disorder*]

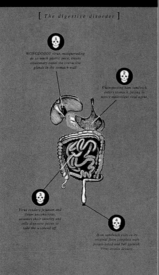

At left, a sampling of past account experience from the folks at the ad agency known as WONGDOODY. With a pedigree of Ogilvy & Mather, Benton & Bowles, Goodby, Silverstein & Partners, Hill-Holiday and Livingston + Co., WONGDOODY offers Northwest advertisers strategic and creative experience seemingly unmatched in this market. This, in turn, might give your competition the affliction diagrammed at right. For more information about the agency WONGDOODY, please contact Pat Doody at 206.624.5325.

FINDING COSTA RICA IS EASY.
IT'S 180° FROM CLUB MED.

Now, that's not to say that one is any better than the other.

It just means that for many of you, a beach and a tan is all you're looking for in a vacation. And there's certainly nothing wrong with that.

But this ad is for the rest of you.

It's for those who want a vacation that does as much for your soul as it does for your skin. That's why we'd like to take this opportunity to tell you what you'll find, if you decide to spend your hard-earned money, in our country.

Essentially, what a Costa Rican vacation comes down to is having, within a day's drive, as many things to do and see as there are Costa Ricans anxious to show them to you.

It's tough to know where to start to tell someone about our country.

Nature might be a good place. Because 25% of our 19,700 square miles is protected rain forest, national parks and wildlife reserves. And while tourism may be our largest industry, our ecosystem is our most important asset.

We believe, the more people who have access to nature, the more educated they'll become about how important it is. Not only here, but around the world.

At last count, Costa Rica was inhabited by 583 species of amphibians, 848 species of birds, 205 species of mammals, around 13,000 species of plants, 400 species of butterflies and 1,500 species of fish.

Unfortunately, it's up to 1 species to ensure these numbers don't decrease.

All this and we haven't even touched on individual stories like the tens of thousands of leatherback turtles that come to Playa Grande like clockwork to lay their eggs. Then there's something called the gar. A creature that's not sure whether it's an alligator or a fish. And neither are we.

So, if you come here, we hope you'll understand if everyone seems to be a little over-zealous about the ecosystem here. As you can see, they've got a lot of reasons to be.

While there's nothing more important to us than the creatures that call Costa Rica home, there are many more reasons to visit.

About 90° worth.

In fact, many people who've come here, often refer to Costa Rica as an island. Despite the fact that it's not surrounded by water.

One of the reasons people think of Costa Rica that way, may have something to do with the fact that we've been a proud democracy since 1948. A country whose civil war lasted only 40 days. Which tells you a lot about the kind of people you'll find here.

It also goes a long way in explaining why Costa Ricans have, over the years, taken pride in their commitment to education instead of militarism. Today, you'll find more teachers here than police. So you won't be surprised when you learn that the literacy rate in our country is 92%.

Speaking of the military, we should also tell you that it's one more way Costa Rica is different.

In that we don't have one.

And we haven't had one for years. So, if you come to Costa Rica and hopefully our capital, San José, make sure you visit our old Army barracks.

Because today, it's one of 28 museums in the country.

A lot has happened since Columbus came here and called it "Rich Coast." But when we think about it, it's what hasn't happened here since then, that makes our country such a popular place to visit.

To this day, you'll find some of the world's most breath-taking sights, unspoiled by so-called progress. Among them is Arenal Volcano which soars 5,358 feet above sea level and has been active since 1968. In one of the many other protected areas, you'll find rocks on the Santa Elena Peninsula that date back 150 million years. The same rocks that have yet to be explored. By humans at least.

And on the world's largest uninhabited island, Coco Island, there are more than 200 waterfalls.

As you can see, with all there is to tell you about our country, this ad could've been a lot bigger. To hear about what we've left out, call your travel agent or Costa Rica Tourism at 1-800-343-6332.

We'd be honored to have you.

By the way, we reluctantly inform you that you can also find 631 miles of beach on the Pacific coast and 131 on the Caribbean for you to relax and soak up some sun.

If you like that sort of thing.

COSTA RICA
TAN YOUR SOUL

THERE ARE VERY FEW
ATHEISTS IN COSTA RICA.

If you didn't already, what would it take to make you believe?

Not necessarily in God, or a god, but a higher being.

For many of you who do, it was easy. It was the day you and your partner brought another human being into the world. The day you stared at your newborn and wondered what could possibly be going through their head.

For others, it was your first eclipse. Or, at the other end of the scale, watching an ant carrying what appeared to be a small loaf of bread up and down the crevices of a sidewalk.

For those who remain unconvinced there's Costa Rica.

In Costa Rica, you can't throw a dart without hitting something that makes you wonder who made it, how long it's existed or how it got here.

That's what happens when you take two large mountain ranges, dozens of volcanoes, two long beaches, hundreds of waterfalls, a rain forest and squeeze it all into a country the size of West Virginia.

But it's the other things that make you rub your eyes and look to the sky for answers.

Take for example, a single rock at the foot of Mount Chirripó. While the mountain itself, standing at 12,529 feet above sea level, leaves you breathless, it's a simple rock that makes you think.

Because this rock is a mirror image of Mount Chirripó itself.

Nobody knows how it got here. Nobody knows how it got this way. Some believe it was native Indians who carved it, others are convinced that the wind shaped it over millions of years, using Mount Chirripó as its model.

All we know for sure is that it sits near the town of San Gerardo, minding its own business, doing nothing more than provoking thought.

The same can be said for Costa Rica's stone spheres.

More than a thousand of them are spread over the flood plains of Río Térraba. Many more are buried.

More impressive than their size, (some are as large as six feet in diameter) is how perfect they are.

There are as many theories on how they got here as there are stones themselves. The only thing the experts seem to agree on is that it's highly unlikely they'll ever figure them out.

If you decide to come to Costa Rica and spend some of your hard-earned money in our beautiful little country, we feel we should also tell you you won't find here. Like a compass that works.

On certain parts of Mount Chirripó, as a result of energies that've been detected there, you'll find your compass will be more useful as a paper weight than to determine the direction you're heading. Some natives refer to Mount Chirripó as a "power place." And while they can't explain why it does what it does, their best guess is that the minerals and metals found in and around the mountain are responsible.

But when it comes to evidence of a higher being, you really need look no further than the living creatures who call Costa Rica their home. The sheer numbers alone are impressive enough.

At last count, Costa Rica was inhabited by 583 species of amphibians, 848 species of birds, 205 species of mammals, around 13,000 species of plants 400 species of butterflies and 1,580 species of fish.

Which brings us to something called a "gaspar."

Something that appears to be part fish and part alligator. Then there's the Costa Rican reptile that's affectionately known as a "Jesus Christ" lizard which can actually run on top of the water.

Whatever they are, they're two more things that'll make you scratch your head and, for a split second, reach for the remote control.

For every single being seen in Costa Rica that makes people realize what a priviledge it is to be on this planet, there's something you can hear that'll bring you to the same conclusion.

The pounding of a waterfall, the howl of a monkey in the middle of the jungle. In Costa Rica, you'll find your senses so heightened, the smack of a single drop of rain hitting the leaf of a mangrove tree can be deafening.

The natives call it "pura vida." Pure life. And in Costa Rica, it's everywhere you turn.

It's all of the above, and things we haven't told you, that'll not only have you convinced in a higher being, but that they spent a little more time here than anywhere else.

We invite you to call your travel agent or Costa Rica Tourism at 1-800-343-6332.

And see for yourself why some things here are so incredible, you won't believe what you're seeing. But you'll believe in something.

COSTA RICA
TAN YOUR SOUL

COSTA RICA HAS NO MILITARY.

Don't laugh.

This 68 year-old teacher has without a doubt, shaped more lives, had more effect on people in this part of the world than anyone ever has in a uniform.

Come to think of it, she has probably struck more fear in the hearts of more Costa Ricans too. If you've ever been in one of her classrooms, you'll know why.

We understand that unless you're related to her, Mrs. Sánchez, as wonderful as she is, isn't reason enough to rush to the airport, buy an airline ticket and hop on the next flight to Costa Rica.

But the kind of country that allows Mrs. Sánchez to be Mrs. Sánchez, might be.

It's been said by many that while Costa Rica is not surrounded by water it is, philosophically speaking, an island. We're a 174 year-old democracy right in the middle of things in Central America.

Costa Ricans first heard the news of their independence by horseback. Three years later, we had our first president. Back then, he was called Chief of State and his name was Juan Mora Fernández. It should come as no surprise for you to learn that Mr. Fernández was, that's right, a teacher.

It seems to make sense that a country whose first leader was a teacher would turn out the way it has. If Juan Mora Fernández was an Army General, a blacksmith, or a lawyer, we'd hazard a guess that Costa Rica would be a very different country than it is today.

BUT THERE'S ALWAYS MRS. SÁNCHEZ.

We know for sure we wouldn't find ourselves with more teachers than police officers as we do today.

It starts to make us wonder about other things. If our Army barracks in San José would be in the state they're in now. That state being a museum. Or, would we find ourselves in a country that, while it condones bullfighting, rewards the bull for its efforts rather than kill it?

Would Costa Rica still have more government-protected rain forest, parks and wildlife reserves per acre than anyone else on the planet? And would thousands of leatherback turtles still be welcome to virtually take over the beach at Playa Grande and lay their eggs in peace?

We're happy to say that we'll never find out. That all these things and everything else that makes our beautiful little country what it is, will stay the same.

We'd be honored if you called us at 1-800-343-6332. So we can tell you the other things that make Costa Rica such a nice place to visit, you might want to live here.

That's if Mrs. Sánchez likes you of course.

COSTA RICA
TAN YOUR SOUL

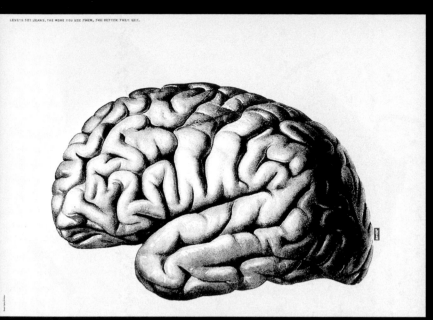

Gold Medalist/Spain

CAMPAIGN
Levi's 501 Trendsetters
ART DIRECTOR *David Ruiz*
CREATIVE DIRECTORS *Gustavo Calda*
David Ruiz
COPYWRITER *Gustavo Caldas*
PHOTOGRAPHERS *Arara Pelegrin,*
Horrillo i Riola, Carlos Suarez
AGENCY *Bassat, Ogilvy and Mather*
CLIENT *Levi Strauss, España, S.A.*

...dalist/U.S.A.

CAMPAIGN
Kent Street, Laurie Schechter, Mike Yalden
ART DIRECTORS *K. C. Arriwong, Mark Figliulo*
CREATIVE DIRECTOR *Mark Figliulo*
COPYWRITERS *Paul Meyer, Kit Cramer*
PHOTOGRAPHER *Chuck Shotwell*
AGENCY *Leo Burnett Company, Chicago*
CLIENT *Rockport*

WE'D LIKE to TELL YOU a LITTLE ABOUT an
INSURANCE COMPANY THAT BELIEVES in FOCUSING on the FUTURE.
To START, LET'S GO BACK to 1810.

COMMERCIAL INSURANCE
ASSET MANAGEMENT
LIFE INSURANCE & ANNUITIES
AUTO & HOMEOWNERS
DISABILITY INSURANCE

ITT HARTFORD

An ENTIRE ARMY COULDN'T STOP our AGENTS from
TAKING CARE of THEIR CUSTOMERS.
Do YOU REALLY THINK a LITTLE WIND is GOING TO?

PROPERTY & CASUALTY
FROM SECRETLY BURYING POLICIES DURING THE CIVIL WAR TO HANDING OUT CASH ADVANCES AFTER HURRICANE ANDREW, OUR AGENTS HAVE ALWAYS DONE WHATEVER IT TAKES TO HELP OUR CUSTOMERS IN TIMES OF CRISIS.

ITT HARTFORD

OUR FINANCIAL STRENGTH has STOOD UP
to the SCRUTINY of STANDARD & POOR'S,
MOODY'S and A. M. BEST.
NOT to MENTION the WRATH of ANDREW,
HUGO and GLORIA.

HURRICAN
23 AUGUS
5 PM EDT
MAX. WIN
923 MB

COMMERCIAL INSURANCE
ASSET MANAGEMENT
LIFE INSURANCE & ANNUITIES
AUTO & HOMEOWNERS

ITT HARTFORD

Silver Medalist/U.S.A.

CAMPAIGN
Time Line, Civil War, Financial Strength
ART DIRECTOR *Kirk Mosel*
CREATIVE DIRECTORS *Dean Stefanides,*
Larry Hampel
COPYWRITER *Chris Jacobs*
PHOTOGRAPHY *Stock*
AGENCY *Hampel/Stefanides*
CLIENT *ITT Hartford*

ADDITIONAL AWARDS

Distinctive Merit
MAGAZINE, CONSUMER, FULL PAGE OR SPREAD
Civil War

Merit
NEWSPAPER, CONSUMER, LESS THAN A FULL PAGE
Civil War

Merit
NEWSPAPER, TRADE, LESS THAN A FULL PAGE
Time Line

Merit
NEWSPAPER, CONSUMER, LESS THAN A FULL PAGE
Financial Strength

Merit
MAGAZINE, CONSUMER, FULL PAGE OR SPREAD
Time Line

Merit
MAGAZINE, CONSUMER, FULL PAGE OR SPREAD
Financial Strength

Andy Markel first laid eyes on his Taylor
at a music store on Long Island.

He wrote us a letter about it, and admitted
that he doesn't usually write letters to companies.

But he had to tell us that his Taylor guitar
was more than a guitar.

It was like a good friend.

He also admitted he was a
little embarrassed to tell us something else.

When he brought his Taylor home that first night,
he kissed it before he put it in the case.

Kissed it twice, in fact.

That's the thing about friends. Some of them
are friends, right from the beginning.

There are a lot of music stores between
Virginia and Missouri.

For two years, in 1988 and 1989, Ray Roberts
began "poking his nose" into a lot of them.

He was looking for a guitar he
could fall in love with.

Finally, at a store in Charlotte,
North Carolina, he found his Taylor.

He could finally stop visiting music stores.

Well, not quite. Two stores in
Lynchburg did ask him to come by.

They asked if he could bring in his
Taylor. They wanted to see if everything
they had heard was true.

Harlan Howard already had five guitars.

But one day he walked into a music
store in Nashville.

I have a problem, he told Richard,
the owner. All my guitars have dried up.

Richard started to talk about the low humidity.

No, not that, said Harlan. There aren't any
more songs left in them. They're dry.

I need a guitar with some fresh songs in it.

A few hours later,
he walked out with a new Taylor.

We're glad to say that each Taylor comes
with a lifetime supply of new songs.

Provided, of course, that your
lifetime is filled with fair amounts of joy,
pain, tenderness and heartache.

One overcast day in Idaho Falls,
Skip Watkins, a happily married man, walked
into a music store and promptly fell in love.

The object of his desire was a Taylor guitar.

But Skip's wife was a problem. In Skip's words,
he knew he'd "have to smooth-talk her."

She handled the family finances, you see.

The next day, they both came
into the store.

To Skip's amazement, she listened
to the sweet tone of the Taylor for less than
30 seconds before she said, "Let's get it."

Skip loves his Taylor, and he loves his wife.

And he never was much of a smooth-talker.

Which is what his wife loves
about him.

David Pearl remembers playing
a Taylor for the first time.

He had strolled into a local music store,
with a few hours of spare time on his hands.

And, just for the heck of it, he started playing
his way through their entire inventory.

David wrote us about it. "I left my
romantic period behind me years ago. Nevertheless,
as I played your instrument I fell in love."

He played, and kept playing, and kept
playing, until, in his words, "They had to
ask me to leave at closing time."

He even came back the next day,
hoping it wasn't just a one-time feeling, a fluke.

And just to be safe, he even made
a point of getting there early.

Silver Medalist/U.S.A.

CAMPAIGN
Taylor Guitars Campaign
ART DIRECTOR *John Vitro*
CREATIVE DIRECTORS *John Vitro, John Robertson*
COPYWRITER *John Robertson*
PHOTOGRAPHER *Chris Wimpey*
AGENCY *VITROROBERTSON*
CLIENT *Taylor Guitars*

FOR EVERY TROOPER SOLD
THERE ARE 23 PEOPLE
WAITING TO BORROW IT.

THE 38TH UNWRITTEN LAW OF DRIVING

THE ROAD IS PAVED
WITH IDIOTS.

THE 60TH UNWRITTEN LAW OF DRIVING

CONCRETE PARKING BARRIERS
WERE INVENTED
TO TAKE OUT OIL PANS.

Silver Medalist/U.S.A.

CAMPAIGN
*Waiting to Borrow, With Idiots,
Take Out Oil Pans*
ART DIRECTOR *Michael Mazza*
CREATIVE DIRECTOR *Michael Mazza*
COPYWRITERS *Dave O'Hare, Chuck McBride*
PHOTOGRAPHER *Graham Westmoreland*
ILLUSTRATOR *Alan Daniels*
AGENCY *Goodby Silverstein & Partners*
CLIENT *Isuzu Motors*

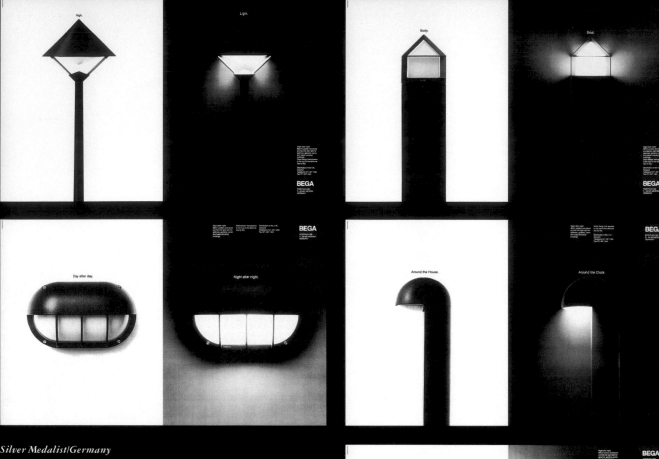

Silver Medalist/Germany

CAMPAIGN
BEGA Campaign
ART DIRECTOR *Gertrud Eisele*
CREATIVE DIRECTOR *Waldemar Meister*
COPYWRITER *Karl Böhm*
DESIGNER *Karin Bausch*
PHOTOGRAPHER *Rolf Herkner*
AGENCY *Leonhardt & Kern Beta GmbH*
CLIENT *BEGA Gatenbrink – Leuchten GmbH & Co.*

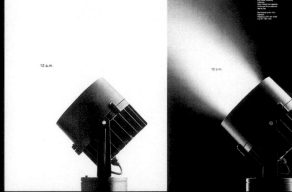

Dishwashers, washing machines, driers. Hand creams, moisturisers, conditioners, nail varnish... everything to avoid your hands being ruined.

We never forgave me for throwing out my old armchair. Everything in furniture and home decoration.

Frying pans, saucepans, plates, carving knives, rolling pins... We arm brides with everything they need to make their marriages work. Wedding lists.

He didn't want the dummy, or the bottle, or the teddy bear or even the musical nursery rhyme...when he saw her he opened his eyes. Could he be hungry? A whole floor for Newborns.

Mattresses, futons, beds, bedrooms...everything so you can sleep like never before.

Silver Medalist/Spain

CAMPAIGN
Specialists in You
ART DIRECTORS *Ramón Roda, Josep Marín,*
Ana Albizuri
CREATIVE DIRECTORS *Jose Pujol,*
Jose Roca de Viñals
PHOTOGRAPHER *Sisco Soler*
AGENCY *Casadevall Pedreño & PRG*
CLIENT *El Corte Inglés*

EL MOROCHITO TRAVEL DEPARTING HAVANNA BETWEEN 10 A.M. AND 12 NOON FOR SANTIAGO DE CUBA, STOPPING AT ALAMAR, SANTA CRUZ DEL NORTE, VARADERO, CÁRDENAS, CORRALILLO, RANCHO VELOZ, QUEMADO DE GÜINES, LA ISABELA, SAGUA LA GRANDE, ENCRUCIJADA, CAIBARIEN, PUERTO MANATÍ, BACARDI & EVERYTHING, GUARDALAVACA, BANES, ANTILLA, GUATEMALA, NICARO, CAYO MANBÍ, MOA, CAÑETE, BARACOA, PUERTA CALETA, BOQUERÓN, DAIQUIRI, ARRIVING SANTIAGO DE CUBA WHEN IT PLEASES GOD.

WITH JAZZ & MODELS & VIDEOCLIPS & LEMON & BLUES & JEANS & JOCKEYS & RACING & TELEVISION & ROCK 'N' ROLL & BOOTS & LEATHER JACKETS & FUSION & RAP & LIGHTS & CAMERAS & RHYTHM & MUSICIANS & WINNERS & VICTORIES & ACTORS & FILMS & SHOWS & CONCERTS & ART & CULTURE & TRADITION & MODERNITY & OPINIONS & WIDE BOYS & TRAVELLERS & SENSUALITY & INTIMACY & COCA-COLA & MATES & DATES & GET-TOGETHERS & FRIENDS & ACQUAINTANCES & LOVERS & YOU & BACARDI & EVERYTHING.

PARA BAILAR LA BAMBA, SE NESESITA UNA POCA DE GRASIA, UNA POCA DE GRASIA Y OTRA COSITA, AY ARRIBA Y ARRIBA. AY ARRIBA Y ARRIBA, YO NO SOY MARINERO, SOY CAPITÁN, SOY CAPITÁN. BAMBA, LA BAMBA, BAMBA, LA BAMBA, PARA SUBIR AL CIELO, PARA SUBIR AL CIELO, SE NESESITA UNA ESCALERA MUY GRANDE, UNA ESCALERA MUY GRANDE Y OTRA CHIQUITA. AY ARRIBA Y ARRIBA. BACARDI & EVERYTHING. AY ARRIBA Y ARRIBA, POR TI SERÉ, POR TI SERÉ. BAMBA, LA BAMBA, BAMBA, LA BAMBA.

THE TURKEY. THE TREE. THE DECORATIONS. THE CHRISTMAS CARDS. GREETINGS. BEST WISHES. FOR HAPPINESS. FOR PROSPERITY. GET TOGETHERS. THE TABLE. CANDLES ALIGHT. SHINING GLASSES. THE PREPARATIONS. THE SHOPPING. FATHER CHRISTMAS IS GOING TO COME. LADEN WITH PRESENTS. TIES, PERFUME, SHIRTS, GAMES, TOYS, TRINKETS, RECORDS, BOOKS, BACARDI & EVERYTHING. A FAMILY GATHERING. CHATTER. GETTING TO KNOW ONE ANOTHER. GETTING CLOSER. LETTING THE DAY SLIP BY. IN NO HURRY. VISITING FRIENDS. TREATING ONESELF. IT'S CHRISTMAS.

Silver Medalist/Spain

CAMPAIGN
Bacardi & Everything
ART DIRECTORS *Ramón Roda, Josep Marín*
CREATIVE DIRECTORS *Luis Casadevall,*
Xavi García, Ramón Roda
COPYWRITER *Nacho Raventós*
PHOTOGRAPHERS *Ramón Eguiguren,*
Antón Eguiguren
AGENCY *Casadevall Pedreño & PRG*
CLIENT *Bacardi*

The End

Of cocoa-butter stained paperbacks
flying kites in the dunes
and lighter-fluid tinged hamburgers.
Junk drawers fill with seashells.
Volleyballs hibernate.
Fahrenheit goes from plus to minus.
Say goodbye to cheap sunglasses
bar-car Friday friendships
and the feeling of tan skin
with sand in the bed.
The best remedy for this depressing news?

New clothes.

Come see the new Fall Collection. **BARNEYS NEW YORK**

300 SERIES
STAINLESS
STEEL

Every Hinge Should Open This Quietly

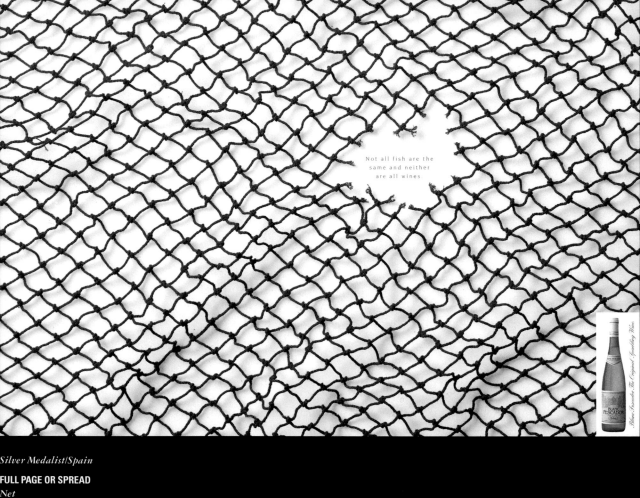

Not all fish are the
same and neither
are all wines.

Best of Show/Gold Medalist/Spain

TELEVISION COMMERCIAL, 30 SECONDS OR LESS, CAMPAIGN
Blonde, Sorry, Trouble, Ready, Cheat
ART DIRECTOR *Paul Shearer*
COPYWRITER *Rob Jack*
PHOTOGRAPHER *Joe Nacoe*
PRODUCER *Laura Gregory*
DIRECTOR *Andy Morahan*
MUSIC *The Blue Hawaiians*
STUDIO *Great Guns Ltd.*
AGENCY *Paul Marciano Advertising Inc.*
CLIENT *Guess?*

ADDITIONAL AWARDS

Gold Medalist
CINEMA COMMERCIAL, OVER 30 SECONDS
Cheat

Gold Medalist
CINEMATOGRAPHY
Cheat

Cheat
FIANCÉE (TO P.I.): *I need to know he's going to be faithful. It's a matter of trust.*
P.I. (VOICEOVER): *You know, an awful lot of people do not like what I do. That's their problem. I mean if a guy's going to drop his pants you'd wanna know, right?*
VISUAL: *P.I. in his office, talking to Julie, the "decoy."*
JULIE: *So, what've you got?*
P.I.: *They've got a kid, wanna get married. She wants him checked out first….Think you can handle it?*
JULIE: *Oh, I think so.*
VISUAL: *P.I. wiring mini-mic onto Julie.*
VISUAL: *Julie seated at a bar. The man sits next to her.*
MAN (TO JULIE): *Are you alone?*
JULIE: *I'm always alone.*
MAN: *Mind if I join you?*
JULIE: *Well, it looks like you already have. So, do you have someone special in your life?*
VISUAL: *P.I. in car, listening on his earpiece, watching a security camera.*
P.I.: *Oh…she's good.*
VISUAL: *Inside bar.*
JULIE: *Are you married?*
MAN: *No. What can I tell you? The relationship just didn't work out.*
VISUAL: *P.I. in his office with Fiancée as she listens to the tape.*
P.I.: *I'm sorry. (To camera) My girls look so good people ask me, Is it fair? And I always say, Quite frankly…no!*
SUPER: *Guess logo.*

TELEVISION COMMERCIAL, 30 SECONDS OR LESS
Love Note
ART DIRECTOR *Sharon McDaniel Azula*
CREATIVE DIRECTOR *John Boone*
COPYWRITER *David Oakley*
PRODUCER *Betsy Barnum*
DIRECTOR *Thom Higgins*
STUDIO *Dektor Higgins & Associates*
AGENCY *Price McNabb*
CLIENT *Weyerhaeuser*

VISUAL: *In an elementary-school classroom.
After stealing glances at a girl, a lovestruck boy
passes a note to her. "I love you. Do you love me?
Check yes or no." She opens the note, thinks for
a moment, then checks a box and passes the note
back. The answer is no. The boy is crushed. As he
begins to crumple the note, he looks up from his
desk and notices another young lady smiling at
him. He uncrumples the note, erases the check
mark of girl #1 and passes it to girl #2.*
SUPER: *You're never too young to start recycling.*
SUPER: *Weyerhaeuser logo.*

TELEVISION COMMERCIAL, 30 SECONDS OR LESS, CAMPAIGN
Neya, Alien Hat Man, UFO Couple
ART DIRECTOR *Jerry Gentile*
CREATIVE DIRECTOR *Steve Rabosky*
COPYWRITER *Scott Vincent*
PRODUCER *Michelle Burke*
DIRECTOR *Jeff Gorman*
STUDIO *Johns & Gorman Films*
AGENCY *TBWA Chiat/Day Inc. Advertising*
CLIENT *Sunkist California Pistachios*

ADDITIONAL AWARDS

Distinctive Merit
TELEVISION COMMERCIAL, 30 SECONDS OR LESS
Neya

Merit
TELEVISION COMMERCIAL, 30 SECONDS OR LESS
Alien Hat Man

Neya
VISUAL: *Woman on couch.*
SUPER: *Romayne Riddell. Trance channeler.*
SUPER: *Everybody knows the best nuts come from California.*
VISUAL: *Bag of pistachios.*
SUPER: *California Pistachios.*
ROMAYNE: *Well, I started trance channeling about six years ago. It's almost like my body was suddenly filled with love. (In high-pitched voice) Hello, Peter. How are you today?*
PETER: *Very good, Neya. How are you?*
ROMAYNE: *Very fine, thank you. So, what is it you wanted to know?*
PETER: *Where are you from?*
ROMAYNE: *I'm from Jupiter.*

EVERYBODY KNOWS

THE BEST NUTS COME

FROM CALIFORNIA.

CALIFORNIA PISTACHIOS

TELEVISION COMMERCIAL, 30 SECONDS OR LESS
Hedgehogs
ART DIRECTOR *Willie Sonnenberg*
CREATIVE DIRECTOR *Willie Sonnenberg*
COPYWRITER *Terry Murphy*
PRODUCER *Esther Campbell*
DIRECTOR *Giacomo Angelini*
MUSIC *Library Music*
PUPPETEERING *The Creative Shop*
STUDIO *The Vision Corporation*
AGENCY *Sonnenberg Murphy Leo Burnett*
CLIENT *Mercedes-Benz of South Africa*

VISUAL: *Cars whizz by in both directions on a fairly busy country road. On the grassy verge are three hedgehogs—a mother and two youngsters—all wearing gas masks. The mother looks to her left. So do the youngsters. They all take off their masks. A Mercedes C-Class appears and drives past. Once the car has gone, the hedgehogs put their masks back on.*
SUPER: *The new C-Class diesels.*
ANNCR: *Emission levels that were already low have been further reduced by up to fifteen percent in the new C-Class diesels. Hopefully one day all diesels will be this clean.*

Gold Medalist/Canada

TELEVISION COMMERCIAL, OVER 30 SECONDS
Snowball
ART DIRECTOR *George Gilewski*
CREATIVE DIRECTORS *Larry Tolpin,*
Neil McOstrich
COPYWRITER *Jon Freir*
PRODUCER *Mike Cooper*
DIRECTOR *Richard D'Alessio*
MUSIC *Jungle Music*
PRODUCTION HOUSE *Imported Artists*
AGENCY *BBDO Canada*
CLIENT *Chrysler Canada, Ltd.*

ADDITIONAL AWARD

Distinctive Merit
**TELEVISION COMMERCIAL, OVER 30 SECONDS,
CAMPAIGN**
Window, Hockey Reunion, Snowball

VISUAL: *On a typical residential street, a minivan approaches. Behind a snowbank, a mischievous neighborhood kid meticulously packs a snowball. He gives a "thumbs up" to a second kid behind a snowbank on the other side of the street. The minivan approaches, then pulls up to a stop sign. When the minivan stops, the kids rear back and let fly with their snowballs. The snowballs head toward the van's windows. Inside the minivan, a hand pulls open a door. From head-on, we see the snowballs proceed directly through the van and out their opposite sides. Just as the kids realize what is happening, the snowballs hit the two of them, sending them into the snow. The doors close up, and the van casually drives off.*
SUPER: *The new originals from Chrysler Canada.*

hungry?

Gold Medalist/Japan

TELEVISION COMMERCIAL, 30 SECONDS OR LESS, CAMPAIGN
Father Tries to Throw a Rock, Father Saw Stars, Father Returns
ART DIRECTOR *Takuya Onuki*
CREATIVE DIRECTOR *Susumu Miyazaki*
COPYWRITERS *Masahiko Ishii, Tomomi Maeda*
DESIGNER *Kazuhiro Suda*
PHOTOGRAPHER *Satoshi Seno*
PRODUCERS *Seiichiro Horii, Kazuyuki Machida*
DIRECTOR *Shinya Nakajima*
AGENCY *Hakuhodo Inc.*
CLIENT *Nissin Food Products Co. Ltd.*

ADDITIONAL AWARDS

Silver Medalist
TELEVISION COMMERCIAL, 30 SECONDS OR LESS
Father Tries to Throw a Rock

Merit
TELEVISION COMMERCIAL, 30 SECONDS OR LESS
Father Returns

Father Tries to Throw a Rock
VISUAL: *Three members of a caveman family sit in a cave. The child throws a stone at a large bird, but the stone falls short. Mom tries a larger stone, but this one fails as well. Dad lifts a huge rock to throw, but it falls on his head, squashing him.*
ANNCR: *Hungry? Nissin Cup Noodle.*

Silver Medalist/U.S.A.

TELEVISION COMMERCIAL, 30 SECONDS OR LESS
Amish
ART DIRECTOR *Jason Gaboriau*
CREATIVE DIRECTOR *Gary Goldsmith*
COPYWRITER *Tom Miller*
PHOTOGRAPHY *Stock*
AGENCY *Goldsmith/Jeffrey*
CLIENT *Crain's New York Business*

ANNCR: *In the foothills of Pennsylvania, in the Amish town of Minst, the people live a carefree life. They don't worry about hostile takeovers. They aren't concerned with being ambushed by competitors. Or blindsided by unexpected information. It is a town of joy, friendliness, and boundless love. And when you move there... you can cancel your subscription to Crain's.*

Silver Medalist/U.S.A.

TELEVISION COMMERCIAL, 30 SECONDS OR LESS
Beer Fu
ART DIRECTOR *Scott Smith*
CREATIVE DIRECTORS *Dan Heagy, Terry Baker*
COPYWRITER *Steve Romanenghi*
PRODUCER *Cary Potterfield*
DIRECTOR *Kevin Smith*
MUSIC *Ad Music, Los Angeles*
AGENCY *Leo Burnett Company, Chicago*
CLIENT *Miller Brewing Company*

VISUAL: *Two guys in a bar get zapped into a bad, poorly dubbed Kung Fu movie after hitting the television with a Miller Lite bottle.*
WARLORD (TO MAIDENS): *No one can save you now!*
GUY #1: *Hey, bet we could.*
WARLORD: *Fools! We will defeat you and take your Miller Lite.*
GUY #1: *Not if we choose the weapon.*
VISUAL: *Guy #1 rapidly folds a piece of paper, Kung Fu-style, into a paper football.*
WARLORD: *Paper football! Very clever. You kick off.*
VISUAL: *Guys and warlord's benchmen begin playing. Guys score touchdown, then send the football through the goalposts for the winning score.*
MAIDEN #1/MAIDEN #2: *It's good!/We are saved!*
VISUAL: *Miller Lite bottles on ice.*
ANNCR: *When you've got the great taste of an ice-cold Miller Lite, life is good.*

Silver Medalist/U.S.A.

TELEVISION COMMERCIAL, 30 SECONDS OR LESS, CAMPAIGN
Talk Show, Happy Gary, Wide Load
ART DIRECTORS *John Staffen, Gary Rozanski*
EXECUTIVE CREATIVE DIRECTOR *Mike Rogers*
CREATIVE DIRECTORS *Mike Rogers, John Staffen*
COPYWRITERS *Mike Rogers, Thom Baginski*
PRODUCER *Eric Herrmann*
DIRECTOR *John Lloyd*
MUSIC *Lavsky Music*
STUDIO *BFCS, Inc.*
AGENCY *DDB Needham Worldwide, New York*
CLIENT *New York State Lottery*

ADDITIONAL AWARD

Merit
TELEVISION COMMERCIAL, OVER 30 SECONDS
Wide Load

Wide Load
VISUAL: *Row of houses, man mowing lawn. One house begins to move. House has "Wide Load" sign on its back. Pulls into street, drives by on the back of a truck. Truck stops and "Mel" the mover gets out, goes to front door of the house, and knocks. Occupant opens door, smiles.*
MEL: *Is this O.K.?*
VISUAL: *Whole family runs outside.*
KIDS (SIMULTANEOUSLY): *Yeaaaaaaaaaaahhhhhhh!*
VISUAL: *View of house sitting on beach.*
ANNCR: *Hey, you never know. New York Lotto.*

NEW YORK
LOTTO
Hey, you never know.

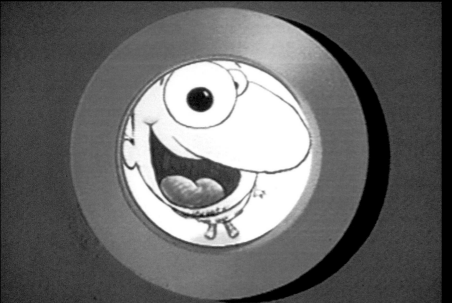

Silver Medalist/U.S.A.

TELEVISION COMMERCIAL, OVER 30 SECONDS, CAMPAIGN
Training Camp, Rotoscope, Prosperous Stroll
ART DIRECTORS *Matt Vescovo, Greg Bell*
CREATIVE DIRECTORS *Arthur Bijur, Cliff Freeman*
COPYWRITERS *Cliff Freeman, Arthur Bijur, Steve Dildarian, Tina Hall, Harold Einstein*
PRODUCERS *Anne Kurtzman, Mary Ellen Duggan*
DIRECTORS *David Kellogg, Jeff Gorman, Charles Wittenmeier*
MUSIC *Michael Carroll Music*
STUDIOS *Propaganda Films, Johns & Gorman Films, Harmony Pictures*
AGENCY *Cliff Freeman & Partners*
CLIENT *Little Caesars*

ADDITIONAL AWARD

Silver Medalist
TELEVISION COMMERCIAL, OVER 30 SECONDS
Training Camp

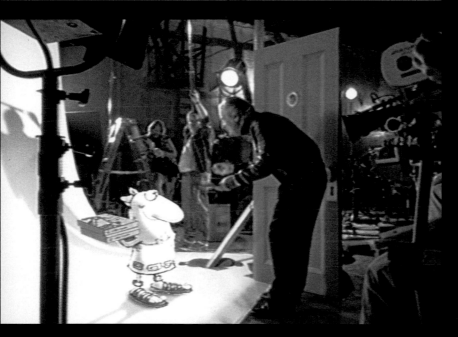

Silver Medalist/U.S.A.

TELEVISION COMMERCIAL, LOW BUDGET
Youth Basketball
ART DIRECTOR *Dan O'Donnell*
CREATIVE DIRECTOR *Edward Boches*
COPYWRITER *Jim Elliott*
PRODUCER *Alyson Singer*
DIRECTOR *Neil Salley*
STUDIO *September Productions*
AGENCY *Mullen*
CLIENT *YMCA*

VISUAL: *Shot of a basketball stuck on a hoop.*
From outside the frame, someone attempts to
knock it down by throwing a tennis shoe at it.
Several more people attempt to do the same.
SUPER: *Beverly YMCA Youth Basketball...*
SUPER: *Needs Volunteers.*
VISUAL: *Shot of basket with ball and several*
tennis shoes in it.

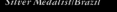

TELEVISION COMMERCIAL, 30 SECONDS OR LESS
The Scream
ART DIRECTOR *Aurélio Julianelli*
CREATIVE DIRECTORS *Eduardo Fischer,*
Cláudio Carillo
COPYWRITER *Ricardo Braga*
PHOTOGRAPHERS *Breno da Silveira,*
Joel Alves Lopes
DIRECTOR *Andrew Waddington*
MUSIC *Jorge Saldanha*
PRODUCTION *EB Produções*
STUDIO *Casa Blanca*
AGENCY *Fisher Justus Comunicações Ltda.*
CLIENT *IRB Industrias Reunidas de Bebidas*
Tatuzinho – 3 Fazendas

VISUAL: *As a soprano sings, she shatters several*
glasses. She then attempts to shatter a bottle but
does not succeed, and ends up shattering herself.
SUPER: *Now in crash-proof bottle.*

TELEVISION COMMERCIAL, 30 SECONDS OR LESS
Ex-Boyfriends
ART DIRECTORS *Elspeth Lynn, Lorraine Tao*
CREATIVE DIRECTOR *Jeff Finkler*
COPYWRITERS *Lorraine Tao, Elspeth Lynn*
PRODUCER *Aggie Brook*
DIRECTOR *Ron Baxter Smith*
MUSIC *Rosnick MacKinnon*
CLIENT CONTACT *Mike Sherlock*
AGENCY *Leo Burnett Company, Toronto*
CLIENT *Fruit of the Loom*

VISUAL: *Pair of lacy red underwear on a clothesline.*
SUPER: *For Jim.*
VISUAL: *Black underwear comes into frame.*
SUPER: *For Mike.*
VISUAL: *Underwear with garters comes into frame.*
SUPER: *For Jeff.*
VISUAL: *Furry, leopard-print underwear comes into frame.*
SUPER: *For Bernie.*
VISUAL: *Fruit of the Loom underwear comes into frame.*
SUPER: *For you.*
ANNCR: *Isn't it time you bought underwear that turns you on, not just them?*

FOR BERNIE.

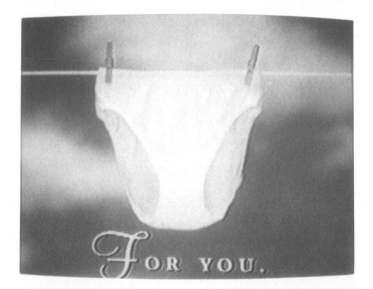

FOR YOU.

Really, really comfortable
~ U N D E R W E A R ~

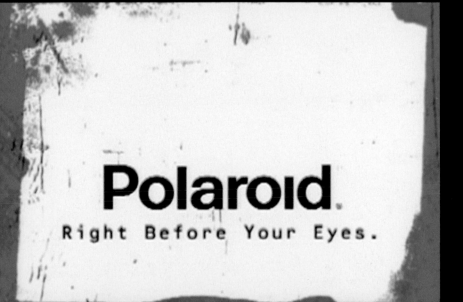

Silver Medalist/Canada

TELEVISION COMMERCIAL, 30 SECONDS OR LESS, CAMPAIGN
Fishing, Puppies, Stereo
ART DIRECTOR *Jamie Way*
CREATIVE DIRECTOR *Larry Tolpin*
COPYWRITER *Randy Diplock*
PRODUCER *Henry Lu*
DIRECTOR *Pier Luca DeCarlo*
MUSIC *Chris Stone Audio*
PRODUCTION HOUSE *Ritts/Hayden*
AGENCY *BBDO Canada*
CLIENT *Polaroid Canada Inc.*

TELEVISION COMMERCIAL, LOW BUDGET
Dogs
ART DIRECTOR *Erik Kessels*
CREATIVE DIRECTORS *Jay Pond-Jones,
Robert Saville*
COPYWRITER *Johan Kramer*
PRODUCER *Spots*
DIRECTORS *Erik Kessels, Johan Kramer*
MUSIC *Marcel Walvisch*
AGENCY *GGT London*
CLIENT *Ariston*

Gold Medalist/U.S.A.

COMMERCIAL, OVER 30 SECONDS, CAMPAIGN
Cow, Irish Humor, Gab, Unlucky, Fighting
COPYWRITERS *Jack Lowe, Bob Adsit*
PRODUCER *Andy Lerner*
DIRECTORS *Jack Lowe, Andy Lerner*
STUDIO *Soundtrack, New York*
AGENCY *Pedone & Partners Advertising Inc.*
CLIENT *Genesee Brewing Company*

Cow
SOUND: *Bar ambiance.*
ANNCR: *They say all Irishmen are born storytellers. Not true. Case in point, Mr. Cormac McMurphy. Now Cormac, do you have a tale you'd like to share with us?*
CORMAC: *"The Cow of Clonakilty."*
ANNCR: *Lay it on me, Cormac.*
CORMAC: *Well, there was a man, Dan his name was, who went to market to sell a cow...*
ANNCR: *Uh huh.*
CORMAC: *And he sold it there to a man named Finn...*
ANNCR: *Uh huh.*
CORMAC: *Who traded the cow to a man named O'Reilly...*
ANNCR: *Uh huh.*
CORMAC: *And the cow and O'Reilly lived happily ever after.*
(A long, uncomfortable pause.)
ANNCR: *That's it?*
CORMAC: *That's it.*
ANNCR: *Well, there you have it, folks, an Irishman who can't tell a story to save his life. But he can tell a good beer when he sees one. Michael Shea's Irish Amber. A rich, hearty beer that tastes great. End of story.... That was deep, Cormac.*
CORMAC: *Thank you.*
ANNCR: *Tell me, is the cow symbolic of O'Reilly's Oedipus complex, or am I reading too much into this?*
TAG ANNCR: *Taste the real spirit of Ireland with Michael Shea's Irish Amber.*

Silver Medalist/U.S.A.

COMMERCIAL, OVER 30 SECONDS
Valentine Candyman
CREATIVE DIRECTOR *Mark Hillman*
COPYWRITER *Mark Hillman*
PRODUCER *Michael LeFevre*
STUDIO *Bert Berdis & Company*
AGENCY *Mars Communications*
CLIENT *Warner Cable/Columbus*

ANNCR: *This is Jim with Warner Cable and today we're talking with the Valentine Candy Man.*
CANDY MAN: *Hey, Sexy.*
ANNCR: *Uh, hi. I understand that you only speak by using the phrases on those little candy hearts.*
CANDY MAN: *Dig me.*
ANNCR: *And that you don't have Warner Cable.*
CANDY MAN: *Wanna cuddle?*
ANNCR: *No, no, no can do, Candy Man. I want to know why a happening guy like you hasn't signed up for Warner Cable.*
CANDY MAN: *Bad boy.*
ANNCR: *Lucky for you, Warner Cable is having a Valentine's Day special offer.*
CANDY MAN: *Hot Mama.*
ANNCR: *There's never been a better time to get all those great news, sports, education, and movie channels.*
CANDY MAN: *Far out.*
ANNCR: *You get Showtime and the Movie Channel for the price of one during the first month.*
CANDY MAN: *Crazy.*
ANNCR: *We're even throwing in 15 minutes of free long-distance calling— for a total savings of over 30 bucks.*
CANDY MAN: *Call me.*
ANNCR: *Ah, you call us. 481-5320.*
CANDY MAN: *I want you.*
ANNCR: *I'm glad you decided to get Warner Cable.*
CANDY MAN: *Hug me.*
ANNCR: *You call Warner Cable at 481-5320 and...I'll think about it.*
CANDY MAN: *Groovy.*
ANNCR: *(Laughs uncomfortably).*

Silver Medalist/U.S.A.

COMMERCIAL, PUBLIC SERVICE, CAMPAIGN
Bob Mehrman Campaign
CREATIVE DIRECTORS *Rich Herstek, Peter Favat*
COPYWRITER *Mark Nardi*
PRODUCER *Lisa Sulda*
STUDIO *Soundtrack, Boston*
AGENCY *Houston Effler Herstek Favat*
CLIENT *Massachusetts Department of Public Health*

ADDITIONAL AWARD

Silver Medalist
RADIO COMMERCIAL, PUBLIC SERVICE
Alphabet

Alphabet
BOB MEHRMAN: *A, B, C, D, E, F, G,...I, J...It is impossible for me to pronounce that missing letter. It is impossible for me to do a lot of things. My name is Bob Mehrman and I must use this Electro larynx because I lost my voice. I got throat cancer from smoking cigarettes and my larynx was removed. I strongly recommend that you keep your larynx. It makes life so much easier. For example, people won't suddenly turn around in restaurants when you talk. If you call someone on the phone, they won't cut you off because they think you are a machine. And if a little nine-year-old girl comes to your front door selling candy for a school project, she won't stare at you and ask if you were a robot. You know, it's too bad I can't pronounce that certain letter I talked about earlier, because there were so many times I wanted to tell the cigarette industry to go to —ell.*
ANNCR: *The Massachusetts Department of Public Health.*

Gold Medalist/U.S.A.

BILLBOARD
Vultures
ART DIRECTOR *Vince Aamodt*
CREATIVE DIRECTOR *Larry Postaer*
COPYWRITER *Vince Aamodt*
PHOTOGRAPHERS *Gary McGuire, Juni Banico*
AGENCY *Rubin Postaer & Associates*
CLIENT *American Lung Association*

Gold Medalist/The Netherlands

BILLBOARD
Pokon Plant Food
ART DIRECTOR *Marsel Van Oosten*
CREATIVE DIRECTOR *Ton Van Hecke*
COPYWRITER *Arjen De Jong*
PHOTOGRAPHER *Edo Kars*
ACCOUNT DIRECTOR *Gé Key*
AGENCY *HVR Advertising*

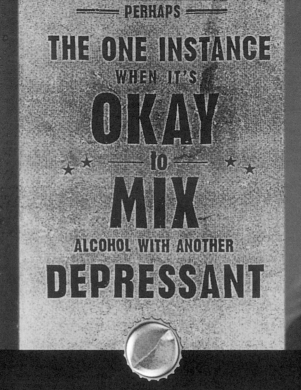

PERHAPS
THE ONE INSTANCE
WHEN IT'S
OKAY
to
MIX
ALCOHOL WITH ANOTHER
DEPRESSANT

THE FIRST ANNUAL ST. LOUIS MICROBREW AND BLUES FESTIVAL.

Silver Medalist/U.S.A.

PROMOTIONAL
Depressant
ART DIRECTOR *Dan Bryant*
CREATIVE DIRECTORS *Eric Tilford, Todd Tilford*
COPYWRITER *Chad Rea*
PHOTOGRAPHER *James Schwartz*
AGENCY *CORE/R & D/The Richards Group*
CLIENT *St. Louis Microbrew and Blues Festival*

ADDITIONAL AWARD

Merit
POSTER, ENTERTAINMENT OR SPECIAL EVENT

(facing page)
Silver Medalist/Japan

POINT-OF-PURCHASE
N.G. Inc Rikuyo-Sha
ART DIRECTOR *Hiroaki Nagai*
DESIGNER *Kyoko Iida*
PHOTOGRAPHER *Katsuhiro Ichikawa*

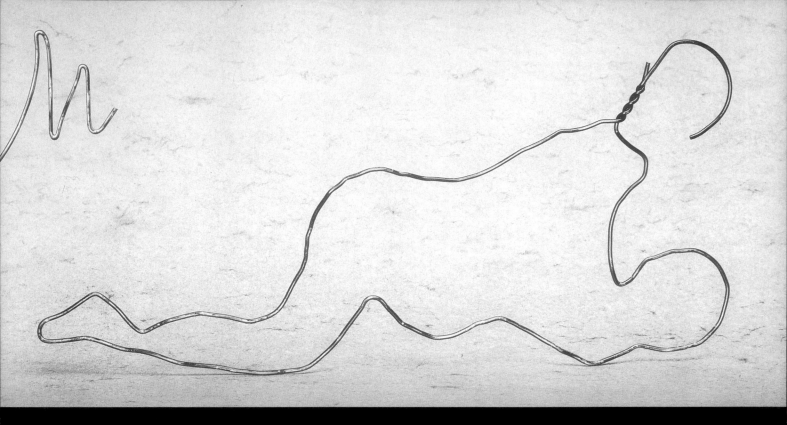

1895 1995

AT ONE POINT,
HE WANTED TO BECOME A PRIEST. HE SETTLED FOR
BEING A GOD.

In 1902, a rowdy 7-year-old named George Herman Ruth was sent off to St. Mary's School for boys, a Catholic reform school in Baltimore. A teacher there named Brother Matthias taught Babe to play baseball and had such an influence on the youth that he considered entering the priesthood.

Fortunately for baseball fans (and Catholics everywhere), he opted for pinstripes over a frock. Ruth went on to be the most revered athlete in history. And how worthy of worship was he? To put his dominance into perspective, consider that in 1920, Ruth out-homered not just every player, but 14 out of 15 teams.

(To approach this feat today, Ken Griffey Jr. would have to hit well over 200 home runs a season.) Ruth was so good, even scientists of the day studied him. One physicist from Columbia University named Professor Hodges reported that Ruth "had a near magical facility for hitting a baseball." He calculated that when Ruth swung his 54 oz. bat (the heaviest in history), he applied 24,000 foot pounds of energy. (Pardon us for slipping over the math.)

You'll learn a lot about the Babe you didn't know when you visit The Babe Ruth Museum. Sundays are a particularly good day to stop in and pay your respects.

Celebrating 100 years. 216 Emory Street Baltimore, Maryland. Open daily, admission $5. For more information call (410) 727-1539. Photos courtesy of the National Baseball Library in Cooperstown, New York.

THE BABE RUTH MUSEUM

1895 1995

WHEN BABE GOT
CAUGHT IN A RUNDOWN, IT WAS USUALLY BETWEEN
1ST AND 142ND.

Millions knew him as the Sultan of Swat. But to those who had to ride in a car with him, Babe's lead foot earned him another nickname, "The Ghost of Riverside Drive."

One incident in 1921 left Babe in jail and 2 hours late for a game. En route to the Polo Grounds, Ruth was hauled in for speeding. Facing the same judge who had fined him before, Babe was locked up with some of New York's finest felons for several hours. Changing into his uniform from jail, Ruth was finally released after paying a $100 fine. (He then drove 9 miles through New York City traffic in 16 minutes reaching speeds

far greater than the one for which he was fined.)

Many times though, the Babe's speeding cost him a lot more than a hundred bucks. He wrecked countless Cadillacs and Packards. He even survived one collision with a trolley. Though Yankee teammate Tony Lazzari later commented, "He wasn't really that bad a driver, just a bit reckless." Ironically, Ruth later took part in a New York safe driving campaign. Babe rode around in an open touring car waving safety signs. (Wisely, somebody else drove the car.)

There's a lot about Babe you don't know, so stop by. Just watch out for speed traps on Pratt Street.

Celebrating 100 years. 216 Emory Street Baltimore, Maryland. Open daily, admission $5. For more information call (410) 727-1539. Photos courtesy of the National Baseball Library in Cooperstown, New York.

THE BABE RUTH MUSEUM

1895 1995

HIS BIGGEST DAY
EVER AT THE PLATE?
18 HOT DOGS.

You won't find this statistic in any official box score. But the Babe did wolf down 18 wieners once at a New Jersey State Fair eating contest.

Yankee reporter Art Robinson recalled another time Babe stayed up all night playing cards and probably ate 14 sirloin sandwiches with some odds and ends thrown in. The next day on just two hours of sleep, he hit two homers over the center field wall.

Of course, the Bambino didn't always wait until after games to indulge. He was known to order hot dogs and ice cream from a vendor right in the middle of a game when his hearty appetite beckoned. (Babe kept a jar of

bicarbonate soda handy in the dugout just in case of any unexpected gastronomical emergencies.)

His legendary eating habits even led to the creation of Yankee pinstripes. In spring of 1925, Yankee team owner Colonel Jacob Ruppert requested pinstripes be added to the Yankee uniform, reportedly to make Ruth look thinner to the team's fans. Amazingly enough, while the Bambino's waistline topped out at a whopping 49 3/4 inches in 1952, his most impressive career numbers came from the end of a bat, not a fork.

To see those numbers for yourself, stop by. Our sincere apologies to Babe, but no food allowed.

Celebrating 100 years. 216 Emory Street Baltimore, Maryland. Open daily, admission $5. For more information call (410) 727-1539. Photos courtesy of the National Baseball Library in Cooperstown, New York.

THE BABE RUTH MUSEUM

1895 1995

HE WAS THE
FIRST ATHLETE TO ENDORSE UNDERWEAR. LUCKILY, WE COULDN'T LOCATE
ANY PICTURES.

In 1924, *The New York Times* listed Babe Ruth as the most photographed person of the day, ahead of the president and Mickey Mouse. Capitalizing on his popularity, the All-American Underwear Company paid the Babe to endorse their 100% cotton briefs. (Actually, when playing ball he wore no underwear, but that's another story.)

Ruth's other endorsements included everything from cereal to chewing tobacco. He was also the first star athlete to endorse athletic shoes. (Had television been invented yet, the Babe would have made Michael Jordan and Joe Montana look underexposed.)

Though not every endorsement came with the Babe's approval. Curtiss Candy Company introduced a candy bar they called "Baby Ruth." To this day, the company claims it was named after President Grover Cleveland's daughter Ruth. (She's no doubt who you think of every time you unwrap one.) Babe even endorsed the country's National Guard. For his publicity photographs with General Pershing though, they couldn't find an army uniform big enough and the Babe had to be fitted with a khaki suit instead.

To see the Bambino in a uniform that did fit, stop by today for a visit to the Babe Ruth Museum.

Celebrating 100 years. 216 Emory Street Baltimore, Maryland. Open daily, admission $5. For more information call (410) 727-1539. Photos courtesy of the National Baseball Library in Cooperstown, New York.

THE BABE RUTH MUSEUM

Panasonic

カミさんは忘れた

※たまりにたまった行きツケも

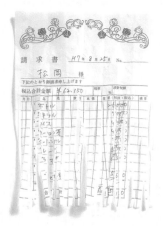

※ゴルフ場へ"休日出社"も

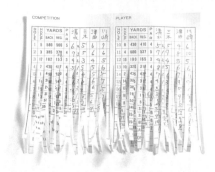

松下電器産業株式会社

Silver Medalist/Japan

TRANSIT
My Wife Is Good at Finding Things I've Tried
Hard to Lose
ART DIRECTORS *Takanori Yasukouchi,*
Naoki Nakano
CREATIVE DIRECTORS *Katsunori Tsuyama,*
Masayuki Bundo
COPYWRITERS *Ryoji Matsuoka,*
Kiyoharu Shimizu
DESIGNERS *Mitsuaki Inaba, Yoshiyuki Miyoshi,*
Kenichi Mori
PHOTOGRAPHER *Kazuo Miki*
PRINTER *Mutsumi Create Ltd.*
AGENCY *Dentsu Inc., Osaka*
CLIENT *Matsushita Electric Industrial Co. Ltd.*

ろに見つけ出す。

Silver Medalist/Austria

PUBLIC SERVICE
Stop AIDS Now
CREATIVE DIRECTOR *Claudio Alessandri*
DESIGNERS *Momix, Cordula Alessandri,*
Marcus Sterz
PHOTOGRAPHER *Claudio Alessandri*
AGENCY *Alessandri GmbH*
CLIENT *AIDS-Hilfen Österreichs*

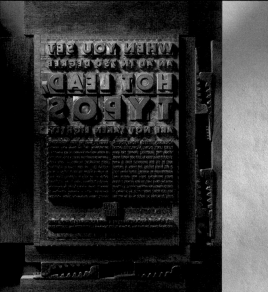

WHEN YOU SET
AN AD IN 750 DEGREE
HOT LEAD, TYPOS
ARE NOT TAKEN LIGHTLY.

FORMING LETTERS FROM MOLTEN LEAD ISN'T DONE NONCHALANTLY. When first practiced around the year 1450, it took time to cast hot metal type. And to do this properly, time is what it still takes today. But there is another requirement to pouring letterforms from lead, arranging them into words, and pressing their images into paper. It takes dedication — something that M & H Type has exhibited since 1915, by offering a rare collection of metal type to suit the tastes of even the most discriminating individuals. And for those who require a more modern approach, we provide a photo-composition service also, using the most advanced technology obtainable today. Call Andrew Hoyem, president, to inquire about the availability of type styles or for help in planning your next project. Because there is an additional benefit from having your typography composed with a greater attention to detail. There are usually fewer mistakes.

M & H TYPE, TYPOGRAPHERS & TYPEFOUNDERS SINCE 1915.
460 Bryant Street, San Francisco, California 94107. Telephone 415-777-0716. Fax: 415-777-2730.

WHEN YOUR
T·Y·P·E
LOOKS LIKE THIS,
IT IS YOUR
VISUAL.

THE LETTERFORMS YOU ARE READING ARE FASHIONED AS those of Johann Gutenberg, who, around the year 1450, worked out a method of casting type and printing so enduring it is practiced today. And nowhere is this craft upheld more than at the oldest and largest typefoundry in the United States, M & H Type. First, we cast letters from molten lead. Next, we cover them with ink and then impress them onto paper. The advantage of this process is an image as crisp as an engraving and as expensive as any work of art. Plus, for individuals who are as equally demanding of typography generated by computer, we now provide an exacting photo-composition service that utilizes the most advanced technologies. Please call Andrew Hoyem, president, to inquire about the availability of types, or for help in planning your next project. We think you will find that what your type is a picture of perfection. It could be the only visual your message requires.

M & H TYPE, TYPOGRAPHERS & TYPEFOUNDERS SINCE 1915.
460 Bryant Street, San Francisco, California 94107. Telephone 415-777-0716. Fax: 415-777-2730.

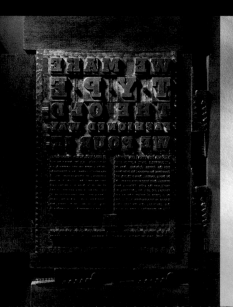

WE MAKE T·Y·P·E THE OLD-FASHIONED WAY. WE POUR IT.

AROUND THE YEAR 1450, JOHANN GUTENBERG CAST MOLTEN LEAD into the Roman alphabet. Then for five years, he arranged his letterforms by hand, covered them with ink, and pressed their images into paper. The result was the Latin Bible — a book revered not only by Christians, but by a group of zealots who became known as typographers. M & H Type has continued this tradition since 1915 by presenting a rare collection of metal types to suit discriminating individuals. And, for those who may desire a more modern approach, we are equally demanding of typography generated by photo-composition. To inquire about the availability of type styles, or for help in planning your next project, please contact Andrew Hoyem, president. Because just as did Gutenberg over five-hundred years ago, we do considerably more than compose typography. We worship it.

M & H TYPE, TYPOGRAPHERS & TYPEFOUNDERS SINCE 1915.
460 Bryant Street, San Francisco, California 94107. Telephone 415-777-0716. Fax: 415-777-2730.

DISTINCTIVE MERIT AWARDS

Distinctive Merit/U.S.A.

FULL PAGE OR SPREAD
The Poe Museum Is Now Preparing for Its Quarterly Wine Tasting
ART DIRECTOR *Cliff Sorah*
CREATIVE DIRECTOR *Mike Hughes*
COPYWRITER *Raymond McKinney*
PRINT PRODUCER *Karen Smith*
AGENCY *The Martin Agency*
CLIENT *The Poe Museum*

ADDITIONAL AWARD

Merit
NEWSPAPER, CONSUMER, CAMPAIGN
*Wine Tasting, Slasher Movies,
Who Is the True Heir to Poe*

Distinctive Merit/U.S.A.

LESS THAN A FULL PAGE
Siskel & Ebert
ART DIRECTORS *Abi Aron, Rob Carducci*
CREATIVE DIRECTOR *Sal DeVito*
COPYWRITERS *Rob Carducci, Abi Aron*
DESIGNER *Leslie Sweet*
AGENCY *DeVito Verdi*
CLIENT *Time Out*

ADDITIONAL AWARD

Merit
POSTER, TRANSIT

Taxicabs

make pretty

good slalom

cones.

The next generation E-Class starts at $39,900.

The new E-Class: Rack-and-pinion steering. Double-wishbone front suspension. Side air bags mounted in the front doors. Dual-zone climate control. What a great way to get around. (Ⓜ) Mercedes-Benz

Distinctive Merit/U.S.A.

FULL PAGE OR SPREAD
Taxicabs Make Pretty Good Slalom Cones
ART DIRECTOR *Mark Fuller*
CREATIVE DIRECTORS *Kerry Feuerman, Ron Huey*
COPYWRITER *Joe Nagy*
PRINT PRODUCER *Tom Maher*
AGENCY *The Martin Agency*
CLIENT *Mercedes-Benz of North America*

Distinctive Merit/U.S.A.

CAMPAIGN
Ozone, Second Million, Securities, Bliss
ART DIRECTOR *Dan Cohen*
CREATIVE DIRECTOR *Rochelle Klein*
COPYWRITER *Payl Hartzell*
AGENCY *Angotti Thomas Hedge, Inc.*
CLIENT *Barron's*

ADDITIONAL AWARDS

Merit
NEWSPAPER, CONSUMER, LESS THAN A FULL PAGE
Ozone

Merit
NEWSPAPER, CONSUMER, LESS THAN A FULL PAGE
Second Million

Merit
NEWSPAPER, CONSUMER, LESS THAN A FULL PAGE
Securities

Given the state of the ozone layer, there's never been a worse time to lose your shirt.

To subscribe, call 1-800-328-6800, Ext. 514. *Barron's. How money becomes wealth.*

It's a lot easier making your second million. But we'll talk about that later.

To sub cribe, call 1-800-328-6800, Ext. 510. *Barron's. How money becomes wealth.*

Whoever named them "Securities" had a wicked sense of humor.

To subscribe, call 1-800-328-6800, Ext. 524. *Barron's. How money becomes wealth.*

Ignorance may be bliss. But bliss won't mail you a dividend check four times a year.

To subscribe, call 1-800-328-6800, Ext. 510. *Barron's. How money becomes wealth.*

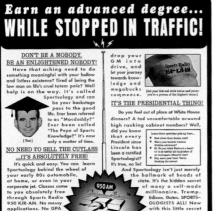

Distinctive Merit/U.S.A.

CAMPAIGN
*Urinal Chat, Study at Home, Traffic,
Radio Waves, Stupid*
ART DIRECTOR *Jason Busa*
CREATIVE DIRECTOR *Wade Koniakowsky*
COPYWRITER *Rob Bagot*
DESIGNER *Wade Koniakowsky*
ILLUSTRATORS *Wade Koniakowsky, Jason Busa*
AGENCY *Big Bang Idea Engineering*
CLIENT *New Century Media/Sports Radio
950 KJR-AM*

*T*HE HORROR STORIES YOU'VE HEARD ABOUT CHEMOTHERAPY ARE TRUE. THEY'RE ALSO A DECADE OLD.

Today, men and women are leading more active lives while undergoing chemotherapy treatment. And that's good news. Recent breakthroughs are helping reduce many of the common side effects of treatment including nausea and even more serious conditions that can develop like a low white blood cell count.

One drug, Neupogen (Filgrastim), is now being prescribed to help certain people on chemotherapy maintain a normal white blood cell count. Specifically, a normal neutrophil count. In short, neutrophils are white blood cells that help your body fight infection. Maintaining a normal neutrophil count during your chemotherapy treatment can be important for two reasons.

First, you have a much greater chance of staying on your chemotherapy schedule. And, that will mean getting your treatment behind you sooner. Secondly, maintaining a normal neutrophil count can help reduce your risk of infection. So you have a better chance of staying out of the hospital. Instead, you can spend more time at home where you belong with family and friends. Even daily activities like shopping and eating out can be more accessible.

Of course, Neupogen isn't appropriate for every patient. Ask your doctor if Neupogen should be a recommended part of your treatment. On the following page, you'll find an explanation of Neupogen and its possible side effects. The most common side effect that patients experience is mild-to-moderate bone pain, which can usually be controlled with a non-aspirin analgesic.

In closing, before we embarked on this educational campaign, we conducted extensive research with people undergoing chemotherapy and with doctors. Among those being treated, we found an overwhelming desire for more information concerning treatment. Doctors, many of whom had initial misgivings about any advertising at all, urged us to be candid and to point out that Neupogen isn't for everyone. We acted on their advice.

We realize that your medical care is a sensitive and personal matter. We'd like to know your feelings about the information presented here. If you would like to receive more information concerning Neupogen and how it might help *NEUPOGEN* in your treatment, please call us at 1-800-333-9777, extension 667.

Bra Fata Morgana

Today's special offer: 3 for 2.

Triumph
INTERNATIONAL

Distinctive Merit/U.S.A.

FULL PAGE OR SPREAD
The Horror Stories
ART DIRECTOR *Mark Fuller*
CREATIVE DIRECTORS *Mike Hughes, Ron Huey*
COPYWRITER *Ron Huey*
PRINT PRODUCER *Tom Maher*
AGENCY *The Martin Agency*
CLIENT *Amgen*

Distinctive Merit/Switzerland

CAMPAIGN
Valentine's, Spring, Today's Special Offer,
Jolly Good, Headache
ART DIRECTOR *Danielle Lanz*
CREATIVE DIRECTOR *André Benker*
COPYWRITER *Hanspeter Schweizer*
PHOTOGRAPHER *Felix Streuli*
AGENCY *Wirz Werbeagentur AG*
CLIENT *Triumph International*

Meet four of the Magnificent Seven. Their story is the stuff movies are made of.

It all began way back in the 60s.

Seven men met. They became firm friends. And being experts in their craft, soon became known as the Magnificent Seven — a title that is now a famous catchphrase.

Sounds vaguely familiar? Then you may have heard our chefs' story before.

If not, read on.

In 1973, we persuaded Vincent Chui, our head chef, and 6 others at a premier Chinese restaurant to come work for us at the Golden Phoenix.

Needless to say, that premier Chinese restaurant no longer exists.

And so the Magnificent Seven came on board.

Four master chefs with 60 years experience among them; another two cutting-board specialists (yes, just to cut meat and vegetables); and the seventh, a food coordinator to organize over 1000 culinary items.

Nothing was too excessive to make the Golden Phoenix the "Best in the West". (West Malaysia, that is.)

Four of them are still with us today, weaving their own brand of magic.

In Chinese culinary circles, they are legends.

The last we heard there was a movie about the Magnificent Seven.

Funny. We haven't sold the film rights yet.

HOTEL EQUATORIAL KUALA LUMPUR. JALAN SULTAN ISMAIL 50250 KUALA LUMPUR. FOR RESERVATIONS, TEL: 261 7777 EXT. 8222

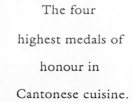

The four highest medals of honour in Cantonese cuisine.

fried rice and noodles; over and over again for 6 long years, perfecting these humble dishes.

A breeze compared to the next level.

The 3rd wok stage. Another 8 years in the art of broiling, baking, steaming, stir-frying and grilling over a hundred dishes to mouthwatering standards.

Not surprisingly, few persevere to 2nd wok status.

As a 2nd wok chef, you'd spend 7 years preparing dishes so delicately flavoured, a slip of your hand sees the

If you seek greatness in the art of Chinese cuisine, you'd pursue the same goal many do.

To enter the "4 Wok Hierarchy" in the kitchens of the Golden Phoenix.

You begin your culinary career with the 4th wok, the lowest in the pecking order.

(But only after 8 years cleaning and cutting meat and vegetables.)

At this stage, you'd prepare noodles and fried rice,

dish end up in a rubbish bin instead of a serving plate.

Finally, after as much time as it takes to earn 4 medical degrees, you earn 1st wok status.

Now you become an artist in specialties like thousand-ringgit abalone dishes, some of which take up to 5 hours to prepare.

Not for the faint-hearted, this punishing 35-year test.

But then, when were medals ever awarded to the faint-hearted?

HOTEL EQUATORIAL KUALA LUMPUR. JALAN SULTAN ISMAIL 50250 KUALA LUMPUR. FOR RESERVATIONS, TEL: 261 7777 EXT. 8222

You're looking at our entry for the Guinness Book of World Records.

One fateful day in 1973, we accepted a reservation for a table at the Golden Phoenix.

At the time, it seemed no more than an ordinary lunch reservation for eight people. Little did we know the reservation would stand until today.

Every weekday for the past 22 years, a few or all of our original eight patrons have returned to enjoy lunch at the same table. Each even has his own designated seat.

Their routine never varies.

They walk in, graciously allow our head chef to decide their menu for the day, go Dutch, then leave.

A practice that may well establish the Golden Phoenix as record holder for the world's longest-running lunchtime reservation.

But what keeps them coming back? There are many theories concerning their unwavering loyalty.

The position of our table being good 'feng shui' perhaps?

Or a diabolical marketing ploy to attract more guests to the Golden Phoenix?

Our eight patrons will simply tell you it's the consistently high standard of our cuisine.

So the next time you walk in to enjoy the same cuisine, look out for legendary table No. 7.

Believe it or not, they'll be there.

Now does that qualify us for Ripley's too?

HOTEL EQUATORIAL KUALA LUMPUR. JALAN SULTAN ISMAIL 50250 KUALA LUMPUR. FOR RESERVATIONS, TEL: 261 7777 EXT. 8222

Distinctive Merit/Malaysia

CAMPAIGN

Magnificent Seven, Cantonese Cuisine, Guinness Book of World Records
ART DIRECTOR *Cheong Yew Fei*
CREATIVE DIRECTOR *Basil Antonas*
COPYWRITER *Dharma Somasundram, T. C.*
PHOTOGRAPHY *Adam Photo*
AGENCY *Dentsu Young & Rubicam, Malaysia*
CLIENT *Hotel Equatorial*

Distinctive Merit/Switzerland

CAMPAIGN
Individual Numbers
ART DIRECTOR *Erik Voser*
CREATIVE DIRECTOR *Jean Etienne Aebi*
COPYWRITER *Matthias Freuler*
PHOTOGRAPHER *Hans Pieler*
AGENCY *Aebi Strebel*
CLIENT *ELVIA*

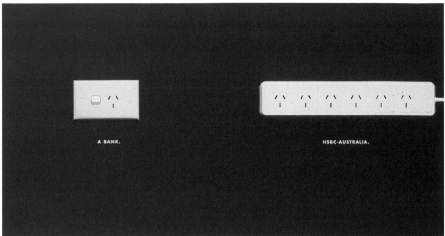

Distinctive Merit/Australia

CAMPAIGN
Hong Kong Bank
ART DIRECTOR *Tony Leishman*
CREATIVE DIRECTOR *Nick Trumble*
COPYWRITER *Nick Trumble*
PHOTOGRAPHER *Stuart Crossett*
TYPOGRAPHER *John Pungercar*
AGENCY *Clemenger Haruie*
CLIENT *Hong Kong Bank*

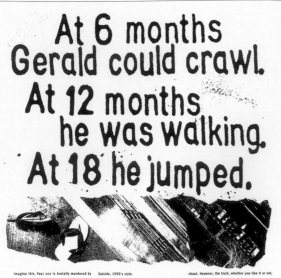

At 6 months Gerald could crawl. At 12 months he was walking. At 18 he jumped.

Imagine this. Your son is brutally murdered by someone who has the same clothes, same finger-prints and same name as him.

But as far as you're concerned it's not him. It can't be him.

This is exactly how Gerald's mother felt when she learnt of her son's suicide. "That person up there wasn't my son. I don't know what got into him. I thought everything was fine."

There is nothing quite as despairing as being unable to recognise a family member crying out for help. Especially one's own flesh and blood.

Unfortunately, that is the way it usually happens.

Last year, on a windy day in April, a lone figure was loitering on the roof-top of a 10 storey HDB block.

Only two hours later, local police discovered a lifeless body between two cars in the carpark below.

Another day. Another tragedy.

Welcome to the not-so pretty side of reality.

Suicide, 1990's style.

To you dear reader, this incredible story about an 18-year old jumping off a high building may look as if it was written with the sole intention of getting your attention.

Well, you're absolutely right.

We hope you saw this ad and we hope you'll spare a few minutes to read it. For one very simple reason. Suicide is robbing this nation of the unfulfilled talent, contribution and genius of a generation in the most productive years of their lives.

Such loss is immeasurable and it's high time we as a nation came to terms with it.

Before the end of this day, fifteen Singaporeans, people just like Gerald will try to end their life prematurely.

Out of the fifteen, one will never need to try again.

It's a shocking statistic and one you may not have known about. Or felt that you'd rather not know

about. However, the truth, whether you like it or not, is still the truth.

Every day our volunteers are swamped with calls. Some are suicidal, others just need a shoulder to cry on.

Either way it's not a happy job.

We are trying our best, but to be honest, we feel that there are a lot more people out there who are too afraid to call us.

If you're one of them. Don't be.

Experience has taught us that when left alone, suicidal feelings don't go away. They get worse and in the end become all consuming.

If you're feeling suicidal or know anyone you suspect is suicidal, please get in touch with us. We can help.

Our phone lines are in operation 24 hours, every day of the year.

All calls are confidential and our service is totally free of charge. When life gets too much, call us.

THE SAMARITANS
1800 2214444

To stop her uncle from climbing into her bed again, Shirley bought two bottles of sleeping pills.

Apparently not everyone who calls the Samaritans of Singapore wants to commit suicide.

Some callers have bigger problems.

Like the true story of Shirley. A bright, fifteen year old JC student whose uncle moved in with her family last year.

One afternoon, she awoke to find him lying on top of her. As she recalls: he was heavier, stronger and threatened to hurt her if she tried to resist. It was to be the worst twenty minutes of her life.

One month later she missed her period.

Too terrified to tell her mother or anyone, she phoned SOS. According to the Samaritan who took the call, not many words were exchanged during that first contact call.

For most of it she just cried.

You might imagine, that for an organisation which deals specifically with suicide, calls like this are few and far between.

Sadly, the truth is a different matter. Our volunteers come into contact with people who have problems equally as distressing as Shirley's. And on a daily basis.

Some we refer to other organisations. The remainder we try to untangle ourselves.

We openly admit, not every caller is suicidal. But then again, we've come to learn that nothing is ever what it seems.

That's why we spend months on end, training Samaritans to listen to what people are really saying. To listen between the lines.

Looking back, although it wasn't at first immediately obvious, Shirley had been thinking of suicide. She was just too embarrassed to tell anyone. Or perhaps no one had ever enquired.

You see unlike what people believe; to ask a child if they're suicidal does not put the idea in their head.

Shirley's two large bottles of pills confirmed that.

So besides giving her advice about her pregnancy, legal rights and family counselling, our volunteers also did the job they were trained for. They listened.

Shirley was lucky. There are others who aren't.

Each day 15 Singaporeans try to kill themselves. Out of that, one usually succeeds.

It's a shocking statistic we know, and one we're trying to lower. But in all honesty, it's not easy. There are still people out there who are too afraid or perhaps too embarrassed to call us.

If you're one of them. Don't be.

Experience has taught us that when left alone, suicidal feelings don't get better. They get worse.

If you're feeling suicidal or know anyone who you think is suicidal, please get in touch with us. We can help.

Our phone lines operate 24 hours, every day of the year.

All calls are confidential and our service is totally free of charge.

When life gets too much, call us.

THE SAMARITANS
1800 2214444

Distinctive Merit/Singapore

CAMPAIGN
Gerald, Shirley, Jolene
ART DIRECTOR *Low Phong Thia*
CREATIVE DIRECTOR *Eugene Cheong*
COPYWRITER *Glendon Mar*
DESIGNER *Low Phong Thia*
PHOTOGRAPHER *Low Phong Thia*
AGENCY *Euro RSCG Ball Partnership Singapore*
CLIENT *The Samaritans*

Jolene's boyfriend never wants to see her again. He won't.

Although a small minority of our teenagers die from cancer, strokes and heart attacks, more are being taken by another killer.

One that's more unpredictable, more fickle and more difficult to pin down than even AIDS.

Their emotions.

Today, more Singaporean teenagers contemplate suicide than any other teenage generation in history.

It's a distressing fact, and one we wish wasn't true.

Unfortunately, wishing doesn't change the truth.

Last year, two-thirds of the calls we received from teenagers were classified suicidal. (That's a one hundred per cent increase of the ratio of calls, in just three short years.)

On top of that, the total number of calls has doubled. Never before have we had so many.

Our counsellors are swamped.

Now more than ever, children aged 13 to 19 urgently need our help.

Teenagers just like Jolene.

Last year, on a lonely night in May, sixteen year old Jolene made sure she'd never have another broken heart. Ever again.

That night, her parents found the door to her room tightly locked.

Nothing strange about this they thought; she'd locked herself in on a few occasions.

However the next morning, the door was still locked. With no response from her, the worried parents broke into her room.

That moment, is a moment they'll never forget

for as long as they live.

There, hanging by a piece of thick cord was the still, lifeless body of their darling daughter.

She'd been dead for over eight hours.

No one had known.

Nothing on earth will ever prepare a parent for such a sight. Nor should it. No parent ever deserves to outlive their own children.

Sadly, such tragedies are becoming commonplace in Singapore.

It's time the slaughter stopped.

Everyday fifteen Singaporeans try to kill themselves. People just like you and I. Young people, old people, rich and poor. Suicide is a respecter of no-one.

Out of the fifteen, one person never needs to try again.

It's a shocking statistic and one we're desperately trying to lower. But to be honest, we can't do it alone.

There's still a great many people who are too afraid or too embarrassed to call us.

If you're one of them. Don't be.

Experience has taught us that when left alone, suicidal feelings don't get better. They get worse and in the end become all consuming.

The most effective way to fight suicide is to talk to somebody. Anybody.

At the Samaritans of Singapore we can help.

Our phone lines operate 24 hours, every day of the year. All calls are confidential and our service is free.

When life gets too much, call us.

THE SAMARITANS
1800 2214444

Distinctive Merit/U.S.A.

FULL PAGE OR SPREAD
Helps Stop Squeaks
ART DIRECTORS *John Morton, Robert Shaw West*
CREATIVE DIRECTOR *Robert Shaw West*
COPYWRITER *Bo Coyner*
DESIGNER *Robert Shaw West*
PHOTOGRAPHER *Steve Belkowitz*
ILLUSTRATOR *Drew Townsend*
PRODUCER *Lee Davis*
PRINTER *Square One Studio*
AGENCY *West & Vaughan*
CLIENT *Snap, Inc.*

ADDITIONAL AWARD

Merit
POSTER, POINT-OF-PURCHASE

Distinctive Merit/U.S.A.

CAMPAIGN
Surveillance, Precision, Stealth
ART DIRECTOR *Rob Palmer*
CREATIVE DIRECTOR *David Lubars*
COPYWRITER *Max Gdsil*
PHOTOGRAPHY *Stock*
ILLUSTRATOR *Howard Lim*
PRODUCER *Denise Casstevens*
PRINTER *Gore Graphics*
AGENCY *BBDO West*
CLIENT *Northrop Grumman Corporation*

ADDITIONAL AWARD

Merit
MAGAZINE, CONSUMER, FULL PAGE OR SPREAD
Surveillance

(facing page)
Distinctive Merit/U.S.A.

LESS THAN A FULL PAGE
No Bugs
ART DIRECTOR *Todd Grant*
CREATIVE DIRECTOR *Michael Mazza*
COPYWRITER *Bo Coyner*
PHOTOGRAPHER *Gil Smith*
PRODUCER *Suzee Barrabee*
AGENCY *Goodby Silverstein & Partners*
CLIENT *Isuzu Motors*

ADDITIONAL AWARD

Merit
MAGAZINE, CONSUMER, CAMPAIGN
No Bugs, Peanut Butter, Human Robots

Distinctive Merit/U.S.A.

FULL PAGE OR SPREAD
Screaming Orgasm
ART DIRECTOR *Whit Friese*
CREATIVE DIRECTOR *Mark Figliulo*
COPYWRITER *John Coveny*
PHOTOGRAPHER *Robert Whitman*
AGENCY *Leo Burnett Company, Chicago*
CLIENT *Schieffelin & Somerset Co.*

ADDITIONAL AWARD

Merit
MAGAZINE, CONSUMER, CAMPAIGN
Need We Say More, Screaming Orgasm,
Trust Us

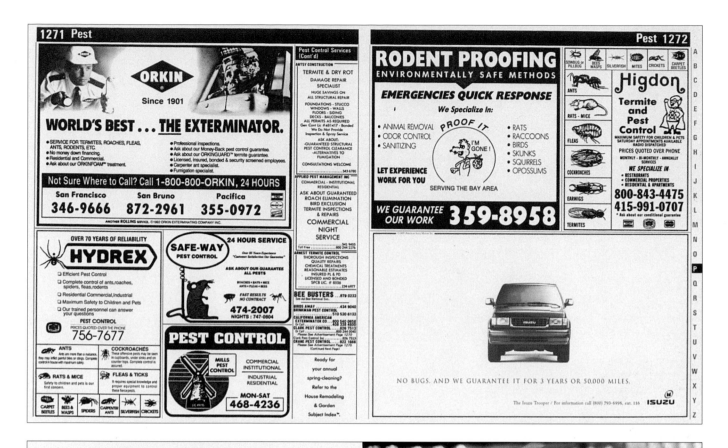

NO BUGS. AND WE GUARANTEE IT FOR 3 YEARS OR 50,000 MILES.

The Isuzu Trooper / For information call (800) 793-6996, ext. 116 ISUZU

Do you really want to ask this guy to give you a "Screaming Orgasm"?

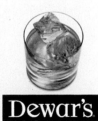

Dewar's

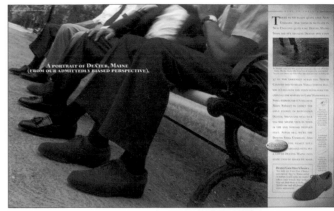

Distinctive Merit/U.S.A.

CAMPAIGN
Porch, Park Bench, All-Terrain, Boat
ART DIRECTOR *Hal Curtis*
CREATIVE DIRECTOR *Woody Kay*
COPYWRITER *Steve Bautista*
PHOTOGRAPHERS *Paul Clancy, Susie Cushner,*
Harry DeZitter, Jack Richmond
ILLUSTRATOR *Peter Hall*
PRODUCER *Marita Stapleton*
AGENCY *Pagano Schenck & Kay*
CLIENT *Dexter Shoe Company*

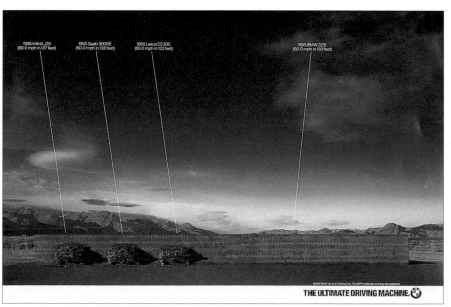

Distinctive Merit/U.S.A.

CAMPAIGN
Ice Fishing, Feather, Brick Wall
ART DIRECTOR *Keith Weinman*
CREATIVE DIRECTORS *Keith Weinman, Jack Fund*
COPYWRITERS *Peter Pappas, Jack Fund*
PHOTOGRAPHERS *Jim Hall, Garry Owens*
AGENCY *Mullen*
CLIENT *BMW of North America, Inc.*

ADDITIONAL AWARDS

Distinctive Merit
MAGAZINE, CONSUMER, FULL PAGE OR SPREAD
Ice Fishing

Merit
MAGAZINE, CONSUMER, FULL PAGE OR SPREAD
Feather

Distinctive Merit
MAGAZINE, CONSUMER, FULL PAGE OR SPREAD
Brick Wall

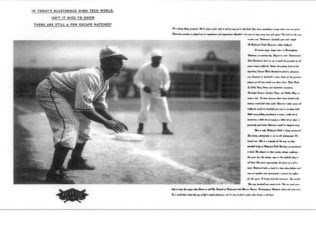

AT MOST BASEBALL PARKS
A HOT DOG AND SODA WILL SET YOU BACK'S.
AT RICKWOOD FIELD
IT WILL SET YOU BACK 85 YEARS.

FOR THOSE HOPELESS ROMANTICS
STILL IN LOVE, BUT A LITTLE DISENCHANTED,
WITH THE GAME OF BASEBALL,
THIS IS THE PLACE TO RENEW YOUR VOWS.

Distinctive Merit/U.S.A.

CAMPAIGN
Rickwood
ART DIRECTOR *Gregg McGough*
CREATIVE DIRECTOR *Terry Slaughter*
COPYWRITERS *Laura Holmes, Don Harbor*
PHOTOGRAPHER *John Huet*
AGENCY *Slaughter Hanson*
CLIENT *The Friends of Rickwood*

EN? WANNEER GAAN WE NAAR DE OPTICIEN?
ONGEMERKT KUNNEN UW OGEN ACHTERUIT GAAN. REDEN GENOEG OM ZE EENS PER JAAR TE LATEN CONTROLEREN. STICHTING BETER ZIEN.

EN? WANNEER GAAN WE NAAR DE OPTICIEN?
ONGEMERKT KUNNEN UW OGEN ACHTERUIT GAAN. REDEN GENOEG OM ZE EENS PER JAAR TE LATEN CONTROLEREN. STICHTING BETER ZIEN.

EN? WANNEER GAAN WE NAAR DE OPTICIEN?
ONGEMERKT KUNNEN UW OGEN ACHTERUIT GAAN. REDEN GENOEG OM ZE EENS PER JAAR TE LATEN CONTROLEREN. STICHTING BETER ZIEN.

Distinctive Merit/The Netherlands

CAMPAIGN
Fish, Slippers, Toilet
ART DIRECTOR *Diederick Hillenius*
COPYWRITER *Lysbeth Bijlstra*
PHOTOGRAPHER *Paul Ruigrok*
AGENCY *TBWA/Campaign Company*
CLIENT *Stichting Beter Zien*

Distinctive Merit/Germany

CAMPAIGN
Homemakers, Students, University Professors
ART DIRECTOR *Heiner Rogge*
COPYWRITER *Oliver Voss*
AGENCY *Jung von Matt Werbeagentur GmbH*
CLIENT *Noah Vereinigung gegen Tierversuche*

Liebe Hausfrauen:
Kaufen Sie sich Putz- und Reinigungsmittel.
Reiben Sie sich damit das Gesicht ein. Nach einigen
Stunden bilden sich Pusteln und Beulen. Kratzen
Sie diese blutig. Bestreichen Sie die Wunden mit
weiterem Putzmittel.

Liebe Studenten:
Nehmen Sie eine Rasierklinge in Ihre Hand.
Trennen Sie damit die Haut Ihres Handgelenks ab.
Nehmen Sie nun eine Säge, und durchtrennen
Sie damit langsam Ihr gesamtes Handgelenk.
Werfen Sie die Hand in den Mülleimer.

Liebe Universitätsprofessoren:
Nehmen Sie eine heiße Häkelnadel. Stechen Sie diese
durch die Pupille Ihres Auges. Drehen Sie sie zu
allen Seiten, bis Sie keinen Widerstand mehr spüren.
Und reißen Sie dann den Augapfel heraus.

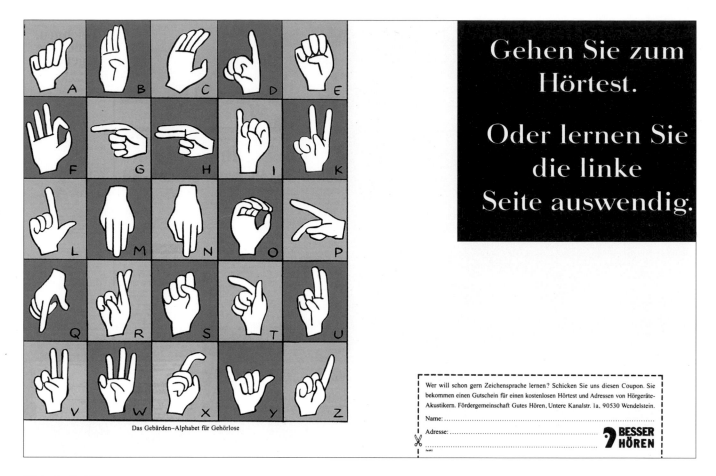

Das Gebärden–Alphabet für Gehörlose

Gehen Sie zum Hörtest.

Oder lernen Sie die linke Seite auswendig.

Wer will schon gern Zeichensprache lernen? Schicken Sie uns diesen Coupon. Sie bekommen einen Gutschein für einen kostenlosen Hörtest und Adressen von Hörgeräte-Akustikern. Fördergemeinschaft Gutes Hören, Untere Kanalstr. 1a, 90530 Wendelstein.

Name: ....

Adresse: ....

BESSER HÖREN

Distinctive Merit/Germany

FULL PAGE OR SPREAD
Sign Language
ART DIRECTOR *Daniela Sautter*
CREATIVE DIRECTOR *Deneke von Weltzien*
COPYWRITERS *Hartwig Keuntje, Jana Liebig*
ILLUSTRATOR *Philippe Petit-Roulet*
AGENCY *Jung von Matt Werbeagentur GmbH*
CLIENT *Fördergemeinschaft Gutes Hören*

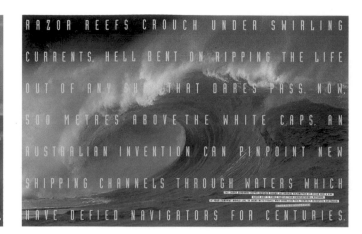

Distinctive Merit/Singapore

CAMPAIGN
Traffic, Wave, Lightning, Fish, Kelly
ART DIRECTOR *John Finn*
CREATIVE DIRECTOR *Jim Aitchison*
COPYWRITERS *Jim Aitchison, Antony Redman*
PHOTOGRAPHY *Stock*
TYPOGRAPHER *John Finn*
AGENCY *Batey Kazoo, Singapore and Sydney*
CLIENT *Australian Department of Foreign Affairs and Trade*

水が、いのちを枯らせている。

環境問題のひとつとして水質汚染があげられるが、その具体的な
原因について、多くは知られていない。ひとつの例として、洗剤や現像液などに含まれているキレート剤がある。
キレート剤とは、難分解性物質で、水中で金属イオンと結合し、重金属を包み込む性質をもっている。
川や海に流れ込むと、自然界のバランスを崩してしまうことになるのだ。さらに、人間の体内に蓄積されると、貧血などの症状を
引き起こすため、近年ヨーロッパでは大きな問題として取り上げられている。杉江さんは、
微生物を利用して、このキレート剤を分解する研究を行っている。難分解性物質を分解する微生物を理解すると、
そこから純粋分離操作という方法で微生物を探索し、水を浄化する実験を繰り返しているのだ。
好奇心旺盛な杉江さんは、「未知の能力をもつ微生物を発見して、その可能性を追求していきたい」と、
文明と自然の共存を基本に、環境問題を真正面から見つめている。

杉江利子

環境と生命を見つめる人になる。
東京農業大学

自然が、捨てられている。

多くの人々がリサイクルという言葉から、空き缶や紙のリサイクルを連想する。
しかし、この他にも、資源を有効利用する方法はあらゆる分野で求められている。例えば、森林資源のリサイクルとして、
杉の端材をチップ状にして、固め、建材として役立つ木質ブロックをつくる研究が進められている。
台風で倒されてしまった木や家屋、住宅建材などのリサイクルとしても期待される研究だ。山田さんは、この杉の研究を基盤に、
カラマツの有効利用を考えている。カラマツは、軽強、繊維によって増えたが、建材としては利用しにくく、
間伐材としても有効に活用できず、捨てられていた。なんとかこのカラマツを利用できないかと山田さんは、蒸気噴射の
カリュレゲを使ったり、硬化剤の量などを細かに調節しようとその可能性を追求している。
山田さんは、「人間の都合で自然を壊してはいけない。人間がしたことは、最後まで責任をとるべきだ」と、
進行しつづける自然破壊に対し、資源の大切さと再利用の必要性を強く訴えている。

山田和弘

環境と生命を見つめる人になる。
東京農業大学

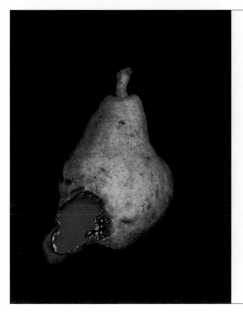

栄養が、衰弱している。

食料についての問題は、人間が生きるうえで最も重要な問題である。
単に作物を生産するのではなく、栄養に重点をおいた作物の生産が求められている。例えば、赤道直下の
乾燥地域では、作物が持に育たない。つまり、ビタミンやカロチンなど、栄養分に多く
含まれている栄養素が、極端に不足してしまうのだ。乾燥地域に住む人々の栄養不足は、今、生命にかかわる深刻な問題と
なっている。大柳さんは、そんな環境状況でも育つ作物の、より適した品種の選定やより効果的な栽培技術を
研究している。小松菜やモロヘイヤを対象として、土の水分量を調節することで乾燥ストレスを与え、乾燥に強く、
栄養価の高い作物をつくっているのだ。大柳さんは、「ノウハウを提供するだけでなく、
現地の人々の手によって、そこに必要な作物を生産できるように、技術を根付かせるのが重要なんです」と、
食料問題に悩む人々の立場にたった発見を、熱い瞳で持っている。

大柳由紀子

環境と生命を見つめる人になる。
東京農業大学

Distinctive Merit, Japan

CAMPAIGN
Tokyo University of Agriculture
ART DIRECTOR *Norio Kudo*
CREATIVE DIRECTORS *Norio Kudo, Chiaki Kasahara*
COPYWRITER *Chiaki Kasahara*
DESIGNER *Yoshifumi Hioki*
PHOTOGRAPHER *Motonobu Okada*
PRODUCER *Kumi Ogou*
AGENCY *Magna, Inc. Advertising*
CLIENT *Tokyo University of Agriculture*

Distinctive Merit/U.S.A.

TELEVISION COMMERCIAL, 30 SECONDS OR LESS
Genie
ART DIRECTOR *Jerry Gentile*
CREATIVE DIRECTORS *Steve Rabosky, Steve Sweitzer*
COPYWRITER *Ed Crayton*
PRODUCER *Helen Erb*
DIRECTOR *Gerard de Thame*
MUSIC *Elias & Associates*
AGENCY *TBWA Chiat/Day Inc. Advertising*
CLIENT *Eveready Battery*

Distinctive Merit/U.S.A.

TELEVISION COMMERCIAL, 30 SECONDS OR LESS
Baby Animals
ART DIRECTOR *Roy Grace*
CREATIVE DIRECTORS *Roy Grace, Diane Rothschild*
COPYWRITER *Diane Rothschild*
PRODUCER *Barbara Benedict*
DIRECTOR *Carl Furuta*
MUSIC *Look Music*
AGENCY *Grace & Rothschild Advertising*
CLIENT *Land Rover North America, Inc.*

Distinctive Merit/U.S.A.

TELEVISION COMMERCIAL, 30 SECONDS OR LESS
Dentist
ART DIRECTOR *Sig Gross*
CREATIVE DIRECTOR *Rochelle Klein*
COPYWRITER *Bob McPheron*
PRODUCER *Pane Ferman*
DIRECTOR *David Kellogg*
MUSIC *Bob Ponann*
AGENCY *Angotti Thomas Hedge, Inc.*
CLIENT *Foster's*

VISUAL: *Standing outside an ancient tomb, where he has unearthed an ancient lamp, an archaeologist rubs the lamp and a genie appears out of an impressive puff of smoke.*
GENIE: *Master, for freeing me, I shall grant thee three wishes.*
MAN (SKEPTICAL): *Okay, I want enormous wealth.*
VISUAL: *Large piles of money fill the tomb.*
MAN: *Unbelievable! Uh, let me see. I want to be adored by women.*
VISUAL: *Several stunning women appear.*
GENIE: *You have one final wish. Use it wisely.*
MAN: *Long life…*
VISUAL: *The genie looks concerned. A big puff of smoke appears. When it clears, we see that the genie has turned the guy into the Energizer Bunny.*
SUPER: *Simulated demonstration.*
ANNCR: *Still going. Long-lasting Energizer batteries keep going and going and…*

ANNCR: *Every species has its own method of transporting its young…some means of getting offspring from one place to another…safely, comfortably, and reliably.*
VISUALS: *Kangaroo with baby in pouch. Baboon with baby on its back. Penguins with a baby who falls. Koala with baby on its back. Spotted rat with many babies on its back. Leopard carrying cub in mouth. Big chimp tapping little chimp on behind. Baby baboon hopping from tree to big baboon's back. Lion picking up cub in mouth. Baby chimp being dragged by a hand.*
ANNCR: *And human beings are no exception. The Land Rover Discovery. Far superior to carrying your children in your mouth.*
VISUAL: *Land Rover Discovery, seen through trees.*
SUPER: *Land Rover logo.*

ANNCR: *How to speak Australian: Dentist. Foster's: Australian for beer.*

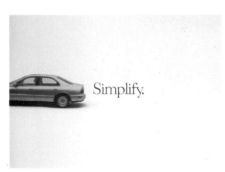  

Distinctive Merit/U.S.A.

TELEVISION COMMERCIAL, 30 SECONDS OR LESS
Eraser
ART DIRECTOR *Vince Aamodt*
CREATIVE DIRECTORS *Larry Postaer, Mark Erwin*
COPYWRITER *Todd Carey*
AGENCY PRODUCER *Gary Paticoff*
PRODUCTION PRODUCER *Chris Whitney*
EFFECTS PRODUCER *Robin Skirboll*
DIRECTOR *Richard Kizu-Blair*
SPECIAL EFFECTS *Jonathan Keeton, Simon Mowbray*
SOUND DESIGN *Ken Dahlinger of Framework Sound*
STUDIO *Colossal Pictures*
AGENCY *Rubin Postaer & Associates*
CLIENT *American Honda Motor Co., Inc.*

ADDITIONAL AWARD

Merit
**GRAPHIC DESIGN, TELEVISION, FILM, AND VIDEO,
SPECIAL EFFECTS**

VISUAL: *Honda Accord sedan in congested city traffic.
In foreground, a cab driver yells out of his window and
honks his horn. An eraser enters the frame and removes
the cab. In background, a truck sounds its horn. The
eraser removes the truck. The eraser continues to remove
images until only the Accord remains against a white
background. The Accord pulls forward.*
SUPER: *Simplify.*

Distinctive Merit/U.S.A.

TELEVISION COMMERCIAL, 30 SECONDS OR LESS
The Offer
ART DIRECTORS *Greg Wells, Everett Wilder*
CREATIVE DIRECTORS *Mark Cacciatore,
Carl Warner*
COPYWRITERS *Mark Cacciatore, Carl Warner*
PRODUCER *Chelle McDonald*
DIRECTOR *Robert Hannant*
MUSIC *Jud Haskins*
AGENCY *DDB Needham Worldwide, Dallas Group*
CLIENT *Southern Methodist University*

ANNCR: *Not long ago, Mustang Athletic Director
Jim Copeland made Mike Dement an offer he couldn't
refuse. We suggest you come see SMU's new coach in
action. Your absence could be taken as an insult.*

Distinctive Merit/Japan

TELEVISION COMMERCIAL, 30 SECONDS OR LESS
Exchange–No Questions Asked
CREATIVE DIRECTOR *Kunihiko Tainaka*
COPYWRITER *Tatsuya Ishii*
PHOTOGRAPHER *Yutaka Kobayashi*
PRODUCER *Momoko Mieda*
DIRECTOR *Satoshi Kawarabayashi*
AGENCY *Dentsu Inc., Tokyo*
CLIENT *Fast Retailing Co. Ltd.*

WOMAN (TO STORE CLERK): *Hi, handsome.
These make me look too old. I want to exchange them.
I'll find something else. Let's exchange.*
SUPER: *Exchange. No questions asked.*
ANNCR: *Casual clothes. Uni-Qlo.*

Distinctive Merit/New Zealand

TELEVISION COMMERCIAL, 30 SECONDS OR LESS
Yellow Pages—Focus
ART DIRECTOR *Todd McCracken*
CREATIVE DIRECTOR *Andy Lish*
COPYWRITER *Andy Lish*
PRODUCER *Neil Stichbury*
DIRECTOR *Simon Mark-Brown*
STUDIO *Republic Films*
AGENCY *Bates New Zealand*
CLIENT *John G. Adam, Optometrist*

VISUAL: *Blurry yellow image. Camera moves in and out, trying to pull the image into focus. It fails.*
SUPER: *John G. Adam, Optometrist. Ask a friend to find us in the Yellow Pages.*

Distinctive Merit/Spain

TELEVISION COMMERCIAL, 30 SECONDS OR LESS
Voices
ART DIRECTORS *Beat Keller, Francesc Talamino*
CREATIVE DIRECTORS *Jorge Villena, Beat Keller*
COPYWRITERS *Jorge Villena, Kilian Asensio*
PRODUCER *María Rius*
AGENCY *Bassat, Ogilvy and Mather*
CLIENT *Orbis*

HUGH GRANT: *They've changed my voice again…. Shit.*
GARY OLDMAN: *But they've given me the same voice as Hugh Grant!!!!*
MICHELLE PFEIFFER: *This is not my voice.*
ANTHONY HOPKINS: *Listen to this voice they've given me…*
ANNCR: *Orbis presents films in their original versions with subtitles in Spanish.*
WOODY ALLEN: *I'm calling to see what voice I have in tomorrow's movie.*

Distinctive Merit/Spain

TELEVISION COMMERCIAL, 30 SECONDS OR LESS
Alarm Clock
ART DIRECTOR *Oscar Pla*
CREATIVE DIRECTORS *Gustavo Caldas, Oscar Pla*
COPYWRITER *Gustavo Caldas*
PRODUCER *Joaquím Margrinyà*
AGENCY *Bassat, Ogilvy and Mather*
CLIENT *Lotto Catalunya*

AUDIO: *Alarm clock rings.*
ANNCR: *Listen…listen very carefully…concentrate on this sound…on this unbearable sound. Because if you win the Lotto, you will never hear it again.*
AUDIO: *Alarm clock stops ringing.*
VISUAL: *Lotto. Make your dreams come true.*

Distinctive Merit/Sweden

TELEVISION COMMERCIAL, 30 SECONDS OR LESS
Sofa
ART DIRECTOR *Olle Mattson*
CREATIVE DIRECTOR *Bo Rönnberg*
COPYWRITER *Carl Lewenhaupt*
PHOTOGRAPHER *Stefan Kullänger*
PRODUCER *Mary Lee Copeland*
AGENCY *Rönnberg McCann*
CLIENT *Ikea*

SUPER: *A question for Sweden's biggest sofa expert:*
VISUAL: *Close-up of a woman's bottom.*
ANNCR: *If I were to say that you could buy five of Sweden's highest-quality sofas at Ikea prices, how would you react?*
BOTTOM: *Mmmmm!*
VISUAL: *Ikea sofa.*
ANNCR: *Buy one of Sweden's finest sofas interest-free at Ikea.*

Distinctive Merit/Brazil

TELEVISION COMMERCIAL, 30 SECONDS OR LESS
Real Road
CREATIVE DIRECTORS *Alexandre Gama, Marcello Serpa*
COPYWRITER *Alexandre Gama*
PRODUCER *Luiza Jatobá*
DIRECTOR *Clovis Mello*
STUDIO *Cine 21*
AGENCY *ALMAP/BBDO*
CLIENT *Senna Import*

Distinctive Merit/Brazil

TELEVISION COMMERCIAL, 30 SECONDS OR LESS
Peanut
CREATIVE DIRECTORS *Alexandre Gama, Marcello Serpa*
COPYWRITER *Alexandre Gama*
PRODUCER *Luiza Jatobá*
DIRECTOR *Sergio Mastroccola*
MUSIC *V.U. Estudio*
STUDIO *Jere Moreira Filmes*
AGENCY *ALMAP/BBDO*
CLIENT *Senna Import*

Distinctive Merit/Germany

TELEVISION COMMERCIAL, 30 SECONDS OR LESS
Mice
ART DIRECTOR *Klaus Hoffmann*
CREATIVE DIRECTOR *Klaus Hoffmann*
COPYWRITER *Klaus Hoffmann*
PRODUCER *Thorsten Levermann*
DIRECTOR *Andreas Kayales*
STUDIO *FBI Hamburg*
AGENCY *Bates Frankfurt*
CLIENT *DG Bank Frankfurt*

Distinctive Merit/U.S.A.

TELEVISION COMMERCIAL, 30 SECONDS OR LESS, CAMPAIGN
Quarters, Future, Peewee
ART DIRECTOR *Young Kim*
CREATIVE DIRECTOR *John Jay*
COPYWRITER *Jimmy Smith*
PRODUCERS *Jon Kamen, Robert Fernandez*
DIRECTOR *Robert Leacock*
STUDIO *@radical.media*
AGENCY *Wieden & Kennedy*
CLIENT *Nike*

Peewee
PEEWEE: *Then I bring it back out because I want to embarrass him...I shake him and fake him and I'm looking at his face saying, what you want me to do, make a lay-up, make a jump shot, make up your mind what you want me to do...bam, bam, bam, I'm going through my legs, twice, then I'm gonna reverse, hesitate, stop, I freeze him then I pull up on him, then I back up on him, yeah, yeah, come on now, now, now, oh, oh, you ain't guarding me here, I go, now I'm back again, now you, I thought you was guarding me, I'm saying now, push up now, push up, up, he's in the air, I done faked him, but I come up to fake him again, I'm going to the basket, laying it up, behind my back, double reverse fake, head fake, I'm looking at him saying man you can't guard me, I've got so many moves, last game I shook myself.*

Distinctive Merit/U.S.A.

TELEVISION COMMERCIAL, 30 SECONDS OR LESS, CAMPAIGN
Injury, Balloon, Taxi, Suit
ART DIRECTOR *Rick McQuiston*
CREATIVE DIRECTORS *Larry Frey, Jerry Cronin*
COPYWRITER *Hank Perlman*
PRODUCERS *Jon Kamen, Robert Fernandez*
DIRECTORS *Bryan Buckley, Frank Todaro*
STUDIO *@radical.media*
AGENCY *Wieden & Kennedy*
CLIENT *ESPN*

Suit
MIKE RICHTER: *Hey, I'm the first to admit it, Boston's a good team, but this Friday nothing, and I mean nothing, is getting by me.*
PIZZA DELIVERY BOY: *Hey, here's your pizza.*
MIKE RICHTER: *This isn't a large.*

  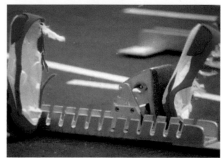

 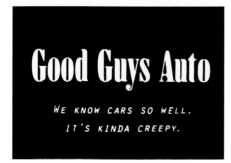  

Good Guys Auto

WE KNOW CARS SO WELL,
IT'S KINDA CREEPY.

Better buy
sports shoes at
MIGROS.

Distinctive Merit/U.S.A.

**TELEVISION COMMERCIAL, 30 SECONDS OR LESS,
CAMPAIGN**
Spark Plug, Oil, Car Door
ART DIRECTOR *Rohitash Rao*
CREATIVE DIRECTOR *Rob Shapiro*
COPYWRITER *Eric Silver*
PRODUCER *Nancy Hacohen*
DIRECTOR *Jesse Dylan*
AGENCY *Earle Palmer Brown*
CLIENT *Good Guys Auto*

ADDITIONAL AWARDS

Distinctive Merit
TELEVISION COMMERCIAL, 30 SECONDS OR LESS
Oil

Merit
TELEVISION COMMERCIAL, 30 SECONDS OR LESS
Car Door

Oil
VISUAL: *Mechanic holds glass up to the light.*
MECHANIC: *It's an American car, Cadillac. Power
windows…power steering…*
VISUAL: *Mechanic dips finger into glass and tastes oil.*
MECHANIC: *And the air conditioning is on the fritz.*
SUPER: *Good Guys Auto. We know cars so well, it's
kinda creepy.*

Distinctive Merit/U.S.A.

**TELEVISION COMMERCIAL, 30 SECONDS OR LESS,
CAMPAIGN**
Intern, Peeking, Bib
ART DIRECTORS *Matt Vescovo, Rohitash Rao,
John Leu, Henriette Lienke*
CREATIVE DIRECTOR *Arthur Bijur*
COPYWRITERS *Michelle Roufa, Jenny Noble,
Arthur Bijur, Tina Hall*
PRODUCERS *Mary McInerney, Catherine Abate,
Mary Ellen Duggan*
DIRECTORS *Jeff Gorman, Charles Wittenmeier*
STUDIOS *Johns & Gorman Films, Harmony Pictures*
AGENCY *Cliff Freeman & Partners*
CLIENT *Staples*

ADDITIONAL AWARD

Merit
TELEVISION COMMERCIAL, 30 SECONDS OR LESS
Peeking

Distinctive Merit/Switzerland

**TELEVISION COMMERCIAL, 30 SECONDS OR LESS,
CAMPAIGN**
Psycho, Tandem, Sprinter, Copper
ART DIRECTOR *Mathias Babst*
CREATIVE DIRECTOR *Hansjörg Zürcher*
COPYWRITER *Hanjörg Zürcher*
DIRECTOR *Ernst Wirz*
PRODUCTION *Wirz & Fraefel Productions*
AGENCY *Advico Young & Rubicam, Zurich*
CLIENT *Migros Genossenschafts-Bund*

Distinctive Merit/U.S.A.

TELEVISION COMMERCIAL, OVER 30 SECONDS
Mirage
ART DIRECTOR *Roy Grace*
CREATIVE DIRECTORS *Roy Grace, Diane Rothschild*
COPYWRITER *Diane Rothschild*
PRODUCER *Barbara Benedict*
DIRECTOR *Barry Meyers*
MUSIC *Danny Troob of Look Music*
STUDIOS *Spots Films, @radical.media*
AGENCY *Grace & Rothschild Advertising*
CLIENT *Land Rover North America, Inc.*

ADDITIONAL AWARD

Merit
TELEVISION COMMERCIAL, 30 SECONDS OR LESS

VISUAL: *Two men stagger through a desert.*
MAN #1/MAN #2: *I see a lake./With a waterfall…*
MAN #1: *And little whitecaps shaped by the breeze.*
MAN #2: *Ah, there's a hotel.*
MAN #1: *With hundreds of air-conditioned rooms.*
MAN #2: *And minibars, no doubt…*
VISUAL: *They stumble uphill, toward a Range Rover and a couple picnicking.*
MAN #1: *Look! A Range Rover!*
MAN #2: *Ah, yes. A 4.0 SE. And a smashing woman giving caviar to that chap.*
VISUAL: *They continue walking into the desert.*
SUPER: *Land Rover logo.*
MAN #1: *I see an igloo…*

Distinctive Merit/Italy

TELEVISION COMMERCIAL, OVER 30 SECONDS
A Telephone Call Prolongs Life
ART DIRECTOR *Mauro Mortaroli*
CREATIVE DIRECTOR *Mauro Mortaroli*
COPYWRITERS *Erminio Perocco, Mauro Mortaroli*
DIRECTOR *Alessandro D'Alatri*
LIGHTING DIRECTOR *Franco Di Giacomo*
SET DESIGNER *Giuseppe Mangano*
MUSIC *Gabriele Ducros*
TESTIMONIAL *Massimo Lopez*
EDITOR *Roberto Crescenzi*
PRODUCTION *Filmmaster*
AGENCY *Armando Testa S.p.A.*
CLIENT *Telecom Italia S.p.A.*

VISUAL: *Massimo Lopez — a famous Italian comic actor — is facing a firing squad. The officer asks if he has a final request.*
MASSIMO LOPEZ: *Could I make a telephone call?*
VISUAL: *The call goes on, and on, and on…until the firing squad heads off on patrol. After a sequence of unending, very amusing conversations, Lopez is still talking on the phone.*
SUPER: *A telephone call prolongs life.*

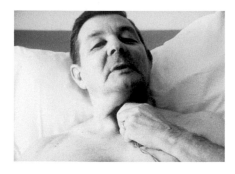

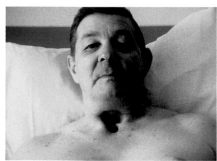

Distinctive Merit/U.S.A.

TELEVISION COMMERCIAL, PUBLIC SERVICE
Happy Birthday
ART DIRECTOR *Peter Favat*
CREATIVE DIRECTORS *Rich Herstek, Peter Favat*
COPYWRITER *Stu Cooperrider*
PRODUCER *Amy Feenan*
DIRECTOR *Tony Kaye*
PRODUCTION COMPANY *Tony Kaye Films*
AGENCY *Houston Effler Herstek Favat*
CLIENT *Massachusetts Department of Public Health*

AUDIO: *Happy birthday to you. Happy birthday to you. Happy birthday dear…*
SUPER: *Happy birthday to the tobacco industry. Celebrating 121 years of fine tobacco products.*
AUDIO: *Happy birthday to you.*
SUPER: *It's time we made smoking history. Massachusetts Department of Public Health.*

Distinctive Merit/England

CINEMA COMMERCIAL, PUBLIC SERVICE
Tears
ART DIRECTOR *Jan Dirk Bouw*
CREATIVE DIRECTORS *Robert Saville, Jay Pond-Jones*
COPYWRITER *David Bell*
PRODUCER *De Schiettent*
DIRECTOR *Lex Brand*
MUSIC *Marcel Walvisch*
AGENCY *GGT London*
CLIENT *St. Patrick's Church*

VISUAL: *Inside St. Patrick's Church, we see a statue of the Virgin Mary. A tear seems to fall from the statue's eye. We follow this tear, and other droplets that seem to come from the statue's eye, down the length of its body until they drip from the statue's foot and into a bucket underneath. As we cut to the head of the statue, we see drips of water falling onto the head and over the face. We follow the drips up and see that the water is coming from a hole in the ceiling above the statue. Cut to exterior shot of the St. Patrick's Church sign. It's raining heavily.*
SUPER: *Donations needed for urgent repairs.*
0171 437 2010.

Distinctive Merit/U.S.A.

COMMERCIAL, OVER 30 SECONDS
Things I'd Like to See
CREATIVE DIRECTOR *Mike Renfro*
COPYWRITER *Mike Renfro*
PRODUCER *David Rucker, Jessica Coats*
STUDIO *Real To Reel Studios*
AGENCY *The Richards Group*
CLIENT *The Auto Show*

MAN: *And now, things I'd really like to see on TV. I'd really like to see Regis and Kathie Lee go toe-to-toe in a No-Holds-Barred Championship Texas Death Match. I'd like to see a Family Feud where everybody packs heat. I'd like to see Judge Wapner after a couple of drinks. I'd like to see The Commish get his butt kicked by a couple of mimes. I'd like to see what happens if you flush while that guy in the boat's in your toilet. I'd like to see the Skipper cold-cock Mr. Howell....*
ANNCR: *Of all the things you'd like to see on TV, at least one actually makes it onto your screen every week. The Auto Show. Nothing but cars for sale and trade. You see the car you like, you call the number on your screen. It's the one show on TV you can actually have an effect on. The Auto Show. Coming this spring to Channel 39. Think of it as PBS for the car enthusiast.*
MAN: *...I'd like to see Mr. Whipple get knocked around a little. I'd like to see Lucy and Ricky sleep in the same bed. I'd like to see Mr. Ed's family tree. I'd like to see Laverne file a lawsuit against Shirley....*

Distinctive Merit/South Africa

COMMERCIAL, 30 SECONDS OR LESS, CAMPAIGN
Guzzler, Doggy Drive-Thru, Barry
CREATIVE DIRECTOR *Jono Shubitz*
COPYWRITER *Alistair King*
PRODUCER *Fiona Abbott*
DIRECTOR *Tully McCullagh*
STUDIO *Spaced Out Sound*
AGENCIES *Ogilvy & Mather, Rightford Searle-Tripp & Makin*
CLIENT *Ramsay Son & Parker*

ADDITIONAL AWARD

Merit
RADIO COMMERCIAL, 30 SECONDS OR LESS
Doggy Drive-Thru

Doggy Drive-Thru
MAN #1: *Hey, Eddie, how you doing?*
MAN #2: *Fine, Neville, strong man.*
MAN #1: *Good, good. Where's Dusty?*
MAN #2: *He went for a drive.*
MAN #1: *Your dog is out driving?*
MAN #2: *Yeah, well, I read in the September Car Magazine about this drive-in burger shack for dogs. So I lent him my car.*
MAN #1: *Your dog can drive? That's incredible.*
MAN #2: *No, not really, it's an automatic.*
ANNCR: *Read about the doggy drive-thru restaurant in the September Car Magazine, out now.*
MAN #1: *Oh, here he is now.*
MAN #2: *I can't believe it.*
MAN #1: *Me neither, look what he's doing on my tire...Hey! (whistles)...voetsek!*

Distinctive Merit/Canada

BILLBOARD, CAMPAIGN
Plastic Bags: The Beach, The Mountainside, The Sea,
The Countryside
ART DIRECTOR *Antoine Autin*
COPYWRITER *Thomas Reichlin-Meldegg*
PHOTOGRAPHER *Thierry Desouches*
AGENCY *CLM BBDO*
CLIENT *Leclerc*

Distinctive Merit/Canada

BILLBOARD, CAMPAIGN
IOU Beer, Unmatched Brewski, Get Me a Beer
ART DIRECTORS *Dean Hore, Paul Hains*
CREATIVE DIRECTOR *Paul Hains*
COPYWRITER *Dean Hore*
PHOTOGRAPHER *Shin Sugino*
TYPOGRAPHER *Ron Hooft*
PRINT PRODUCERS *Al Hilts, Kim Burchiel*
STUDIO *Mediacom*
AGENCY *Bozell Palmer Bonner*
CLIENT *Labatt Breweries of Canada*

Distinctive Merit/Japan

PROMOTIONAL, CAMPAIGN
Ginza-Aster
ART DIRECTOR *Takao Kajiyama*
COPYWRITER *Mitsuho Abe*
DESIGNER *Takao Kajiyama*
PHOTOGRAPHER *Megumu Wada*
PRINTER *Kashimura Printing Co. Ltd.*
AGENCY *ASATSU Inc.*
CLIENT *Ginza-Aster Co. Ltd.*

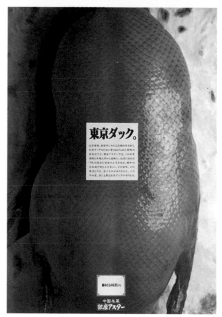

Distinctive Merit/U.S.A.

ENTERTAINMENT OR SPECIAL EVENT
Mighty Aphrodite
ART DIRECTOR *Burt Kleeger*
CREATIVE DIRECTOR *Burt Kleeger*
DESIGNER *Burt Kleeger*
PHOTOGRAPHER *Dennis Martin*
STUDIO *Burt Kleeger Inc.*
CLIENTS *Miramax Films,*
Jean Doumanian Productions

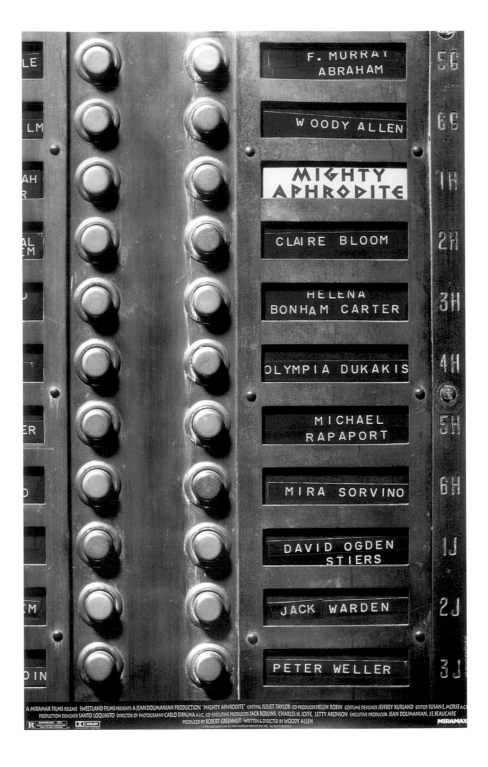

Distinctive Merit/Singapore

ENTERTAINMENT OR SPECIAL EVENT, CAMPAIGN
The Night Safari
ART DIRECTOR *Rashid Salleh*
CREATIVE DIRECTOR *Rashid Salleh*
COPYWRITERS *Rashid Salleh, Glendon Mar*
DESIGNER *Rashid Salleh*
TYPOGRAPHER *Winston Teh*
ILLUSTRATOR *Rashid Salleh*
AGENCY *shid...!*
CLIENT *The Night Safari*

ADDITIONAL AWARDS

Merit
POSTER, ENTERTAINMENT OR SPECIAL EVENT
Rhino

Merit
POSTER, ENTERTAINMENT OR SPECIAL EVENT
Hog

Distinctive Merit/U.S.A.

PUBLIC SERVICE, CAMPAIGN
1995 Boy Scout Print Campaign
ART DIRECTOR *Christopher Gyorgy*
CREATIVE DIRECTOR *Jim Ferguson*
COPYWRITERS *Mark Cacciatore, Clay Hudson,*
Marshall Twinam
PHOTOGRAPHER *John Katz*
AGENCY *DDB Needham Worldwide, Dallas Group*
CLIENT *Circle Ten Council/Boy Scouts of America*

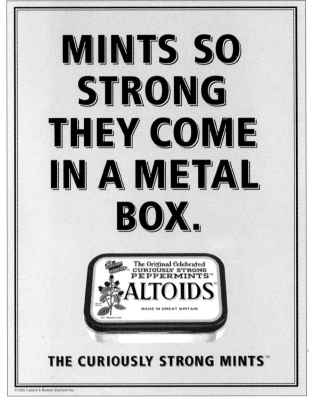

Distinctive Merit/U.S.A.

TRANSIT, CAMPAIGN
Nice Altoids, Practice on Other Mints, Metal Box
ART DIRECTOR *Mark Faulkner*
CREATIVE DIRECTOR *Ute Brantsch*
COPYWRITER *Steffan Postaer*
PHOTOGRAPHER *Tony D'Orio (Nice Altoids)*
AGENCY *Leo Burnett Company, Chicago*
CLIENT *Callard & Bowser-Suchard Inc.*

ADDITIONAL AWARDS

Merit
POSTER, TRANSIT
Nice Altoids

Merit
POSTER, TRANSIT
Metal Box

*Chelsea
and
Derrick*

*. . . have no taste
and wouldn't know
a well-designed card
if it came up and
bit them on the ass.*

*That's why their
piece-of-crap wedding invitation
which looks exactly like this won't win
at
The One Club's 2nd Annual Card Party.
But perhaps something you did will.
Something with style.
Something with concept.
Something with no hideous, shiny purple script
that
induces projectile vomiting.
And since The One Show sadly
no longer has a category
for invitations, announcements, or cards,
this is your only chance to
make sure that your creativity doesn't go to waste.
One Show judges will award
Gold, Silver and Bronze certificates.
And winners will be displayed in the gallery.
So send in your wedding, birth, class reunion,
bar mitzvah or whatever invitation/announcement,
and come see cards that people with names like
Chelsea and Derrick would,
and could,
never do.
Entries are due December 22.
The One Club*

Distinctive Merit/U.S.A.

SPECIAL-EVENT MARKETING KIT
Chelsea and Derrick
ART DIRECTOR *Chuck Finkle*
CREATIVE DIRECTOR *Gary Goldsmith*
COPYWRITER *Tom Miller*
DESIGNER *Chuck Finkle*
AGENCY *Goldsmith/Jeffrey*
CLIENT *The One Club*

(facing page)
Distinctive Merit/U.S.A.

SELF-PROMOTION
Palm Size Design
ART DIRECTOR *Toshiki Saito*
COPYWRITER *Toshiki Saito*
DESIGNER *Yutaka Murakami*
ILLUSTRATOR *Asako Yoshida*
STUDIO *Toshiki Saito Design Room*
CLIENT *Toshiki Saito Design Room*

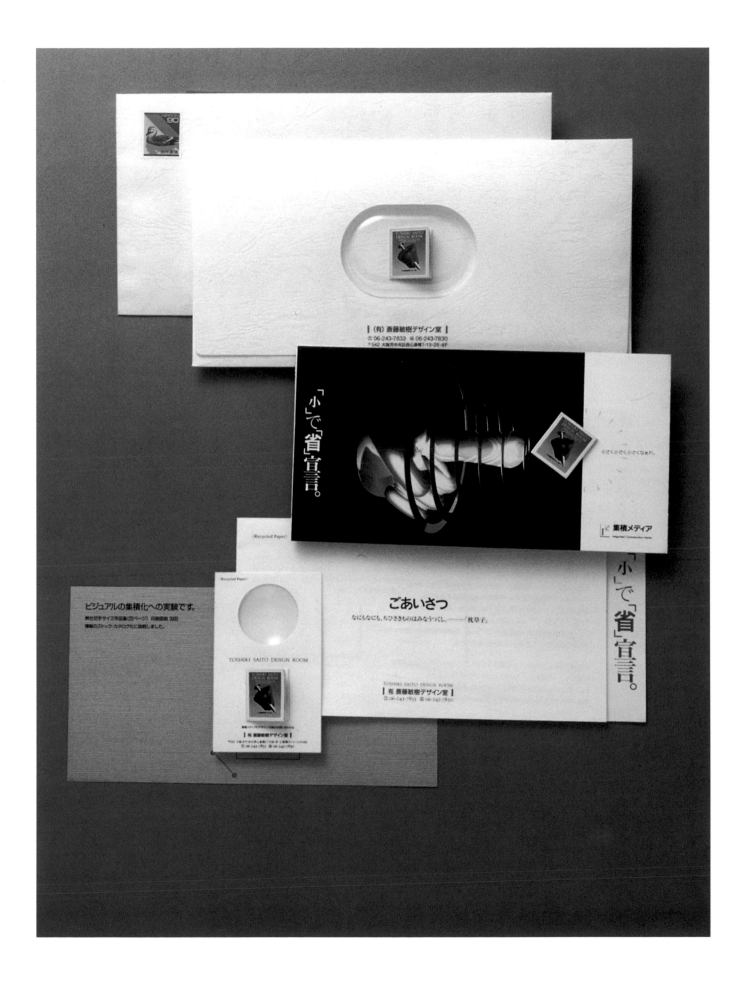

MERIT AWARDS

"My parents went on vacation and all I got was this stupid ceremonial tunic."

LAND ROVER
DISCOVERY

Keeping people off the endangered species list since 1948.

LAND ROVER
DEFENDER 90

Merit/U.S.A.

LESS THAN A FULL PAGE
Ceremonial Tunic
ART DIRECTOR *Allen Richardson*
CREATIVE DIRECTOR *Roy Grace*
COPYWRITER *Gary Cohen*
PHOTOGRAPHER *Vic Huber*
AGENCY *Grace & Rothschild Advertising*
CLIENT *Land Rover North America, Inc.*

Merit/U.S.A.

LESS THAN A FULL PAGE
Endangered Species
ART DIRECTOR *Allen Richardson*
CREATIVE DIRECTOR *Roy Grace*
COPYWRITER *Gary Cohen*
PHOTOGRAPHER *Vic Huber*
AGENCY *Grace & Rothschild Advertising*
CLIENT *Land Rover North America, Inc.*

Merit/U.S.A.

LESS THAN A FULL PAGE
Cheeseburger
ART DIRECTOR *Terence Reynolds*
CREATIVE DIRECTOR *Todd Tilford*
COPYWRITER *Todd Tilford*
PHOTOGRAPHER *Robb Debenport*
PRODUCTION MANAGER *Gail Beckman*
AGENCY *R & D/The Richards Group*
CLIENT *94.5 FM/The Edge*

94.5 THE EDGE

A BIG, GREASY CHEESEBURGER IN A VAST WASTELAND OF TOFU.

Priced so you can feel the wind in your hair while you still have your hair.

Don't be surprised to find yourself behind the wheel of your dream car a little ahead of schedule. With the Encore Program, you can buy or lease a pre-owned Mercedes that has passed a rigorous inspection. And includes a zero-deductible limited warranty and 24-hour roadside assistance. Take a test drive. And feel free to put the top down.

ENCORE
PRE-OWNED MERCEDES-BENZ

Merit/U.S.A.

LESS THAN A FULL PAGE
Priced So You Can Feel the Wind in Your Hair
While You Still Have Your Hair
ART DIRECTOR *Barney Goldberg*
CREATIVE DIRECTORS *Kerry Feuerman, Ron Huey*
COPYWRITER *Anne Marie Floyd*
PHOTOGRAPHER *Brad Miller*
PRINT PRODUCER *Tom Maher*
AGENCY *The Martin Agency*
CLIENT *Mercedes-Benz of North America*

Take the
mobile
phone off
the hook.

The 1996 E-Class: Spacious interior. Dual-zone climate control. Burl walnut. Double-wishbone front suspension. Side air bags mounted in front doors. No wonder you don't want to be reached.   Mercedes-Benz

Merit/U.S.A.

LESS THAN A FULL PAGE
Take the Mobile Phone Off the Hook
ART DIRECTOR *Barney Goldberg*
CREATIVE DIRECTORS *Kerry Feuerman, Ron Huey*
COPYWRITER *Jeff Ross*
PRINT PRODUCER *Linda Locks*
AGENCY *The Martin Agency*
CLIENT *Mercedes-Benz of North America*

The sense of
timelessness one
gets here in winter is
pretty amazing.

When you visit Wisconsin in winter, it's like going back in time to the pristine beauty of the Ice Age. But with all the skiing, sledding, snowmobiling, shopping and dining you can pack into a modern day. **For your free guide to** winter in Wisconsin, call us at **1-800-432-8747.** And whatever you do, keep an eye out for wildlife.   **WISCONSIN**

Merit/U.S.A.

LESS THAN A FULL PAGE
Mastodon
ART DIRECTOR *John Kirchen*
CREATIVE DIRECTOR *Steve Laughlin*
COPYWRITER *Sheldon Rusch*
PHOTOGRAPHERS *Richard Hamilton Smith,*
Mike Huibregste
AGENCY *Laughlin/Constable*
CLIENT *Wisconsin Tourism*

IN THE INTEREST OF FAIRNESS, ISN'T IT TIME WE VISITED THEIR PLANETS?

Welcome, Earthlings, to our new Planetarium. Our enhanced image technology puts you right there: aboard a spaceship, speeding toward a black hole, alongside a meteoroid. Interactive controls at your seat and a new telescope mounted on the roof add to the fun.

THE NEW PLANETARIUM
MUSEUM OF SCIENCE

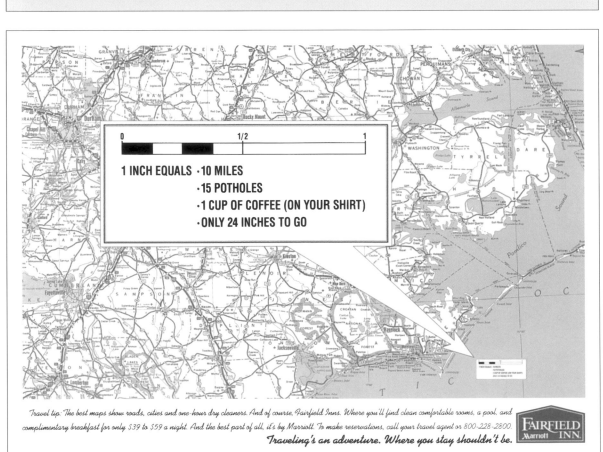

1 INCH EQUALS
- 10 MILES
- 15 POTHOLES
- 1 CUP OF COFFEE (ON YOUR SHIRT)
- ONLY 24 INCHES TO GO

Travel tip: The best maps show roads, cities and one-hour dry cleaners. And of course, Fairfield Inns. Where you'll find clean comfortable rooms, a pool, and complimentary breakfast for only $39 to $59 a night. And the best part of all, it's by Marriott. To make reservations, call your travel agent or 800-228-2800.

FAIRFIELD INN
Marriott

Traveling's an adventure. Where you stay shouldn't be.

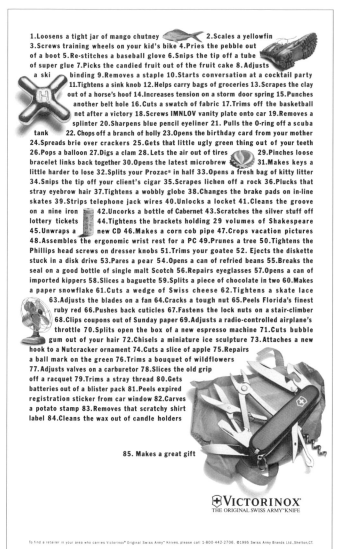

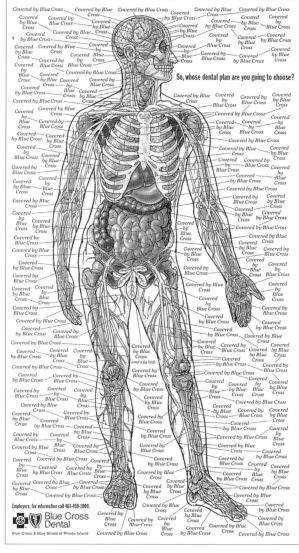

(facing page)
Merit/U.S.A.

LESS THAN A FULL PAGE
Aliens
ART DIRECTORS *Todd Riddle, Mark Nardi*
CREATIVE DIRECTORS *Rich Herstek, Peter Favat*
COPYWRITERS *Mark Nardi, Todd Riddle*
ILLUSTRATOR *Emily Sassano*
ENGRAVING *Unigraphic*
AGENCY *Houston Effler Herstek Favat*
CLIENT *Museum of Science, Boston*

Merit/U.S.A.

LESS THAN A FULL PAGE
Map: 1 inch Equals 10 Miles
ART DIRECTOR *Jamie Mahoney*
CREATIVE DIRECTOR *Kerry Feuerman*
COPYWRITER *Raymond McKinney*
PRINT PRODUCER *Linda Locks*
AGENCY *The Martin Agency*
CLIENT *Fairfield Inn by Marriott*

Merit/U.S.A.

LESS THAN A FULL PAGE
Makes a Great Gift
ART DIRECTOR *Jeff Compton*
CREATIVE DIRECTORS *Marty Weiss, Nat Whitten*
COPYWRITER *Howard Lenn*
AGENCY *Weiss, Whitten, Stagliano, Inc.*
CLIENT *Victorinox Original Swiss Army Knives*

Merit/U.S.A.

LESS THAN A FULL PAGE
So, Whose Dental Plan Are You Going to Choose?
ART DIRECTOR *Robert Hamilton*
CREATIVE DIRECTOR *Steve Bautista*
COPYWRITER *Bob Shiffrar*
ILLUSTRATOR *Sharon Ellis*
PRODUCER *Marita Stapleton*
AGENCY *Pagano Schenck & Kay*
CLIENT *Blue Cross & Blue Shield of Rhode Island*

To place your free personal ad, or for information on our latest listings, call 1-800-474-9046.
Person to Person. In your local paper.

Merit/U.S.A.

LESS THAN A FULL PAGE
Baywatch
ART DIRECTOR *Jennifer Pitt*
CREATIVE DIRECTORS *Mike Fornwald, Daryl Travis*
COPYWRITER *Shannon Lavin*
AGENCY *Arian, Lowe & Travis*
CLIENT *Brite Voice Systems*

Merit/U.S.A.

LESS THAN A FULL PAGE
Ignoring Something
ART DIRECTOR *Alison Cannon*
CREATIVE DIRECTOR *Mike Bevil*
COPYWRITER *Jonathan Balser*
AGENCY *T3*
CLIENT *Texoma Medical Center*

Merit/U.S.A.

LESS THAN A FULL PAGE
Football
ART DIRECTOR *Kirk Mosel*
CREATIVE DIRECTORS *Dean Stefanides,*
Larry Hampel
COPYWRITER *Chris Jacobs*
PHOTOGRAPHY *Jim Salsano, Stock*
AGENCY *Hampel/Stefanides*
CLIENT *ITT Hartford*

Ignoring something won't make it go away.

Chest pain can be caused by something as simple as indigestion or it can be a symptom of a much more serious problem. Simply ignoring it can have dire consequences. If you experience any pain or discomfort at all, please come in and see us. The TMC Chest Pain Center is backed by the most comprehensive open heart surgery and cardiology services in the Texoma region. We can diagnose your chest pain and treat the problem right here at Texoma Medical Center. Life is too short to take a chance with chest pain. If you have it, don't ignore it. Let us help.

 TEXOMA HEALTHCARE SYSTEM

It's Your Life...Live It Well.

WE'VE INSURED ORGANIZATIONS that were TOUGH, AGGRESSIVE and FULL of EGOS.

SOUND ANYTHING like YOUR COMPANY?

COMMERCIAL INSURANCE

Taking on the Green Bay Packers™ is enough to intimidate anyone. Particularly an insurance company. But at ITT Hartford, we've welcomed the challenge of insuring many of the world's largest and most aggressive organizations. From Fortune 500, companies to Super Bowl™ contenders.

Naturally, it takes a great deal of expertise to handle risks of that magnitude. And that's precisely what we bring to the table. Whether it means delivering unique cost containment methods or a full range of commercial products and services.

At ITT Hartford, we believe in taking a proactive approach to problem solving. After all, the best defense is a good offense.

ITT HARTFORD

Our living rooms are so comfortable, you may forget that they come with bedrooms.

Imagine stretching out on a plump sofa after a long, hard day away from home. As your eyes slowly begin to close, you smile thinking how smart you were for paying only $75-$105 a night. Sound good? Call your travel agent or 800-331-3131.

Residence Inn
The next best thing to home.

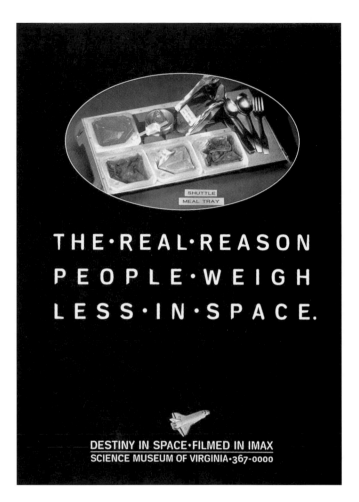

THE·REAL·REASON
PEOPLE·WEIGH
LESS·IN·SPACE.

DESTINY IN SPACE·FILMED IN IMAX
SCIENCE MUSEUM OF VIRGINIA·367-0000

THINK OF ME

Exorcising haunting coughs from theatres everywhere.

Vicks tasty throat soother. Sweet relief for both your throat and the rest of the audience.

Merit/U.S.A.

LESS THAN A FULL PAGE
Our Living Rooms Are So Comfortable
ART DIRECTOR *Bob Meagher*
CREATIVE DIRECTOR *Kerry Feuerman*
COPYWRITERS *John Mahoney, Dean Hawthorne*
PRINT PRODUCER *Kay Franz*
AGENCY *The Martin Agency*
CLIENT *Residence Inn by Marriott*

Merit/U.S.A.

LESS THAN A FULL PAGE
The Real Reason People Weigh Less in Space
ART DIRECTOR *Sean Riley*
CREATIVE DIRECTOR *Hal Tench*
COPYWRITER *Joe Alexander*
PRINT PRODUCER *Tom Maher*
AGENCY *The Martin Agency*
CLIENT *Science Museum of Virginia*

Merit/Hong Kong

LESS THAN A FULL PAGE
Think of Me
ART DIRECTOR *Kendal Yim*
CREATIVE DIRECTORS *Christine Pong, Milker Ho*
COPYWRITER *Christine Pong*
AGENCY *D'Arcy Masius Benton & Bowles*
CLIENT *Procter & Gamble Hong Kong*

Merit/Philippines

LESS THAN A FULL PAGE
Resort
ART DIRECTOR *Mario B. Serrano*
ASSOCIATE ART DIRECTOR *Anthony C. Ligot*
CREATIVE DIRECTOR *Teresita P. Filipinia*
COPYWRITER *Joel C. Macaventa*
PRODUCER *Ponso Tolosa*
AGENCY *Basic Advertising*
CLIENT *Bahay Tuluyan*

Merit/U.S.A.

FULL PAGE OR SPREAD
Professional Driver on Closed Road
ART DIRECTOR *Mark Fuller*
CREATIVE DIRECTORS *Kerry Feuerman, Ron Huey*
COPYWRITER *Joe Nagy*
PRINT PRODUCER *Tom Maher*
AGENCY *The Martin Agency*
CLIENT *Mercedes-Benz of North America*

Merit/U.S.A.

FULL PAGE OR SPREAD
Sends Chills Down Your Orthopedically
Supported Spine
ART DIRECTOR *Barney Goldberg*
CREATIVE DIRECTORS *Kerry Feuerman, Ron Huey*
COPYWRITER *Jeff Ross*
PRINT PRODUCER *Linda Locks*
AGENCY *The Martin Agency*
CLIENT *Mercedes-Benz of North America*

Look at the bright side, Mr. Castro. Tonight you can have steak.

The quintessential New York City steakhouse.
49th St. & 3rd Ave. (212) 753-1530
We accept all major credit cards and only American currency.

Since you're in town for the fall fashion shows,
why not stop by and put a little meat on your bones?

The quintessential New York City steakhouse.
49th St. & 3rd Ave. (212) 753-1530

Merit/U.S.A.

FULL PAGE OR SPREAD
Smith & Wollensky/Castro
ART DIRECTOR *Moe VerBrugge*
CREATIVE DIRECTORS *Dean Stefanides,*
Larry Hampel
COPYWRITER *Josh Miller*
DESIGNER *Moe VerBrugge*
AGENCY *Hampel/Stefanides*
CLIENT *New York Restaurant Group*

Merit/U.S.A.

FULL PAGE OR SPREAD
Smith & Wollensky/Model
ART DIRECTOR *Moe VerBrugge*
CREATIVE DIRECTORS *Dean Stefanides,*
Larry Hampel
COPYWRITER *Josh Miller*
PHOTOGRAPHER *Tiff Pemberton*
AGENCY *Hampel/Stefanides*
CLIENT *New York Restaurant Group*

TO FIND OUT IF
you need to read
Food Day,
simply answer the following question:

This resembles food.

☐ Yes.　　☐ No.

The Oregonian

If you answered yes, you need some serious help. Rush at top speed to your nearest Tuesday Oregonian for the Food Day section. It's got a huge selection of recipes, complete with nutritional details, plus coupons, home ideas and more. If you answered no, well, we suggest you read Food Day anyway. After all, you did just stop to stare at a TV dinner.

FOOD DAY. TUESDAYS.

Child mauled
by
tiger.
(And other hilarious stories.)

The Oregonian

Every day, The Oregonian gives you two full pages of comics. Plus eight color pages every Sunday. Because what better way is there to start the day than with a sled crash, a spaceship explosion, or an attack by Tyrannosaurus Rex?

COMICS. DAILY.

Merit/U.S.A.

FULL PAGE OR SPREAD
Food Day
ART DIRECTOR *David Ayriss*
CREATIVE DIRECTOR *David Ayriss*
COPYWRITER *Mark Waggoner*
PHOTOGRAPHER *Mark Ehsen*
AGENCY *Cole & Weber*
CLIENT *The Oregonian*

Merit/U.S.A.

FULL PAGE OR SPREAD
Tiger
ART DIRECTOR *David Ayriss*
CREATIVE DIRECTOR *David Ayriss*
COPYWRITER *Mark Waggoner*
AGENCY *Cole & Weber*
CLIENT *The Oregonian*

POE CONSTRUCTED HIS POEMS MATHEMATICALLY BEFORE HE WROTE THEM. HERE'S AN EARLY DRAFT OF "THE RAVEN": 2X+Y=B.

There are critics and naysayers aplenty who would like to believe that Poe's haunting works were the uninhibited ramblings of an irrational mind.

The truth, as is the usual case in matters concerning Poe, is far stranger. Consider the following quote from his "The Philosophy of Composition": "It is my design to render it manifest that no one point in "The Raven's" composition is referrible either to accident or intuition - that the work proceeded, step by step, to its comple-

tion with the precision and rigid consequence of a mathematical problem."

Aha! Right there in black and white, a method to the madness! But wait, there's much, much more.

Not only would he structure the work in accordance to mathematical principles, he would also

labor over the character of each word. The relationship of each letter to the other. The audible marriage between vowel and consonant. Oh, and there was a small matter of devising characters and a plot that would smoothly flesh out this whole underlying formula.

An odd philosophy, admittedly. But then again, Poe was an odd fellow. To find out more about the quirky nature of his genius, we invite you to visit The Poe Museum at 1914 E. Main St. You can tour the Enchanted Garden, study original manuscripts and letters, and stand beneath the eerie gaze of rare portraits.

For more information, give us a call by working your way through this mathematical formula: (804) 648-3523.

THE POE MUSEUM

POE FANTASIZED ABOUT A WOMAN WHO WAS JUST LIKE HIS MOTHER: DEAD.

Poe, like every red-blooded man, aspired towards beauty. He compared this yearning to "the desire of the moth for the star."

But, Poe's concept of beauty, was how shall we say this, tilted a bit toward the morbid. To put things in a modern perspective, the supermodels in the *Sports Illustrated* Swimsuit Issue would not have been his cup of tea.

He was obsessed with the beauty outside of this world. The "Beauty above...the glories beyond the grave." In other words, Poe pictured Cupid not as

a good-natured, chubby cherub, but as a dark-cloaked Grim Reaper. To him, nothing was more poetical than the death of a beautiful woman.

Here, take a look at his poem "Annabel Lee." The narrator's girlfriend dies one cloudy night, chilled by a wind supposedly sent down by jealous angels. The narrator goes on to say that even death cannot kill the love the two feel for each other: "And so, all the night-tide, I lay down by the side/ Of my darling - my darling - my life and my bride. In her

tomb by the sounding sea."

And don't think this behavior was isolated to characters in his stories. Poe himself even went so far as to propose marriage to a woman in a cemetery. (Relax, she was alive at the time.)

What triggered this obsession? The death of his mother when he was a child? The loss of his young wife to tuberculosis? Or was it a culmination of many incidents? The death or loss of the women he loved was one of the most constant factors that Poe faced in his life. No one knows for sure. Stop by the Poe Museum at 1914 East Main Street right here in Richmond. Or give us a call at 648-5523 to learn about other of Poe's strange obsessions. We have letters, manuscripts and other assorted oddities. And don't worry. All of the women who work here are alive and well.

THE POE MUSEUM

VISITORS SAY THE CREAKING IS THE GHOST OF POE. ACTUALLY WE'RE IN NEED OF RENOVATION.

Come, enter into our museum. Come on, don't be afraid. There, do you hear that? The moaning seeping through the rooms. Do you feel the cold, sudden drafts in the halls? Do you notice the lights flickering out of the corner of your eye?

Is this the tormented spirit of our own Edgar Allan Poe come to share the icy secrets of the grave?!

Alas, the truth is much scarier. Our museum is badly in need of a bit of upgrading. For starters, we're looking for more effective ways of

not only preserving, but of displaying to the public, Poe's writings: manuscripts, letters, notes and other assorted keepsakes. (Alas, while Poe's words are immortal, the yellowing, crumbling paper they're printed on is not.)

On a more mundane front, our building itself needs a thorough going over, from an inspection of our plumbing fixtures to possible roofing repairs to

custodians, we're not well-versed in the field of structural inspection.)

We're also looking to create a new common meeting room in, appropriately enough, our basement. Unfortunately, these improvements cost money (hey, shackles and Iron Maidens don't come cheap). We could certainly use your help. Drop us a check, if you have a mind to. Or give us a call at (804) 648-5523 for more information. Better yet, come by The Poe Museum at 1914 East Main Street right here in Richmond and see for yourself the truly frightening condition of our museum, if you dare.

THE POE MUSEUM

Merit/U.S.A.

FULL PAGE OR SPREAD
Raven
ART DIRECTOR *Cliff Sorah*
CREATIVE DIRECTOR *Mike Hughes*
COPYWRITER *Raymond McKinney*
PRINT PRODUCER *Karen Smith*
AGENCY *The Martin Agency*
CLIENT *The Poe Museum*

Merit/U.S.A.

FULL PAGE OR SPREAD
Poe Fantasized About a Woman Who Was Just Like His Mother: Dead
ART DIRECTOR *Cliff Sorah*
CREATIVE DIRECTOR *Mike Hughes*
COPYWRITER *Raymond McKinney*
PRINT PRODUCER *Karen Smith*
AGENCY *The Martin Agency*
CLIENT *The Poe Museum*

Merit/U.S.A.

FULL PAGE OR SPREAD
Renovation
ART DIRECTOR *Cliff Sorah*
CREATIVE DIRECTOR *Mike Hughes*
COPYWRITER *Raymond McKinney*
PRINT PRODUCER *Karen Smith*
AGENCY *The Martin Agency*
CLIENT *The Poe Museum*

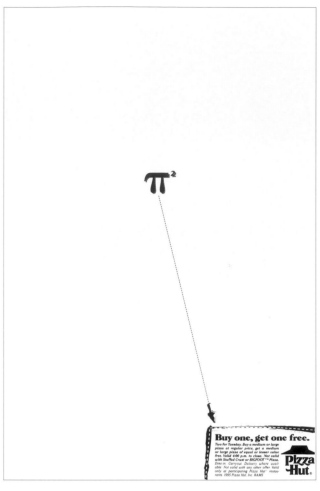

Merit/U.S.A.

FULL PAGE OR SPREAD
Hold An Empty Rainier Can Up to Your Ear
ART DIRECTOR *John Payne*
CREATIVE DIRECTORS *Ron Henderson, Jeff Hopfer*
COPYWRITER *Gary Pascoe*
PHOTOGRAPHER *John Katz*
AGENCY *The Richards Group*
CLIENT *G. Heilman Brewing/Rainier Beer*

Merit/U.S.A.

FULL PAGE OR SPREAD
Pi Squared
ART DIRECTOR *Lola Carlisle*
CREATIVE DIRECTOR *Jim Spruell*
COPYWRITER *Cathy Lepik*
ILLUSTRATOR *Dave Misconish*
AGENCY *Austin Kelley Advertising*
CLIENT *Pizza Hut*

YOU'VE JUST FOUND OUT YOU HAVE CANCER. LET'S BEGIN BY REDUCING THE LUMP IN YOUR THROAT.

In recent years, new breakthroughs have been made in helping people with cancer better manage their treatment. New drugs are helping reduce many of the common side effects of chemotherapy treatment. Including nausea and even more serious conditions that can develop like a low white blood cell count.

One drug, Neupogen (Filgrastim), is now being prescribed to help certain people on chemotherapy maintain a normal white blood cell count. Specifically, a normal neutrophil count. In short, neutrophils are white blood cells that help your body fight infection. Maintaining a normal neutrophil count during your chemotherapy treatment can be important for two reasons.

First, you have a much greater chance of staying on your chemotherapy schedule. And, that will mean getting your treatment behind you sooner. Secondly, maintaining a normal neutrophil count can help reduce your risk of infection. So you have a better chance of staying out of the hospital. Instead, you can spend more time at home where you belong with family and friends. Even daily activities like shopping and eating out can be more accessible.

Of course, Neupogen isn't appropriate for every patient. Ask your doctor if Neupogen should be a recommended part of your treatment. On the following page, you'll find an explanation of Neupogen and its possible side effects. The most common side effect that patients experience is mild-to-moderate bone pain, which can usually be controlled with a non-aspirin analgesic.

In closing, before we embarked on this educational campaign, we conducted extensive research with people undergoing chemotherapy and with doctors. Among those being treated, we found an overwhelming desire for more information concerning treatment. Doctors, many of whom had initial misgivings about any advertising at all, urged us to be candid and to point out that Neupogen isn't for everyone. We acted on their advice.

We realize that your medical care is a sensitive and personal matter. We'd like to know your feelings about the information presented here. If you would like to receive more information concerning Neupogen and how it might help **NEUPOGEN** in your treatment, please call us at 1-800-333-9777, extension 667.

Merit/U.S.A.

FULL PAGE OR SPREAD
You've Just Found Out
ART DIRECTOR *Mark Fuller*
CREATIVE DIRECTORS *Mike Hughes, Ron Huey*
COPYWRITER *Ron Huey*
PRINT PRODUCER *Tom Maher*
AGENCY *The Martin Agency*
CLIENT *Amgen*

ADDITIONAL AWARD

Merit
MAGAZINE, CONSUMER, FULL PAGE OR SPREAD

Merit/Belgium

FULL PAGE OR SPREAD
State of the Art
ART DIRECTOR *Stephane Abinet*
CREATIVE DIRECTOR *Gaston Kooymans*
COPYWRITER *Gaston Kooymans*
ILLUSTRATOR *Pierre Servais*
AGENCY *Moors Bloomsbury N.V.*
CLIENT *Rotring*

SOME PRESIDENTS WOULD HAVE SENT IN THE POLICE. JOHN KENNEDY SENT COFFEE AND DOUGHNUTS.

It's a damp, chilly afternoon in 1962. In front of the White House, a Ban the Bomb demonstration is taking place. Among the protesters is a two-time Nobel Prize winning scientist. John Kennedy is notified. Immediately, he sends out an urn of coffee, a plate of doughnuts and an invitation to the leaders to come inside and state their case.

Unusual actions for a Commander in Chief? Maybe. But John Kennedy didn't see merely another group of protesters that day. He saw a chance to encourage debate and dissent. The fact is, he often played host at small dinners with artists, scientists, writers and poets, because it gave him a chance to listen, provoke, and most importantly, learn. At The New Museum at the John F. Kennedy Library, you too will be invited to debate the issues of his presidency. Because here, you'll learn about the man and how he handled each moment. Call 617-929-4523 to learn more. Or visit today. Then stop by our coffee shop. Because, like those protesters in '62, you'll have a lot to talk about.

THE NEW MUSEUM AT THE JFK LIBRARY

COMMUNISM. NUCLEAR WAR. THE STRUGGLE FOR CIVIL RIGHTS. NO WONDER HIS BACK HURT.

From the moment he took office in January of 1961, John F. Kennedy wrestled with one gigantic, history-making issue after another. Castro and the Bay of Pigs. George Wallace and Alabama. The Cuban missile crisis. The Berlin Wall. Space exploration. The Nuclear Test Ban Treaty. The conflict  *in Southeast Asia. No wonder these words from JFK were so inspirational: "The tasks before us are vast, the problems difficult. The challenges unparalleled. But we*

Nikita Khrushchev

carry with us the vision of a new and better world, and the unlimited power of free men guided by free government." At The New Museum at the John F. Kennedy Library, you'll retrace each and every one of these vital moments. Through video, interviews, and re-creations of the original settings, you'll debate Nixon. Face off with Castro. Challenge Khrushchev. Cheer for Glenn. As you step into the past, an interesting thing will happen. You'll step into the present and future, too. Because as you learn how Kennedy handled critical issues, you'll develop a keener perspective on how leaders of today handle foreign affairs. And how past issues are still playing out today. Plan to visit soon. Or call 617-929-4523 to learn more. After all, as JFK said, "we celebrate the past to awaken the future."

THE NEW MUSEUM AT THE JFK LIBRARY

Merit/U.S.A.

CAMPAIGN
Coffee and Doughnuts, Back Hurt, Moon
ART DIRECTOR *Cliff Sorah*
CREATIVE DIRECTOR *Hal Tench*
COPYWRITERS *Joe Alexander, Tripp Westbrook*
PRINT PRODUCER *Kay Franz*
AGENCY *The Martin Agency*
CLIENT *John F. Kennedy Library Foundation*

ADDITIONAL AWARDS

Merit
NEWSPAPER, CONSUMER, LESS THAN A FULL PAGE
Back Hurt

Merit
NEWSPAPER, CONSUMER, LESS THAN A FULL PAGE
Moon

Merit
MAGAZINE, CONSUMER, FULL PAGE OR SPREAD
Coffee and Doughnuts

Merit
MAGAZINE, CONSUMER, FULL PAGE OR SPREAD
Back Hurt

Merit
MAGAZINE, CONSUMER, LESS THAN A FULL PAGE
Moon

JOHN KENNEDY WASN'T THE FIRST POLITICIAN TO PROMISE HIS CONSTITUENTS THE MOON. BUT HE WAS THE FIRST TO DELIVER IT.

Rice University. 1962. John F. Kennedy makes a bold promise: Before the decade of the 60s is over, the United States will place a man on the moon. JFK is determined to build a strong NASA – not only because of  *the scientific advances, but because space rockets double as morale boosters to the American public. Eight years later, with the strong support of Presidents Lyndon Johnson and Richard Nixon, astronaut Neil Armstrong plants the American flag on the lunar surface. At The New Museum at the John F. Kennedy Library, the space program is just one of the many important moments*

"The task of every generation is to build a road for the next generation." JFK, 1962.

in JFK's life you'll witness. You'll be there applauding at Rice. Voting at the 1960 Democratic Convention. Probing at a press conference. Waving an American flag under the Berlin Wall. As you do, you'll gain a much keener understanding of the man's optimism, vigor, and passion. Who knows, maybe you'll even be inspired to join in John F. Kennedy's call for public service. Plan to visit soon. Or simply call us at 617-929-4523 to learn more about the museum. We'll promise you an enlightening time. And, of course, we'll promise you the moon.

See an original NASA space suit.

THE NEW MUSEUM AT THE JFK LIBRARY

SINGLES
BAR

PICK UP TANTALISING TOBLERONE, THE CHOCOLATE BAR YOU'LL WANT TO SAVOUR ALL BY YOURSELF.

BAR
NONE

CHUNKY, HUGELY DELICIOUS TOBLERONE IS THE CHOCOLATE BAR NO OTHER MEASURES UP TO.

TOBLERONE

BAR
TENDER

TOBLERONE ... THE CHOCOLATE CONCOCTION SO SMOOTH, SO POTENT, IT'S INTOXICATING.

Merit/Malaysia

CAMPAIGN
Bar Series
ART DIRECTOR *Lim Hock Chuan*
CREATIVE DIRECTOR *Basil Antonas*
COPYWRITER *Suzanne Schokman*
PHOTOGRAPHY *Studio Pashe*
AGENCY *Dentsu Young & Rubicam, Malaysia*
CLIENT *Kraft Foods International*

Merit/Taiwan

CAMPAIGN
Baboon, Elephant, Porcupine
ART DIRECTORS *Jolene Hsieh, Randy Larsen*
CREATIVE DIRECTOR *Randy Larsen*
COPYWRITERS *Randy Larsen, Tim Brantingham*
ILLUSTRATOR *Roy Tsai*
AGENCY *Dentsu Young & Rubicam, Taiwan*
CLIENT *Tender Tissue*

Being a baboon butt isn't easy. Imagine! Hot chaffing rocks. Prickly thorn bushes. It's rough. But thankfully, your hiney is a human one. And you can nurse those sore and sensitive areas with the loving care of tender tissues. Don't monkey around, caress yourself with the silky best.

Tender to the touch

Being an elephant butt isn't easy. Imagine! Sandpaper-like tree bark. Prodding antelope horns. It's rough. But thankfully, your hiney is a human one. And you can nurse those sore and sensitive areas with the loving care of tender tissues. Don't be snooty, caress yourself with the silky best.

Tender to the touch

Being a porcupine butt isn't easy. Imagine! Self-stabbing appendages. Big-jawed borrowing insects. It's rough. But thankfully, your hiney is a human one. And you can nurse those sore and sensitive areas with the loving care of tender tissues. Don't be poky, caress yourself with the silky best.

Tender to the touch

There are those who say Sayaji Hotel is a tad too big for its boots. We tend to agree.

You see, we're a three star hotel in Baroda that behaves like a five star hotel in New York.

Our head waiters might not be quite at home at The Plaza on Park Avenue, but they're terribly popular with all our guests. Our head chef is as adept at Chocolate Mousse as he is at Gulab Jamun. (He's won himself quite a following in Baroda - if you ever want to eat at our restaurant, you'd do well to book in advance.) And finally, our service borders on pure pampering. Our bank of computers helps us remember every little detail about every guest who's ever visited. We never forget a name, a birthday or a preference.

All of the above have made us very popular. And rather profitable. 70% of our guests come back to us again and again. Our occupancy rate stays at 100%, round the year. Our home delivery service is a flourishing business on its own. Our restaurants are always packed to bursting. Our second hotel at Gandhidham has recently doubled its capacity within six months of commencing operations. The one-of-its-kind Sayaji Club at Indore was inaugurated just a few days ago. And the adjoining hotel will open its doors in mid-1995, nine months ahead of schedule.

The truth of the matter is, we do have a slightly inflated ego. We also happen to have a balance sheet to back it up.

SAYAJI
HOTELS LTD.
*A 5 Star
Business Strategy*

YOU CAN ALWAYS TELL A GOOD HOTEL BY THE SIZE OF ITS EGO.

At the Sayaji Hotel, we've found that pampering our guests does wonders for business.

It's the little things we do. Like never forgetting a face, a name or a birthday. Like serving morning tea and coffee at a piping 83° celsius, precisely 8 minutes after the order is placed. Like remembering that Mr. Gupta prefers his Dal Makhani extra *makhani*. And that Mr. Ramanathan likes his bedcovers turned down *just* so.

Little things that make big business sense.

Consider the facts : 70% of our guests come back to us again and again. Our occupancy rate stays at 100%, round the year. Our home delivery service is a flourishing business on its own. Our restaurants are always packed to bursting. Our second hotel at Gandhidham has recently doubled its capacity within six months of starting operations. The one-of-its-kind Sayaji Club at Indore was inaugurated just a few days ago. And the adjoining hotel will open its doors in mid-1995, nine months ahead of schedule.

The fact is, whoever said flattery doesn't get you anywhere didn't know his stuff. It's got us a thriving balance sheet.

SAYAJI
HOTELS LTD.
*A 5 Star
Business Strategy*

CONTRARY TO POPULAR BELIEF, FLATTERY *WILL* GET YOU ANYWHERE.

Nobody runs hotels better than the Swiss. Nobody knows more about fine cuisine than the French.

We should know. We've been studying them for years. And we've adapted what we've learned to create standards not far behind the finest in the world.

Our head chef, for instance, is as renowned for his Sauteed Mushrooms as for his Aloo Makhani. As a matter of fact, his Cream of Malabar Soup recently won us accolades in the Times of India.

Then there's our service, which borders on pure pampering. Our bank of computers helps us remember every little detail about every guest who's ever visited. We never forget a name, a face, a birthday or a preference.

Our efforts have made the Sayaji both very popular and very profitable. 70% of our guests come back to us again and again. Our occupancy rate stays at 100%, round the year. Our home delivery service is a flourishing business on its own. Our restaurants are always packed to bursting. Our second hotel at Gandhidham has recently doubled its capacity within six months of commencing operations. The one-of-its-kind Sayaji Club at Indore was inaugurated just a few days ago. And the adjoining hotel will open its doors in mid-1995, nine months ahead of schedule.

All in all, we've learned a lot from our friends in Europe. Our balance sheet, however, remains hearteningly Gujarati.

SAYAJI
HOTELS LTD.
*A 5 Star
Business Strategy*

EVERYTHING WE KNOW, WE LEARNT FROM FUNNY LITTLE MEN WITH ACCENTS.

Merit/India

CAMPAIGN
Ego, Flattery, Funny Little Men
ART DIRECTOR *Suresh Babu*
CREATIVE DIRECTOR *Maia Katrak Patel*
COPYWRITER *Maia Katrak Patel*
DESIGNER *Suresh Babu*
ILLUSTRATOR *Avinash Mukund Gavandalkar*
PRINTER *Liberty Graphics*
AGENCY *Options Trikaya Grey*
CLIENT *Sayaji Hotels Ltd.*

Merit/Singapore

CAMPAIGN
Nissan March Campaign
ART DIRECTOR *Terrence Tan*
CREATIVE DIRECTORS *Rita Haque, Peter Soh*
COPYWRITER *Rex Hu*
DESIGNER *Terrence Tan*
PHOTOGRAPHER *Alex Kai Keong of Amoeba*
ILLUSTRATOR *Terrence Tan*
PRINT PRODUCER *Angie Ang*
AGENCY *Fong Haque & Soh Pte. Ltd.*
CLIENT *Nissan*

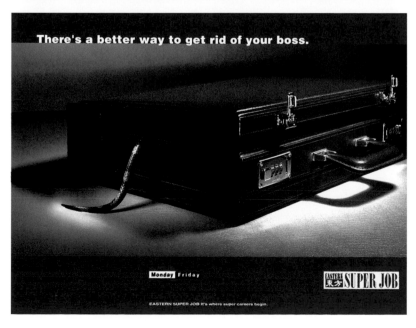

Merit/Hong Kong

CAMPAIGN
Get Rid of Your Boss: Cake, Seat, Snake
ART DIRECTOR *Willie Chan*
CREATIVE DIRECTORS *Graham Woodall, Milker Ho,*
Christine Pong
COPYWRITER *Graham Woodall*
PHOTOGRAPHER *Stephen Cheung*
AGENCY *D'Arcy Masius Benton & Bowles*
CLIENT *Oriental Press Group*

Merit/Korea

CAMPAIGN
Oh, It's Alive
ART DIRECTOR *Eui-Chul Lee*
CREATIVE DIRECTOR *Ho-Lim Jung*
COPYWRITER *Yong-Hyun Park*
DESIGNER *Hyunf-Woo Lee*
PHOTOGRAPHER *Gam Hu*
AGENCY *LG AD Inc.*
CLIENT *LG Electronic Co.*

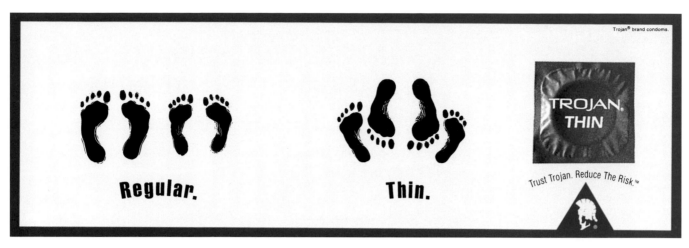

Merit/Canada

CAMPAIGN
Feet, Door Knob, Football
ART DIRECTOR *John Terry*
CREATIVE DIRECTOR *Brad Riddoch*
COPYWRITER *Ashley O'Brien*
ILLUSTRATOR *Bill Russell*
STUDIO *Norman*
AGENCY *Bates Canada, Inc.*
CLIENT *Carter Products*

Merit/U.S.A.

LESS THAN A FULL PAGE
Backbone
ART DIRECTOR *Robert Hamilton*
CREATIVE DIRECTOR *Woody Kay*
COPYWRITER *Bob Shiffrar*
PRODUCER *Marita Stapleton*
AGENCY *Pagano Schenck & Kay*
CLIENT *Pagano Schenck & Kay*

Today's fan: more passion, more intensity, more make-up.

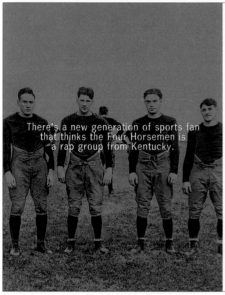

There's a new generation of sports fan that thinks the Four Horsemen is a rap group from Kentucky.

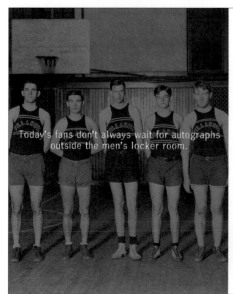

Today's fans don't always wait for autographs outside the men's locker room.

Merit/U.S.A.

CAMPAIGN
Today's Fan, Four Horsemen, Men's Locker Room
ART DIRECTOR *Jason Gaboriau*
CREATIVE DIRECTOR *Gary Goldsmith*
COPYWRITER *Eddie Van Bloem*
PHOTOGRAPHY *Ilan Rubin, Stock*
ILLUSTRATOR *Mike Samuel*
AGENCY *Goldsmith/Jeffrey*
CLIENT *ESPN2*

ADDITIONAL AWARDS

Merit
NEWSPAPER, TRADE, FULL PAGE OR SPREAD
Today's Fan

Merit
NEWSPAPER, TRADE, FULL PAGE OR SPREAD
Four Horsemen

Merit
MAGAZINE, CONSUMER, FULL PAGE OR SPREAD
Today's Fan

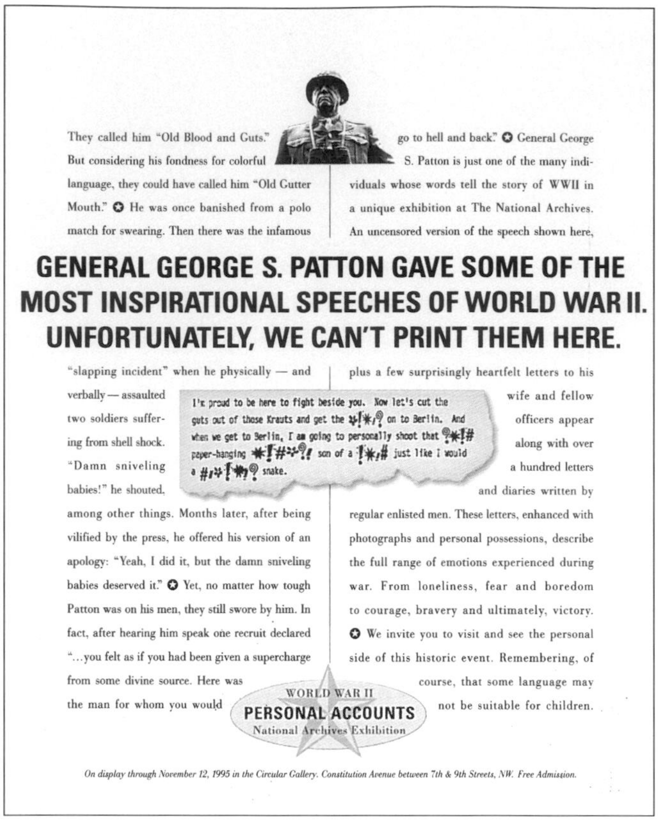

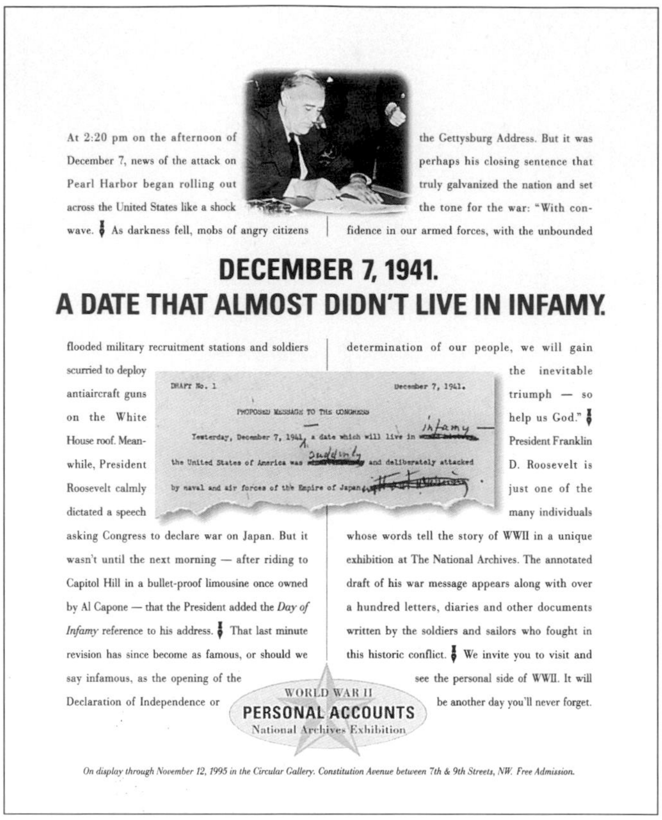

They called him "Old Blood and Guts." But considering his fondness for colorful language, they could have called him "Old Gutter Mouth." ❂ He was once banished from a polo match for swearing. Then there was the infamous go to hell and back." ❂ General George S. Patton is just one of the many individuals whose words tell the story of WWII in a unique exhibition at The National Archives. An uncensored version of the speech shown here,

GENERAL GEORGE S. PATTON GAVE SOME OF THE MOST INSPIRATIONAL SPEECHES OF WORLD WAR II. UNFORTUNATELY, WE CAN'T PRINT THEM HERE.

"slapping incident" when he physically — and verbally — assaulted two soldiers suffering from shell shock. "Damn sniveling babies!" he shouted, among other things. Months later, after being vilified by the press, he offered his version of an apology: "Yeah, I did it, but the damn sniveling babies deserved it." ❂ Yet, no matter how tough Patton was on his men, they still swore by him. In fact, after hearing him speak one recruit declared "…you felt as if you had been given a supercharge from some divine source. Here was the man for whom you would

> I'm proud to be here to fight beside you. Now let's cut the guts out of those Krauts and get the *!#*;⚐ on to Berlin. And when we get to Berlin, I am going to personally shoot that ⚐*!# paper-hanging ✳!#*⚐!¢ son of a !*¢# just like I would a #!⚐!*¢⚐ snake.

plus a few surprisingly heartfelt letters to his wife and fellow officers appear along with over a hundred letters and diaries written by regular enlisted men. These letters, enhanced with photographs and personal possessions, describe the full range of emotions experienced during war. From loneliness, fear and boredom to courage, bravery and ultimately, victory. ❂ We invite you to visit and see the personal side of this historic event. Remembering, of course, that some language may not be suitable for children.

WORLD WAR II
PERSONAL ACCOUNTS
National Archives Exhibition

On display through November 12, 1995 in the Circular Gallery. Constitution Avenue between 7th & 9th Streets, NW. Free Admission.

At 2:20 pm on the afternoon of December 7, news of the attack on Pearl Harbor began rolling out across the United States like a shock wave. ⬇ As darkness fell, mobs of angry citizens the Gettysburg Address. But it was perhaps his closing sentence that truly galvanized the nation and set the tone for the war: "With confidence in our armed forces, with the unbounded

DECEMBER 7, 1941. A DATE THAT ALMOST DIDN'T LIVE IN INFAMY.

flooded military recruitment stations and soldiers scurried to deploy antiaircraft guns on the White House roof. Meanwhile, President Roosevelt calmly dictated a speech asking Congress to declare war on Japan. But it wasn't until the next morning — after riding to Capitol Hill in a bullet-proof limousine once owned by Al Capone — that the President added the *Day of Infamy* reference to his address. ⬇ That last minute revision has since become as famous, or should we say infamous, as the opening of the Declaration of Independence or

> DRAFT No. 1   December 7, 1941.
> PROPOSED MESSAGE TO THE CONGRESS
> Yesterday, December 7, 1941, a date which will live in ~~world history~~ *Infamy*
> the United States of America was *suddenly* and deliberately attacked
> by naval and air forces of the Empire of Japan

determination of our people, we will gain the inevitable triumph — so help us God." ⬇ President Franklin D. Roosevelt is just one of the many individuals whose words tell the story of WWII in a unique exhibition at The National Archives. The annotated draft of his war message appears along with over a hundred letters, diaries and other documents written by the soldiers and sailors who fought in this historic conflict. ⬇ We invite you to visit and see the personal side of WWII. It will be another day you'll never forget.

WORLD WAR II
PERSONAL ACCOUNTS
National Archives Exhibition

On display through November 12, 1995 in the Circular Gallery. Constitution Avenue between 7th & 9th Streets, NW. Free Admission.

Merit/U.S.A.

CAMPAIGN
Patton, Infamy, World War III
ART DIRECTOR *Don Schramek*
CREATIVE DIRECTOR *Jeff Millman*
COPYWRITER *Jim Lansbury*
PRODUCER *Patty Snyder*
AGENCY *Gray Kirk/VanSant Advertising*
CLIENT *National Archives*

ADDITIONAL AWARD

Merit
NEWSPAPER, TRADE, FULL PAGE OR SPREAD
World War III

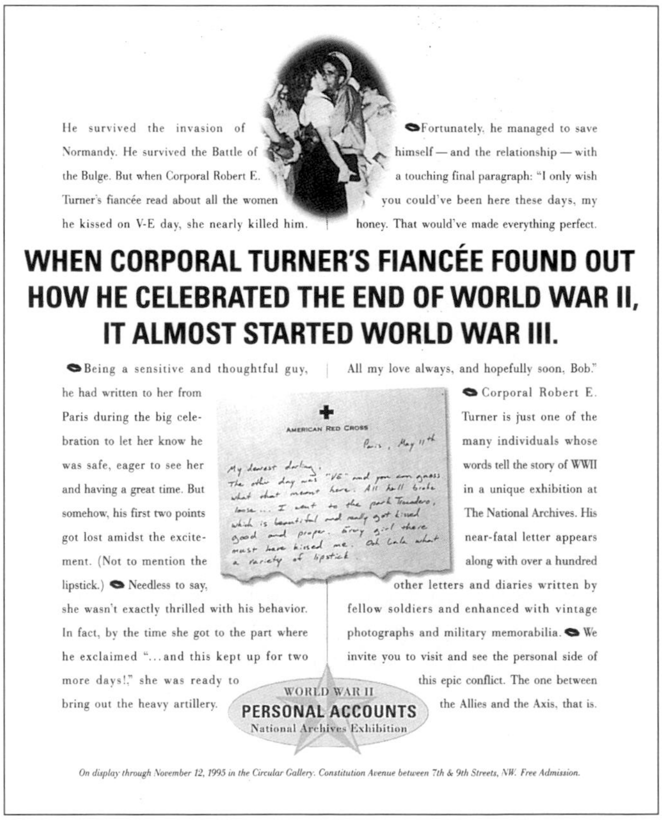

He survived the invasion of Normandy. He survived the Battle of the Bulge. But when Corporal Robert E. Turner's fiancée read about all the women he kissed on V-E day, she nearly killed him. ◖Fortunately, he managed to save himself — and the relationship — with a touching final paragraph: "I only wish you could've been here these days, my honey. That would've made everything perfect.

WHEN CORPORAL TURNER'S FIANCÉE FOUND OUT HOW HE CELEBRATED THE END OF WORLD WAR II, IT ALMOST STARTED WORLD WAR III.

◖Being a sensitive and thoughtful guy, he had written to her from Paris during the big celebration to let her know he was safe, eager to see her and having a great time. But somehow, his first two points got lost amidst the excitement. (Not to mention the lipstick.) ◖ Needless to say, she wasn't exactly thrilled with his behavior. In fact, by the time she got to the part where he exclaimed "…and this kept up for two more days!," she was ready to bring out the heavy artillery.

> AMERICAN RED CROSS
> Paris, May 11th
> My dearest darling,
> The other day was "VE" and you can guess what that means here. All hell broke loose… I went to the park Trocadero, which is beautiful and really got kissed good and proper. Every girl there must have kissed me. Oh Lala what a variety of lipstick.

All my love always, and hopefully soon, Bob." ◖ Corporal Robert E. Turner is just one of the many individuals whose words tell the story of WWII in a unique exhibition at The National Archives. His near-fatal letter appears along with over a hundred other letters and diaries written by fellow soldiers and enhanced with vintage photographs and military memorabilia. ◖ We invite you to visit and see the personal side of this epic conflict. The one between the Allies and the Axis, that is.

WORLD WAR II
PERSONAL ACCOUNTS
National Archives Exhibition

On display through November 12, 1995 in the Circular Gallery. Constitution Avenue between 7th & 9th Streets, NW. Free Admission.

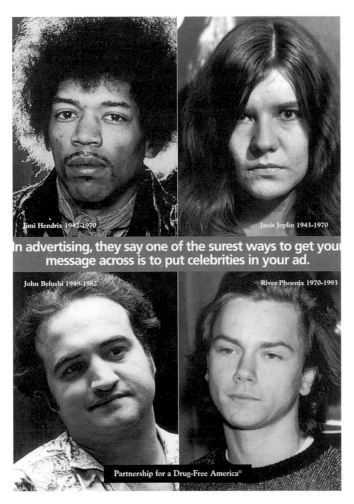

Merit/U.S.A.

FULL PAGE OR SPREAD
Celebrities
ART DIRECTOR *Matthew Schwartz*
CREATIVE DIRECTOR *Stan Becker*
COPYWRITER *David George*
ART BUYER *Francis Timoney*
PRINT SERVICES DIRECTOR *Joe Pedone*
AGENCY *Saatchi & Saatchi Advertising*
CLIENT *Partnership for a Drug-Free America*

Merit/U.S.A.

LESS THAN A FULL PAGE
Baby Lungs
ART DIRECTORS *Todd Riddle, Mark Nardi*
CREATIVE DIRECTORS *Rich Herstek, Peter Favat*
COPYWRITERS *Mark Nardi, Todd Riddle*
ENGRAVING *Unigraphic*
AGENCY *Houston Effler Herstek Favat*
CLIENT *Massachusetts Department of Public Health*

Merit/Canada

FULL PAGE OR SPREAD
Jesus Will Love You for Free
ART DIRECTOR *Duncan Bruce*
CREATIVE DIRECTOR *Duncan Bruce*
COPYWRITER *Aubrey Singer*
PRODUCER *Sheila Proctor*
FILM HOUSE *Partners Imaging Inc.*
AGENCY *TBWA Chiat/Day*
CLIENT *The Billy Graham Mission*

Merit/U.S.A.

LESS THAN A FULL PAGE
Assa Kickerata
ART DIRECTOR *Mark Faulkner*
CREATIVE DIRECTOR *Ute Brantsch*
COPYWRITER *Steffan Postaer*
AGENCY *Leo Burnett Company, Chicago*
CLIENT *Callard & Bowser-Suchard Inc.*

Merit/U.S.A.

LESS THAN A FULL PAGE
KKK Robe
ART DIRECTOR *Troy King*
CREATIVE DIRECTOR *Rudy Fernandez*
COPYWRITER *Rudy Fernandez*
DESIGNER *Troy King*
PHOTOGRAPHER *William F. Hull*
PRODUCER *Wendy Silver*
AGENCY *Hughes Advertising Inc.*
CLIENT *Atlanta History Center*

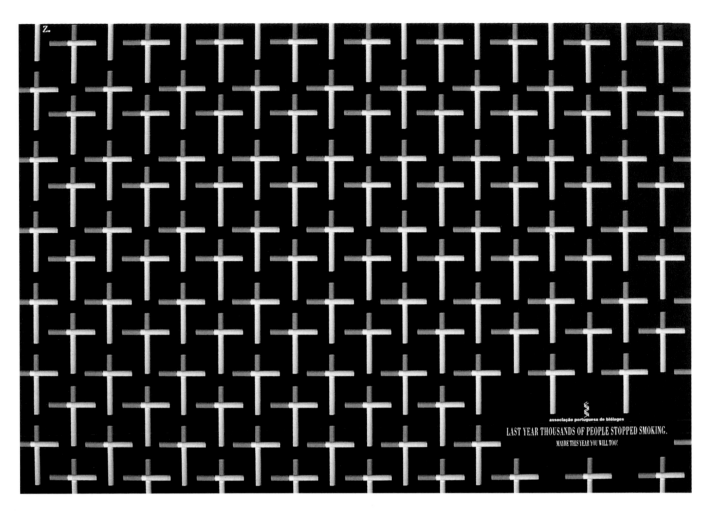

Merit/Portugal

FULL PAGE OR SPREAD
Cigarette Crosses
ART DIRECTOR *Miguel Coibra*
CREATIVE DIRECTOR *Luis Christello*
COPYWRITER *Ricardo Adolfo*
PHOTOGRAPHER *Ana Urban*
AGENCY *Z.cdp europe*
CLIENT *Associação Portuguesa de Biólogos*

You could hire a
straight decorator. People in Kansas
do it all the time.

DAVID ALEXANDER DESIGN

You've got to be gay to be a good decorator.
303.329.9695

Merit/U.S.A.

LESS THAN A FULL PAGE
David Alexander Design: Kansas
ART DIRECTOR *Brandt Wilkins*
CREATIVE DIRECTOR *Brandt Wilkins*
COPYWRITER *Brandt Wilkins*
PRINTER *Expose*
AGENCY *Reece & Company*
CLIENT *David Alexander Design*

One o... letter.

The letter is B. The wine is quite brilliant. Brancott Estate
Sauvignon Blanc is an exceptional example of this variety from Montana,
New Zealand's leading winemaker. An elegant wine, with powerful fruit flavours
and hints of Nevers oak, Brancott "B" is a letter that you'll relish opening.

MONTANA ESTATES

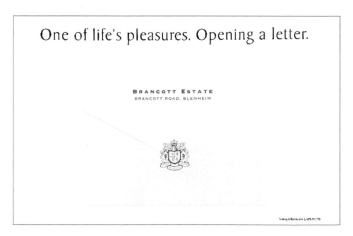

One of life's pleasures. Opening a letter.

BRANCOTT ESTATE
BRANCOTT ROAD, BLENHEIM

Merit/New Zealand

LESS THAN A FULL PAGE
Letter
ART DIRECTOR *Carl van Wijk*
CREATIVE DIRECTOR *Dave Henderson*
COPYWRITER *Dave Henderson*
DESIGNERS *Carl van Wijk, Tom van der Loos*
PRODUCER *Greg Owen*
AGENCY *Young & Rubicam Ltd.*
CLIENT *Montana Wines Ltd.*

Merit/U.S.A.

LESS THAN A FULL PAGE
Here Comes the Leash
ART DIRECTOR *Gary Goldsmith*
CREATIVE DIRECTOR *Gary Goldsmith*
COPYWRITER *Tom Miller*
PRINTER *AGT*
AGENCY *Goldsmith/Jeffrey*
CLIENT *Barneys New York*

Merit/U.S.A.

FULL PAGE OR SPREAD
Just Released
ART DIRECTOR *Warren Johnson*
CREATIVE DIRECTORS *Jack Supple, Jud Smith*
COPYWRITER *Jim Nelson*
PHOTOGRAPHER *Graham Westmoreland*
PRODUCER *Brenda Clemons*
AGENCY *Carmichael Lynch*
CLIENT *Harley-Davidson*

Merit/U.S.A.

FULL PAGE OR SPREAD
World
ART DIRECTOR *Eric Tilford*
CREATIVE DIRECTORS *Todd Tilford, Eric Tilford*
COPYWRITER *Todd Tilford*
PHOTOGRAPHER *John Huet*
AGENCY *R & D/The Richards Group*
CLIENT *Pick-Up Hoops Magazine*

Merit/U.S.A.

FULL PAGE OR SPREAD
The Road Kill Diaries: Harp Music
ART DIRECTOR *Rob Palmer*
CREATIVE DIRECTOR *David Lubars*
COPYWRITER *Kathy Hepinstall*
PHOTOGRAPHERS *Lars Topelman, Helen Trotman*
ILLUSTRATORS *Joe Saputo, Snatar Dayal*
PRODUCER *Denise Casstevens*
PRINTER *George Rice & Sons*
AGENCY *BBDO West*
CLIENT *Pioneer Electronics U.S.A. Inc.*

Merit/U.S.A.

FULL PAGE OR SPREAD
Ben Hur
ART DIRECTOR *Jason Gaboriau*
CREATIVE DIRECTOR *Gary Goldsmith*
COPYWRITER *Eddie Van Bloem*
PHOTOGRAPHER *Scott Clark*
ILLUSTRATOR *Mike Samuel*
AGENCY *Goldsmith/Jeffrey*
CLIENT *ESPN2*

Merit/U.S.A.

FULL PAGE OR SPREAD
Sunset
ART DIRECTORS *Earl Cavanah, Tom Thomas*
CREATIVE DIRECTOR *Lee Garfinkel*
COPYWRITER *Tom Thomas*
AGENCY *Lowe & Partners/SMS*
CLIENT *Western Union*

Merit/U.S.A.

FULL PAGE OR SPREAD
10, 10, 10, 10, 9.9, 10
ART DIRECTOR *Allen Richardson*
CREATIVE DIRECTOR *Roy Grace*
COPYWRITER *Ari Merkin*
PHOTOGRAPHER *Vic Huber*
AGENCY *Grace & Rothschild Advertising*
CLIENT *Land Rover North America, Inc.*

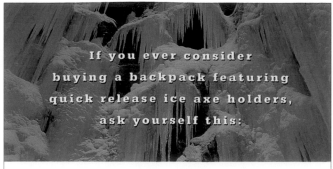

If you ever consider buying a backpack featuring quick release ice axe holders, ask yourself this:

Do I own an ice axe?

Clever features on outdoor equipment are great. Unless they're features you'll never use. At Peak 1, we design our gear with features you'll need. Take our 5.6 pound Ocala™ backpack. It's designed to hold everything you need. Our patented Kevlar™ reinforced Next Generation

Frame can support a heavy load and still flex with you as you hike. The EVA foam molded suspension keeps the Ocala comfortable. Even the price is easy to carry. Find out more. Call us at 1-800-835-3278 for a copy of our technical product guide.

Merit/U.S.A.

FULL PAGE OR SPREAD
Children Are Seldom Seen
ART DIRECTOR *Heidi Flora*
CREATIVE DIRECTOR *Kevin Jones*
COPYWRITER *Kevin Jones*
PHOTOGRAPHER *Robert Whitman*
AGENCY *Cole & Weber*
CLIENT *Westin Hotels & Resorts*

ADDITIONAL AWARD

Merit
POSTER, TRANSIT

Merit/U.S.A.

FULL PAGE OR SPREAD
Ice Axe
ART DIRECTOR *Jon Montgomery*
CREATIVE DIRECTOR *Lyle Wedemeyer*
COPYWRITER *Tom Kelly*
PHOTOGRAPHER *Buck Holzemer*
AGENCY *Martin/Williams*
CLIENT *Coleman*

Merit/U.S.A.

FULL PAGE OR SPREAD
Weenies
ART DIRECTOR *Wayne Best*
CREATIVE DIRECTORS *Tony Gomes, Tod Seisser*
COPYWRITER *Ian Reichenthal*
PHOTOGRAPHER *Aaron Rezny*
ILLUSTRATOR *Michiko Stehrenberger*
AGENCY *Ammirati Puris Lintas*
CLIENT *Hillshire Farm*

Some devote their lives to charity. Others, to science. For us, it's cocktail weenies.

Hillshire Farm. Taste the difference.

What to drive in places where you're the food.

The Defender 90 from Land Rover is one of the most sought-after vehicles in the world.

Which is why it's designed to keep whatever's out there, out there.

It offers the comfort of a front passenger safari cage, permanent four-wheel drive, and a brisk 3.9-liter V8 engine that can put just the right distance between you and a stomping, hungry, salivating who-knows-what.

With an immensely rugged 14-gauge

steel chassis and phenomenally resilient coil spring suspension, it can climb over boulders, splash through a muddy gulch, power up a mountain, and curl down a twisted gorge.

Leaving a predator dumbstruck back at the gulch.

And now that the Defender comes with an optional removable hard top, a dangling green tree boa can't even drop in unannounced.

So why not call 1-800-FINE 4WD for the nearest dealer?

While it's not exactly the least expensive 4x4, the Defender offers you that invaluable old English option.

To be or not to be.

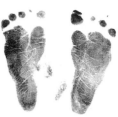 **DEFENDER 90**

Nutrition Facts

Serving Size: depends. So how was your day?
Servings Per Container: see above.

Amount Per Serving	
Calories huh?	
	% Daily Value
Total Euphoria	94%
Rapture	82%
Ecstasy	89%
Bliss	90%
Indulgence	100%
Decadence	75%
Fulfillment	97%
Thiamin	0%
Niacin	0%

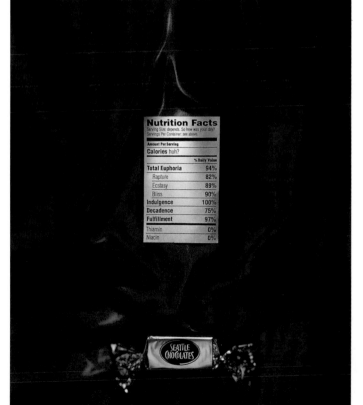

Seattle Chocolates are available in seven flavors: espresso, passion fruit, mint, toffee, hazelnut, raspberry and white chocolate orange. For more information, call 1-800-334-3600.

It doesn't take long

for a child

to need Dove.

Dove' is milder

on your baby's skin

than any soap.

Which is why it's the

#1 pediatrician

recommended cleanser

for babies.

Five minutes and older.

Dove

Merit/U.S.A.

FULL PAGE OR SPREAD
Where You're the Food
ART DIRECTORS *Allen Richardson, Gerard Vaglio*
CREATIVE DIRECTOR *Roy Grace*
COPYWRITER *Gary Cohen*
PHOTOGRAPHER *Vic Huber*
AGENCY *Grace & Rothschild Advertising*
CLIENT *Land Rover North America, Inc.*

Merit/U.S.A.

FULL PAGE OR SPREAD
Baby Feet
ART DIRECTOR *Ron Rosen*
CREATIVE DIRECTOR *Mylene Pollock*
COPYWRITER *Deborah Kasher*
AGENCY *Ogilvy & Mather, New York*
CLIENT *Lever Brothers Company*

Merit/U.S.A.

FULL PAGE OR SPREAD
Nutrition Facts
ART DIRECTOR *Tracy Wong*
CREATIVE DIRECTOR *Tracy Wong*
COPYWRITERS *Ken Bennett, Ben Wiener*
DESIGNER *Tracy Wong*
PHOTOGRAPHER *Randy Allbritton*
PRODUCER *Kathy Blakley*
PRINTER *Sunset Magazine*
AGENCY *WONGDOODY*
CLIENT *Seattle Chocolates*

Merit/U.S.A.

FULL PAGE OR SPREAD
Heimlich Maneuver
ART DIRECTOR *Jimmy Olson*
CREATIVE DIRECTORS *Tom McConnaughy,*
Jim Schmidt
COPYWRITER *Jim Schmidt*
DESIGNER *Jimmy Olson*
ILLUSTRATION *Stock*
PRINTER *Lake Shore Imaging*
AGENCY *McConnaughy Stein Schmidt Brown*
CLIENT *321 East*

HOW GOOD IS OUR STEAK?

LAST WEEK A MAN WHO WAS

CHOKING ON A PIECE

——— REFUSED ———

THE HEIMLICH MANEUVER.

321 EasT

For the very best in American cuisine come to 321 East. The food is so good it sometimes leaves people speechless. 321 Division, Elgin IL. (708)468-0612

Merit/U.S.A.

FULL PAGE OR SPREAD
Toe Hair
ART DIRECTOR *Wade Koniakowsky*
CREATIVE DIRECTOR *Wade Koniakowsky*
COPYWRITER *Joe Cladis*
PHOTOGRAPHY *Peter Samuels, Stock*
AGENCY *dGWB Advertising*
CLIENT *Vans Shoes*

Feel the wind in your toe hair.

Introducing VANS Sandals.

Mahatma   Dali   Caesar Sport   Zen   Monk   Shaman

Merit/U.S.A.

FULL PAGE OR SPREAD
Cowboy Cut Jeans
ART DIRECTOR *Bob Meagher*
CREATIVE DIRECTOR *Mike Hughes*
COPYWRITER *Joe Nagy*
PHOTOGRAPHER *Mark Scott*
PRINT PRODUCER *Jenny Schoenherr*
AGENCY *The Martin Agency*
CLIENT *Wrangler Company*

ADDITIONAL AWARDS

Merit
MAGAZINE, TRADE, FULL PAGE OR SPREAD

Merit
POINT-OF-PURCHASE

Merit/U.S.A.

FULL PAGE OR SPREAD
How Could We Fit 50 Patents Inside?
ART DIRECTOR *Cliff Sorah*
CREATIVE DIRECTOR *Kerry Feuerman*
COPYWRITERS *Joe Alexander, Kerry Feuerman*
PHOTOGRAPHERS *Terry Neifield, Dean Hawthorne*
PRINT PRODUCER *Kay Franz*
AGENCY *The Martin Agency*
CLIENT *Seiko Corporation of America*

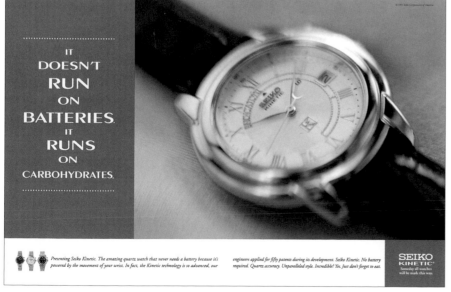

Merit/U.S.A.

FULL PAGE OR SPREAD
It Doesn't Run on Batteries
ART DIRECTOR *Cliff Sorah*
CREATIVE DIRECTOR *Kerry Feuerman*
COPYWRITER *Joe Alexander*
PHOTOGRAPHERS *Terry Niefield, Dean Hawthorne*
PRINT PRODUCER *Kay Franz*
AGENCY *The Martin Agency*
CLIENT *Seiko Corporation of America*

Merit/U.S.A.

FULL PAGE OR SPREAD
Fire
ART DIRECTOR *Margaret Johnson*
CREATIVE DIRECTOR *Todd Tilford*
COPYWRITER *Vinnie Chieco*
PHOTOGRAPHER *Jamie Stillings*
PRODUCTION MANAGER *Gail Beckman*
AGENCY *R & D/The Richards Group*
CLIENT *Muratec*

Merit/U.S.A.

FULL PAGE OR SPREAD
Resurface
ART DIRECTOR *Bob Perman*
CREATIVE DIRECTOR *Michael Winslow*
COPYWRITER *David Salmon*
PHOTOGRAPHER *Ray Barbour*
PRINTER *Laser Tech Color Inc.*
AGENCY *Rockett, Burkhead, Lewis & Winslow*
CLIENT *Volvo GM Heavy Truck Corporation*

Merit/U.S.A.

FULL PAGE OR SPREAD
Balloon
ART DIRECTOR *Allen Richardson*
CREATIVE DIRECTOR *Roy Grace*
COPYWRITER *Ari Merkin*
PHOTOGRAPHER *Jerry Cailor*
AGENCY *Grace & Rothschild Advertising*
CLIENT *Land Rover North America, Inc.*

(facing page)
Merit/South Africa

FULL PAGE OR SPREAD
Mudpack
ART DIRECTOR *Theo Ferreira*
CREATIVE DIRECTOR *Mike Schalit*
COPYWRITER *Bryn Puchert*
PHOTOGRAPHER *Mark Lanning*
PRINTER *Beith Process*
PRODUCTION MANAGER *Clinton Mitri*
AGENCY *Net Work*
CLIENT *Nissan South Africa*

Row,

Row,

Row

your boat

pathetically

whimpering

like a

little weenie

down the

stream.

WHITEWATER IN
NORTH CAROLINA.
1-800-VISIT-NC

Nobody

will

ever

know

it wasn't

the water

that

made

your pants

wet.

WHITEWATER IN
NORTH CAROLINA.
1-800-VISIT-NC

Getting on.

Repeatedly

screaming

out the name

of the

Supreme Being.

Then,

weak-kneed,

getting off.

Kinda like sex,

huh?

WHITEWATER IN
NORTH CAROLINA.
1-800-VISIT-NC

Merit/U.S.A.

CAMPAIGN
Row, Row, Row, Wet Pants, Supreme Being
ART DIRECTOR *Jim Mountjoy*
CREATIVE DIRECTOR *Jim Mountjoy*
COPYWRITER *Ed Jones*
AGENCY *Loeffler Ketchum Mountjoy*
CLIENT *North Carolina Travel and Tourism*

ADDITIONAL AWARDS

Merit
NEWSPAPER, CONSUMER, LESS THAN A FULL PAGE
Row, Row, Row

Merit
MAGAZINE, CONSUMER, LESS THAN A FULL PAGE
Row, Row, Row

FISHING ISN'T A HOBBY.

A HOBBY IS

SOMETHING YOU DO IN

YOUR SPARE TIME.

Fishing is an addiction. And being addicts ourselves, we spend every waking moment either fishing for walleye or designing tackle to catch more walleye. Our latest obsession is the Spirex®. We started by giving it Dyna Balance® and the patented QuickFire II® trigger for easy one-handed casting. Add to that an aluminum spool, four stainless steel · *ball bearings, a self-centering bail with Super Roller™ and a choice of front drag or rear Fightin' Drag®. Making the Spirex the smoothest, toughest, mid-priced spinning reel there is. At least from our compulsive, obsessive, infatuated point of view. For a free Shimano Catalog and a dealer near you, call 1-800-833-5540, Dept. 506T.*

SHIMANO

*Spirex 500 Ultralight not included.

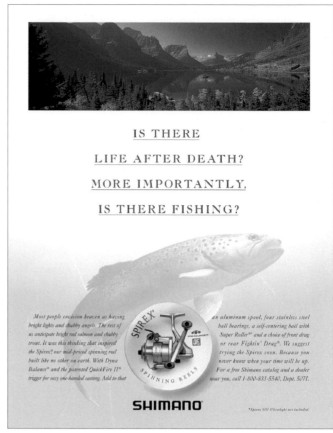

IS THERE

LIFE AFTER DEATH?

MORE IMPORTANTLY,

IS THERE FISHING?

Most people envision heaven as having bright lights and chubby angels. The rest of us anticipate bright red salmon and chubby trout. It was this thinking that inspired the Spirex®, our mid-priced spinning reel built like no other on earth. With Dyna Balance® and the patented QuickFire II® trigger for easy one-handed casting. Add to that · *an aluminum spool, four stainless steel ball bearings, a self-centering bail with Super Roller™ and a choice of front drag or rear Fightin' Drag®. We suggest trying the Spirex soon. Because you never know when your time will be up. For a free Shimano catalog and a dealer near you, call 1-800-833-5540, Dept. 507I.*

SHIMANO

*Spirex 500 Ultralight not included.

FOR THE RICH

THERE'S THERAPY.

FOR THE REST OF US,

THERE'S BASS.

The Coriolis® is built with care and precision by people who, just like you, would go crazy if they couldn't fish. In addition to its two stainless steel ball bearings, the new Coriolis has a Super Stopper® one-way roller bearing for solid hooksets, plus a · *Power Handle® 5.1:1 gear ratio, aluminum spool and tough graphite frame. Maybe we could've cut corners on this mid-priced reel, but we would've gone nuts. For a free Shimano catalog and a dealer near you, call 1-800-833-5540, Department 505K.*

SHIMANO

Merit/U.S.A.

CAMPAIGN
Hobby, Life After Death, Therapy
ART DIRECTOR *Jon Gothold*
CREATIVE DIRECTORS *Jon Gothold, Al Christensen, Wade Koniakowsky*
COPYWRITERS *Eric Springer, Al Christensen*
DESIGNERS *Jeff Labbe, Jon Gothold*
PHOTOGRAPHY *Tom Hollar, Stock*
AGENCY *dGWB Advertising*
CLIENT *Shimano*

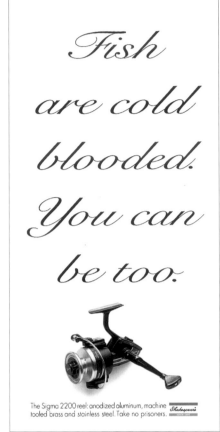

Fish are cold blooded. You can be too.

The Sigma 2200 reel: anodized aluminum, machine-tooled brass and stainless steel. Take no prisoners.

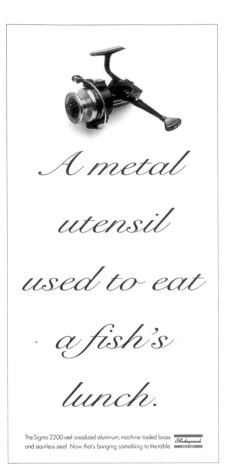

A metal utensil used to eat a fish's lunch.

The Sigma 2200 reel: anodized aluminum, machine-tooled brass and stainless steel. Now that's bringing something to the table.

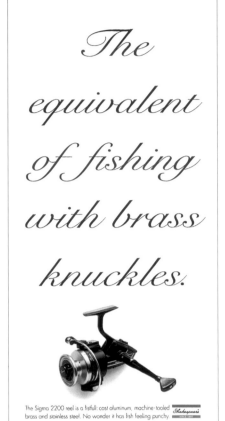

The equivalent of fishing with brass knuckles.

The Sigma 2200 reel is a fistfull: cast aluminum, machine-tooled brass and stainless steel. No wonder it has fish feeling punchy.

Merit/U.S.A.

CAMPAIGN
Cold Blooded, Metal Utensil, Brass Knuckles
ART DIRECTOR *Jim Mountjoy*
CREATIVE DIRECTOR *Jim Mountjoy*
COPYWRITER *Steve Lasch*
PHOTOGRAPHER *Jim Arndt*
AGENCY *Loeffler Ketchum Mountjoy*
CLIENT *Shakespeare*

ADDITIONAL AWARD

Merit
MAGAZINE, CONSUMER, LESS THAN A FULL PAGE
Cold Blooded

Merit/U.S.A.

CAMPAIGN
Zippers, There She Goes, Paintbrush
ART DIRECTOR *Jamie Mahoney*
CREATIVE DIRECTORS *Mike Hughes, Joe Alexander*
COPYWRITER *Joe Alexander*
PHOTOGRAPHY *Dublin Productions*
PRINT PRODUCERS *Kay Franz, Jenny Schoenherr*
AGENCY *The Martin Agency*
CLIENT *Healthtex, Inc.*

ADDITIONAL AWARDS

Merit
MAGAZINE, CONSUMER, FULL PAGE OR SPREAD
Paintbrush

Merit
MAGAZINE, CONSUMER, FULL PAGE OR SPREAD
There She Goes

Merit/U.S.A.

CAMPAIGN
Doggie Bag, Imaginary Friends,
The Baby Will Now Count
ART DIRECTORS *Carolyn McGeorge, Jamie Mahoney*
CREATIVE DIRECTORS *Mike Hughes, Joe Alexander*
COPYWRITER *Raymond McKinney*
PHOTOGRAPHY *Dublin Productions*
PRINT PRODUCERS *Kay Franz, Jenny Schoenherr*
AGENCY *The Martin Agency*
CLIENT *Healthtex, Inc.*

ADDITIONAL AWARDS

Merit
MAGAZINE, CONSUMER, FULL PAGE OR SPREAD
Doggie Bag

Merit
MAGAZINE, CONSUMER, FULL PAGE OR SPREAD
Imaginary Friends

Merit/U.S.A.

CAMPAIGN
Not on Our Mountain, Vail, Wrong Exit
ART DIRECTOR *Bob Pullum*
CREATIVE DIRECTORS *Kirk Citron, Matt Haligman*
COPYWRITER *Bryan Behar*
PHOTOGRAPHER *Marc Muench*
PRINTER *Pixxon*
AGENCY *Citron Haligman Bedecarre*
CLIENT *Copper Mountain*

ADDITIONAL AWARD

Merit
MAGAZINE, CONSUMER, FULL PAGE OR SPREAD
Wrong Exit

Becoming a man doesn't have to involve beating drums or hugging a tree.

Dewar's

Merit/U.S.A.

CAMPAIGN
Becoming a Man, Goatee, Nothing Artificial
ART DIRECTOR *Whit Friese*
CREATIVE DIRECTOR *Mark Figliulo*
COPYWRITER *John Coveny*
PHOTOGRAPHER *Robert Whitman*
AGENCY *Leo Burnett Company, Chicago*
CLIENT *Schieffelin & Somerset*

Okay, you've done the goatee thing.

Now can we all just move on.

Dewar's

There should be nothing artificial about what you drink or who you marry.

Dewar's

Merit/U.S.A.

CAMPAIGN
Trust, Nap, Heart
ART DIRECTOR *Jamie Mahoney*
CREATIVE DIRECTOR *Hal Tench*
COPYWRITER *Joe Alexander*
PHOTOGRAPHER *Jonathan LeVine*
PRINT PRODUCER *Linda Locks*
AGENCY *The Martin Agency*
CLIENT *KinderCare Learning Centers, Inc.*

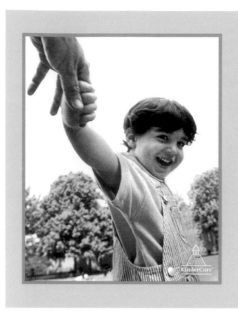

YOU'RE GOING TO LEAVE YOUR CHILD WITH US FOR 8 HOURS, EVERY DAY, ALL YEAR. (MAYBE THIS IS A GOOD TIME TO TALK ABOUT TRUST.)

YOU WANT YOUR CHILD TO BE ACTIVE, SMART, TOLERANT, LOVED, EMOTIONALLY STABLE, SELF-AWARE, ARTISTIC, AND GET A 2-HOUR NAP. ANYTHING ELSE?

IF THE BRAIN IS THE MOST IMPORTANT THING TO DEVELOP WHEN YOU'RE TWO YEARS OLD, THE HEART CAN'T BE FAR BEHIND.

YOU KNOW ALL ABOUT THE LAST DAY IN JOHN KENNEDY'S LIFE. BUT WHAT ABOUT THE 16,979 DAYS BEFORE IT?

May 29th, 1917. Rose Kennedy of Brookline, Massachusetts gives birth to her second son, John Fitzgerald Kennedy. July 23, 1935, JFK's acceptance letter from Harvard arrives in the mail. August 2, 1943, PT-109, with JFK on board as commander, is sunk by a Japanese destroyer. May 6, 1957, "Profiles in Courage", written by JFK, is awarded the Pulitzer Prize for biography. January 20, 1961, he becomes the youngest elected President of the United States.

At The New Museum at the John F. Kennedy Library, these are just a few of the many important days you'll learn about in the life of our 35th President. As you watch rare footage of a football game at Hyannis Port, stand in the middle of a mock TV studio, listen to real speeches and interviews, and study old photos, you'll hear yourself repeat over and over, "I didn't know that." The fact is, you'll come away just as many Americans did after meeting JFK for the first time: with a renewed passion and vigor for American politics. Why not call us at 617-929-4523 to learn more. Then plan to visit us. It will be a day you won't soon forget.

THE NEW MUSEUM AT THE JFK LIBRARY

HE WAS WELL-READ ON MANY SUBJECTS. THE STRIFE IN GERMANY. THE CONFLICT IN SOUTHEAST ASIA. THE TRIALS OF GOLDILOCKS.

In a typical day, John Kennedy would read newspapers from New York, Washington and Los Angeles. He would read foreign policy briefs and domestic white papers. Drafts of two or three speeches. He might steal

some time on Air Force One to read Keats. More briefs. Another draft. All the time, he would be reading the moods of foes, the whims of voters, the motives of special interests. And then after a long day at the Office, he would walk down the hall and attend to one more important domestic issue: bedtime stories for

Caroline and John Jr. At The New Museum at the John F. Kennedy Library, you'll learn what it was like to raise a family in the White House. You'll see rare footage of President Kennedy with his children and wife Jacqueline. You'll find out details about the President's own youth and how his upbringing had a profound influence on his later years. All presented in a way that makes you feel as if you were there yourself underneath JFK's desk in the "secret hideout" with Caroline and a friend. Just call 617-929-4523 to learn more. Or plan a visit soon. Bring your children. And we'll tell them a story about a man whose optimism and vigor inspired an entire generation.

Macaroni, Caroline's pony, on the White House lawn.

THE NEW MUSEUM AT THE JFK LIBRARY

BEFORE JOHN KENNEDY ENTERED POLITICS, HE WANTED TO BE A TEACHER. THIRTY YEARS LATER, HE HAS HIS WISH.

By the time John Kennedy was 14 years old, he was reading "The New York Times" daily. A friend at Choate once found him reading "The World Crisis," Churchill's six-volume history of WWI. His senior thesis at Harvard, "Why England Slept," was turned into a book and sold 90,000 copies. Many thought of him as the family intellectual and believed he would become a writer or, even more appropriately, a teacher. In fact, the title of "politician" belonged to JFK's older brother Joe, a gifted speaker and charismatic leader. But when Joe Jr. died in World War II, the course of JFK's life changed forever. Hesitant but encouraged by his father, Joseph, JFK decided to enter public service by running for Congress in 1946. And his dreams of becoming a teacher were put on hold. Or so it seemed.

At The New Museum at the John F. Kennedy Library, one of our country's greatest politicians has now been transformed into one of our greatest history teachers. Here, through rare footage,

The New Museum at the JFK Library is located on Columbia Point in the Dorchester section of Boston, the same area where Rose Kennedy lived as a young girl. Many believe the building itself, designed by I.M. Pei, is as inspirational as the man it honors.

intimate interviews, and dramatic settings, you'll see him face off with Khrushchev. Take on Nixon in the first televised debates. Tackle tough questions in the White House pressroom. Even cheer for astronaut John Glenn. And it's all presented in a way that makes you feel as if you were there. Visit today. Or call 617-929-4523 to learn more. Think of it as a field trip with a very experienced history professor.

THE NEW MUSEUM AT THE JFK LIBRARY

Merit/U.S.A.

CAMPAIGN
The Last Day, Goldilocks, Teacher
ART DIRECTOR *Cliff Sorah*
CREATIVE DIRECTOR *Hal Tench*
COPYWRITERS *Joe Alexander, Tripp Westbrook*
PRINT PRODUCER *Kay Franz*
AGENCY *The Martin Agency*
CLIENT *John F. Kennedy Library Foundation*

Merit/U.S.A.

CAMPAIGN
The Rack, Shoes, Black Diamonds
ART DIRECTOR *Terry Schneider*
CREATIVE DIRECTOR *Terry Schneider*
COPYWRITER *Greg Eiden*
DESIGNER *Shelley Stout*
PHOTOGRAPHER *Mark Ebsen*
AGENCY *Borders, Perrin & Norrander*
CLIENT *Columbia Sportswear Company*

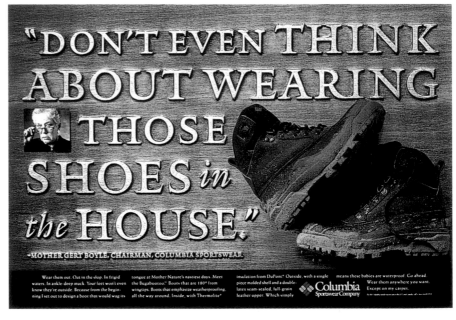

Three-time All-American Reid Jackson could have played lacrosse for just about any school in the country. Instead, he stuck it out with 19th ranked Rutgers. "You got a problem with Rutgers?"

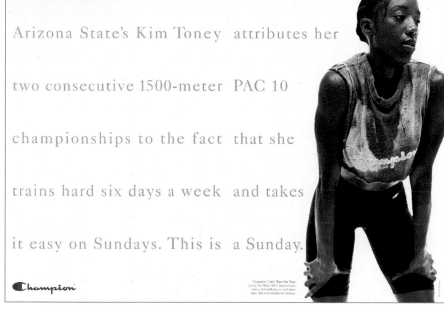

Arizona State's Kim Toney attributes her two consecutive 1500-meter PAC 10 championships to the fact that she trains hard six days a week and takes it easy on Sundays. This is a Sunday.

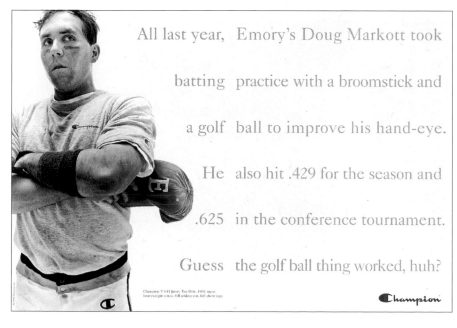

All last year, Emory's Doug Markott took batting practice with a broomstick and a golf ball to improve his hand-eye. He also hit .429 for the season and .625 in the conference tournament. Guess the golf ball thing worked, huh?

Merit/U.S.A.

CAMPAIGN
Reid Jackson, Kim Toney, Doug Markott
ART DIRECTOR *David Fox*
CREATIVE DIRECTOR *Parry Merkley*
COPYWRITER *David Corr*
PHOTOGRAPHER *Christian Witkin*
AGENCY *Merkley Newman Harty*
CLIENT *Champion*

Merit/U.S.A.

CAMPAIGN
Navel, Man's Back, Foot
ART DIRECTORS *David Angelo, Paul Hirsch*
CREATIVE DIRECTOR *David Angelo*
COPYWRITERS *Cliff Freeman, David Buckingham*
PHOTOGRAPHERS *Herb Ritts, Steve Hellerstein*
AGENCY *Cliff Freeman & Partners*
CLIENT *Sauza Gold Tequila*

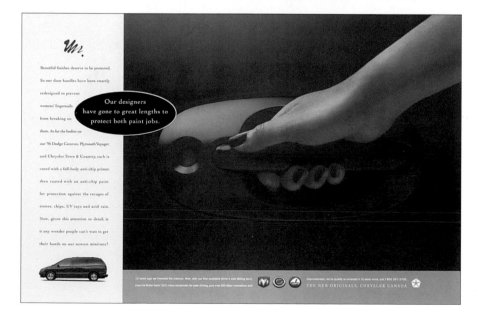

Merit/Canada

CAMPAIGN
Starry Night, Window, Nail Polish
ART DIRECTORS *Bill Newberry, Jim Brown,*
Richard Williams
CREATIVE DIRECTORS *Larry Tolpin, Neil McOstrich*
COPYWRITER *Neil McOstrich*
PHOTOGRAPHER *George Simhoni*
AGENCY *BBDO Canada*
CLIENT *Chrysler Canada Limited*

179

Merit/Germany

CAMPAIGN
Paris, Houston, Barcelona, Mexico City,
Havanna, Rome
ART DIRECTOR *Claudia Hammerschmidt*
CREATIVE DIRECTORS *Claudia Hammerschmidt,*
Hajo Depper
COPYWRITER *Hajo Depper*
PHOTOGRAPHER *Franklin Berger*
AGENCY *RG Wiesmeier Werbeagentur GmbH*
CLIENT *Eduard Dressler GmbH*

Merit/Hong Kong

CAMPAIGN
Reclamation, Miracle, Peg
ART DIRECTOR *Stanley Wong*
CREATIVE DIRECTORS *Stanley Wong, Paul Regan*
COPYWRITER *Paul Regan*
ILLUSTRATOR *Bernard Chau*
AGENCY *J. Walter Thompson Company Ltd.,*
Hong Kong
CLIENT *Friends of the Earth*

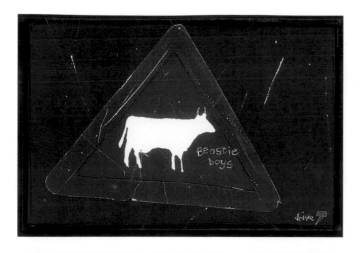

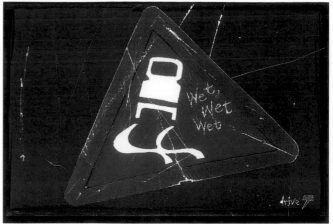

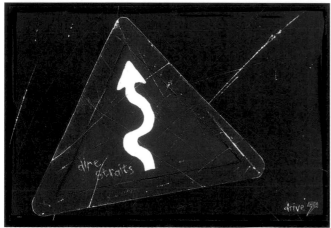

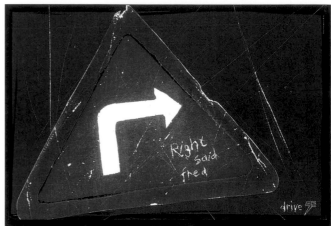

Merit/South Africa

CAMPAIGN
Beastie Boys, Wet Wet Wet, Dire Straits,
Right Said Fred, Spin Doctors
ART DIRECTOR *James Daniels*
CREATIVE DIRECTOR *Graham Warsop*
COPYWRITER *David Selikow*
ILLUSTRATOR *James Daniels*
PRINTER *City Graphics*
AGENCY *The Jupiter Drawing Room*
CLIENT *5 FM*

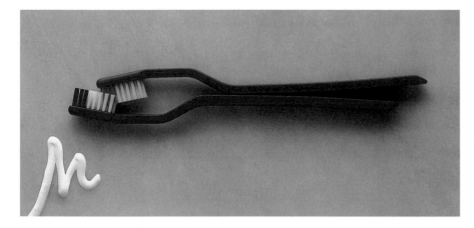

Merit/England

CAMPAIGN
Toothbrushes, Mondrian, Jigsaw, Clothing, Coat Hanger
ART DIRECTOR *Andy Ray*
CREATIVE DIRECTOR *Paul Delaney*
COPYWRITER *Paul Delaney*
PHOTOGRAPHERS *Kathy Curshen,*
Martin Thompson, Steve Thompson, John Wallace
ILLUSTRATOR *Mike Lister of Up to Scratch*
MODELMAKERS *Andy Ray, Kathy Curshen*
ACCOUNT SUPERVISOR *Stuart Leach*
AGENCY *Knight Leach Delaney*
CLIENT *Mates Condom*

ADDITIONAL AWARDS

Silver Medalist
POSTER, PRODUCT OR SERVICE
Coat Hanger

Merit
POSTER, PRODUCT OR SERVICE
Toothbrushes

Merit
POSTER, PRODUCT OR SERVICE
Mondrian

Merit/U.S.A.

INSERT
Cavity
ART DIRECTORS *David Angelo, Matt Vescovo*
CREATIVE DIRECTOR *David Angelo*
COPYWRITERS *John Miller, Donna Weinheim*
PRODUCERS *Lee Crum, Craig Cutler*
AGENCY *Cliff Freeman & Partners*
CLIENT *Sauza Conmemorativo Tequila*

Merit/U.S.A.

INSERT
OK 12-Pack
ART DIRECTOR *Todd Waterbury*
CREATIVE DIRECTORS *Todd Waterbury, Peter Wegner*
COPYWRITER *Peter Wegner*
DESIGNER *Todd Waterbury*
ILLUSTRATOR *Todd Waterbury*
AGENCY *Wieden & Kennedy*
CLIENT *The Coca-Cola Company*

10% OF YOUR CLIENTS WOULD LOVE BERMUDA
THIS WINTER. IF FOR NO OTHER REASON THAN TO
AVOID THE OTHER 90%.

*Mopeds instead
of traffic*

Bermuda from November through March isn't for everyone. And thank goodness. Our overworked visitors have always enjoyed our uncrowded paradise, its winding walks and pastel landscapes. Not to mention the absence of the thong-wearing, "I live to be bronze" population found at the sun resorts. ◆ In fact, 80% of our winter visitors are couples, sophisticated and weary clients that come through your door every day. To them club hopping means going from a 5 wood to a 3 iron. Drinking conjures up visions of high tea at 4:00. And tanning? Well, that's perfectly acceptable for leather. ◆ But please, don't think our guests are unsocial. It's just that they don't travel to find themselves surrounded by the same people they left in the first place. For more information contact your Bermuda Department of Tourism representative.

*Not just teatime,
tee-time*

BERMUDA
NOVEMBER THROUGH MARCH
A DIFFERENT KIND OF WARMTH™

We debated whether it even needed a top button.

Soft. Comfortable. Relaxing. Flyshacker Clothing Co. 6 Homestead Rd. Greenwich, CT 06831. (203) 531-1797

WE CAN'T BELIEVE HOW MUCH MONEY
YOU'RE SPENDING ON ENERGY EITHER.

If wall sockets could talk, they'd probably chastise you for using too much energy. The purpose of Energy Smart Design, on the other hand, is to enlighten you with hundreds of energy-saving ideas for your existing or planned commercial building. From which kinds of lighting, windows and motors are the most energy efficient, to what are the most frugal and effective ways to cool, heat and insulate your building.

The process begins with a meeting between the owner or developer, lead design team members, the electric

utility and its Energy Smart Design analysts. After which you'll receive a design analysis report recommending specific measures that will significantly reduce your building's monthly energy usage. These measures will also improve the look and feel of your building without radically altering its design.

Just call your local electric utility and ask for more information about the Energy Smart Design program. For ideas on how to lower your long-term operating cost, it's definitely your best outlet.

ENERGY SMART DESIGN ⸺▶ *GOOD ADVICE FROM YOUR ELECTRIC UTILITY*
└▶ *Sponsored by Bonneville Power Administration and participating electric utilities.*

Merit/U.S.A.

FULL PAGE OR SPREAD
10% of Your Clients
ART DIRECTOR *Renee Melnick*
EXECUTIVE CREATIVE DIRECTOR *Mike Rogers*
CREATIVE DIRECTORS *Dennis Stevens,
Joanna Quinn-Templeton*
COPYWRITER *Lisa Rettig-Falcone*
PHOTOGRAPHER *Harry DeZitter*
AGENCY *DDB Needham Worldwide, New York*
CLIENT *Bermuda Department of Tourism*

Merit/U.S.A.

FULL PAGE OR SPREAD
Top Button
ART DIRECTOR *Doug Trapp*
CREATIVE DIRECTOR *Lyle Wedemeyer*
COPYWRITER *Tom Kelly*
PHOTOGRAPHER *Chuck Smith*
AGENCY *Martin Williams*
CLIENT *Flyshacker Clothing Co.*

Merit/U.S.A.

FULL PAGE OR SPREAD
Wall Socket
ART DIRECTOR *Chris Toland*
CREATIVE DIRECTOR *David Ayriss*
COPYWRITER *Steve Morris*
PHOTOGRAPHER *Mark Hooper*
FABRICATOR *DillonWorks*
AGENCY *Cole & Weber*
CLIENT *Bonneville Power Administration*

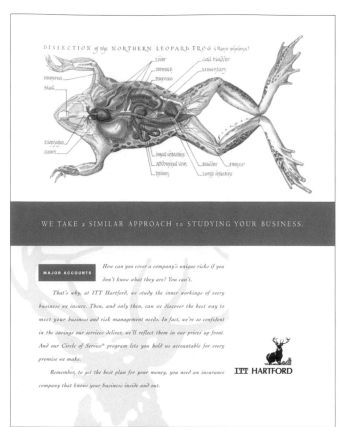

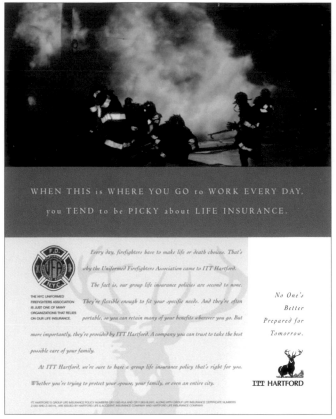

Merit/U.S.A.

FULL PAGE OR SPREAD
Frog Dissection
ART DIRECTOR *Leeanna Golden*
CREATIVE DIRECTORS *Dean Stefanides,*
Larry Hampel
COPYWRITER *Chris Jacobs*
ILLUSTRATOR *Dugal Stermer*
AGENCY *Hampel/Stefanides*
CLIENT *ITT Hartford*

Merit/U.S.A.

FULL PAGE OR SPREAD
Fire
ART DIRECTOR *Kirk Mosel*
CREATIVE DIRECTORS *Dean Stefanides,*
Larry Hampel
COPYWRITER *Chris Jacobs*
PHOTOGRAPHY *Stock*
AGENCY *Hampel/Stefanides*
CLIENT *ITT Hartford*

Merit/U.S.A.

FULL PAGE OR SPREAD
Stapler
ART DIRECTOR *Jason Stinsmuehlen*
CREATIVE DIRECTORS *Tony Gomes, Bill Schwab*
COPYWRITER *Scott Habetz*
PHOTOGRAPHER *Ilan Rubin*
AGENCY *Ammirati Puris Lintas*
CLIENT *Stanley*

Merit/U.S.A.

FULL PAGE OR SPREAD
The One Show
ART DIRECTORS *Robert Reitzfeld, Allan Beaver*
CREATIVE DIRECTORS *Robert Reitzfeld,*
Allan Beaver
COPYWRITERS *Robert Reitzfeld, Allan Beaver*
DESIGNERS *Robert Reitzfeld, Allan Beaver*
PHOTOGRAPHER *Peter Reitzfeld*
AGENCY *Beaver Reitzfeld*
CLIENT *The One Club for Art and Copy*

ADDITIONAL AWARDS

Merit
POSTER, ENTERTAINMENT OR SPECIAL EVENT

Merit
SALES PROMOTION

Merit/U.S.A.

FULL PAGE OR SPREAD
Cha-Ching
ART DIRECTOR *Wayne Thompson*
CREATIVE DIRECTOR *Lyle Wedemeyer*
COPYWRITER *Tom Kelly*
PHOTOGRAPHER *Eric Emmings*
AGENCY *Martin Williams*
CLIENT *3M*

Merit/U.S.A.

FULL PAGE OR SPREAD
Must've Been Something He Ate
ART DIRECTOR *Barney Goldberg*
CREATIVE DIRECTOR *Hal Tench*
COPYWRITER *Anne Marie Floyd*
ILLUSTRATOR *Stan Watts*
PRINT PRODUCER *Karen Smith*
AGENCY *The Martin Agency*
CLIENT *FMC Corporation*

 Must've been something he ate.

Next time uninvited guests show up for dinner, serve Thiodan Insecticide from FMC. Nothing controls early to mid-season insects more effectively. Not Guthion, Bolstar or any other organophosphate. Ask your dealer for information. Or give us a call at 1-800-468-0441. Seconds anyone? Hello? Anyone?

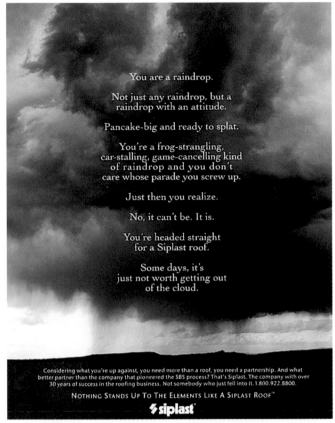

You are a raindrop.

Not just any raindrop, but a
raindrop with an attitude.

Pancake-big and ready to splat.

You're a frog-strangling,
car-stalling, game-cancelling kind
of raindrop and you don't
care whose parade you screw up.

Just then you realize.

No, it can't be. It is.

You're headed straight
for a Siplast roof.

Some days, it's
just not worth getting out
of the cloud.

Considering what you're up against, you need more than a roof, you need a partnership. And what
better partner than the company that pioneered the SBS process? That's Siplast. The company with over
30 years of success in the roofing business. Not somebody who just fell into it. 1.800.922.8800.

NOTHING STANDS UP TO THE ELEMENTS LIKE A SIPLAST ROOF™

≶ siplast

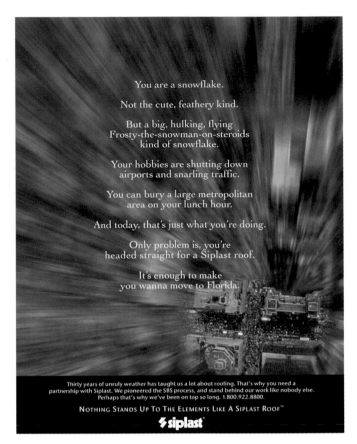

You are a snowflake.

Not the cute, feathery kind.

But a big, hulking, flying
Frosty-the-snowman-on-steroids
kind of snowflake.

Your hobbies are shutting down
airports and snarling traffic.

You can bury a large metropolitan
area on your lunch hour.

And today, that's just what you're doing.

Only problem is, you're
headed straight for a Siplast roof.

It's enough to make
you wanna move to Florida.

Thirty years of unruly weather has taught us a lot about roofing. That's why you need a
partnership with Siplast. We pioneered the SBS process, and stand behind our work like nobody else.
Perhaps that's why we've been on top so long. 1.800.922.8800.

NOTHING STANDS UP TO THE ELEMENTS LIKE A SIPLAST ROOF™

≶ siplast

You are a ray of sunlight.

You've traveled
umpteen million miles and you're
about to hit L.A.

You're ecstatic.

You figure you'll fry eggs
on the sidewalk. Melt a car
dashboard or two.

Maybe even help
George Hamilton with his tan.

Then you realize you're
headed straight for a Siplast roof.

Hollywood
can be a tough town.

In a place where it's hard to stay on top for very long, Siplast SBS roofs are doing just that. That's why
you need a partnership with Siplast. We pioneered the SBS process and have over 30 years of success in the
roofing business. Which is the kind of performance you don't find just anywhere. 1.800.922.8800.

NOTHING STANDS UP TO THE ELEMENTS LIKE A SIPLAST ROOF™

≶ siplast

Merit/U.S.A.

CAMPAIGN
Raindrop, Snowflake, Ray of Sunlight
ART DIRECTORS *Jim Baldwin, Mike Renfro*
CREATIVE DIRECTORS *Jim Baldwin, Mike Renfro*
COPYWRITERS *Jim Baldwin, Mike Renfro*
PHOTOGRAPHER *Peter Kaplan*
AGENCY *R & D/The Richards Group*
CLIENT *Siplast Roofing Co.*

Merit/U.S.A.

CAMPAIGN
Lightolier, Delta, Genzyme
ART DIRECTOR *Andrew Lewis*
CREATIVE DIRECTORS *Rich Herstek, Peter Favat*
COPYWRITERS *Mike Sheehan, Ken Lewis*
PHOTOGRAPHER *Bill Miles*
AGENCY *Houston Effler Herstek Favat*
CLIENT *Massachusetts Office of Business Development*

Tax credits. Development incentives. Relocation assistance. (Is there no limit to what we'd do to make Lightolier a fixture in Massachusetts?)

There's a fair chance you're reading this ad by the light of a Lightolier light fixture. Lightolier is, after all, the fifth largest manufacturer of lighting fixtures in the entire world.

So it's probably not a big surprise that the residents of Massachusetts are proud that Lightolier now calls Fall River, MA home. And to a large degree, they've got the Massachusetts Office of Business Development and the city of Fall River to thank. You see, when Lightolier was considering moving their headquarters from New Jersey, MOBD directed and coordinated the efforts of city and state officials and agencies in assembling an incentive package that Lightolier, quite frankly, couldn't say "no" to.

The package included a variety of tax credits (the state has the highest research and development tax credit in the United States), financing, development incentives, relocation assistance and even employee training programs.

And Massachusetts' highly educated and skilled workforce was another key reason Lightolier moved their entire R&D, engineering, marketing, and senior management operations to Fall River. (The Commonwealth boasts some 122 institutions of higher learning.)

Lightolier is just one of the many forward-thinking companies that call the Commonwealth of Massachusetts home. Not only because of a climate that's conducive to sailing, to skiing, and to sightseeing. But in addition, because of a climate that's conducive to business. (Six tax cuts in three years prove it.)

You, too, can see what a bright idea locating a business in Massachusetts is. For more information, simply contact the Massachusetts Office of Business Development at 1-800-5-CAPITAL.

[Lightolier is the fifth-largest manufacturer of lighting fixtures in the world.]

MASSACHUSETTS
The Venture Capital

Maybe it was their unique perspective, but Delta found a pretty healthy business environment in Massachusetts.

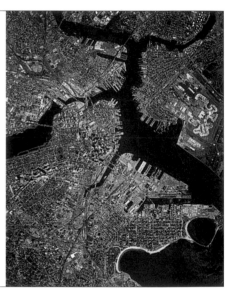

In 1992, Delta Air Lines announced that they were planning to consolidate both their Boston and New York Reservations Centers into one central location.

Almost immediately, the Massachusetts Office of Business Development went to work creating a strong incentive package the airline would find attractive.

Of course, you don't impress a company like Delta just by promising the sky. (They already own that.)

What Delta management was look-ing for were concrete solutions. More specifically, they sought low-cost building financing and tax incentives.

That's what they found in Massachusetts. Working hand-in-hand, several state and city agencies, along with the Massachusetts Port Authority (the agency that operates Boston's Logan International Airport) arranged a deal that was not just attractive, but irresistible.

Due for completion later this year, the new Reservations Center will be a true state-of-the-art telecommunications facility that will provide close to 750 jobs for the people of Massachusetts.

Landing an economic boon like the Delta Reservations Center requires plenty of cooperation between cities, the state, and business. As well as an administration that supports the efforts of business.

For more information about how our approach to business can help benefit your business, please call the Massachusetts Office of Business Development at 1-800-5-CAPITAL.

You'll find that we have a rather unique way of looking at things, too.

[Delta Air Lines located their Northeast Reservations Center at Logan International Airport.]

MASSACHUSETTS
The Venture Capital

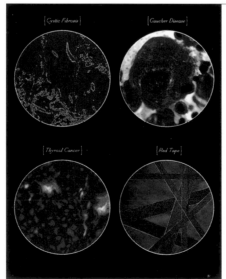

[Cystic Fibrosis] *[Gaucher Disease]*

[Thyroid Cancer] *[Red Tape]*

In Massachusetts, Genzyme found the perfect location to fight some of mankind's most painful afflictions.

There are numerous diseases that adversely affect the health and well-being of mankind. Genzyme, one of America's fastest growing biotechnology companies, devises therapies to combat and ultimately eliminate them.

There are also afflictions that can potentially affect the health and well-being of a successful company like Genzyme. Namely, red tape.

Which explains why Genzyme approached the Massachusetts Office of Business Development when it came time to build their new $125 million manufacturing facility.

Genzyme wanted to locate in a state that was decidedly pro-business. (Under the current Administration, the state has passed nine tax cuts in the past three years alone.) Because of the company's rapid growth, they also needed to move quickly. Numerous state and local government agencies worked together to accelerate the permitting process, negotiate leases, even work out tax and financial agreements, including a $4 million grant for critical highway and road construction.

Today, Genzyme's Boston facility sits upon the banks of the Charles River, within five miles of three interstate high-ways, a deep-water seaport, and a major, international airport. Thanks in part to a state that knows what it takes to support business. And, in the case of red tape, what it doesn't take.

For more information on locating a business in the Commonwealth, simply contact the Massachusetts Office of Business Development at 1-800-5-CAPITAL

[Genzyme's Boston facility is within five miles of three interstate highways.]

MASSACHUSETTS
The Venture Capital

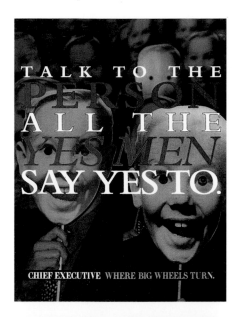

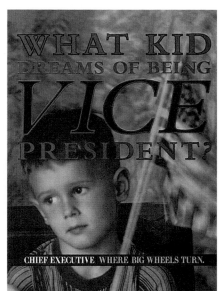

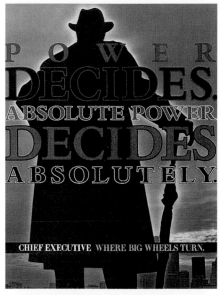

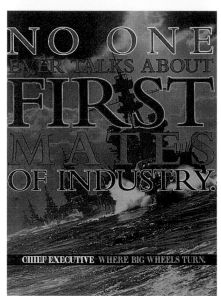

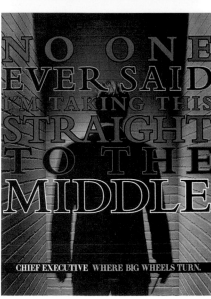

Merit/U.S.A.

CAMPAIGN
*Yes Men, Vice President, Power, First Mates,
Straight to the Middle*
ART DIRECTOR *Casey Grady*
CREATIVE DIRECTOR *Jeff Weiss*
COPYWRITER *Fred Stesney*
DESIGNER *Casey Grady*
PHOTOGRAPHERS *Roxanne Lowitt, Moshe Brakha,
Ralph Meatyard*
TYPOGRAPHER *Pat Starace*
AGENCY *McCann Amster Yard*
CLIENT *Chief Executive Magazine*

ADDITIONAL AWARD

Merit
MAGAZINE, TRADE, FULL PAGE OR SPREAD
Straight to the Middle

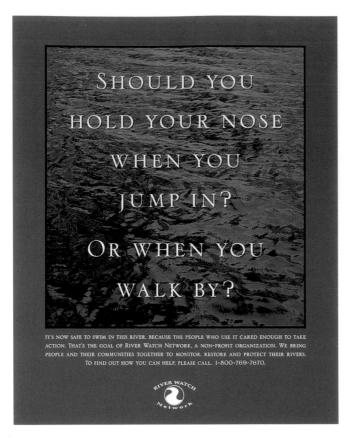

There is a fountain of youth. You just have to swim laps in it.

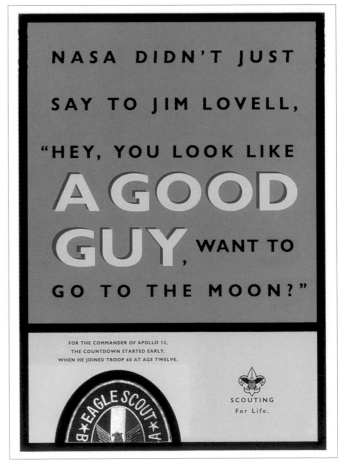

Merit/U.S.A.

FULL PAGE OR SPREAD
Hold Your Nose
ART DIRECTORS *Todd Riddle, Mark Nardi*
CREATIVE DIRECTORS *Rich Herstek, Peter Favat*
COPYWRITERS *Mark Nardi, Todd Riddle*
PHOTOGRAPHER *Joseph Holmes*
PRINTER *Unigraphic*
AGENCY *Houston Effler Herstek Favat*
CLIENT *River Watch Network*

Merit/U.S.A.

INSERT
Fountain of Youth
ART DIRECTORS *Robert Shaw West, Wayne Best*
CREATIVE DIRECTOR *Robert Shaw West*
COPYWRITER *Ian Riechenthal*
DESIGNER *Wayne Best*
PRODUCER *Drew Townsend*
PRINTER *Square One Studio*
AGENCY *West & Vaughan*
CLIENT *YMCA*

Merit/U.S.A.

FULL PAGE OR SPREAD
Jim Lovell
ART DIRECTORS *George Capuano, Glenn Price*
CREATIVE DIRECTOR *Larry Cadman*
COPYWRITER *Sean Looney*
DESIGNERS *George Capuano, Glenn Price*
PRINTER *I.I.C.*
AGENCY *Bozell Worldwide, Inc., New York*
CLIENT *Boy Scouts of America*

Merit/U.S.A.

TELEVISION COMMERCIAL, 30 SECONDS OR LESS
Tuxedo
ART DIRECTOR *Andy Hirsch*
CREATIVE DIRECTOR *Lee Garfinkel*
COPYWRITER *Barbara Siegel*
PRODUCER *Diane Jeremias*
DIRECTOR *Jeff Preiss*
EDITOR *Lin Polito of Dennis Hayes & Associates*
MUSIC *David Horowitz of DHMA*
AGENCY *Lowe & Partners/SMS*
CLIENT *Citibank ENA Cards Group*

Merit/U.S.A.

TELEVISION COMMERCIAL, 30 SECONDS OR LESS
Sprite: Crisp and Clean
ART DIRECTOR *C.J. Waldman*
CREATIVE DIRECTOR *Lee Garfinkel*
COPYWRITER *Todd Godwin*
PRODUCER *Teri Altman*
DIRECTOR *Peter Elliot*
AGENCY *Lowe & Partners/SMS*
CLIENT *The Coca-Cola Company*

Merit/U.S.A.

TELEVISION COMMERCIAL, 30 SECONDS OR LESS
1-800-COLLECT
ART DIRECTOR *Craig Silverman*
CREATIVE DIRECTOR *Ron Berger*
COPYWRITER *Israel Garber*
DIRECTOR *Graham Henman*
AGENCY *Messner Vetere Berger Mcnamee Schmetterer*
CLIENT *MCI*

Merit/U.S.A.

TELEVISION COMMERCIAL, 30 SECONDS OR LESS
Revenge
ART DIRECTOR *Bryan Burlison*
CREATIVE DIRECTOR *Lee Clow*
COPYWRITER *Josh Gold*
PRODUCER *Richard O'Neill*
DIRECTOR *Charles Wittenmeier*
MUSIC *Elias & Associates*
STUDIO *Harmony Pictures*
AGENCY *TBWA Chiat/Day Inc. Advertising*
CLIENT *Heal the Bay*

Merit/U.S.A.

TELEVISION COMMERCIAL, 30 SECONDS OR LESS
Reveal
ART DIRECTOR *Damian Dodd*
CREATIVE DIRECTOR *Jeff Millman*
COPYWRITER *Chuck Meehan*
PRODUCER *John Noble*
DIRECTOR *Lee Bonner*
STUDIO *Bonner Films, Inc.*
AGENCY *Gray Kirk/VanSant Advertising*
CLIENT *True Temper Hardware*

Merit/U.S.A.

TELEVISION COMMERCIAL, 30 SECONDS OR LESS
Lassie
ART DIRECTOR *Tom Quaglino*
CREATIVE DIRECTOR *John Russo*
COPYWRITER *Jack Lowe*
PRODUCER *Matt Pedone*
DIRECTORS *Scott Carlson, Tom Godici*
AGENCY *Pedone & Partners Advertising Inc.*
CLIENT *Genesee Brewing Company*

Merit/U.S.A.

TELEVISION COMMERCIAL, 30 SECONDS OR LESS
Jelly-Filled
ART DIRECTOR *Richard Bess*
CREATIVE DIRECTOR *Larry Postaer*
COPYWRITER *Jon Pearce*
PRODUCER *Jack Epsteen*
DIRECTOR *Craig Henderson*
SOUND DESIGNER *Chris Bell*
STUDIO *Stiegel & Co.*
AGENCY *Rubin Postaer and Associates*
CLIENT *American Honda Motor Co., Inc.*

Merit/U.S.A.

TELEVISION COMMERCIAL, 30 SECONDS OR LESS
Psycho Trainer II
ART DIRECTOR *Mickey Paxton*
CREATIVE DIRECTORS *Rich Herstek, Peter Favat*
COPYWRITER *Mike Wilson*
PRODUCER *Harry McCoy*
DIRECTOR *J. J. Sedelmaier*
STUDIO *J. J. Sedelmaier Productions*
AGENCY *Houston Effler Herstek Favat*
CLIENT *Converse*

ADDITIONAL AWARDS

Merit
**GRAPHIC DESIGN, TELEVISION, FILM,
AND VIDEO, ANIMATION, SERIES**
Psycho Trainer I, II

Merit
**GRAPHIC DESIGN, TELEVISION, FILM,
AND VIDEO, ANIMATION**
Psycho Trainer II

Merit/U.S.A.

TELEVISION COMMERCIAL, 30 SECONDS OR LESS
Elephants
CREATIVE DIRECTORS *Roy Grace, Diane Rothschild*
PRODUCERS *Frank Scherma, Jon Kamen*
DIRECTOR *Jeff Zwart*
MUSIC *Look Music*
STUDIO *@radical.media*
AGENCY *Grace & Rothschild Advertising*
CLIENT *Land Rover North America, Inc.*

Merit/U.S.A.

TELEVISION COMMERCIAL, 30 SECONDS OR LESS
Party
ART DIRECTOR *David Page*
CREATIVE DIRECTORS *Brent Bouchez, David Page*
COPYWRITER *Brent Bouchez*
PRODUCER *Susan Shipman*
DIRECTOR *Mark Coppos*
MUSIC *Trivers Myers Music*
AGENCY *Ammirati Puris Lintas*
CLIENT *Compaq Computer Corporation*

Merit/U.S.A.

TELEVISION COMMERCIAL, 30 SECONDS OR LESS
Recipe
ART DIRECTOR *Mike MacNeill*
CREATIVE DIRECTORS *Brent Bouchez, David Page*
COPYWRITER *Keith Klein*
PRODUCER *Susan Shipman*
DIRECTOR *Mark Coppos*
MUSIC *Trivers Myers Music*
AGENCY *Ammirati Puris Lintas*
CLIENT *Compaq Computer Corporation*

Merit/U.S.A.

TELEVISION COMMERCIAL, 30 SECONDS OR LESS
Homework
ART DIRECTOR *Mike MacNeill*
CREATIVE DIRECTORS *Brent Bouchez, David Page*
COPYWRITER *Keith Klein*
PRODUCER *Susan Shipman*
DIRECTOR *Mark Coppos*
MUSIC *Trivers Myers Music*
AGENCY *Ammirati Puris Lintas*
CLIENT *Compaq Computer Corporation*

  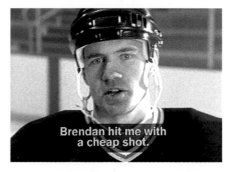

Merit/U.S.A.

TELEVISION COMMERCIAL, 30 SECONDS OR LESS
Dime
ART DIRECTOR *Chris Poulin*
CREATIVE DIRECTOR *Fred Bertino*
COPYWRITER *David Wecal*
PHOTOGRAPHER *John Schwarzman*
PRODUCER *David Verhoef*
DIRECTOR *Geoff McGann*
MUSIC *Mark Villa of Lany Music*
STUDIO *O Pictures*
AGENCY *Hill, Holliday, Connors, Cosmopulos, Inc.*
CLIENT *Spalding*

Merit/U.S.A.

TELEVISION COMMERCIAL, 30 SECONDS OR LESS
Wake Up
ART DIRECTOR *Jonathan Moore*
CREATIVE DIRECTORS *Jonathan Moore,*
John Immesoete
COPYWRITER *John Immesoete*
DIRECTOR *Simon Cheek*
COMPOSER *Joel Raney*
AGENCY *Leo Burnett Company, Chicago*
CLIENT *McDonald's*

Merit/U.S.A.

TELEVISION COMMERCIAL, 30 SECONDS OR LESS
Teammates
ART DIRECTOR *Robert Hamilton*
CREATIVE DIRECTOR *Jay Williams*
COPYWRITER *Josh Caplan*
PRODUCER *Jim Vaughan*
DIRECTOR *Jesse Peretz*
AGENCY *Arnold Fortuna Lawner & Cabot*
Advertising, Inc.
CLIENT *World Junior Hockey Championships*

Merit/U.S.A.

TELEVISION COMMERCIAL, 30 SECONDS OR LESS
Germany
ART DIRECTOR *Michael Fazende*
CREATIVE DIRECTORS *Michael Fazende,*
Stan Richards
COPYWRITER *Chris Sekin*
PRODUCER *Jessica Coats*
DIRECTOR *Peter Kagan*
MUSIC *Mark Boardman*
STUDIO *Stieffel & Company*
AGENCY *The Richards Group*
CLIENT *Continental Airlines*

Merit/U.S.A.

TELEVISION COMMERCIAL, 30 SECONDS OR LESS
Hypnotize
ART DIRECTOR *Jim Baldwin*
CREATIVE DIRECTORS *Jim Baldwin, Ron Henderson*
COPYWRITER *Ron Henderson*
MUSIC *Tom Faulkner*
AGENCY *The Richards Group*
CLIENT *Motel 6*

Merit/U.S.A.

TELEVISION COMMERCIAL, 30 SECONDS OR LESS
9 Iron
ART DIRECTOR *Jim Henderson*
CREATIVE DIRECTOR *Lyle Wedemeyer*
COPYWRITER *Tom Kelly*
PRODUCER *Rebecca Keller*
DIRECTOR *Chuck Statler*
AGENCY *Martin Williams*
CLIENT *Play It Again Sports*

Dear God,

Nevermind.

HOW WILL IT
AFFECT YOU?

Merit/U.S.A.

TELEVISION COMMERCIAL, 30 SECONDS OR LESS
Trucker
ART DIRECTOR *Kevin Kehoe*
CREATIVE DIRECTOR *Scott Rockwood*
COPYWRITER *Steve Dolbinski*
PRODUCER *Brian Robinson*
DIRECTOR *David Dobkin*
STUDIO *A + R Group*
AGENCY *Williams & Rockwood*
CLIENT *Utah Symphony*

Merit/U.S.A.

TELEVISION COMMERCIAL, 30 SECONDS OR LESS
Dear God
ART DIRECTOR *Melanie Menkemeller*
CREATIVE DIRECTORS *Wade Koniakowsky,*
Jon Gothold
COPYWRITERS *Joe Cladis, Kirt Gentry*
DIRECTOR *Brian Blak*
AGENCY *dGWB Advertising*
CLIENT *Quiksilver*

Merit/U.S.A.

TELEVISION COMMERCIAL, 30 SECONDS OR LESS
Pizza
ART DIRECTOR *Jay Giesen*
CREATIVE DIRECTOR *Rob Schapiro*
COPYWRITER *Dave Kwasnick*
PRODUCER *Marilyn Salley*
DIRECTOR *John Rice*
EDITOR *Chuck Aikman*
MUSIC *Sue Hartford*
AGENCY *Ketchum Advertising*
CLIENT *The Carnegie Museum*

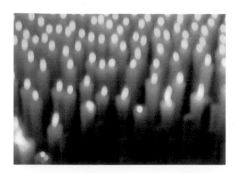

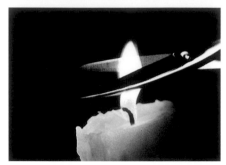

Merit/Brazil

TELEVISION COMMERCIAL, 30 SECONDS OR LESS
The Queen's Guard
ART DIRECTOR *Paulo Pretti*
CREATIVE DIRECTORS *Eduardo Fischer,*
Cláudio Carillo
COPYWRITER *Fábio Bologna*
DIRECTOR *Paula Trabulssi*
PHOTOGRAPHER *Rodolfo Sanches*
MUSIC *Fax So Funny*
PRODUCTION *Adrenalina Filmes*
PUBLISHER *Charles Miller*
STUDIO *Post Point*
AGENCY *Fischer Justus Comunicaçoes Ltda.*
CLIENT *Prever S/C Seguro e Previdência*

Merit/Singapore

TELEVISION COMMERCIAL, 30 SECONDS OR LESS
Candles
ART DIRECTOR *Andy Fackrell*
CREATIVE DIRECTOR *Tim Evill*
COPYWRITER *Kash Sree*
PRODUCERS *Leonie Schiroli, Cora Chee*
DIRECTOR *Tony Johns*
MUSIC *Song Zu*
STUDIO *Renaissance Films*
AGENCY *Batey Ads Singapore*
CLIENT *Sony Singapore*

Merit/Canada

TELEVISION COMMERCIAL, 30 SECONDS OR LESS
Baseball
ART DIRECTOR *Sam Sitt*
CREATIVE DIRECTOR *Jeff Finkler*
COPYWRITER *Dan Zimerman*
PRODUCER *Colleen Floyd*
DIRECTOR *Phil Kates*
MUSIC *Ted Rosnick*
CLIENT CONTACT *Brock Furlong*
AGENCY *Leo Burnett Company, Toronto*
CLIENT *Pillsbury Canada Ltd.*

  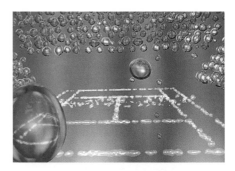

Merit/Switzerland

TELEVISION COMMERCIAL, 30 SECONDS OR LESS
Krankenkasse
ART DIRECTOR *Heinz Schwegler*
CREATIVE DIRECTOR *Mike Krüll*
COPYWRITER *Iwan Weidmann*
DIRECTOR *Ron Eichhorn*
PRODUCTION *PPM Filmproduktions AG*
AGENCY *Dubach Werbeagentur*
CLIENT *Telekurs AG*

Merit/Brazil

TELEVISION COMMERCIAL, 30 SECONDS OR LESS
Prensa
ART DIRECTOR *Paschoal Fabra Neto*
CREATIVE DIRECTORS *Paschoal Fabra Neto,*
Fernando Luna
COPYWRITER *Fernando Luna*
PHOTOGRAPHER *Raul Pedreira*
PRODUCER *Daniel Jotta Barbosa*
DIRECTOR *Carlos Mendes*
MUSIC *Emilio Carrera*
STUDIO *Piano*
AGENCY *ADD Comunicações*
CLIENT *Gruppo Bom Dia*

Merit/New Zealand

TELEVISION COMMERCIAL, 30 SECONDS OR LESS
Tennis
ART DIRECTOR *Basil Christensen*
CREATIVE DIRECTORS *Damon O'Leary,*
Basil Christensen
COPYWRITER *Damon O'Leary*
PRODUCER *Treza Conway*
DIRECTORS *Damon O'Leary, Basil Christensen,*
Job Kline
AGENCY *Saatchi & Saatchi Advertising*
CLIENT *CCA Beverages NZ Limited*

Merit/Australia

TELEVISION COMMERCIAL, 30 SECONDS OR LESS
Sheep
ART DIRECTOR *Fred Madderom*
CREATIVE DIRECTOR *Fred Madderom*
COPYWRITER *Russell Smyth*
DIRECTOR *David London*
MUSIC *Ken Francis*
STUDIO *Omnicon*
AGENCY *Batey Kazoo*
CLIENT *Royal Agricultural Society*

Merit/South Africa

TELEVISION COMMERCIAL, 30 SECONDS OR LESS
Blown Away
ART DIRECTOR *Sybi Rossouw*
CREATIVE DIRECTOR *Errol Denman*
PRODUCER *David Elton*
DIRECTOR *Jeremy Goodall*
MUSIC *Dallas Fraser*
STUDIO *Cinergy Cape Town*
AGENCY *Berry Bush De Villiers Di Bella Bellamy*
CLIENT *Stuttaford Van Lines*

Merit/New Zealand

TELEVISION COMMERCIAL, 30 SECONDS OR LESS
Pregnant
ART DIRECTOR *Alf Nadin*
CREATIVE DIRECTOR *Rob Sherlock*
COPYWRITER *Rob Sherlock*
PRODUCER *Lynette Gordon*
DIRECTOR *Barry Fawcett*
PHOTOGRAPHER *Garry Wapshot*
STILL PHOTOGRAPHER *David Ogden*
STUDIO *Airdate Films*
AGENCY *Foote Cone & Belding, Auckland*
CLIENT *Hanimex (NZ) Ltd.*

Merit/Canada

TELEVISION COMMERCIAL, 30 SECONDS OR LESS
Tornado
ART DIRECTOR *Scott Bradford*
CREATIVE DIRECTOR *Kurt Hagan*
COPYWRITER *David Daga*
PRODUCER *Martha Scandrett*
DIRECTOR *David McNally*
MUSIC *Louder Music*
STUDIO *Players Film Co.*
AGENCY *DDB Needham Canada*
CLIENT *Helene Curtis*

Merit/Hong Kong

TELEVISION COMMERCIAL, 30 SECONDS OR LESS
Sleeper
ART DIRECTOR *Jamie Pfaff*
CREATIVE DIRECTORS *Jamie Pfaff, Simon Jenkins,*
Gladys Lam
COPYWRITER *Mark Birman*
PRODUCER *Yvonne Ho*
DIRECTOR *David Tsui*
EDITOR *Adrian Brady*
MUSIC *Romeo Diaz*
AGENCY *Leo Burnett Ltd.*
CLIENT *McDonald's*

Merit/Hong Kong

TELEVISION COMMERCIAL, 30 SECONDS OR LESS
Darkness
ART DIRECTOR *Pau Tak Yan*
CREATIVE DIRECTOR *Graham Woodall*
COPYWRITERS *Graham Woodall, Jacqueline Chau*
PRODUCER *Jamie Lee*
DIRECTOR *Humberto Lai*
AGENCY *D'Arcy Masius Benton & Bowles*
CLIENT *Project Orbis Flying Eye Hospital*

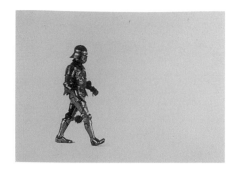

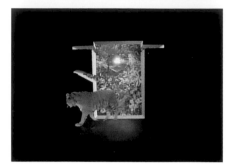

Merit/Australia

TELEVISION COMMERCIAL, 30 SECONDS OR LESS
Don't Knock Yourself Out
ART DIRECTOR *James Rickard*
CREATIVE DIRECTOR *James Rickard*
COPYWRITER *P. J. Smith*
PRODUCER *Heather McBride*
DIRECTOR *John Studley*
MUSIC *Best Fx*
AGENCY *Robertson Leo Burnett*
CLIENT *Australian Central Credit Union*

Merit/Brazil

TELEVISION COMMERCIAL, 30 SECONDS OR LESS
Bird
ART DIRECTOR *Paulo de Almeida*
CREATIVE DIRECTOR *Ruy Lindenberg*
PHOTOGRAPHER *Abraam Metri*
DIRECTOR *Roberto Laguna*
MUSIC *Play It Again*
PRODUCTION COMPANY *5.6*
AGENCY *Young & Rubicam*
CLIENT *Kaiser*

Merit/Japan

TELEVISION COMMERCIAL, 30 SECONDS OR LESS
Deer
ART DIRECTOR *Ryo Honda*
CREATIVE DIRECTORS *Ryo Honda, Koichi Sawada*
COPYWRITERS *Konosuke Kamitani, Koichi Sawada*
DESIGNER *Teiji Fujioka*
PHOTOGRAPHER *Etsuo Itoyama*
PRODUCER *Yuji Shibasaki*
DIRECTOR *Kenya Tauchi*
MUSIC *Sound City*
STUDIO *Dentsu Prox Inc.*
AGENCY *Dentsu Inc., Tokyo*
CLIENT *Fuji Xerox*

  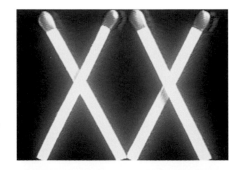

  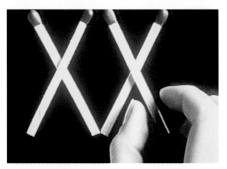

  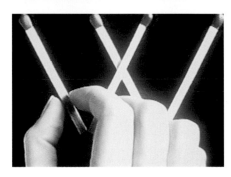

Merit/South Africa

TELEVISION COMMERCIAL, 30 SECONDS OR LESS
Abuser
ART DIRECTOR *Marc Volkwyn*
CREATIVE DIRECTOR *Clive Loxton*
COPYWRITER *Claire Harrison*
PRODUCER *Maggie Post*
DIRECTOR *Jeremy Goodall*
AGENCY *BLGK*
CLIENT *P.O.W.A.*

Merit/Switzerland

TELEVISION COMMERCIAL, 30 SECONDS OR LESS
The Fly
ART DIRECTORS *Martin Spillmann, Roland Scotoni*
CREATIVE DIRECTOR *Martin Spillmann*
COPYWRITERS *Martin Spillmann, Urs Schrepfer*
PRODUCER *Olivier Delahaye*
DIRECTOR *Paul Meijer*
MUSIC *Michel Hardy*
AGENCY *Advico Young & Rubicam, Zurich*
CLIENT *Hakle AG, Reichenburg*

Merit/Brazil

TELEVISION COMMERCIAL, 30 SECONDS OR LESS
Matches
CREATIVE DIRECTORS *Alexandre Gama,*
Marcello Serpa
COPYWRITERS *Alexandre Gama, Adherbal Rocha*
PRODUCER *Luiz Jatobá*
DIRECTOR *Clovis Mello*
MUSIC *Play It Again*
STUDIO *Cine 21*
AGENCY *ALMAP/BBDO*
CLIENT *Volkswagen*

Merit/Norway

TELEVISION COMMERCIAL, 30 SECONDS OR LESS
Travel Insurance
ART DIRECTOR *Kjell Bryngell*
COPYWRITER *Morten Andresen*
PHOTOGRAPHER *G. B. Alessandri*
DIRECTOR *Ubbe Haavind*
SOUND *David Gjester*
PRODUCTION *Kraftwerk Productions*
AGENCY *Saatchi & Saatchi Advertising*
CLIENT *Europeiske Reiseforsikring*

Merit/Brazil

TELEVISION COMMERCIAL, 30 SECONDS OR LESS
Fly
ART DIRECTOR *Julio Andery*
CREATIVE DIRECTOR *Fabio Fernandes*
COPYWRITER *Eduardo Lima*
PRODUCER *Licia Contoli*
DIRECTOR *Bia Flecha*
MUSIC *Play It Again*
STUDIO *Filmmakers*
AGENCY *F/NAZCA S&S Publicidade Ltda.*
CLIENT *Antenna 1*

Merit/U.S.A.

TELEVISION COMMERCIAL, 30 SECONDS OR LESS, CAMPAIGN
Big Commercial, Modelmaker, Yes Men
ART DIRECTOR *Jerry Gentile*
CREATIVE DIRECTORS *Steve Rabosky, Steve Sweitzer*
COPYWRITER *Jeff Watzman*
PRODUCER *Michelle Burke*
DIRECTOR *Jeff Gorman*
MUSIC *Elias & Associates*
STUDIO *Johns & Gorman Films*
AGENCY *TBWA Chiat/Day Inc. Advertising*
CLIENT *Unocal*

Merit/U.S.A.

TELEVISION COMMERCIAL, 30 SECONDS OR LESS, CAMPAIGN
Mystery, Driving, Bathroom Cleaner
ART DIRECTOR *Eric Olis*
CREATIVE DIRECTORS *Gail Offen, Dave Michalak*
COPYWRITER *Craig Pines*
PRODUCER *Rob DeMilner*
DIRECTOR *Larry August*
MUSIC *Stock*
AGENCY *W. B. Doner and Company*
CLIENT *F&M Super Drug Store*

ADDITIONAL AWARD

Merit
TELEVISION COMMERCIAL, 30 SECONDS OR LESS
Bathroom Cleaner

Merit/U.S.A.

TELEVISION COMMERCIAL, 30 SECONDS OR LESS, CAMPAIGN
Bosnia, Haiti, Central America
ART DIRECTOR *Jason Gaboriau*
CREATIVE DIRECTOR *Gary Goldsmith*
COPYWRITER *Justin Rohrlich*
PRODUCER *Sadie Pollack*
DIRECTOR *Noam Murro*
AGENCY PRODUCER *Noam Murro*
MUSIC *Avi Oron, John Califra*
STUDIO *Aniforms*
AGENCY *Goldsmith/Jeffrey*
CLIENT *The Robin Hood Foundation*

ADDITIONAL AWARD

Merit
TELEVISION COMMERCIAL, 30 SECONDS OR LESS
Central America

Merit/U.S.A.

TELEVISION COMMERCIAL, 30 SECONDS OR LESS, CAMPAIGN
Indiana, Kansas, UCLA
CREATIVE DIRECTORS *Larry Frey, Jerry Cronin*
COPYWRITER *Ernest Lupinacci*
PRODUCERS *Frank Scherma, Robert Fernandez*
DIRECTOR *Alan White*
AGENCY *Wieden & Kennedy*
CLIENT *ESPN*

Merit/U.S.A.

TELEVISION COMMERCIAL, 30 SECONDS OR LESS, CAMPAIGN
Mystic Woman, Burns Boy, Abstract Woman
ART DIRECTOR *Todd Waterbury*
CREATIVE DIRECTORS *Todd Waterbury, Peter Wegner*
COPYWRITER *Peter Wegner*
PRODUCER *Amy Davenport*
DIRECTORS *Donna Pittman, Mark Hensley*
DESIGNER *Todd Waterbury*
ILLUSTRATORS *Dan Clowes, Charles Burns, David Cowles*
MUSIC *John Zorn*
AGENCY *Wieden & Kennedy*
CLIENT *The Coca-Cola Company*

Merit/U.S.A.

TELEVISION COMMERCIAL, 30 SECONDS OR LESS, CAMPAIGN
Choke, Sinatra, Petition
CREATIVE DIRECTORS *Bryan Buckley, Frank Todaro*
PRODUCERS *Jon Kamen, Robert Fernandez*
DIRECTORS *Bryan Buckley, Frank Todaro*
STUDIO *@radical.media*
AGENCY *@radical.media*
CLIENT *ESPN*

Merit/U.S.A.

TELEVISION COMMERCIAL, OVER 30 SECONDS
Diner
ART DIRECTOR *Don Schneider*
CREATIVE DIRECTORS *Michael Patti, Don Schneider*
COPYWRITER *Michael Patti*
PRODUCERS *Regina Ebel, Maria Amato*
DIRECTOR *Joe Pytka*
STUDIO *Crew Cuts*
AGENCY *BBDO New York*
CLIENT *Pepsi-Cola Co.*

Merit/U.S.A.

TELEVISION COMMERCIAL, OVER 30 SECONDS
Graduation Party
ART DIRECTOR *Rich Ostroff*
CREATIVE DIRECTOR *Lee Garfinkel*
COPYWRITERS *Lee Garfinkel, John Brockenbrough*
PRODUCER *Bob Nelson*
DIRECTOR *Mark Coppos*
EDITOR *Craig Warner of Bender Editorial*
AGENCY *Lowe & Partners/SMS*
CLIENT *Hanson Industries*

Merit/U.S.A.

TELEVISION COMMERCIAL, OVER 30 SECONDS
Tickets
ART DIRECTOR *Rick McQuiston*
CREATIVE DIRECTORS *Larry Frey, Jerry Cronin*
COPYWRITER *Hank Perlman*
PRODUCERS *Jon Kamen, Robert Fernandez*
DIRECTORS *Bryan Buckley, Frank Todaro*
AGENCY *Wieden & Kennedy*
CLIENT *ESPN Hockey*

Merit/South Africa

TELEVISION COMMERCIAL, PUBLIC SERVICE
Cell
ART DIRECTOR *Neil Dawson*
CREATIVE DIRECTOR *Ricardo De Carvalho*
COPYWRITER *Clive Pickering*
PRODUCER *Ken McKenzie*
DIRECTOR *Ricardo De Carvalho*
MUSIC *Sue Greally*
PRODUCTION COMPANY *McKenzie Rudolphe Films*
ACCOUNT SUPERVISOR *Gerrie Heyneke*
AGENCY *The White House*
CLIENT *United Nations Committee, New York*

Merit/Brazil

TELEVISION COMMERCIAL, PUBLIC SERVICE
Farra
ART DIRECTOR *Wladimir Cardoso*
CREATIVE DIRECTORS *Paschoal Fabra Neto,*
Fernando Luna
COPYWRITER *Eduardo Di Lascio*
PRODUCER *Daniel Jotta Barbosa*
DIRECTOR *Jorge Solari*
MUSIC *Mauricio Tagliardi*
STUDIO *Y. B. do Brazil*
AGENCY *ADD Comunicações*
CLIENT *UIPA (International Union of Animal*
Protection)

Merit/U.S.A.

TELEVISION COMMERCIAL, LOW BUDGET,
CAMPAIGN
Tree, Turtle, Mushroom
ART DIRECTOR *Sean Riley*
CREATIVE DIRECTOR *Hal Tench*
COPYWRITER *Joe Alexander*
PRODUCER *Mike Henry*
AGENCY *The Martin Agency*
CLIENT *Sierra Club*

Merit/U.S.A.

COMMERCIAL, 30 SECONDS OR LESS
Girl Scream
CREATIVE DIRECTOR *Kurt Tausche*
COPYWRITERS *Sally Williams, Andrew Payton*
PRODUCER *Danica Walker*
PRODUCTION *Doppler Studios,*
oooka oooka eek eek Productions
AGENCY *Tausche Martin Lonsdorf*
CLIENT *Hotlanta*

Girl Scream
GIRL: *(Screaming at the top of her lungs,*
all in one breath)
Aaaaaaaaaaaaaaaaaaaaaaaaaaaaaaaaa
aaaaaaaaaaaaaaaaaaaaaaaaaaaaaaaaa
aaaaaaaaaaaaaaaaaaaaaaaaaaaaaaaaa
aaaaaaaaaaaaaaaaaaaaaaaaaaaaaaaaa
aaaaaaaaaaaaaaaaaaaaaaaaaaaaaaaaa
aaaaaaaaaaaaaaaaahhhhhhhhhhhhhhhh
hhhhhhhhhhhhhhhhhhhhhhhhhhhhhhhhh
hhhhhhhhhhhhhhhhhhhhhhhhhhhhhhhhh
hhhhhhhhhhhhhhhhhhhhhhhhhhhhhhhhh
hhhhhhhhhhhhhh. Mmm, that's good.
ANNCR: *Hotlanta. Gourmet hot sauces from*
around the world. At the Underground.

Merit/U.S.A.

COMMERCIAL, 30 SECONDS OR LESS
Guy Scream
CREATIVE DIRECTOR *Kurt Tausche*
COPYWRITERS *Sally Williams, Andrew Payton*
DIRECTOR *Danica Walker*
PRODUCTION *Doppler Studios,*
oooka oooka eek eek Productions
AGENCY *Tausche Martin Lonsdorf*
CLIENT *Hotlanta*

Guy Scream
GUY: *(Screaming at the top of his lungs,*
all in one breath)
Aaaaaaaaaaaaaaaaaaaaaaaaaaaaaaaaa
aaaaaaaaaaaaaaaaaaaaaaaaaaaaaaaaa
aaaaaaaaaaaaaaaaaaaaaaaaaaaaaaaaa
aaaaaaaaaaaaaaaaaaaaaaaaaaaaaaaaa
aaaaaaaaaaaaaaaaahhhhhhhhhhhhhhhh
hhhhhhhhhhhhhhhhhhhhhhhhhhhhhhhhh
hhhhhhhhhhhhhhhhhhhhhhhhhhhhhhhhh
hhhhhhhhhhhhhhhhhhhhhhhhhhhhhhhhh
hhhhhhhhhhhhhhh. Boy, that's hot.
ANNCR: *Hotlanta. Gourmet hot sauces from*
around the world. At the Underground.

Merit/U.S.A.

COMMERCIAL, 30 SECONDS OR LESS
Windbag
ART DIRECTOR *Rochelle Klein*
CREATIVE DIRECTOR *Jerry Fields*
PRODUCER *Fran Cosentino*
STUDIO *Romann Sound*
AGENCY *Angotti Thomas Hedge Inc.*
CLIENT *Molson Breweries*

Windbag
SOUND: *A didgeridoo being played.*
ANNCR: *How to speak Australian.*
SOUND: *General bar sounds.*
AUSSIE 1: *How're you goin', Rodg?*
AUSSIE 2: *Not bad.*
ANNCR: *Conversationalist.*
SOUND: *Didgeridoo.*
ANNCR: *How to speak Australian, continued.*
SOUND: *Bar.*
AUSSIE 1: *How're you goin', Dave?*
AUSSIE 3: *Not bad. Not bad at all.*
ANNCR: *Windbag.*
SOUND: *Beer can opens and pours.*
ANNCR: *Foster's. Australian for beer.*
Imported by Century Importers,
Reston, Virginia.

Merit/U.S.A.

COMMERCIAL, OVER 30 SECONDS
Poem
CREATIVE DIRECTOR *Gary Goldsmith*
COPYWRITER *Eddie Van Bloem*
AGENCY PRODUCER *Eddie Van Bloem*
PRODUCTION *McHale/Barone*
STUDIO *Superdupe*
AGENCY *Goldsmith/Jeffrey*
CLIENT *ESPN2*

Poem
SOUND: *Clinking glasses, quiet conversation, etc.*
MAN: *OK, people, next up…a poem, from the lovely Jenny.*
SOUND: *Applause.*
JENNY: *Um, this is a poem about…um, this is a poem.*
SOUND: *Bass accompanies her reading.*
JENNY: *My love is lost and that hurts most. What's left? Burnt toast.*
I melt, I turn to slush,
Like a toilet, unable to flush.
I pour my heart out, he is but a wall,
Watching NCAA hoops, 180 games in all.
If it were a woman, there'd be something I could do.
But it's the devil's network—one called ESPN2.
(Grows increasingly angry and stops rhyming.)
A little affection—all I seek,
But got NHL hockey, three nights a week.
College football, Indy car, NASCAR, too— we never do the things we used to do.
There's even this wrap-up show called RPM 2Nite.
SOUND: *Bass has trouble keeping tempo, finally stops.*
JENNY: *Like it's not enough to watch the races, he's got to watch stupid highlights, and then it's:" Jenny, could you move a little, you're in the way." God, I could kill him, and to think this is the man I was going to procreate with! (Pause.) Thank you.*
SOUND: *Polite applause.*
MAN: *ESPN2. Some will love it. Others, not so much.*

Merit/U.S.A.

COMMERCIAL, OVER 30 SECONDS
Still More Things I'd Like To See
CREATIVE DIRECTOR *Mike Renfro*
COPYWRITER *Mike Renfro*
PRODUCERS *David Rucker, Jessica Coats*
STUDIO *Real To Reel Studios*
AGENCY *The Richards Group*
CLIENT *The Auto Show*

Still More Things I'd Like to See
VO: *And now, things I'd really like to see on TV. I'd really like to see what effect wind shear would have on the Flying Nun. I'd like to see Julia Child in a pool hall. I'd like to see a Melrose Place where all the guys have beer guts. I'd like to see the Care Bears doing time in the Federal pen. I'd like to meet the Incredible Hulk's tailor. I'd like to see Bob Barker give away a couple of furs. I'd like to see golf where you can heckle your opponent. I'd like to see Mr. Whipple get knocked around a little….*
ANNCR: *Wouldn't it be nice if there was something on TV you'd actually like to see? Now there is something. The Auto Show. Nothing but cars and trucks for sale or trade. You see a car you like, you call the number on the screen. It's the one show on TV you can actually have an effect on. The Auto Show. Coming this spring to Channel 39. Think of it as PBS for the car enthusiast.*
VO: *…I'd like to see somebody give Connie Chung a wedgie. I'd like to see Marshall Dillon get rolled by a bunch of bikers. I'd like to see…a baseball game.*

Merit/U.S.A.

COMMERCIAL, OVER 30 SECONDS, CAMPAIGN
Delivery Drama, Harold's Lucky Day, History of Movies
CREATIVE DIRECTOR *Arthur Bijur*
COPYWRITER *Michelle Roufa*
PRODUCERS *Mary Ellen O'Brien, Maresa Wickham*
STUDIOS *Kamen Audio, Clack Sound Studio*
AGENCY *Cliff Freeman & Partners*
CLIENT *Little Caesars*

ADDITIONAL AWARD

Merit
COMMERCIAL, 30 SECONDS OR LESS
Harold's Lucky Day

Harold's Lucky Day
ANNCR: *Today was the luckiest day of Harold's life.*
SOUND: *Walking, tinkling of foot kicking a coin.*
HAROLD: *A silver dollar! Wow!! And what's that shiny rock?*
SOUND: *Pop of rock coming loose.*
HAROLD: *It's gold!!!*
SOUND: *Burbling sound, turns to gush of oil.*
HAROLD: *Whoa!!! I struck oil!!!*
SOUND: *Walking again. Gush gets far away, then feet stop.*
BILL: *Oh, wow—someone dropped a Picasso!!!*
ANNCR: *Just when you thought things couldn't get any better—now, for a limited time, buy two Little Caesars specialty pizzas loaded with cheese and toppings and get free Crazy Bread for only $9.98!*
LITTLE CAESAR: *Pizza! Pizza!*

Merit/U.S.A.

COPYWRITING
Angel
ART DIRECTOR *Ian Harding*
CREATIVE DIRECTORS *Shaun McIlrath, Ian Harding*
COPYWRITER *Shaun McIlrath (inspired by Margaret Powers)*
PRODUCER *Zoe Howard*
STUDIO *The Bridge*
AGENCY *Impact FCA*
CLIENT *Marie Curie Cancer Care*

ADDITIONAL AWARD

Merit
COMMERCIAL, PUBLIC SERVICE

Angel
ANNCR: *A man finds himself on a beach with his guardian angel. As they walk, he notices two sets of footprints. "Whose are those?" he asks. "They are yours," the angel replies. "This is the path of your life." "And who do the other footprints belong to?" "They are mine," the angel answers. "I was there throughout your life." As they walk on, the angel points to a place where one set of footprints begins to limp. "There," he says, "That is where your wife fell ill. You see, I was with you even then." "And what about here?" the man says, indicating a part of the beach where there is only one set of footprints. "That is where your wife died." "Well, where were you then?" the man asked angrily. "Where were you then, when I needed you most?" At that point, the angel replied, "I was carrying you."*
ANNCR: *Every year, thousands of Marie Curie nurses provide free care and 24-hour support to cancer patients in their homes. Contact them through your GP or district nurse or support Marie Curie Cancer Care on Daffodil Day, March the 18th.*

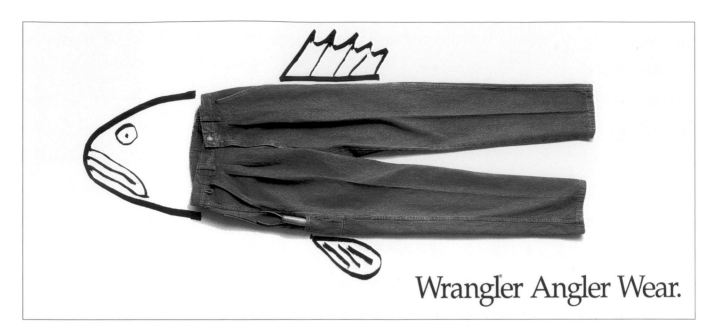

Wrangler Angler Wear.

Put Wrangler Jeans On Your Horse.

Merit/U.S.A.

BILLBOARD
Wrangler Angler Wear
ART DIRECTOR *Hal Tench*
CREATIVE DIRECTOR *Hal Tench*
COPYWRITER *Joe Nagy*
PHOTOGRAPHER *Tim Gabbert*
PRINT PRODUCER *Jenny Schoenherr*
AGENCY *The Martin Agency*
CLIENT *Wrangler Company*

Merit/U.S.A.

BILLBOARD
Put Wrangler Jeans on Your Horse
ART DIRECTOR *Bob Meagher*
CREATIVE DIRECTORS *Mike Hughes, Ron Huey*
COPYWRITER *Joe Nagy*
PRINT PRODUCER *Jenny Schoenherr*
AGENCY *The Martin Agency*
CLIENT *Wrangler Company*

When wit and charm fail.

One should sip, not gulp.

Old surfers never die, they just get jobs. Mercedes-Benz

The C-Class. Starting at $30,950.*

Merit/U.S.A.

BILLBOARD, CAMPAIGN
Wit and Charm, One Should Sip,
Old Surfers Never Die, Soon
ART DIRECTOR *Barney Goldberg*
CREATIVE DIRECTORS *Kerry Feuerman, Ron Huey*
COPYWRITERS *Jeff Ross, Joe Nagy*
PHOTOGRAPHERS *Michael Rausch, Chris Bailey*
PRINT PRODUCER *Tom Maher*
AGENCY *The Martin Agency*
CLIENT *Mercedes-Benz of North America*

ADDITIONAL AWARDS

Merit
POSTER, BILLBOARD
Old Surfers Never Die

Merit
POSTER, BILLBOARD
Soon

Merit/U.S.A.

PROMOTIONAL
Ahh, Yes. That Was a Very Good Year
ART DIRECTOR *Cliff Sorah*
CREATIVE DIRECTOR *Mike Hughes*
COPYWRITER *Raymond McKinney*
PRINT PRODUCER *Karen Smith*
AGENCY *The Martin Agency*
CLIENT *The Poe Museum*

Merit/Japan

PROMOTIONAL
Fourth Antique Grand Fair in Kyoto
ART DIRECTOR *Yasuhiko Kida*
CREATIVE DIRECTOR *Yasuhiko Kida*
DESIGNER *Yasuhiko Kida*
ILLUSTRATOR *Yasuhiko Kida*
PRINTER *Hiyoshi Printing Co.*
CLIENT *Gomokudo Co.*

Merit/Japan

PROMOTIONAL
Fifth Antique Grand Fair in Kyoto
ART DIRECTOR *Yasuhiko Kida*
CREATIVE DIRECTOR *Yasuhiko Kida*
DESIGNER *Yasuhiko Kida*
ILLUSTRATOR *Yasuhiko Kida*
PRINTER *Hiyoshi Printing Co.*
CLIENT *Gomokudo Co.*

Merit/Japan

PROMOTIONAL
How Do You Like the World of Nature
ART DIRECTOR *Hirofumi Yamanaka*
CREATIVE DIRECTOR *Hirofumi Yamanaka*
COPYWRITER *Hiroshi Nagawa*
DESIGNER *Hirofumi Yamanaka*
PHOTOGRAPHER *Shintaro Shiratori*
STUDIO *Creators Group MAC*
CLIENT *Shinchosha Co., Ltd.*

Merit/Japan

PROMOTIONAL
Takashi Fukui
ART DIRECTOR *Takashi Fukui*
CREATIVE DIRECTOR *Takashi Fukui*
DESIGNER *Takashi Fukui*
PHOTOGRAPHER *Kazuhiro Takahashi*
PRINTER *Nissho Co. Ltd.*
AGENCY *Dentsu Inc., Tokyo*
CLIENT *Takashi Fukui*

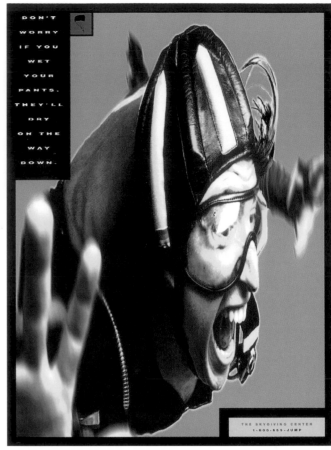

Merit/U.S.A.

POINT-OF-PURCHASE
School Prayer
ART DIRECTOR *Damon Williams*
CREATIVE DIRECTOR *Rudy Fernandez*
COPYWRITER *Chris Jacobs*
DESIGNER *Troy King*
PHOTOGRAPHER *Chris Davis*
PRODUCER *Shay Langgood*
AGENCY *Hughes Advertising, Inc.*
CLIENT *The Skydiving Center*

Merit/U.S.A.

POINT-OF-PURCHASE
Wet Your Pants
ART DIRECTOR *Damon Williams*
CREATIVE DIRECTOR *Rudy Fernandez*
COPYWRITER *Chris Jacobs*
DESIGNER *Troy King*
PHOTOGRAPHER *Chris Davis*
PRODUCER *Shay Langgood*
AGENCY *Hughes Advertising, Inc.*
CLIENT *The Skydiving Center*

Merit/U.S.A.

POINT-OF-PURCHASE
Better than Sex
ART DIRECTOR *Damon Williams*
CREATIVE DIRECTOR *Rudy Fernandez*
COPYWRITER *Chris Jacobs*
DESIGNER *Troy King*
PHOTOGRAPHER *Chris Davis*
PRODUCER *Shay Langgood*
AGENCY *Hughes Advertising, Inc.*
CLIENT *The Skydiving Center*

Man cuts down trees.

Man pollutes rivers.

Man buys cheap bike parts.

Nature gets even.

Merit/U.S.A.

POINT-OF-PURCHASE
Gonzo Poster
ART DIRECTOR *Damon Williams*
CREATIVE DIRECTOR *Rudy Fernandez*
COPYWRITER *Zach Watkins*
PHOTOGRAPHER *Tom Moran*
PRINTER *Claxton Printing*
AGENCY *Hughes Advertising, Inc.*
CLIENT *Gonzo Bicycle Components*

Merit/U.S.A.

POINT-OF-PURCHASE
Star
ART DIRECTOR *Dan O'Donnell*
CREATIVE DIRECTOR *Gary Greenberg*
COPYWRITER *Dave Swartz*
DESIGNER *John Young*
PHOTOGRAPHER *Jack Richmond*
PRINTER *Boston Photo*
AGENCY *Greenberg Seronick & Partners, Inc.*
CLIENT *Shalom Hunan*

Merit/U.S.A.

POINT-OF-PURCHASE
Women's Gun Classes
ART DIRECTOR *Cody Spinadel*
COPYWRITER *Mike Collado*
PHOTOGRAPHER *Tim Schaedler*
DIGITAL RETOUCHING *Alan Davidson*
PRINTER *Color Concepts*
AGENCY *Paradigm Communications*
CLIENT *American Firearms*

AFTER GOOD SEX.

AFTER GREAT SEX.

THE CIGAR BAR AT ARTHUR'S

EVERYTHING YOU NEED FOR A WEEKEND IN NICARAGUA, LEBANON, OR NEW YORK CITY.

GALAXY ARMY & NAVY STORE 859 6TH AVENUE, NYC 736-1166

INTRODUCING OUR FALL FASHION COLLECTION. AS SEEN ON CNN.

GALAXY ARMY & NAVY STORE 859 6TH AVENUE, NYC 736-1166

WHEN THERE'S PEACE ON EARTH AND GOODWILL TOWARD MEN, WE'LL HAVE A GOING OUT OF BUSINESS SALE.

GALAXY ARMY & NAVY STORE 859 6TH AVENUE, NYC 736-1166

Merit/U.S.A.

POINT-OF-PURCHASE, CAMPAIGN
Weekend, Fall Fashion, Peace on Earth
ART DIRECTOR *Moe VerBrugge*
CREATIVE DIRECTORS *Dean Stefanides,*
Larry Hampel
COPYWRITER *Chris Jacobs*
DESIGNER *Moe VerBrugge*
AGENCY *Hampel/Stefanides*
CLIENT *Galaxy Army & Navy Store*

(facing page)
Merit/U.S.A.

POINT-OF-PURCHASE
The Cigar Bar
ART DIRECTOR *Jim Mountjoy*
CREATIVE DIRECTOR *Jim Mountjoy*
COPYWRITER *Ed Jones*
PHOTOGRAPHER *Jim Arndt*
AGENCY *Loeffler Ketchum Mountjoy*
CLIENT *Arthur's*

Merit/U.S.A.

POINT-OF-PURCHASE
Catnip for Men
ART DIRECTOR *Patrick Murray*
CREATIVE DIRECTOR *Todd Tilford*
COPYWRITER *Vinnie Chieco*
PHOTOGRAPHER *Robb Debenport*
AGENCY *R & D/The Richards Group*
CLIENT *Tabu Lingerie*

Merit/Singapore

POINT-OF-PURCHASE, CAMPAIGN
Electric Chair, Foreign Accent, Do the Dishes
ART DIRECTORS *Ong Chek Seng, Jasmine Lim*
CREATIVE DIRECTOR *John Kyriakou*
COPYWRITER *David Shaw*
PHOTOGRAPHER *Alex Kaikeong*
AGENCY *J. Walter Thompson*
CLIENT *Wingain Investment*

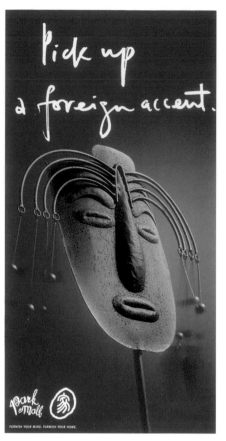

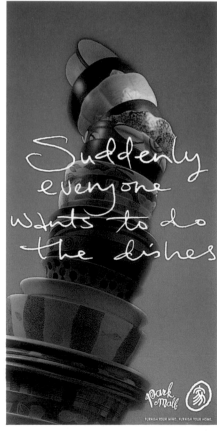

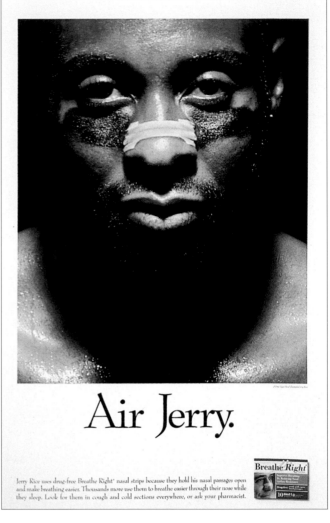

Merit/U.S.A.

PRODUCT OR SERVICE
Man
ART DIRECTOR *Curt Johnson*
CREATIVE DIRECTORS *Brent Bouchez, David Page*
COPYWRITER *Larry Goldstein*
PHOTOGRAPHER *Dennis Manarchy*
AGENCY *Ammirati Puris Lintas*
CLIENT *Compaq Computer Corporation*

Merit/U.S.A.

PRODUCT OR SERVICE
Air Jerry
ART DIRECTOR *Ann Brimacombe*
CREATIVE DIRECTOR *Phil Hanft*
COPYWRITER *Bob Green*
PHOTOGRAPHER *Fred Vanderpoel*
PRODUCER *Norm Lindberg*
AGENCY *Sietsema Engel and Partners*
CLIENT *CNS/Breathe Right*

Merit/U.S.A.

PRODUCT OR SERVICE
No Case Too Small
ART DIRECTOR *Robert Shaw West*
CREATIVE DIRECTOR *Robert Shaw West*
COPYWRITER *Ian Riechenthal*
DESIGNER *Robert Shaw West*
PHOTOGRAPHER *Drew Townsend*
PRINTER *Square One Studio*
AGENCY *West & Vaughan*
CLIENT *Kirshenbaum Law Associates*

Merit/U.S.A.

PRODUCT OR SERVICE
*The Most Popular Drink on the Planet Is Now the Most
Popular Drink off the Planet*
ART DIRECTOR *Bob Meagher*
CREATIVE DIRECTOR *Mike Hughes*
COPYWRITER *Mike Hughes*
AGENCY *The Martin Agency*
CLIENT *The Coca-Cola Company*

(facing page)
Merit/Switzerland

PRODUCT OR SERVICE
Against Risk and Side Effects
ART DIRECTOR *Marco Hert*
CREATIVE DIRECTORS *Edi Andrist, Daniel Meier*
COPYWRITER *Alain Picard*
PHOTOGRAPHER *Bernd Grundmann*
PRODUCER *Marianne Zeller*
AGENCY *McCann-Erickson*
CLIENT *Goodyear (Suisse)*

Merit/Japan

PRODUCT OR SERVICE
Hey, Human Kids I
ART DIRECTOR *Kazumi Murata*
CREATIVE DIRECTOR *Kazumi Murata*
COPYWRITER *Yuji Sugitani*
DESIGNER *Mitsuru Yamamoto*
PHOTOGRAPHER *Takayuki Watanabe*
ILLUSTRATORS *Kazumi Murata, Mitsuru Yamamoto*
PRINTER *Dentsu Actis Inc.*
AGENCY *Dentsu Inc., Tokyo*
CLIENT *Shogakukan Inc.*

ADDITIONAL AWARD

Merit
**ILLUSTRATION, GRAPHIC DESIGN,
POSTER OR CALENDAR**

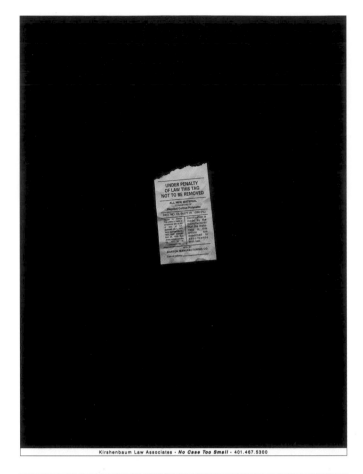

Kirshenbaum Law Associates · *No Case Too Small* · 401.467.5300

Merit/U.S.A.

PRODUCT OR SERVICE, CAMPAIGN
Nixon, Clara, Frank
ART DIRECTOR *Jim Henderson*
CREATIVE DIRECTOR *Lyle Wedemeyer*
COPYWRITER *Alan Marcus*
PHOTOGRAPHER *Peter Wong*
AGENCY *Martin Williams*
CLIENT *Sound 80*

(facing page)
Merit/U.S.A.

PRODUCT OR SERVICE, CAMPAIGN
Suck at Golf, Dr. Doolittle, Sweaters, Llama Dung
ART DIRECTOR *Brock Davis*
CREATIVE DIRECTOR *Joe Milla*
COPYWRITER *Joe Milla*
PHOTOGRAPHER *Joe Milla*
AGENCY *Peterson Milla Hooks*
CLIENT *Elmdale Hills Golf Course*

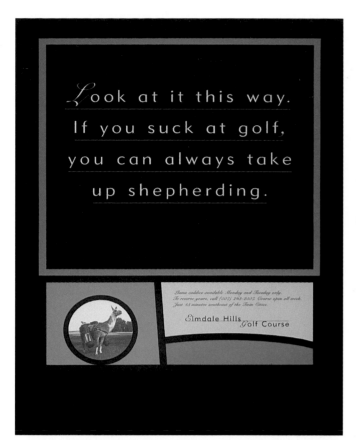

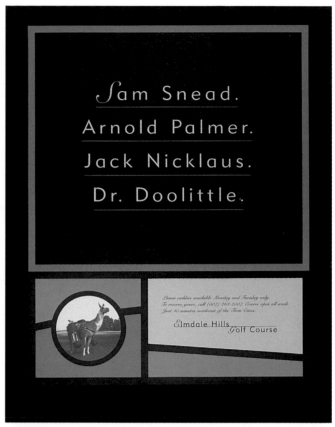

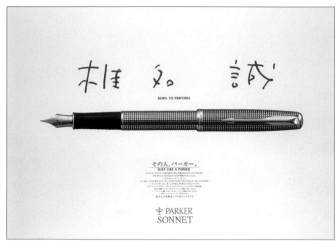

Merit/Japan

PRODUCT OR SERVICE, CAMPAIGN
Parker Signature Series
ART DIRECTOR *Somei Hirai*
CREATIVE DIRECTORS *Keiji Minokura,*
Haruyuki Mita
COPYWRITER *Akihiko Kawai*
DESIGNER *Somei Hirai*
PHOTOGRAPHER *Hiroshi Sato*
AGENCY *McCann-Erickson Inc.*
CLIENT *Gillette Japan*

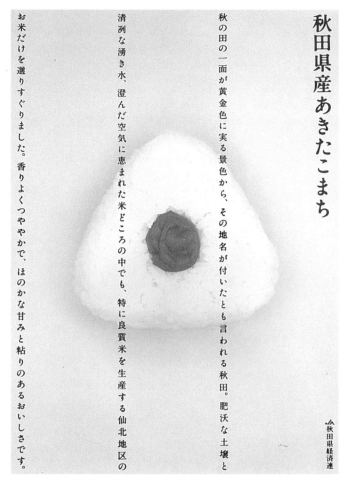

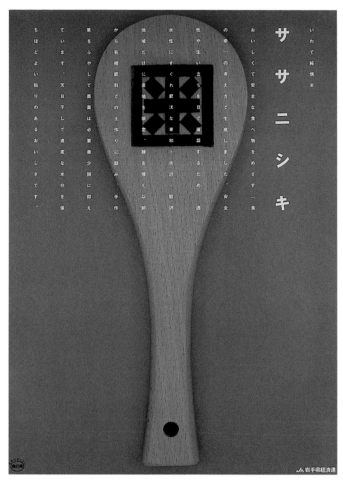

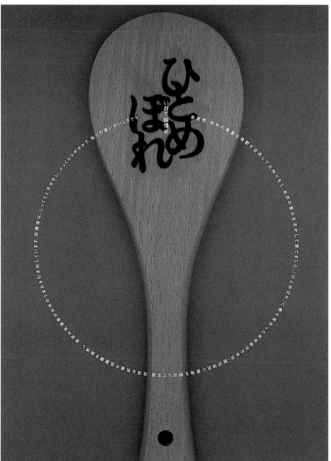

Merit/Japan

PRODUCT OR SERVICE, CAMPAIGN
Akita and Iwate Pure Rice
ART DIRECTOR *Norito Shinmura*
CREATIVE DIRECTOR *Norito Shinmura*
COPYWRITER *Miyuki Tokunaga*
DESIGNER *Norito Shinmura*
PHOTOGRAPHER *Motonobu Okada*
PRODUCER *Nabue Kobayashi*
AGENCY *I&S Corporation*
CLIENT *Japan Agriculture Association*

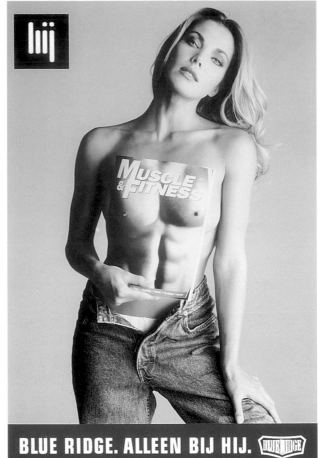

Merit/The Netherlands

PRODUCT OR SERVICE, CAMPAIGN
Man, Muscle and Fitness, Business
ART DIRECTOR *Diederick Hillenius*
COPYWRITER *Lysbeth Bijlstra*
PHOTOGRAPHER *Marcel van der Vlugt*
AGENCY *TBWA/Campaign Company*
CLIENT *We Communications Europe*

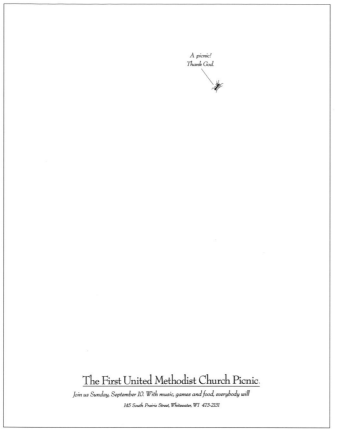

Merit/U.S.A.

ENTERTAINMENT OR SPECIAL EVENT
Ant
ART DIRECTOR *Scott Kirkpatrick*
CREATIVE DIRECTOR *Phil Hänft*
COPYWRITER *Vince Beggin*
PHOTOGRAPHY *Stock*
PRODUCER *Norm Lindberg*
AGENCY *Sietsema Engel and Partners*
CLIENT *First United Methodist Church*

Merit/U.S.A.

ENTERTAINMENT OR SPECIAL EVENT
Happiness
ART DIRECTOR *Eric Tilford*
CREATIVE DIRECTORS *Eric Tilford, Todd Tilford*
COPYWRITER *Todd Tilford*
PHOTOGRAPHER *James Schwartz*
AGENCY *R & D/The Richards Group*
CLIENT *St. Louis Blues Heritage Festival*

Merit/U.S.A.

ENTERTAINMENT OR SPECIAL EVENT
Hawaii International Film Festival
ART DIRECTOR *April Rutherford*
CREATIVE DIRECTOR *Brian McMahon*
COPYWRITER *Richard Tillotson*
DESIGNER *April Rutherford*
PHOTOGRAPHER *Ronnda Heinrich*
PRINTER *Harbor Graphics*
AGENCY *Ogilvy & Mather, Hawaii*
CLIENT *Hawaii International Film Festival*

Merit/U.S.A.

ENTERTAINMENT OR SPECIAL EVENT
Tannhäuser
ART DIRECTORS *Gretchen Burckart, Alison Cannon*
CREATIVE DIRECTOR *Mike Bevil*
COPYWRITERS *Jonathan Balser, Kevin Doyle*
ILLUSTRATOR *Skip Liepke*
AGENCY *T3*
CLIENT *Austin Lyric Opera*

Merit/U.S.A.

ENTERTAINMENT OR SPECIAL EVENT
Lucia di Lammermoor
ART DIRECTORS *Gretchen Burckart, Alison Cannon*
CREATIVE DIRECTOR *Mike Bevil*
COPYWRITERS *Jonathan Balser, Kevin Doyle*
ILLUSTRATOR *Skip Liepke*
AGENCY *T3*
CLIENT *Austin Lyric Opera*

ADDITIONAL AWARD

Merit
SALES PROMOTION

Merit/U.S.A.

ENTERTAINMENT OR SPECIAL EVENT
Banana
ART DIRECTOR *Ed Tajon*
CREATIVE DIRECTOR *F. Byron Tucker*
COPYWRITER *Hugh Carson*
PHOTOGRAPHY *Dave Wilson Studios*
PRODUCER *Jennifer Tiktin*
PRINTER *Alpha Graphics*
AGENCY *Eisner & Associates*
CLIENT *The Baltimore Zoo*

(facing page)
Merit/U.S.A.

ENTERTAINMENT OR SPECIAL EVENT
Farmer Tan
ART DIRECTOR *Randy Hughes*
CREATIVE DIRECTOR *Lyle Wedemeyer*
COPYWRITER *Charlie Callahan*
PHOTOGRAPHER *Shawn Michienzi*
AGENCY *Martin/Williams*
CLIENT *NAMA*

Merit/U.S.A.

ENTERTAINMENT OR SPECIAL EVENT
No Strikes
ART DIRECTOR *Jason Gaboriau*
CREATIVE DIRECTOR *Gary Goldsmith*
COPYWRITER *Eddie Van Bloem*
PHOTOGRAPHER *Richard Elkins*
PRINTER *3D Collators, Inc.*
AGENCY *Goldsmith/Jeffrey*
CLIENT *EDS*

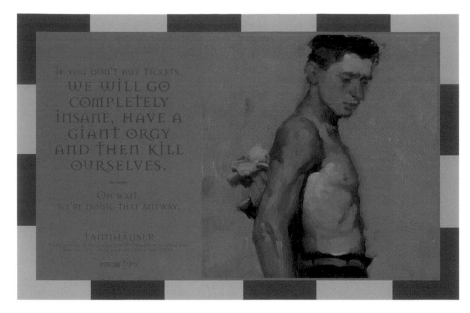

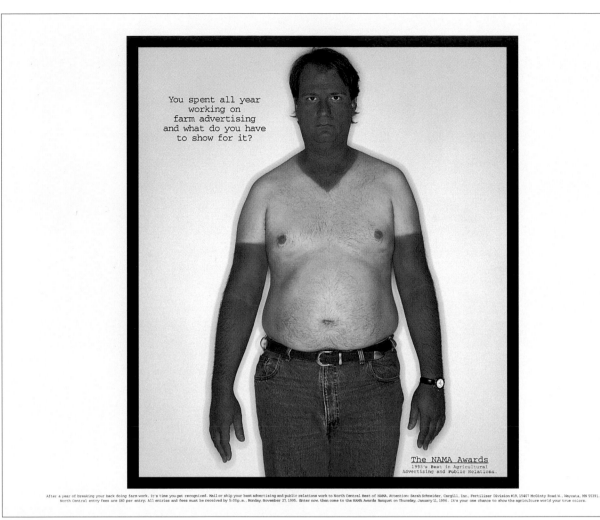

Merit/Canada

PUBLIC SERVICE
The Only Person
ART DIRECTOR *Lance Martin*
CREATIVE DIRECTOR *Jim Ranscombe*
COPYWRITER *Tony Miller*
PHOTOGRAPHER *Chris Gordaneer*
AGENCY *Healthwise Creative Resource Group Inc.*
CLIENT *Searle Canada*

The only person kicking and punching you should be your baby.

Violence Against Women
Stop the Tears.

It doesn't hurt to talk to your doctor.

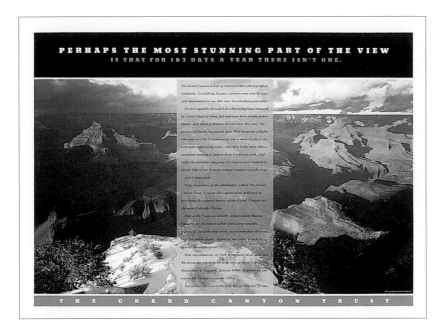

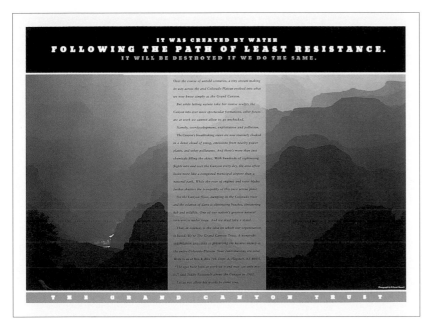

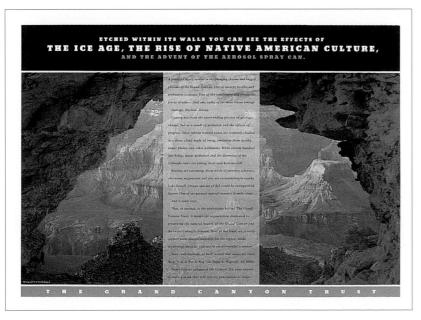

Merit/U.S.A.

PUBLIC SERVICE, CAMPAIGN
Stunning, Resistance, Ice Age
ART DIRECTOR *Hal Curtis*
CREATIVE DIRECTOR *David Lubars*
COPYWRITER *Steve Skibba*
PHOTOGRAPHER *David Meunch*
PRODUCER *Lorraine Alper-Kramer*
PRINTER *Effective Graphics/Gore Engravers*
AGENCY *BBDO West*
CLIENT *The Grand Canyon Trust*

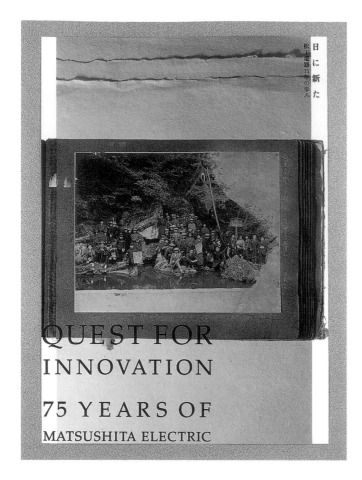

Merit/Japan

PUBLIC SERVICE, CAMPAIGN
Matsushita Electric
ART DIRECTOR *Shinnoske Sugisaki*
CREATIVE DIRECTOR *Katsuhiko Nakamura*
DESIGNER *Shinnoske Sugisaki*
PHOTOGRAPHER *Yasunori Saito*
PRINTER *Nissha Printing*
AGENCY *Shinnoske Inc.*
CLIENT *Matsushita Electric Industrial Co. Ltd.*

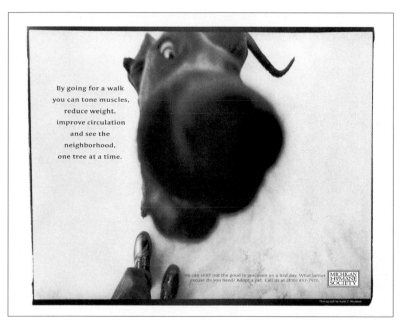

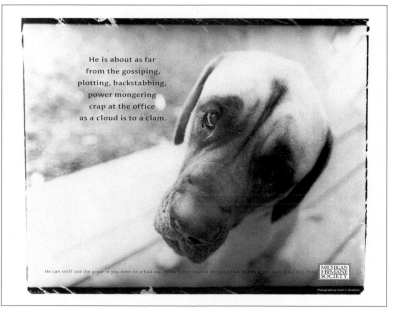

Merit/U.S.A.

PUBLIC SERVICE, CAMPAIGN
Lighten Up, Tree, Clam
ART DIRECTOR *Tracey Ellenberg*
CREATIVE DIRECTOR *Joe Clipner*
COPYWRITER *William J. Hahn*
PHOTOGRAPHER *Scott C. Shulman*
PRINTER *Burch*
AGENCY *TraverRohrback*
CLIENT *Michigan Humane Society*

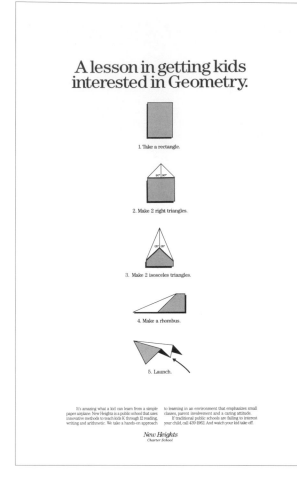

Merit/U.S.A.

PUBLIC SERVICE, CAMPAIGN
Paper Airplane, Egg, Pea Shooter
ART DIRECTOR *Christopher Cole*
COPYWRITER *Carl Pfirman*
ILLUSTRATOR *Scott Moncrief*
PRINTER *Corporate Printing*
AGENCY *HMS Ruhr*
CLIENT *New Heights Charter School*

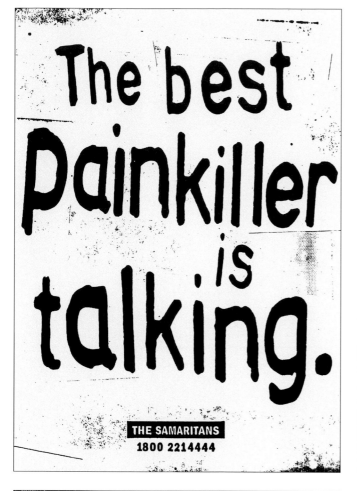

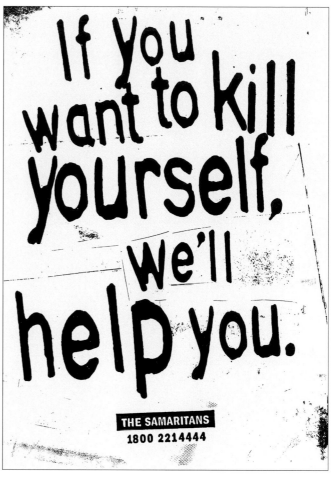

Use the
telephone
to dry
Your tears.

THE SAMARITANS
1800 2214444

Merit/Singapore

PUBLIC SERVICE, CAMPAIGN
Painkiller, Kill Yourself, Dry Your Tears
ART DIRECTOR *Low Phong Thia*
CREATIVE DIRECTOR *Eugene Cheong*
COPYWRITERS *Glendon Mar, Eugene Cheong*
DESIGNER *Low Phong Thia*
AGENCY *Euro RSCG Ball Partnership*
CLIENT *The Samaritans*

kissing butt burns 450 calories an hour. better get some lunch.

be kind. eat true. take out. foodlife Market™
Water Tower Place

Merit/U.S.A.

TRANSIT
Kissing Butt
ART DIRECTOR *Larry Ziegelman*
CREATIVE DIRECTORS *Daryl Travis, Mike Fornwald*
COPYWRITER *Meg Kannin*
AGENCY *Arian, Lowe & Travis*
CLIENT *Lettuce Entertain You Enterprises/*
Foodlife Market

IT'S NOT MONEY AN
IRISHMAN PLAYS FOR.

HARP. A PROUD IRISH LAGER.

HARP

Merit/U.S.A.

TRANSIT
It's Not Money an Irishman Plays For
ART DIRECTOR *Jeff Compton*
CREATIVE DIRECTORS *Marty Weiss, Nat Whitten*
COPYWRITER *Laura Fegley*
AGENCY *Weiss, Whitten, Stagliano, Inc.*
CLIENT *Harp*

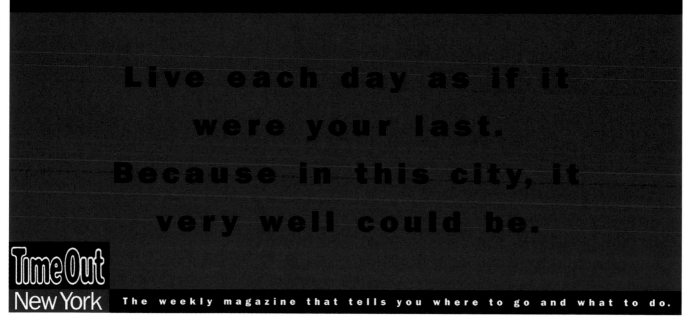

Merit/U.S.A.

TRANSIT, CAMPAIGN
Siskel & Ebert, All the Clubs,
Welcome to New York, Live Each Day,
Average New Yorker
ART DIRECTORS *Abi Aron, Rob Carducci,*
Leslie Sweet, Dan Kelleher, Mark Schruntek,
Vinny Tulley
CREATIVE DIRECTOR *Sal DeVito*
COPYWRITERS *Rob Carducci, Abi Aron, Sal DeVito,*
Mark Schruntek, Dan Kelleher, Dawn Prestom,
Vinny Tulley
DESIGNER *Leslie Sweet*
AGENCY *DeVito Verdi*
CLIENT *Time Out*

ADDITIONAL AWARDS

Merit
POSTER, TRANSIT
Welcome to New York

Merit
POSTER, TRANSIT
Live Each Day

We won't give away
why Mark Fenske
left the Bomb Factory
to join Ayer.

We'll let him
tell you himself
at The Club.

"The Most Powerful Art Form on the Face of the Earth"
or "How I Learned to Stop Time and Wake the Dead."
Monday, December 4th at 6pm.
RSVP 212-979-1900. Members free. Non-members $10.

THE ONE CLUB

32 East 21st Street, New York

Merit/U.S.A.

SPECIAL-EVENT MARKETING KIT
Mark Fenske
ART DIRECTOR *Chuck Finkle*
CREATIVE DIRECTOR *Gary Goldsmith*
DESIGNER *Chuck Finkle*
AGENCY *Goldsmith/Jeffrey*
CLIENT *The One Club*

Merit/U.S.A.

SALES PROMOTION
Leaf
ART DIRECTOR *Jeff Goss*
CREATIVE DIRECTORS *Jim Pringle, Jeff Goss*
COPYWRITER *Bob Morrison*
DESIGNER *Heath Beeferman*
AGENCY *Pringle Dixon Pringle*
CLIENT *Mr. Mow*

Merit/U.S.A.

SALES PROMOTION
U.S. Postal Service
ART DIRECTORS *David Scott, Bill West*
CREATIVE DIRECTOR *Bill West*
COPYWRITERS *David Scott, Don Pausback*
DESIGNER *Bill West*
PRODUCER *Barbara Ketchum*
AGENCY *West & Vaughan*
CLIENT *Polara Roofing Systems*

Merit/U.S.A.

SALES PROMOTION
Coupon
ART DIRECTORS *David Scott, Bill West*
CREATIVE DIRECTOR *Bill West*
COPYWRITERS *David Scott, Don Pausback*
DESIGNER *Bill West*
PRODUCER *Barbara Ketchum*
AGENCY *West & Vaughan*
CLIENT *Polara Roofing Systems*

Merit/U.S.A.

SALES PROMOTION
You Probably Think
ART DIRECTOR *Steve Sandstrom*
CREATIVE DIRECTOR *Steve Sandoz*
COPYWRITER *Steve Sandoz*
DESIGNER *Steve Sandstrom*
PHOTOGRAPHER *Sjef Wildschut*
STUDIO *Sandstrom Design*
AGENCY *Artsy-Fartsy Productions*
CLIENT *Soloflex, Inc.*

Merit/U.S.A.

SALES PROMOTION
Mercedes-Benz E Class Introduction
ART DIRECTOR *Elizabeth Ehrlich-Kellogg*
CREATIVE DIRECTORS *Paul R. Levett, John Young*
COPYWRITER *John Young*
DESIGNER *Elizabeth Ehrlich-Kellogg*
PHOTOGRAPHER *Clint Clemens*
AGENCY *Lowe Direct*
CLIENT *Mercedes-Benz of North America*

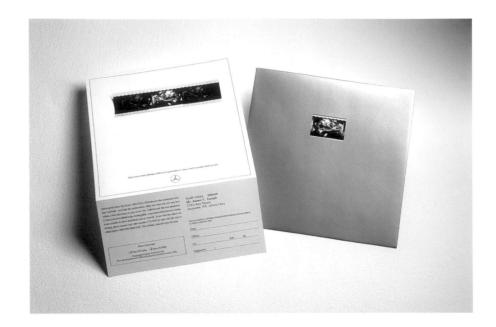

Merit/U.S.A.

SALES PROMOTION
Fifty Million
ART DIRECTOR *Eric Tilford*
CREATIVE DIRECTORS *Todd Tilford, Eric Tilford*
COPYWRITER *Todd Tilford*
PHOTOGRAPHER *Richard Reens*
PRODUCTION MANAGER *Gail Beckman*
AGENCY *CORE/R & D/The Richards Group*
CLIENT *Lombardo Custom Apparel*

Merit/U.S.A.

SALES PROMOTION
Prove to the World
ART DIRECTOR *Phillip Kellogg*
CREATIVE DIRECTOR *Mike Drazen*
COPYWRITER *Vicky Oliver*
AGENCY *Earle Palmer Brown, New York*
CLIENT *Adweek's Best Spots*

1983

Merit/U.S.A.

SALES PROMOTION
Lee Clow (Chiat/Day)—In a Rut?
ART DIRECTOR *Jamie Mahoney*
CREATIVE DIRECTOR *Mike Hughes*
COPYWRITER *Joe Alexander*
PRINT PRODUCER *Jenny Schoenherr*
AGENCY *The Martin Agency*
CLIENT *Dick Gerdes*

Merit/U.S.A.

SALES PROMOTION
Prison
ART DIRECTOR *Joel Nendel*
CREATIVE DIRECTOR *Terry Schneider*
COPYWRITER *Simeon Roane*
AGENCY *Borders, Perrin & Norrander*
CLIENT *Red Lion Hotels & Inns*

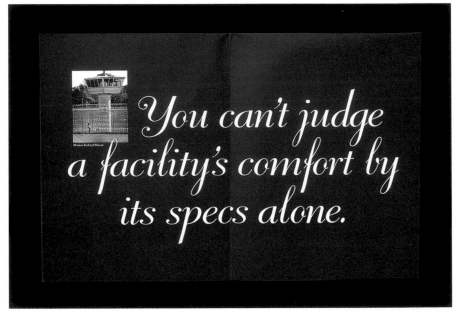

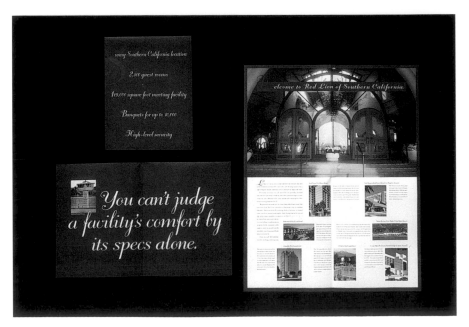

Merit/Austria

SALES PROMOTION
Magno∗Star
ART DIRECTORS *Thomas Maresch, Evelyn Liska*
CREATIVE DIRECTORS *Thomas Maresch,*
Evelyn Liska
COPYWRITER *Romana Huber*
PHOTOGRAPHY *Markl & Schauer*
ILLUSTRATION *Vienna Paint*
AGENCY *Dr. Puttner Bates*
CLIENT *KNP Leykam Gratkorn GmbH*

Merit/Germany

SALES PROMOTION
Vote for the Cow of the Year
ART DIRECTOR *Astrid Franzke*
CREATIVE DIRECTOR *Rosemarie Kreuzer*
COPYWRITER *Wiltraud Neuber*
DESIGNER *Astrid Franzke*
AGENCY *Wächter & Partner Werbeagentur*
CLIENT *Allgäuland Käsereien*

Fig.2
FIRE EXTINGUISHER
(See also AlphaGraphics)

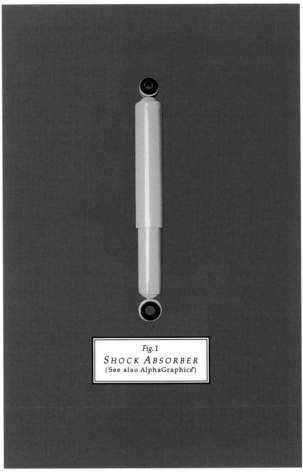

Fig.1
SHOCK ABSORBER
(See also AlphaGraphics)

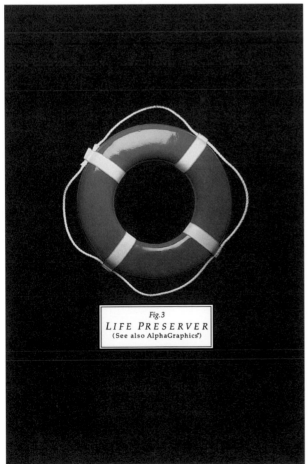

Fig.3
LIFE PRESERVER
(See also AlphaGraphics)

Merit/U.S.A.

SALES PROMOTION, CAMPAIGN
Fire Extinguisher, Shock Absorber, Life Preserver
ART DIRECTOR *John Payne*
CREATIVE DIRECTORS *Jim Baldwin, Mike Renfro*
COPYWRITER *Gary Pascoe*
PHOTOGRAPHER *John Katz*
AGENCY *The Richards Group*
CLIENT *AlphaGraphics*

Merit/Denmark

SALES PROMOTION, CAMPAIGN
Centyl
ART DIRECTOR *Vibeke Nødskov*
COPYWRITERS *Alex Morthorst, Vibeke Nødskov*
ILLUSTRATORS *Alessio Leonardi, Vibeke Nødskov*
PRINTER *Saloprint A/S*
AGENCY *Leo Pharmaceutical In-House*
CLIENT *Leo Pharmaceutical*

Merit/Sweden

SALES PROMOTION, CAMPAIGN
Pull & Push
ART DIRECTOR *Christer Stolpe*
CREATIVE DIRECTOR *Göran Widtfeldt*
COPYWRITER *Berndt Johansson*
PHOTOGRAPHERS *S. J. S. Whiteley,*
G. W. Morrison, J. Jonkers
AGENCY *Lintas AB*
CLIENT *ICA Förlaget*

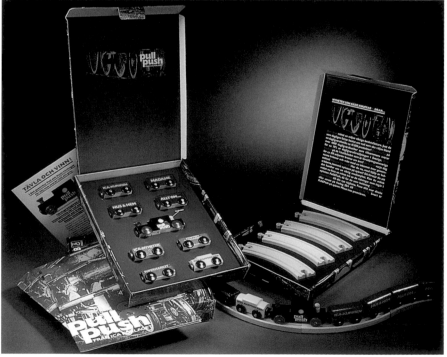

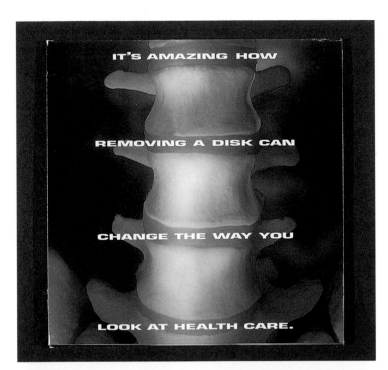

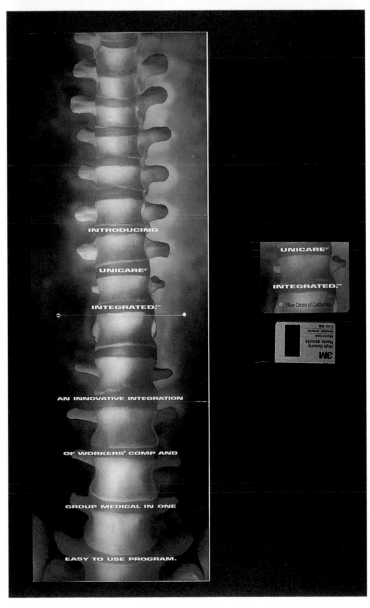

Merit/U.S.A.

SALES PROMOTION
Spine
ART DIRECTOR *Jeff Kemhadjian*
CREATIVE DIRECTOR *Julian Ryder*
COPYWRITER *Ian Macdonald*
PHOTOGRAPHER *Markku*
AGENCY *Highway One Communications*
CLIENT *Blue Cross of California*

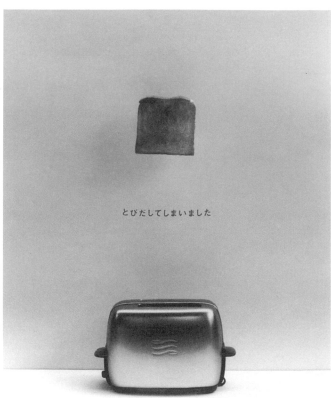

Merit/Japan

SALES PROMOTION, CAMPAIGN
Mousetrap, Toaster
ART DIRECTOR *Kei Saito*
CREATIVE DIRECTOR *Mutsumi Yamaoka*
COPYWRITER *Kei Saito*
DESIGNER *Kei Saito*
PHOTOGRAPHER *Yoshihito Imaizumi*
PRINTER *Seio Printing Co. Ltd.*
AGENCY *Akamura Advertising Office*
CLIENT *Mutsumi Yamaoka*

CHRISTMAS STORIES

Merit/U.S.A.

SELF-PROMOTION
1994 Agency Christmas Card
ART DIRECTOR *Jeff Hopfer*
CREATIVE DIRECTOR *Stan Richards*
COPYWRITER *Kevin Swisher*
DESIGNER *Jeff Hopfer*
PHOTOGRAPHER *Toby Ethridge*
ILLUSTRATORS *John Dawson, Hal Mayforth, Tim Hutchins*
PRINTER *Williamson Printing*
STUDIO *Richards Brock Miller Mitchell & Associates*
AGENCY *The Richards Group*
CLIENT *The Richards Group*

A meteor hits the earth causing atmospheric clouding that eventually kills vegetation used for food. Man's ever increasing need for land encroaches upon nesting habitats. A guy designs an advanced personal computer in his garage that renders existing typesetting equipment completely obsolete.

An abrupt change in a species' environment can be quite catastrophic, indeed. Perhaps even genocidal. Typographers were ‹Dinosaur› a bit luckier than their counterparts. They had the opportunity to adapt to the changes.

Desktop publishing has revolutionized the typography industry. Computers now perform many of the functions typesetters once performed. Which has forced the entire industry to rethink its existence. Either adapt or die.

At Great Faces we did more than simply ‹Dodo Bird› adapt. We've embraced change with some changes of our own. Without compromising the things we've done well for so many years.

We're still the same place you've always turned to for our meticulous approach to typography. We still carry a constantly growing selection of over 20,000 fonts. And our type reps continue ‹Typographer› to boast great relationships with print producers and art directors all over the country.

But the changes we've made go well beyond typography. We're now equipped to play a more complete role in your print production process.

The biggest change we've made is the addition of color separations, retouching and filmwork. Now you can get your type and your separations done under one roof. These days, clients demand faster turnaround. The best way to meet that demand is to reduce the number of resources you use in production.

When you let Great Faces do it all, you won't be left to the whims of couriers and production vendors spread throughout your area. Not to mention how delighted your accounting department will be when they have fewer invoices to deal with.

Great Faces was founded on the dedication to perfect typography. So we knew we'd have to provide that same level of perfection when we added color separations and filmwork. That's why we've hired a full staff of experienced color separators. Placing the most advanced equipment from Scitex at their disposal.

Every day the advertising and design industries are inundated with newer, more powerful computers and software. But we haven't lost sight of the fact that in the end, they're nothing more than tools. And only people with the most experience operate them most effectively.

Somewhere out there is a vast graveyard littered with clunky, obsolete typesetting equipment. We sent our old equipment there a long time ago. But unlike some typographers, we won't be joining it. **Great Faces**

Merit/U.S.A.

SELF-PROMOTION
Extinct
ART DIRECTOR *Christopher Cole*
COPYWRITER *Eric Sorensen*
ILLUSTRATOR *Jerry Gale*
PUBLISHER *Great Faces/The Show '95*
AGENCY *HMS Ruhr*
CLIENT *Great Faces*

Merit/U.S.A.

SELF-PROMOTION
Tibet
ART DIRECTORS *Jacque Taylor, Stan Elder*
CREATIVE DIRECTORS *Peter Taflan,*
David Terrenoire, Hal Kome
COPYWRITERS *David Terrenoire, Hal Kome*
PHOTOGRAPHER *Jim Erickson*
PRINTER *Graphic Technology*
AGENCY *Peter Taflan Marketing Communications*
CLIENT *Erickson Productions*

Merit/U.S.A.

SELF-PROMOTION, CAMPAIGN
R & D
ART DIRECTOR *Terence Reynolds*
CREATIVE DIRECTOR *Todd Tilford*
COPYWRITER *Todd Tilford*
DESIGNER *Terence Reynolds*
PRODUCTION MANAGER *Gail Beckman*
AGENCY *R & D/The Richards Group*
CLIENT *R & D/The Richards Group*

ADDITIONAL AWARD
Merit
GRAPHIC DESIGN, CORPORATE AND PROMOTIONAL
COMMUNICATIONS, BOOKLET OR BROCHURE

(facing page)
Merit/U.S.A.

SELF-PROMOTION, CAMPAIGN
Postcards
ART DIRECTOR *Jon Wyville*
CREATIVE DIRECTORS *Tom McConnaughy,*
Jim Schmidt
COPYWRITER *Jim Schmidt*
DESIGNER *Jon Wyville*
PRINTER *Active Graphics*
AGENCY *McConnaughy Stein Schmidt Brown*
CLIENT *McConnaughy Stein Schmidt Brown*

Merit/Canada

SELF-PROMOTION
Heart
ART DIRECTOR *Daniel Vendramin*
COPYWRITER *Paul Evans*
ILLUSTRATOR *Kam Yu*
AGENCY *Rage Advertising*
CLIENT *Kam Yu Medical Illustration*

WIMP

He's the Neville Chamberlain of the advertising world. Always eager to give away the Sudatenland. At MSSB, we screen carefully for this type of individual. We know full well it's not in your best interest or ours to employ a person who just can't say no to the word yes.

ADVERTISING IS MANURE

Spread it around and watch things grow. Like True Value, up 9%. Or Plochman's Mustard, up 75%. Or even Spiegel requests, up 80%. Clearly the Jolly Green Giant isn't the only one in the ad business with a green thumb.

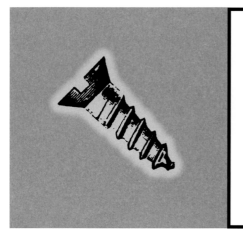

These things happen. True Value has one of their best years ever. Ad Age calls our campaign one of the year's finest. And we get fired. They did, however, keep our tagline (Help is just around the corner) and our positioning. A screw job? Nah, in advertising, it's just another day at the office.

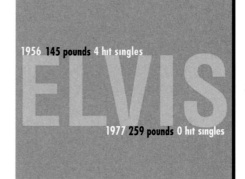

1956 145 pounds 4 hit singles
ELVIS
1977 259 pounds 0 hit singles

Bigger is better? No, better is better. One great art director is worth an army of mediocre ones. At MSSB, we've attracted some of the brightest minds in the business from some of the brightest agencies in the business. All to make our client's advertising shine.

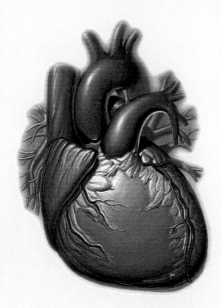

Happy Valentine's Day

KAM YU • MEDICAL ILLUSTRATION • 416~929~7894

Merit/U.S.A.

SELF-PROMOTION, CAMPAIGN
Getting Personal
ART DIRECTORS *Tom Joyce, Steve Stretton*
CREATIVE DIRECTOR *Alan Randolph*
COPYWRITERS *Alan Randolph, David Nobay*
DESIGNER *Samantha Schwemler*
AGENCY *Cohn & Wells*
CLIENT *Cohn & Wells*

Merit/Canada

SELF-PROMOTION
Cost of Newsprint
ART DIRECTOR *John Terry*
CREATIVE DIRECTOR *Brad Riddoch*
COPYWRITER *Brad Riddoch*
AGENCY *Bates Canada Inc.*
CLIENT *Southam Newspapers*

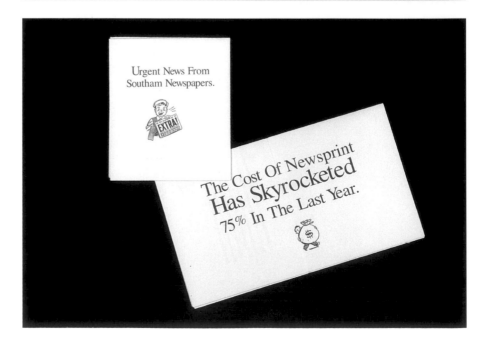

Merit/The Netherlands

SELF-PROMOTION, CAMPAIGN
Sacha Campaign
ART DIRECTORS *Petra Janssen, Edwin Vollebergh*
CREATIVE DIRECTORS *Petra Janssen,*
Edwin Vollebergh
COPYWRITERS *Petra Janssen, Edwin Vollebergh*
DESIGNERS *Petra Janssen, Edwin Vollebergh*
AGENCY *Studio Boot*
CLIENT *Sacha Shoes Holland*

Merit/U.S.A.

MIXED-MEDIA PROMOTION, CAMPAIGN
Ben Day
ART DIRECTORS *Dana Arnett, Bob Rice*
DESIGNERS *Curt Schreiber, Fletcher Martin*
PRINTER *Etheridge Printing*
FIRM *VSA Partners Inc.*
CLIENT *Potlatch Corporation*

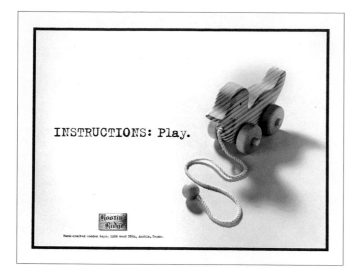

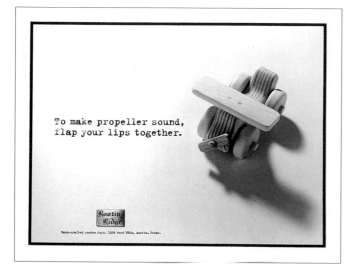

Merit/U.S.A.

POINT-OF-PURCHASE, CAMPAIGN
Instructions, Brain Cells, Flap Your Lips,
State-of-the-Art
ART DIRECTOR *Brent Ladd*
CREATIVE DIRECTORS *Brent Ladd, Brian Brooker*
COPYWRITER *Brian Brooker*
PHOTOGRAPHER *Dennis Fagan*
AGENCY *GSD&M Advertising*
CLIENT *Rootin' Ridge*

Merit/U.S.A.

POINT-OF-PURCHASE, CAMPAIGN
Lights Up the Child, Low-Tech, Rust
ART DIRECTOR *Brent Ladd*
CREATIVE DIRECTORS *Brent Ladd, Brian Brooker*
COPYWRITER *Brian Brooker*
PHOTOGRAPHER *Dennis Fagan*
AGENCY *GSD&M Advertising*
CLIENT *Rootin' Ridge*

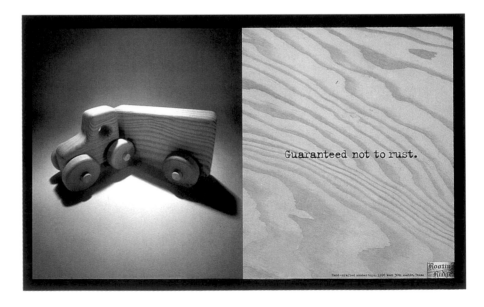

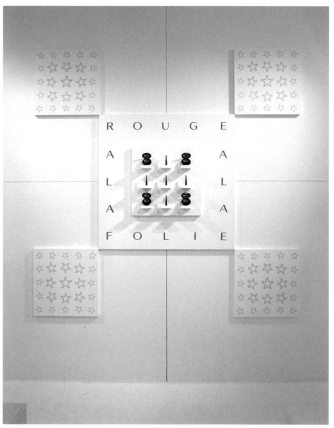

Merit/France

DISPLAY, CAMPAIGN
Shiseido Make-up Press Party
ART DIRECTOR *Aoshi Kudo*
CREATIVE DIRECTOR *Toshio Yamagata*
COPYWRITER *Serge Lutens*
DESIGNERS *Aoshi Kudo, Takayasu Yamada,*
Takao Hirai
ARTIST *Serge Lutens*
CLIENT *Shiseido Co. Ltd.*

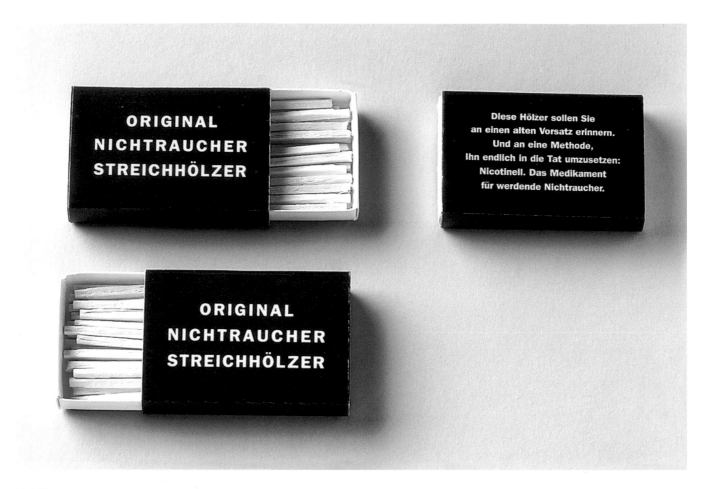

Merit/Germany

PROMOTIONAL CAMPAIGN
Nonsmoking Matches
ART DIRECTOR *Ralph Taubenberger*
CREATIVE DIRECTOR *Ralph Taubenberger*
COPYWRITER *Reinhard Siemes*
PRODUCER *Walter Dittrich*
AGENCY *Heye & Partners GmbH*
CLIENT *Nicotinell (Zyma GmbH)*

GRAPHIC DESIGN

GOLD+SILVER MEDALISTS

J

Jean Reno

It's easy to film sex because you can touch it.
But love, you can't touch.
So it's fantastic if you can film love.

M

Matt Dillon

There's a swirl of anger inside me.
So it's really good for me to have a creative
outlet to let my anger out.

G

Gary Oldman

poupée
de
chair

MAX VADUKUL

Silver Medalist/Japan

MULTIPAGE
Cut No. 38
ART DIRECTOR *Hideki Nakajima*
DESIGNER *Hideki Nakajima*
EDITOR IN CHIEF *Ken Sato*
PHOTOGRAPHERS *Karina Taira, Kei Ogata,
Steve Pyke, Steen Sundland, Max Vadukul*
STUDIO *Nakajima Design*
CLIENT *Rockin' On Inc.*

NO REGRETS

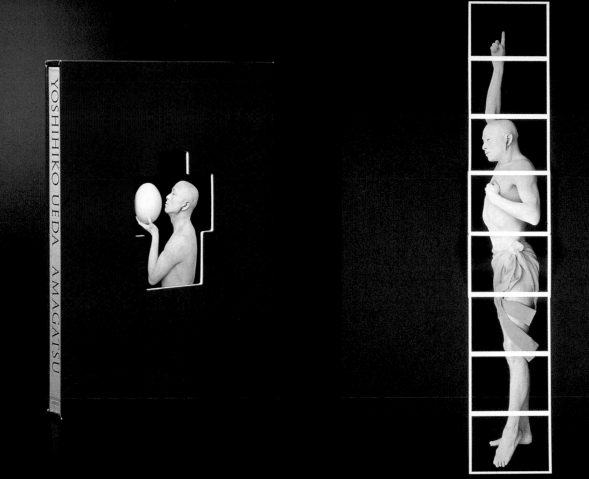

Gold Medalist/Japan

**LIMITED EDITION, PRIVATE OR FINE PRESS,
OR SPECIAL FORMAT**
Amagatsu
ART DIRECTOR *Toshio Yamagata*
CREATIVE DIRECTOR *Toshio Yamagata*
DESIGNER *Toshio Yamagata*
PHOTOGRAPHER *Yoshihiko Ueda*
CLIENT *Korinsha Press & Co., Ltd.*

TYPOGRAPHY

16

1995

THE
ANNUAL
OF THE

TYPE DIRECTORS CLUB

EXHIBITION ST

46

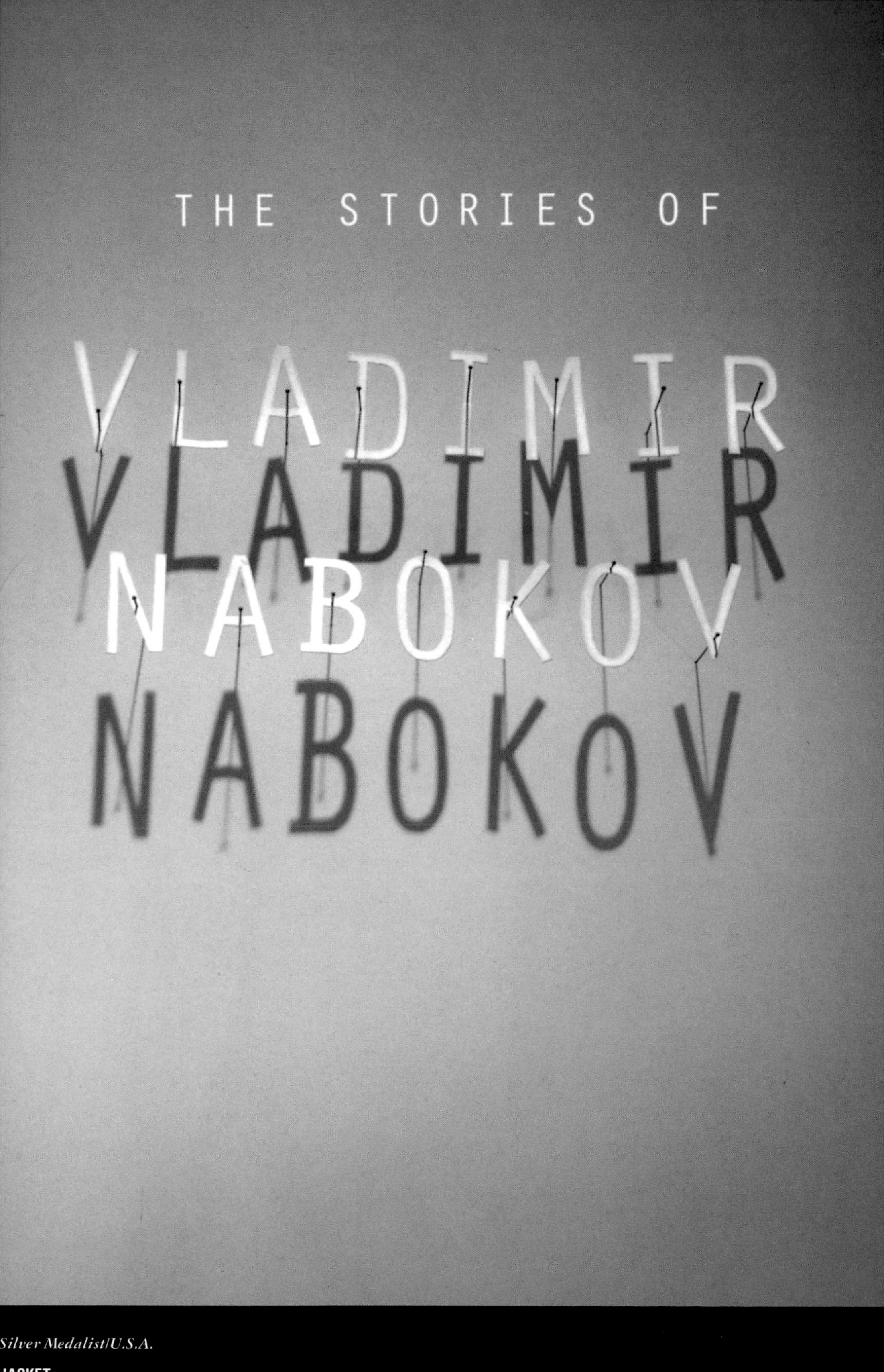

THE STORIES OF

VLADIMIR

VLADIMIR

NABOKOV

NABOKOV

Silver Medalist/U.S.A.

JACKET
The Stories of Vladimir Nabokov
ART DIRECTOR *Stephen Doyle*
DESIGNER *Stephen Doyle*
PHOTOGRAPHER *Geoff Spear*
STUDIO *Drenttel Doyle Partners*
CLIENT *Alfred A. Knopf*

Call

Derivative

Cap

Swap

Option

Gold Medalist/Switzerland

BOOKLET OR BROCHURE
The Centenary of the Swiss National Library
ART DIRECTORS *Gerhard Blättler,*
Martin Gaberthuel, Andreas Netthoevel
CREATIVE DIRECTORS *Gerhard Blättler,*
Martin Gaberthuel, Andréas Netthoevel
COPYWRITERS *Ratus Luck, Peter Edwin Erismann*

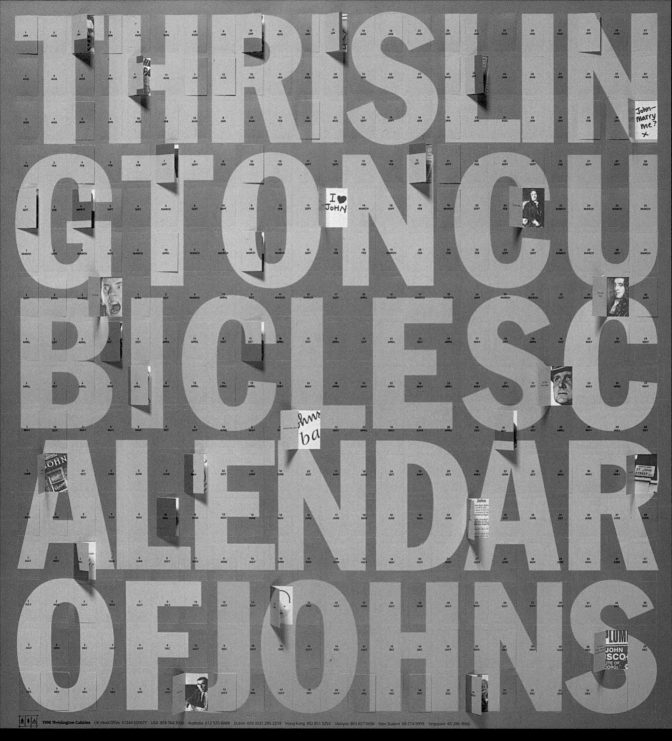

THRISLINGTONCUBICLESCALENDAROFJOHNS

1996 Thrislington Cubicles UK Head Office 01244 520677 USA 818 764 1000 Australia 612 570 8888 Dublin 010 3531 295 2274 Hong Kong 852 811 5253 Malaysia 603 627 0696 New Zealand 09 274 9999 Singapore 65 286 0666

Silver Medalist/England

CALENDAR OR APPOINTMENT BOOK

Calendar of Johns

ART DIRECTOR *Aziz Cami*

(facing page)
Silver Medalist/U.S.A.

MIXED-MEDIA OR SPECIALTY PROMOTION

The Public Theater 1995–96 Season Campaign

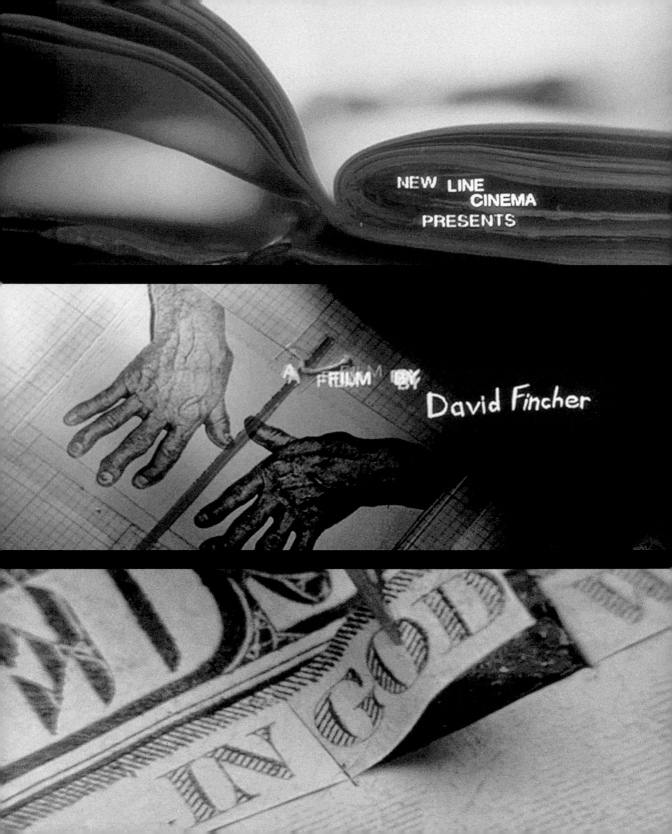

NEW LINE
CINEMA
PRESENTS

A FILM BY David Fincher

Silver Medalist/U.S.A.

ANIMATION
Garden of Regrets
ART DIRECTOR *Jeff Scher*
DESIGNER *Jeff Scher*
PRODUCERS *Jeff Scher, Jennifer Pope*
DIRECTOR *Jeff Scher*
PHOTOGRAPHER *Jeff Scher*
ILLUSTRATOR *Jeff Scher*
EDITOR *Jamie Livingston*
MUSIC *Pablo Ascan*
STUDIO *Crossroad Films*

(facing page)
Best of Show/Gold Medalist/U.S.A.

FILM OR VIDEO TITLE
Seven Opening Title
ART DIRECTOR *Kyle Cooper*
CREATIVE DIRECTOR *Kyle Cooper*
DESIGNER *Kyle Cooper*
CINEMATOGRAPHER *Harris Savides*
PRODUCER *Peter Frankfurt*
DIRECTORS *David Fincher, Kyle Cooper*
SPECIAL IMAGE ENGINEER *Findlay Bunting*
MUSIC *Nine Inch Nails*
STUDIO *R/Greenberg Associates*
CLIENT *New Line Cinema*

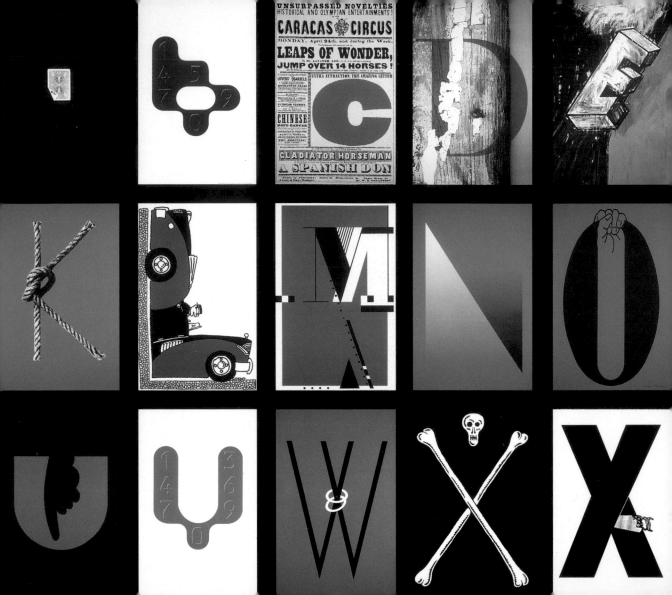

Gold Medalist/U.S.A.

PROMOTIONAL, SERIES
Ambassador Arts Alphabet Poster Series
ART DIRECTOR *Paula Scher*
DESIGNERS *Michael Bierut, Seymour Chwast,*
Paul Davis, Heinz Edelmann, Shigeo Fukuda,
Thomas Geismar, Pierre Mendell, Woody Pirtle,
Peter Saville, Paula Scher, Rosmarie Tissi,
Yarom Vardimon
PRINTER *Ambassador Arts, Inc.*
CLIENT *Ambassador Arts, Inc./*
Champion International

SILENCE,
CUNNING,
EXILE

STARTS FEBRUARY 2

THE

PUBLIC

THEATER

425 LAFAYETTE STREET
(212) 598-7150

WRITTEN BY STUART GREENMAN DIRECTED BY MARK WING-DAVEY

280

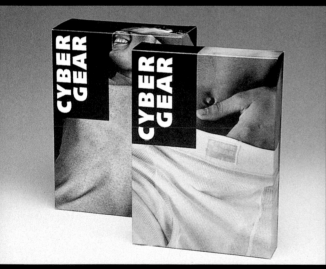

Silver Medalist/Japan

CONSUMER PRODUCT, SERIES
Cyber Gear
ART DIRECTOR *Kan Akita*
CREATIVE DIRECTOR *Rei Ujika*
DESIGNER *Kan Akita*
PHOTOGRAPHER *David LaChapelle*
STUDIO *Akita Design Kan Inc.*
CLIENT *Isokai Co. Ltd.*

Silver Medalist/U.S.A.

PUBLIC INTERIOR
Duncan Aviation NBAA Exhibit
ART DIRECTOR *Mitchell Mauk*
CREATIVE DIRECTOR *Mitchell Mauk*
DESIGNERS *Mitchell Mauk, Adam Brodsley*
PHOTOGRAPHER *Paul Bowen*
FABRICATION *Ironwind*
STUDIO *Mauk Design*
CLIENT *Duncan Aviation*

(facing page)
Gold Medalist/U.S.A.

PUBLIC INTERIOR
Voice of the Homeless
ART DIRECTOR *BJ Krivanek*
DESIGNER *Joel Breaux*
COPYWRITERS *Residents of the Union
Rescue Mission*
PHOTOGRAPHER *Jeff Kurt Petersen*
COMPUTER CONSULTANTS *Martha Najera,
Jesse Milden*
STUDIO *BJ Krivanek Art+Design*
CLIENT *The Union Rescue Mission*

DISTINCTIVE MERIT AWARDS

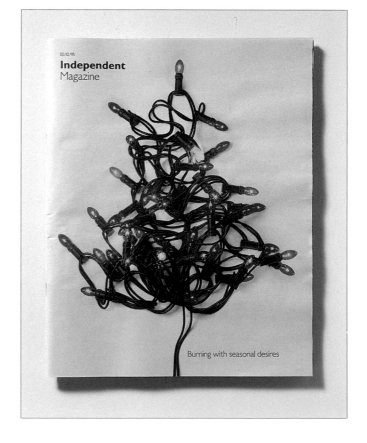

Distinctive Merit/England

COVER, SERIES
Independent Magazine February 12, 1995,
April 11, 1995, November 11, 1995
ART DIRECTOR *Vince Frost*
DESIGNER *Vince Frost*
PHOTOGRAPHER *Matthew Donaldson*
STUDIO *Frost Design*
CLIENT *Mirror Group*

ADDITIONAL AWARD

Merit
MAGAZINE, CONSUMER, FULL ISSUE, SERIES

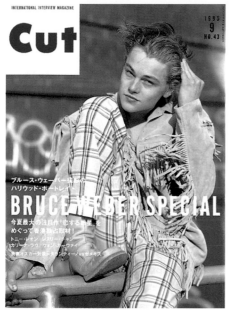

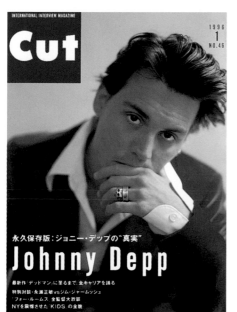

Distinctive Merit/Japan

COVER, SERIES
Cut Nos. 40, 41, 43, 45, 46
ART DIRECTOR *Hideki Nakajima*
DESIGNER *Hideki Nakajima*
EDITOR IN CHIEF *Ken Sato*
PHOTOGRAPHERS *Itaru Hirama, Annie Leibovitz,*
Jean Baptiste Mondino, Cliff Watts, Bruce Weber
STUDIO *Nakajima Design*
CLIENT *Rockin' On Inc.*

ADDITIONAL AWARD

Merit
COVER
Cut No. 40

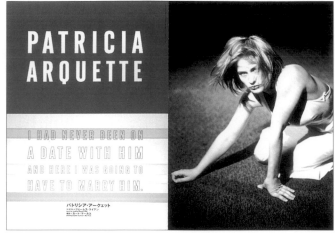

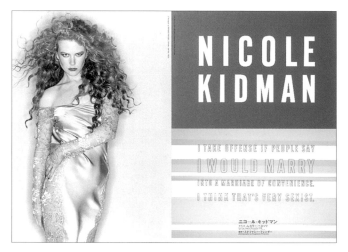

Distinctive Merit/Japan

MULTIPAGE
Cut No. 45
ART DIRECTOR *Hideki Nakajima*
DESIGNER *Hideki Nakajima*
EDITOR IN CHIEF *Ken Sato*
PHOTOGRAPHERS *Kiyohide Hori, Kurt Markus,*
Stephanie Pfriender, Terry Richardson,
Aya Tokunaga
STUDIO *Nakajima Design*
CLIENT *Rockin' On Inc.*

Distinctive Merit/U.S.A.

FULL ISSUE
I.D. Magazine
ART DIRECTOR *Tony Arefin*
CREATIVE DIRECTOR *Tony Arefin*
DESIGNER *Andrea Fella*
PHOTOGRAPHER *James Wojick*
CLIENT *I.D. Magazine*

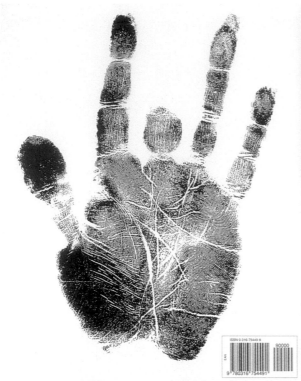

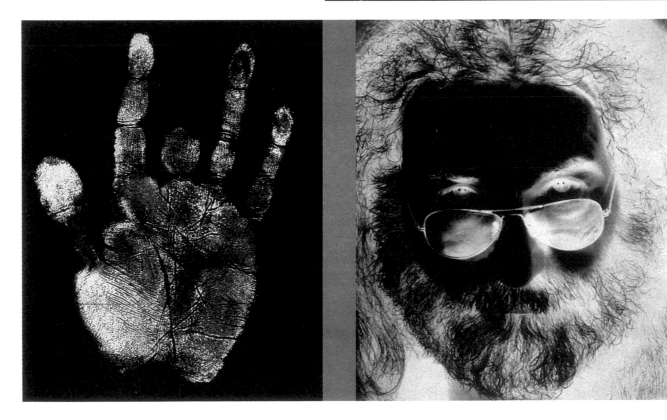

Distinctive Merit/U.S.A.

GENERAL TRADE
Garcia
CREATIVE DIRECTOR *Fred Woodward*
DESIGNERS *Fred Woodward, Gail Anderson,*
Geraldine Hessler, Lee Bearson, Eric J. Siry
PHOTOGRAPHERS *Various*
PHOTO EDITOR *Jodi Peckman*
ARTISTS *Various*
PUBLISHER *Little, Brown and Company*
CLIENT *Rolling Stone Press*

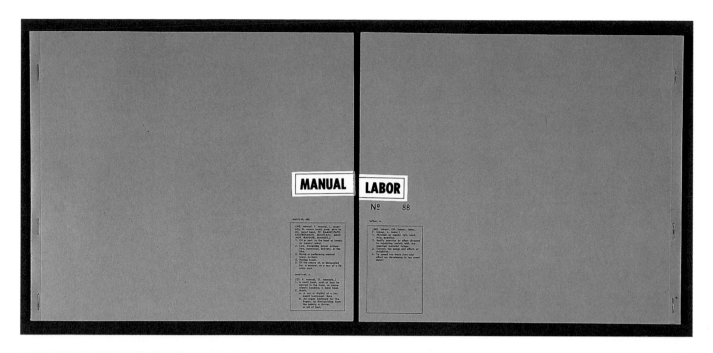

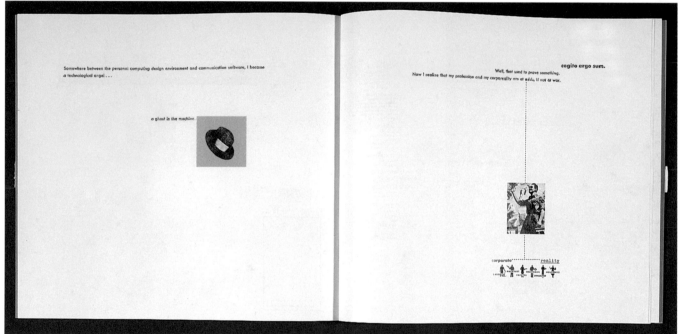

Distinctive Merit/U.S.A.

**LIMITED EDITION, PRIVATE OR FINE PRESS,
OR SPECIAL FORMAT**
Manual Labor
COPYWRITER *Karen Cole*
DESIGNERS *Nan Goggin, Karen Cole*
TYPE COMPOSITOR *Joe Elliot*
TYPESETTERS *Joe Elliot, Nan Goggin, Karen Cole*
PRESSPERSON *Corky Nightlinger*
PRINTER *Office of Printing Services, University of
Illinois at Urbana-Champaign*

Distinctive Merit/U.S.A.

MUSEUM, GALLERY, OR UNIVERSITY PRESS PUBLICATION
Mutant Materials in Contemporary Design
ART DIRECTOR *Eric Baker*
DESIGNER *Jason Godfrey*
STUDIO *Eric Baker Design Associates*
CLIENT *The Museum of Modern Art*

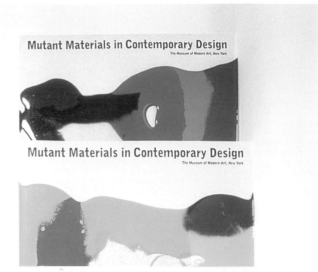

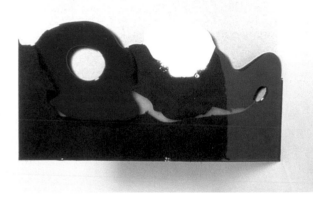

Distinctive Merit/Germany

GENERAL TRADE
Joachim Sartorius, "Atlas der neuen Poesie"
ART DIRECTOR *Walter Hellmann*
CREATIVE DIRECTOR *Walter Hellmann*
COPYWRITER *Rowohlt Verlag GmbH*
DESIGNER *Walter Hellmann*
PRODUCER *Joachim Düster*
CLIENT *Rowohlt Verlag GmbH*

(facing page)
Distinctive Merit/U.S.A.

CHILDREN'S, SERIES
1, 2, 3 and Triangle, Square, Circle
ART DIRECTOR *Stephen Doyle*
DESIGNER *Gary Tooth*
PHOTOGRAPHER *William Wegman*
STUDIO *Drenttel Doyle Partners*
CLIENT *Hyperion Books for Children*

Distinctive Merit/U.S.A.

JACKET
Light Fantastic
ART DIRECTOR *Michael Kaye*
DESIGNER *Paul Davis*
ILLUSTRATOR *Paul Davis*
STUDIO *Paul Davis Studio*
CLIENT *The Dial Press*

Distinctive Merit/U.S.A.

ANNUAL REPORT
Molecular Dynamics 1994 Annual Report
ART DIRECTOR *Bill Cahan*
CREATIVE DIRECTOR *Bill Cahan*
COPYWRITER *Carole Melis*
DESIGNER *Bob Dinetz*
PHOTOGRAPHER *Holly Stewart*
PRINTER *Alan Lithograph*
STUDIO *Cahan & Associates*
CLIENT *Molecular Dynamics*

(facing page)
Distinctive Merit/U.S.A.

BOOKLET OR BROCHURE
Launch Insert
ART DIRECTOR *Todd Waterbury*
CREATIVE DIRECTORS *Todd Waterbury,*
Peter Wegner
COPYWRITER *Peter Wegner*
DESIGNER *Todd Waterbury*
PHOTOGRAPHERS *Various*
PRINTER *Graphic Arts Center*
AGENCY *Wieden & Kennedy*
CLIENT *The Coca-Cola Company*

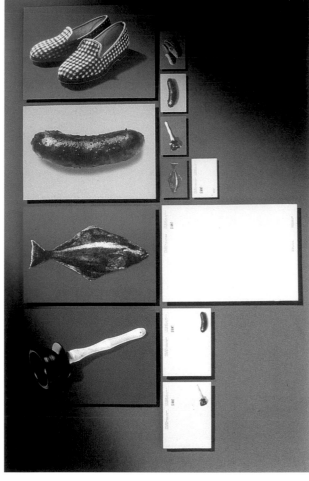

Distinctive Merit/Switzerland

CORPORATE IDENTITY PROGRAM
The Centenary of the Swiss National Library
ART DIRECTORS *Gerhard Blättler,*
Martin Gaberthüel, Andréas Netthoevel
CREATIVE DIRECTORS *Gerhard Blättler,*
Martin Gaberthüel, Andréas Netthoevel
DESIGNERS *Gerhard Blättler, Martin Gaberthüel,*
Andréas Netthoevel
AGENCY *second floor south*
CLIENT *Swiss National Library*

Distinctive Merit/England

STATIONERY
Giant Stationery
ART DIRECTORS *Alan Herron, Martyn Hey,*
Mark Rollinson, Neil Smith
CREATIVE DIRECTORS *Alan Herron, Martyn Hey,*
Mark Rollinson, Neil Smith
DESIGNERS *Alan Herron, Martyn Hey,*
Mark Rollinson, Neil Smith
PHOTOGRAPHER *Ian Skelton*
PRINTER *The Pale Green Press*
AGENCY *Giant Limited*
CLIENT *Giant Limited*

ADDITIONAL AWARD

Merit
CORPORATE AND PROMOTIONAL
COMMUNICATIONS, STATIONERY
Giant Stationery

This is Bandai advertisement was
done this summer vacation.
You win a surprise package
if you find the beaked man on a street corner.

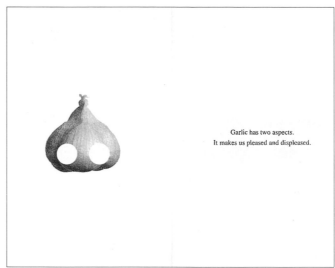

Garlic has two aspects.
It makes us pleased and displeased.

How I wish I could come up with
many ideas like blowing soap bubbles.

Soup. Meat. Soup. Meat. Soup. Meat.
That is the way you use it.

My body is stiff.

Distinctive Merit/Japan

SELF-PROMOTION
Everyday's Stools Are Our Business
ART DIRECTOR *Tatsuo Ebina*
CREATIVE DIRECTOR *Tatsuo Ebina*
DESIGNER *Tatsuo Ebina*
PHOTOGRAPHERS *Tadashi Tomono,*
Touru Kinoshita, Tatsuo Ebina
ILLUSTRATOR *Tatsuo Ebina*
CLIENT *E. Co. Ltd.*

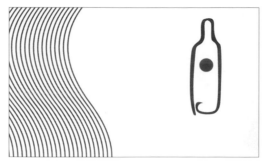

Distinctive Merit/U.S.A.

MUSIC VIDEO

Madonna, "Bedtime Stories"
PRODUCERS *Cean Chaffin, Chip Houghton*
DIRECTOR *Mark Romanek*
PHOTOGRAPHER *Harris Savides*
VISUAL EFFECTS SUPERVISORS *Mike Fink,*
Kevin Hang
ANIMATION *525 Productions*
STUDIO *R/Greenberg Associates, West*
AGENCY *R/Greenberg Associates*
CLIENT *Maverick Recording Company/Satellite*

Distinctive Merit/U.S.A.

ANIMATION

Composition in Op
ART DIRECTOR *Mike Bade*
CREATIVE DIRECTION *McCann Amster Yard*
COPYWRITER *Fred Stesney*
DESIGNER *Mike Bade*
PRODUCER *Natalie Ross*
DIRECTOR *Ellen Kahn*
MUSIC *John Petersen*
STUDIO *Curious Pictures*
AGENCY *McCann Amster Yard*
CLIENT *Bacardi Martini*

Distinctive Merit/Japan

PROMOTIONAL, SERIES
Office "Kurashige"
ART DIRECTOR *Kei Saito*
CREATIVE DIRECTOR *Mutsumi Yamaoka*
COPYWRITER *Kei Saito*
DESIGNER *Kei Saito*
PHOTOGRAPHER *Yoshi Imaizumi*
PRINTER *Seio Printing Co., Ltd.*
AGENCY *Akamaru Advertising Office*
CLIENT *Kurashige*

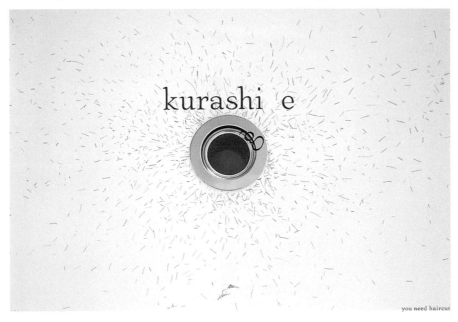

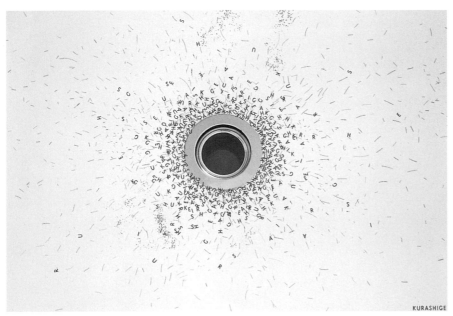

Distinctive Merit/Japan

PROMOTIONAL, SERIES
Ryuichi Sakamoto, "N/Y"
ART DIRECTOR *Hideki Nakajima*
CREATIVE DIRECTOR *Norika Sky Sora*
DESIGNER *Hideki Nakajima*
EDITOR *Shigeo Goto*
PHOTOGRAPHER *Kazunati Tajima*
ARTIST *Ryuichi Sakamoto*
STUDIO *Nakajima Design*
CLIENT *Little More*

ADDITIONAL AWARD

Merit
BOOK, SPECIAL TRADE

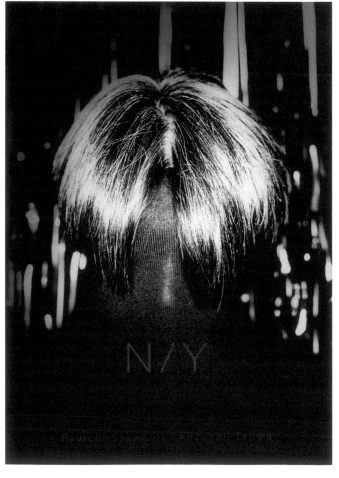

Distinctive Merit/U.S.A.

ENTERTAINMENT OR SPECIAL EVENT
Bring in 'Da Noise, Bring in 'Da Funk
ART DIRECTOR *Paula Scher*
DESIGNERS *Paula Scher, Lisa Mazur*
PHOTOGRAPHER *Peter Harrison*
PRINTER *Teller Graphics*
STUDIO *Pentagram Design*
CLIENT *The Public Theater*

Distinctive Merit/U.S.A.

ENTERTAINMENT OR SPECIAL EVENT, SERIES
1995 New York Shakespeare Festival
ART DIRECTOR *Paula Scher*
DESIGNERS *Paula Scher, Lisa Mazur, Jane Mella*
STUDIO *Pentagram Design*
CLIENT *The Public Theater*

ADDITIONAL AWARD

Merit
POSTER, ENTERTAINMENT OR SPECIAL EVENT
1995 New York Shakespeare Festival: Free Will

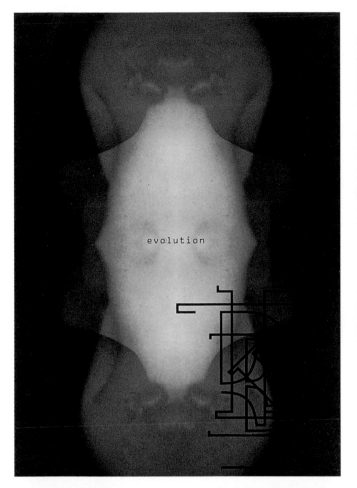

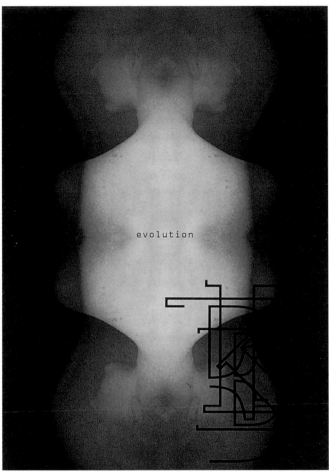

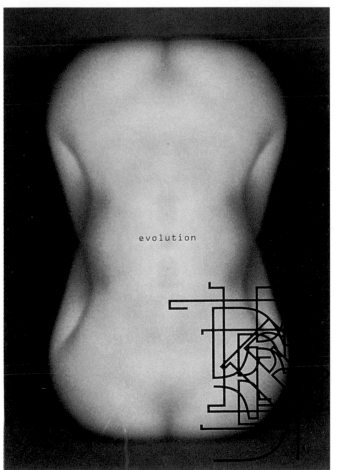

Distinctive Merit/Japan

PUBLIC SERVICE, SERIES
Evolution 1, 2, 3
ART DIRECTOR *Shinnoske Sugisaki*
DESIGNER *Shinnoske Sugisaki*
STUDIO *Shinnoske Inc.*
CLIENT *Ban Garow*

Distinctive Merit/The Netherlands

BILLBOARD OR PAINTED SPECTACULAR
Waardenberg en de Jong, "Naggelwauz"
ART DIRECTORS *Mark de Jong, Pjotr de Jong*
DESIGNERS *Mark de Jong, Pjotr de Jong*
PHOTOGRAPHER *Thijs Wolzak*
PRINTER *Steendrukkerij de Jong & Co.*
STUDIO *gebr de Jong ontwerpen*
CLIENT *Harry Kies Theaterprodukties*

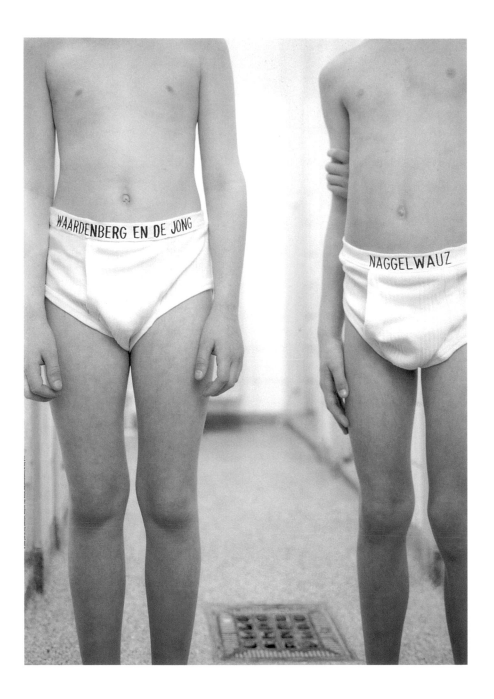

Distinctive Merit/U.S.A.

CONSUMER PRODUCT
Japanese Radio Can
ART DIRECTOR *Kobe*
CREATIVE DIRECTOR *Joe Duffy*
COPYWRITER *Phil Calvit*
DESIGNERS *Kobe, Neil Powell, Alan Leusink*
ILLUSTRATORS *Kobe, Neil Powell, Alan Leusink*
AGENCY *Duffy Design*
CLIENT *The Coca-Cola Company*

Distinctive Merit/U.S.A.

PUBLIC INTERIOR
Minnesota Children's Museum Signage
ART DIRECTOR *Michael Bierut*
DESIGNERS *Michael Bierut, Tracey Cameron*
PHOTOGRAPHERS *Judy Olausen, Michael O'Neill,*
Don F. Wong
FABRICATION *Cornelius Architectural Products*
STUDIO *Pentagram Design*
CLIENT *Minnesota Children's Museum*

Distinctive Merit/U.S.A.

PUBLIC INTERIOR
XIX Amendment Installation
CREATIVE DIRECTORS *Stephen Doyle,*
William Drenttel, Miguel Oks
ARCHITECT *Miguel Oks*
ARCHITECTURAL DESIGNER *James Hicks*
PROJECT MANAGER *Cameron Manning*

MERIT AWARDS

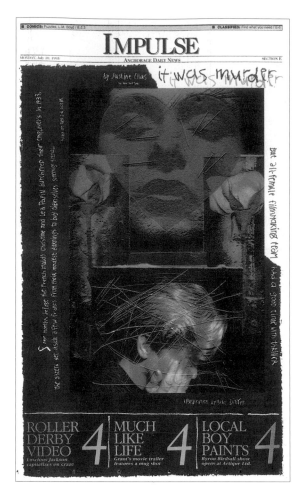

Merit/U.S.A.

FULL PAGE OR SPREAD
It Was Murder
ART DIRECTOR *Galie Jean-Louis*
CREATIVE DIRECTOR *Galie Jean-Louis*
DESIGNER *Dee Boyles*
ILLUSTRATOR *Eric Dinyer*
CLIENT *Anchorage Daily News*

Merit/U.S.A.

FULL PAGE OR SPREAD
American Gothic Horror
ART DIRECTOR *Galie Jean-Louis*
CREATIVE DIRECTOR *Galie Jean-Louis*
DESIGNER *Galie Jean-Louis*
ILLUSTRATOR *Amy Guip*
CLIENT *Anchorage Daily News*

Merit/U.S.A.

FULL PAGE OR SPREAD
Hard Hearing
ART DIRECTOR *Galie Jean-Louis*
CREATIVE DIRECTOR *Galie Jean-Louis*
DESIGNER *Dee Boyles*
PHOTOGRAPHER *Annalisa*
CLIENT *Anchorage Daily News*

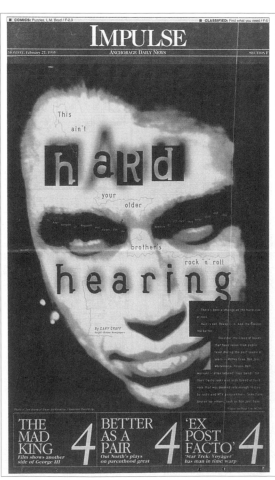

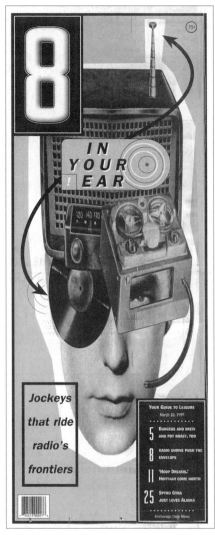

Merit/U.S.A.

FULL PAGE OR SPREAD
Dogg Food
ART DIRECTOR *Galie Jean-Louis*
CREATIVE DIRECTOR *Galie Jean-Louis*
DESIGNER *Galie Jean-Louis*
ILLUSTRATOR *Galie Jean-Louis*
CLIENT *Anchorage Daily News*

Merit/U.S.A.

FULL PAGE OR SPREAD
In Your Ear
ART DIRECTOR *Galie Jean-Louis*
CREATIVE DIRECTOR *Galie Jean-Louis*
DESIGNER *Kevin Ellis*
ILLUSTRATOR *David Plunkert*
CLIENT *Anchorage Daily News*

Merit/U.S.A.

FULL PAGE OR SPREAD
Slant: A Queer History of Rock
ART DIRECTORS *Howard Brown, Mike Calkins*
DESIGN DIRECTOR *Howard Brown*
STUDIO *Urban Outfitters In-House*
CLIENT *Urban Outfitters*

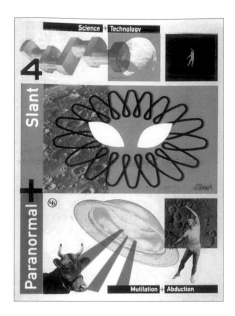

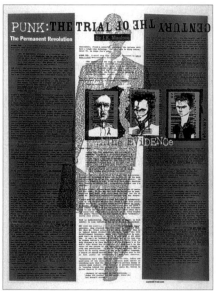

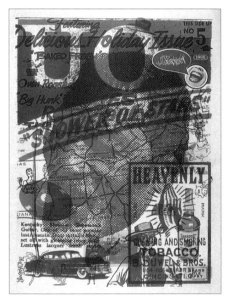

Merit/U.S.A.

FULL ISSUE, SERIES
Slant: Spring, Fall, Holidays
ART DIRECTORS *Howard Brown, Mike Calkins*
DESIGN DIRECTOR *Howard Brown*
DESIGNERS *Anthony Arnold, Howard Brown,*
Mike Calkins, C.S.A. Design, Gary Panter
ILLUSTRATORS *Glen Barr, Mike Calkins,*
Ed Fotheringham, Stephen Kroninger, Gary Panter
STUDIO *Urban Outfitters In-House*
CLIENT *Urban Outfitters*

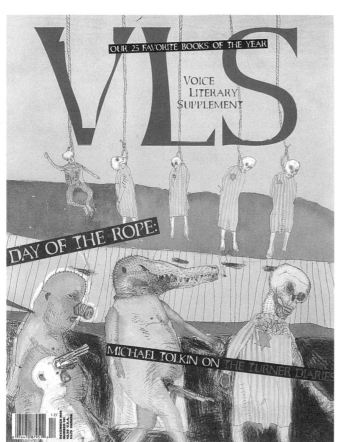

Merit/U.S.A.

COVER
Demi Moore
ART DIRECTOR *Fred Woodward*
DESIGNER *Fred Woodward*
PHOTOGRAPHER *Matthew Rolston*
PHOTO EDITOR *Jodi Peckman*
PUBLISHER *Wenner Media*
CLIENT *Rolling Stone*

Merit/U.S.A.

COVER
Alicia Silverstone
ART DIRECTOR *Fred Woodward*
DESIGNERS *Fred Woodward, Geraldine Hessler*
PHOTOGRAPHER *Peggy Sirota*
PHOTO EDITOR *Jodi Peckman*
TYPOGRAPHER *Eric J. Siry*
PUBLISHER *Wenner Media*
CLIENT *Rolling Stone*

Merit/U.S.A.

COVER
Day of the Rope
ART DIRECTOR *Ted Keller*
CREATIVE DIRECTOR *Audrey Shachnow*
ILLUSTRATOR *Alan E. Cober*
CLIENT *The Village Voice*

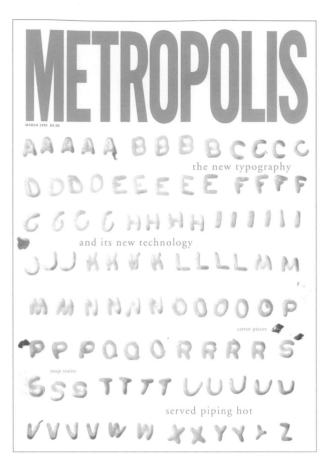

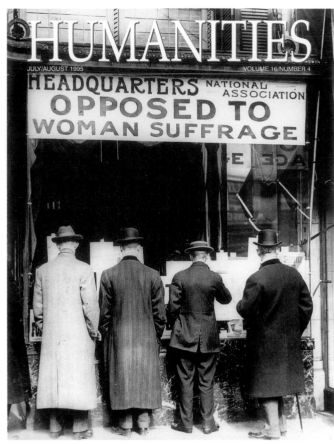

Merit/U.S.A.

COVER
Metropolis March 1995
ART DIRECTORS *Carl Lehmann-Haupt,*
Nancy Kruger Cohen
CREATIVE DIRECTOR *Kevin Slavin*
CLIENT *Metropolis*

Merit/U.S.A.

COVER
Humanities July/August 1995
ART DIRECTOR *Greg Whitlow*
DESIGNER *Greg Whitlow*
PRINTER *Reproductions, Inc.*
STUDIO *Crabtree & Jemison, Inc.*
CLIENT *National Endowment for the Humanities*

Merit/U.S.A.

COVER
The New Jazz Age
ART DIRECTOR *Janet Froelich*
DESIGNER *Lisa Naftolin*
PHOTOGRAPHER *Richard Burbridge*
PHOTO EDITOR *Kathy Ryan*
CLIENT *The New York Times Magazine*

ADDITIONAL AWARD

Merit
PHOTOGRAPHY, GRAPHIC DESIGN, EDITORIAL

Merit/U.S.A.

COVER
Upper & Lower Case
ART DIRECTOR *Ronda Rubinstein*
ILLUSTRATOR *J. Otto Seibold*
STUDIO *R Company, New York*
CLIENT *International Typeface Corporation*

Merit/U.S.A.

FULL PAGE OR SPREAD
Stevie Wonder
ART DIRECTOR *Fred Woodward*
DESIGNERS *Fred Woodward, Geraldine Hessler*
PHOTOGRAPHER *Matt Mahurin*
PHOTO EDITOR *Jodi Peckman*
PUBLISHER *Wenner Media*
CLIENT *Rolling Stone*

Merit/U.S.A.

COVER
UCLA Extension
ART DIRECTOR *George Tscherny*
CREATIVE DIRECTOR *George Tscherny*
DESIGNER *George Tscherny*
ILLUSTRATOR *George Tscherny*
COLOR SEPARATION *Sandy-Alexander Inc.*
PRINTER *Trend Offset Printing*
STUDIO *George Tscherny, Inc.*
CLIENT *UCLA Extension*

Merit/U.S.A.

FULL PAGE OR SPREAD
Foo Fighters
ART DIRECTOR *Fred Woodward*
DESIGNER *Gail Anderson*
PHOTOGRAPHER *Dan Winters*
PHOTO EDITOR *Jodi Peckman*
PUBLISHER *Wenner Media*
CLIENT *Rolling Stone*

Merit/U.S.A.

FULL PAGE OR SPREAD
Jay Leno
ART DIRECTOR *Fred Woodward*
DESIGNERS *Fred Woodward, Gail Anderson*
PHOTOGRAPHER *Mark Seliger*
PHOTO EDITOR *Jodi Peckman*
PUBLISHER *Wenner Media*
CLIENT *Rolling Stone*

Merit/U.S.A.

FULL PAGE OR SPREAD
Faces from the Grave
ART DIRECTOR *Arthur Hochstein*
DESIGNER *Jane Frey*
PHOTOGRAPHY *Photo Archive Group,*
Tuol Sleng Museum
PUBLISHER *Time Inc.*
CLIENT *Time Magazine*

Merit/U.S.A.

FULL PAGE OR SPREAD
Tea
ART DIRECTOR *Eric Pike*
CREATIVE DIRECTOR *Gael Towey*
DESIGNER *Claudia Bruno*
PHOTOGRAPHER *Maria Robledo*
PRODUCER *Claudia Bruno*
PUBLISHER *Time Inc.*
CLIENT *Martha Stewart Living*

Merit/U.S.A.

FULL PAGE OR SPREAD
Act Like Ya Know
ART DIRECTOR *Diddo Ramm*
DESIGNER *Diddo Ramm*
PHOTOGRAPHER *Josef Astor*
CLIENT *Vibe*

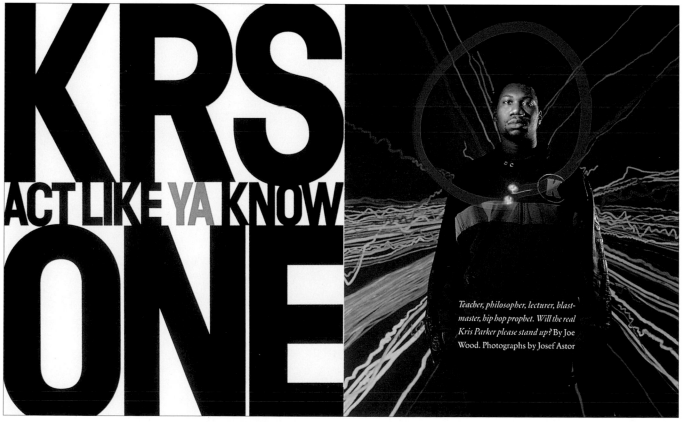

Teacher, philosopher, lecturer, blast-master, hip hop prophet. Will the real Kris Parker please stand up? By Joe Wood. Photographs by Josef Astor

Merit/U.S.A.

FULL PAGE OR SPREAD
Can Major League Sports Survive?
ART DIRECTOR *Mark Geer*
COPYWRITER *Matthew J. Mitten*
DESIGNER *Mark Geer*
ILLUSTRATOR *Ross MacDonald*
STUDIO *Geer Design*
CLIENT *South Texas College of Law*

Merit/U.S.A.

FULL PAGE OR SPREAD
Balancing Act
ART DIRECTOR *Fred Woodward*
DESIGNERS *Fred Woodward, Geraldine Hessler*
PHOTOGRAPHER *Mark Seliger*
PHOTO EDITOR *Jodi Peckman*
PUBLISHER *Wenner Media*
CLIENT *Rolling Stone*

Merit/China

FULL PAGE OR SPREAD
Roman Cieslewicz
ART DIRECTOR *Wang Xu*
DESIGNER *Wang Xu*
PRINTER *Shenzhen Meiguang Color Printing Co., Ltd.*
STUDIO *Wang Xu & Associates*
CLIENT *Exchange Publishing House*

Merit/U.S.A.

FULL PAGE OR SPREAD
Hot List '95
ART DIRECTOR *Fred Woodward*
DESIGNERS *Fred Woodward, Geraldine Hessler*
TYPOGRAPHER *Eric J. Siry*
PUBLISHER *Wenner Media*
CLIENT *Rolling Stone*

Merit/U.S.A.

MULTIPAGE
Name that Game
ART DIRECTOR *Bridget de Socio*
CREATIVE DIRECTOR *Bridget de Socio*
COPYWRITER *Christine Muhlke*
DESIGNERS *Tracie Anglo, John Oleynik*
PHOTOGRAPHER *Judson Baker*
STYLIST *Stefan Campbell*
CLIENT *Paper*

319

Merit/U.S.A.

MULTIPAGE
The Mile around the White House
DESIGN DIRECTOR *Tom Bentkowski*
DESIGNERS *Tom Bentkowski, Mimi Park*
PHOTOGRAPHY DIRECTOR *David Friend*
PHOTOGRAPHERS *David Burnett, Frank Fournier,*
Tomas Muscionico
PUBLISHER *Time Inc.*
CLIENT *Life Magazine*

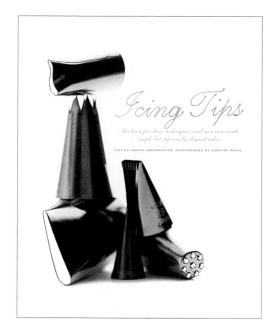

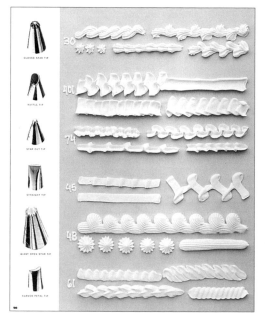

Merit/U.S.A.

MULTIPAGE
Icing Tips
ART DIRECTORS *Eric Pike, Anne Johnson*
CREATIVE DIRECTOR *Gael Towey*
DESIGNER *Anne Johnson*
PHOTOGRAPHER *Carlton Davis*
DIRECTOR *Susan Spungen*
PUBLISHER *Time Inc.*
CLIENT *Martha Stewart Living*

Merit/U.S.A.

MULTIPAGE
Hot Ice
ART DIRECTOR *Janet Froelich*
DESIGNER *Joel Cuyler*
PHOTOGRAPHER *Nadir*
CLIENT *The New York Times Magazine*

[COILED AND READY]

• SLASH takes a working vacation from Guns n' Roses with his new band, Slash's Snakepit •

BY KATHERINE TURMAN

ROLLING STONE, APRIL 20, 1995 · 53

Merit/U.S.A.

MULTIPAGE
Coiled and Ready
ART DIRECTOR *Fred Woodward*
DESIGNERS *Fred Woodward, Gail Anderson*
PHOTOGRAPHER *Matt Mahurin*
PHOTO EDITOR *Jodi Peckman*
PUBLISHER *Wenner Media*
CLIENT *Rolling Stone*

ADDITIONAL AWARD

Merit
PHOTOGRAPHY, GRAPHIC DESIGN, EDITORIAL

VEN UNDER THE BEST of circumstances, the Hamburger Hamlet that anchors the west end of L.A.'s Sunset Strip is lacking in serious ambience. At 3 in the afternoon on a rainy Saturday, though, the venerable if unremarkable restaurant is surprisingly crowded, the day's watery light lending a strangely cozy, slightly surreal air. THE EATERY'S PROXIMITY to the Atlantic and the Geffen record-company offices makes it a humming power-lunch destination during the week. Weekends, however, find plastic-surgeried Beverly Hills matrons quaffing diet sodas and kibitzing in the restaurant's brighter front rooms while the serious drinkers huddle in the welcoming banquette booths or at the bar in the slightly more dissolute atmosphere of the taproom. PERCHED ON A BARSTOOL is one Saul Hudson, colloquially known as Slash, Guns n' Roses' guitar guru. Save for the hefty diamond studs glittering in both ears, Slash — sporting facial scruff, a backward baseball cap, a hoop in his nose and a cigarette dangling from his lips — might be any other wanna-be rock star enjoying a midafternoon cocktail. SLASH ACCIDENTALLY ARRIVED an hour early for his scheduled interview, but unperturbed by the time mix-up, he waves to the waitress — clearly an old acquaintance — grabs his vodka and cranberry from the bar and slides into a booth, leaning forward conspiratorially. "Mr. T is sitting two tables away," he says sotto voce, excitement in his eyes. THOUGH JET-LAGGED AND UNSHAVEN, the guitarist proves loquacious, candid and relaxed. While he's got the slacker-musician vibe in spades, his conversation moves between topics — from piercing {"The next time you see me, I'll have my navel pierced"{ to Les Paul {"He wiped the stage with me once"{ — with frightening rapidity and surprising clarity, never straying far from his current raison d'etre, a down-and-dirty little rock & roll lineup known as Slash's Snakepit. Featured on the band's 14-song debut, *It's Five O'Clock Somewhere*, are ex-Gunner guitarist Gilby Clarke, present Gunner drummer Matt Sorum, Alice in Chains bassist Mike Inez and former Jellyfish background singer and guitarist Eric Dover on lead vocals. SLASH WAVES at the maitre d', who,

kindly, has not asked the guitarist to extinguish his cigarette despite stringent new anti-smoking laws in L.A. "That's Don," Slash says. "He's from the Sherman Oaks Hamburger Hamlet that was destroyed in the earthquake." SLASH DRAGS on his cigarette and downs a shot of Jagermeister. "This is the whole scheme," he says, shifting gears. "Initially I was just writing what I thought was cool. I was a kid in a toy store. I had a studio in my house. Get up in the morning. Literally. Press ON. Plug in your guitar and go. I don't look at stuff from the concept of writing the quintessential hit record. Just guitar riffs. GUNS GOT OFF THE ROAD," Slash continues. "I had the studio built right next to my snake cage, a walk-in with all these 20-foot snakes in it. It's *Slash's* Snakepit at this point, because all of a sudden there's an all-girl band in San Diego called Snake Pit." He laughs. "Don't ask."

MR. T'S VOICE RISES above the din, and Slash peers at him over the heads of the other diners and grins, his eyes crinkling. "If Dean Martin were here, that would be classic," says the 29-year-old guitarist. He settles back into the booth and easily picks up his train of thought. "It's like I'm owned by Guns n' Roses in a way," Slash continues in his intimate, stoner-ish timbre. "It's our band. So if I write something, my first and foremost priority would be to dedicate it to Guns." He draws heavily on his cigarette as the maitre d' hovers. "At the time, no one seemed to be interested in the material. Axl }Rose{ said, 'That's not the kind of music I want to do.' I said, 'OK,' and took it all back. We've had that happen too many times in Guns, when certain songs just didn't make it, and they would have been killer. I didn't want to lose any more material." SLASH WASN'T PLANNING on a solo record — "side project" being the much-preferred term. "It's not a solo project," he says, "because everybody in the band got to play whatever the fuck he wanted." The third original member of Guns n' Roses to release a solo album }following bassist Duff McKagan and ex-guitarist Izzy Stradlin{, Slash wrote all the music to the songs that appear on *It's Five O'Clock Somewhere* in his home studio, completing the initial concepts and tracks in early '94. The LP title was taken from a generous bartender at LAX airport, who gave Slash an early morning drink with the dictum "Hey, it's 5 o'clock somewhere, pal." THE COOLEST OMEN," says Slash, "was the night I recorded three songs and }*Cont. on 96*{

XXL said, 'That's not the music I want to do.' I said, 'OK,' and took it all back. That's happened too many times." —SLASH

• *Photographs by MATT MAHURIN* •

94 · ROLLING STONE, APRIL 20, 1995

ROLLING STONE, APRIL 20, 1995 · 55

Merit/U.S.A.

MULTIPAGE
Aftermath
ART DIRECTOR *Fred Woodward*
DESIGNERS *Fred Woodward, Gail Anderson*
PHOTOGRAPHER *Sebastião Salgado*
PHOTO EDITOR *Jodi Peckman*
PUBLISHER *Wenner Media*
CLIENT *Rolling Stone*

cranberries

OPPOSITE: A bog at harvest. All over the piney lowlands of Plymouth and Barnstable counties in Massachusetts, cranberry bogs are flooded and the berries floated to make collecting easier. The annual harvest begins around the third week of September and peaks in mid-October. The town of Carver, Massachusetts, is the cranberry capital of the world, and the industry hosts an annual harvest festival on Columbus Day weekend, attracting thirty thousand visitors. THIS PAGE: Fresh-picked berries are ready to be dumped into crates and airlifted by helicopter to trucks waiting on solid ground.

a wet harvest There are two ways of harvesting cranberries: wet or dry. Ninety percent are harvested wet and turned into juice or sauce; the rest are grown for fresh fruit. In a wet harvest, the bog is flooded and the berries are knocked off the vines so they float to the surface, where they can be corralled. 1. At John Decas's bog in Carver, Massachusetts, his son Dean drives a water harvesting machine known as an eggbeater over a partially flooded bog. It knocks the berries loose by agitating the water with a whipping action. 2. Once the eggbeater has covered the bog, more water is let in so the berries can float free from the plants. 3. The berries are raked and corralled with floating hounds called booms. 4. Long-handled rakes capture the last of the floating berries. 5. The cranberries are contained within the booms, which form huge circles on the water. This bog is owned by Gary Garrison, one of nine hundred grower-owners for the Ocean Spray cooperative. 6. Once the berries are contained, they can be pumped into trucks. 7, 8. A truck holding $10,000 worth of cranberries takes them to a receiving pool, where berries from different growers are floated so they can be raked onto elevators and lifted to the adjoining cleaning plant.

80

There are few things as lovely as a cranberry bog in autumn, when the berries are red and ripe and the vines heavy for harvest. The bogs are brilliant red, crimson, and scarlet, as if the earth itself were blushing from its own surfeit of fruit. At this time of year—on Cape Cod and in Plymouth County, in the New Jersey Pine Barrens and the wetlands of Wisconsin—the harvest has begun and the bogs are full of frenzied activity. In a few weeks, they must be cleared of their crop, the berries picked, processed, and packaged, all before the first freeze arrives and winter begins in earnest.

It is the perfect season for cranberries, stewed into sauces, sprinkled into stuffing or cake, or used sparingly, like jewels, to dress salad or sorbets. The key to cranberries is restraint, for there is nothing subtle about them. A cranberry is a tart character, a kernel of tang, clean and explosive. Eat a fresh one in autumn and its acids will make your mouth pucker. Its taste is as sharp as a stiletto.

It is perhaps the most North American of all fruits. Native Americans crushed the dried berries and mixed the powder with parched corn and cooked it into cakes. They used them in pemmican, an emergency ration made with deer meat and moose fat, and as a poultice for wounds. They also taught the Pilgrims how, and when, to pick them. Cranberries, in turn, were the first American fruit to be eaten in Europe. The berries, saturated with vitamin C, protected New England sailors from scurvy, and just as English ships were renowned for their limes and German ships for kraut, American vessels were famous for their barrels of cranberries. Over the years the small (CONTINUED ON PAGE 82)

OPPOSITE: There are more than a hundred varieties of cranberries, many named for the families that originally grew them. Late Howes, a berry sold fresh at market, has been one of the most popular since the early nineteenth century because it is especially red and reliably round.

77

Merit/U.S.A.

MULTIPAGE
Cranberries
ART DIRECTOR *Eric Pike*
CREATIVE DIRECTOR *Gael Towey*
DESIGNER *Eric Pike*
PHOTOGRAPHERS *Evan Sklar, Carlton Davis*
DIRECTOR *Hannah Milman*
PUBLISHER *Time Inc.*
CLIENT *Martha Stewart Living*

Merit/U.S.A.

MULTIPAGE
Some Enchanted Evening Clothes
ART DIRECTOR *Janet Froelich*
DESIGNER *Janet Froelich*
PHOTOGRAPHER *Lillian Bassman*
STYLIST *Franciscus Ankoné*
CLIENT *The New York Times Magazine*

ADDITIONAL AWARD

Merit
PHOTOGRAPHY, GRAPHIC DESIGN, EDITORIAL

Some Enchanted Evening Clothes

Just in case you meet a stranger.

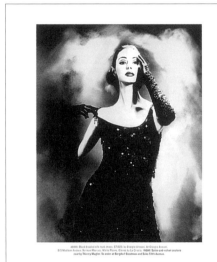

Merit/Japan

MULTIPAGE
Dune Autumn 1995
ART DIRECTOR *Hideki Nakajima*
DESIGNER *Hideki Nakajima*
EDITOR IN CHIEF *Fumihiro Hayashi*
PHOTOGRAPHERS *Kyoji Takahashi, Katsumi Omori,*
François Rotger, Masashi Ohashi
PHOTO EDITOR *Kouichro Yamamoto*
ILLUSTRATOR *Hiroshi Tanabe*
STUDIO *Nakajima Design*
CLIENT *Dune*

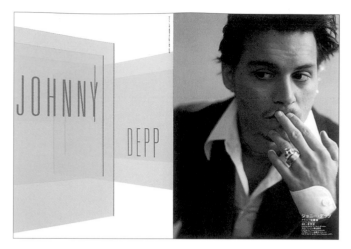

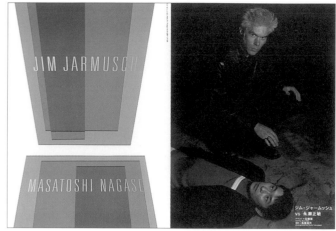

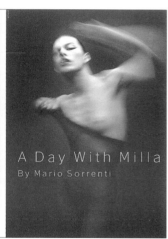

Merit/Japan

MULTIPAGE
Cut No. 46
ART DIRECTOR *Hideki Nakajima*
DESIGNER *Hideki Nakajima*
EDITOR IN CHIEF *Ken Sato*
PHOTOGRAPHERS *Christopher Doyle, Itaru Hirama,*
Mario Sorrenti, Kyoji Takahashi
STUDIO *Nakajima Design*
CLIENT *Rockin' On Inc.*

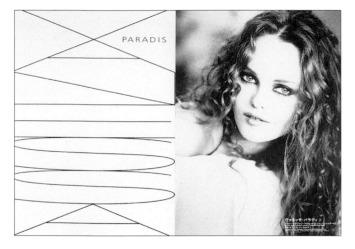

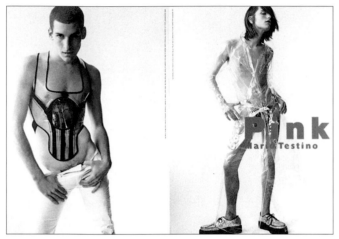

Merit/Japan

MULTIPAGE
Cut No. 40
ART DIRECTOR *Hideki Nakajima*
DESIGNER *Hideki Nakajima*
EDITOR IN CHIEF *Ken Sato*
PHOTOGRAPHER *Dominique Issermann*
STUDIO *Nakajima Design*
CLIENT *Rockin' On Inc.*

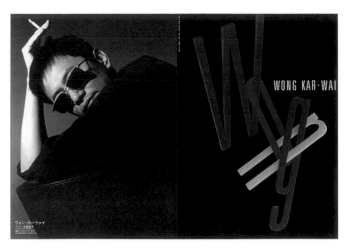

Merit/Japan

MULTIPAGE
Cut No. 43
ART DIRECTOR *Hideki Nakajima*
DESIGNER *Hideki Nakajima*
EDITOR IN CHIEF *Ken Sato*
PHOTOGRAPHERS *Fanco Lai, Shigemi Tsutsumi*
STUDIO *Nakajima Design*
CLIENT *Rockin' On Inc.*

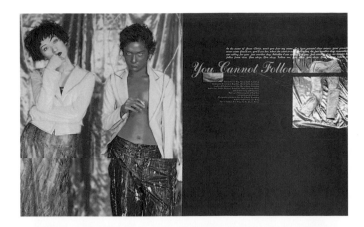

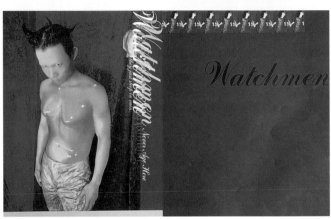

Merit/Hong Kong

MULTIPAGE
You Cannot Follow Me
ART DIRECTOR *Wing Shya*
CREATIVE DIRECTOR *Wing Shya*
DESIGNER *Ivan Choi*
PHOTOGRAPHER *Wing Shya*
RETOUCHING *Tse Chiu Yan*
STUDIO *Double X Workshop*

Merit/U.S.A.

FULL ISSUE
Vibe September 1995
ART DIRECTOR *Diddo Ramm*
DESIGNERS *Diddo Ramm, Ellen Fanning,*
David Harley
CLIENT *Vibe*

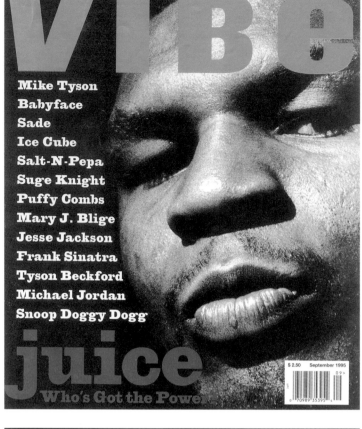

Merit/U.S.A.

FULL ISSUE
Blind Spot Issue 6
ART DIRECTOR *Tony Arefin*
CREATIVE DIRECTOR *Tony Arefin*
DESIGNER *Miranda Dempster*
CLIENT *Blind Spot Photography Inc.*

Merit/U.S.A.

FULL ISSUE
Childhood in America
ART DIRECTOR *Janet Froelich*
DESIGNER *Catherine Gilmore-Barnes*
PHOTOGRAPHERS *Various*
PHOTO EDITORS *Kathy Ryan, Sarah Harbutt*
CLIENT *The New York Times Magazine*

Merit/England

FULL ISSUE
The Sunday Telegraph Magazine
ART DIRECTOR *Derek Copsey*
DESIGNER *Derek Birdsall*
EDITOR *Alexander Chancellor*
ART EDITOR *John Belknap*
VISUAL ARTS CONSULTANT *Bruce Bernard*
CLIENT *The Sunday Telegraph*

Merit/Germany

FULL ISSUE
*Instant: Zeitgenössische Deutsche
Modephotographie 1995*
ART DIRECTOR *Manuela Nyhuis*
CREATIVE DIRECTORS *Thomas Feicht,
Manuela Nyhuis*
COPYWRITER *Daniel Mayer*
DESIGNER *Angela Rädlein*
AGENCY *TRUST Corporate Culture GmbH*
CLIENT *Abele Optik*

Merit/England

FULL ISSUE
Big Magazine No. 11
ART DIRECTOR *Vince Frost*
CREATIVE DIRECTOR *Vince Frost*
DESIGNER *Vince Frost*
PHOTOGRAPHERS *Alan Bevkers, Robin Grierson,*
Giles Revell, Gino Sprio
STUDIO *Frost Design*
CLIENT *Big Magazine*

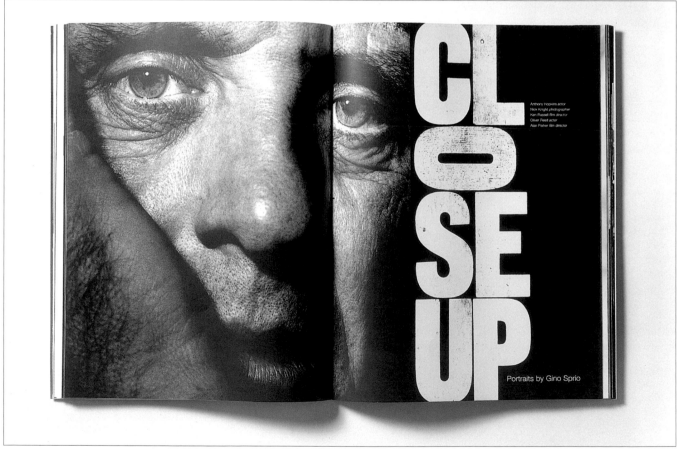

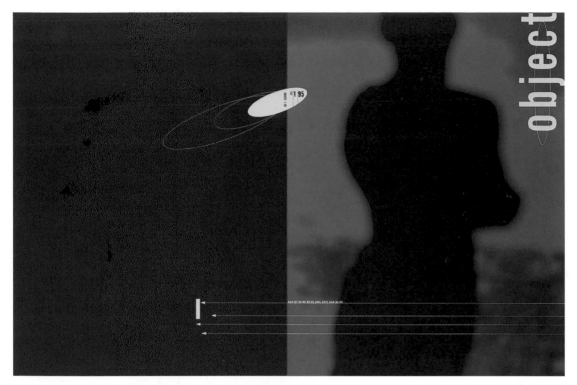

Merit/Australia

FULL ISSUE
Object No. 1
ART DIRECTOR *Zoë Wishart*
CREATIVE DIRECTOR *Zoë Wishart*
DESIGNER *Zoë Wishart*
EDITOR IN CHIEF *Helen Zilko*
PHOTOGRAPHERS *Ian Hobbs, Clayton Glen, Various*
PRINTER *RT Kelly Pty. Ltd.*
STUDIO *Antart*
AGENCY *Direct*
CLIENT *Centre for Contemporary Craft,*
New South Wales

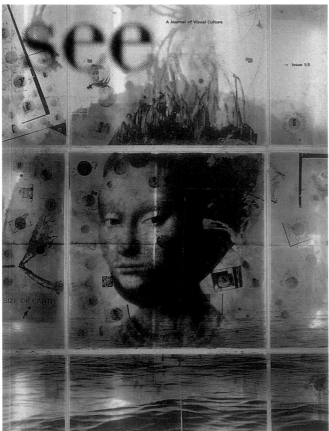

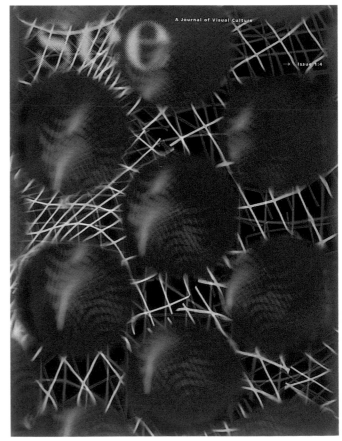

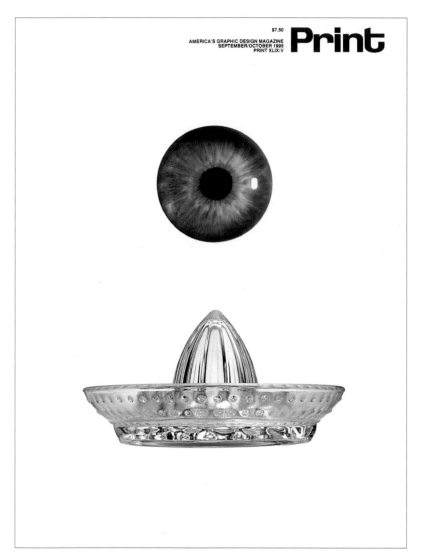

Merit/U.S.A.

COVER
Print September/October 1995
ART DIRECTOR *Andrew Kner*
CREATIVE DIRECTOR *Andrew Kner*
DESIGNER *Benoit Fillion*
PHOTOGRAPHER *Benoit Fillion*
PUBLISHER *RC Publications*
CLIENT *Print Magazine*

Merit/U.S.A.

FULL PAGE OR SPREAD
Stick Magazine
ART DIRECTOR *Scott Clum*
CREATIVE DIRECTOR *Scott Clum*
DESIGNER *Scott Clum*
PHOTOGRAPHER *Scott Clum*
PUBLISHER *Marvin Jarrett of Raygun Publishing*
STUDIO *Ride*
CLIENT *Stick Magazine*

(facing page)
Merit/U.S.A.

FULL ISSUE, SERIES
See Nos. 1:1, 1:2, 1:3, 1:4
ART DIRECTOR *Michiko Toki of Toki Design*
DESIGNER *Michiko Toki of Toki Design*
EXECUTIVE EDITOR *Deborah Klochko*
EDITOR IN CHIEF *Andy Grundberg*
SENIOR EDITORS *Amy Howorth, Steven Jenkins*
PRODUCTION EDITOR *Charlene Rule*
PHOTOGRAPHERS *Various*
ILLUSTRATORS *Various*
STUDIO *Toki Design*
CLIENT *The Friends of Photography*

Merit/U.S.A.

FULL PAGE OR SPREAD
Safe
ART DIRECTOR *Andrew Kner*
CREATIVE DIRECTOR *Andrew Kner*
DESIGNERS *Andrew Kner, Michele Trombley*
EDITOR *Tod Lippy*
PHOTOGRAPHER *Nora Scarlett*
PUBLISHER *RC Publications*
CLIENT *Scenario Magazine*

Merit/U.S.A.

FULL ISSUE
Mohawk: Rethinking Design II
ART DIRECTOR *Michael Bierut*
COPYWRITERS *Various*
DESIGNERS *Michael Bierut, Emily Hayes*
PHOTOGRAPHERS *Various*
ILLUSTRATORS *Various*
STUDIO *Pentagram Design*
CLIENT *Mohawk Paper Mills*

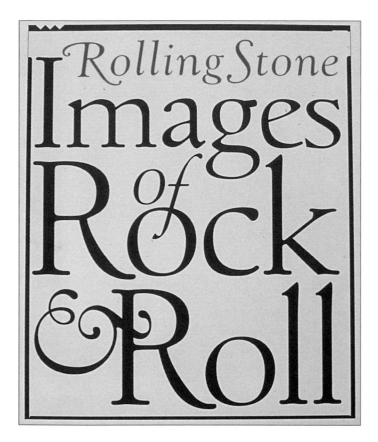

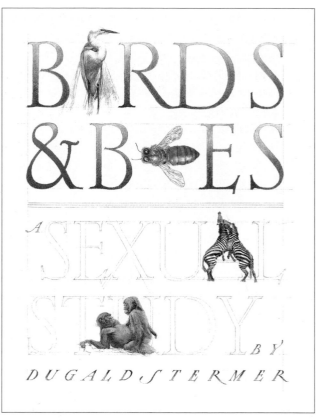

Merit/U.S.A.

GENERAL TRADE
Images of Rock & Roll
ART DIRECTOR *Fred Woodward*
PHOTOGRAPHERS *Various*
PHOTO EDITORS *Denise Sfraga,*
Julie Claire Derscheid
PUBLISHER *Little, Brown and Company*
CLIENT *Rolling Stone Press*

Merit/U.S.A.

SPECIAL TRADE
Birds & Bees
ART DIRECTOR *Dugald Stermer*
COPYWRITER *Dugald Stermer*
DESIGNER *Dugald Stermer*
EDITOR *Jennifer Barry*
ILLUSTRATOR *Dugald Stermer*
PRINTER *Mondadori Ltd.*
CLIENT *HarperCollins*

Merit/U.S.A.

SPECIAL TRADE
Vanishing Flora
ART DIRECTOR *Dugald Stermer*
COPYWRITER *Dugald Stermer*
DESIGNERS *Dugald Stermer, Samuel N. Antupit*
EDITOR *Sharon AvRutick*
PHOTOGRAPHER *Kevin Bond*
ILLUSTRATOR *Dugald Stermer*
PRINTER *Dai Nippon*
CLIENT *Harry N. Abrams, Inc.*

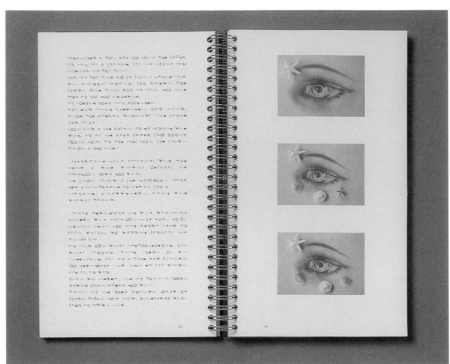

Merit/Japan

SPECIAL TRADE
Mizuumi
ART DIRECTOR *Tomohiro Itami*
CREATIVE DIRECTOR *Takashi Asai*
DESIGNER *Tomohiro Itami*
ILLUSTRATOR *Sawako Goda*
PRINTER *Uplink Ltd.*
STUDIO *It Is Design Ltd.*

Merit/U.S.A.

PAPERBACK
A Good Day for Soup
ART DIRECTOR *Sharon Werner*
CREATIVE DIRECTOR *Jill Jacobson*
COPYWRITERS *Jeanette Ferrary, Louise Fiszer*
DESIGNERS *Sharon Werner, Sarah Nelson*
PHOTOGRAPHER *Darrell Eager*
ILLUSTRATORS *Sharon Werner, Sarah Nelson*
STUDIO *Werner Design Werks Inc.*
CLIENT *Chronicle Books*

Merit/U.S.A.

PROMOTIONAL
Vera Wang Spring Preview
ART DIRECTOR *Bridget de Socio*
CREATIVE DIRECTOR *Deborah Moses*
COPYWRITER *Deborah Moses*
PHOTOGRAPHER *Ruven Afanador*
STUDIO *Socio X*
CLIENT *Vera Wang*

Merit/Switzerland

PROMOTIONAL
Zehndergeschichte
ART DIRECTOR *Jürg Brühlmann*
COPYWRITER *Andreas Steigmeier*
PHOTOGRAPHY *Lucia Degonda, Michael Richter,*
Zehnder Archive
PRODUCER *Hans Peter Zehnder*
PRINTER *Grafische Betriebe Aargauer Tagblatt*
STUDIO *Atelier Jürg Brühlmann*
CLIENT *Zehnder Holding AG*

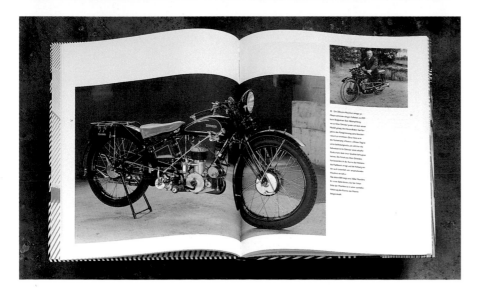

Merit/Japan

PROMOTIONAL
Hallelujah's Flowers
ART DIRECTOR *Katsuhiro Kinoshita*
CREATIVE DIRECTORS *Keiko Murakami,*
Takako Suzuki
DESIGNER *Katsuhiro Kinoshita*
PHOTOGRAPHERS *Masataka Nakano,*
Masahiko Takeda
PRINTING DIRECTOR *Seiji Tajima*
BINDING DIRECTOR *Toshihiro Fujita*
STUDIO *Design Club Inc.*
CLIENT *Hallelujah*

Merit/U.S.A.

LIMITED EDITION, PRIVATE OR FINE PRESS,
OR SPECIAL FORMAT
Rebus Redux
ART DIRECTOR *Eric Baker*
DESIGNER *Eric Baker*
PUBLISHER *Eric Baker Design Associates*
STUDIO *Eric Baker Design Associates*

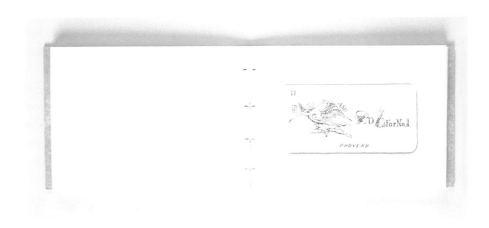

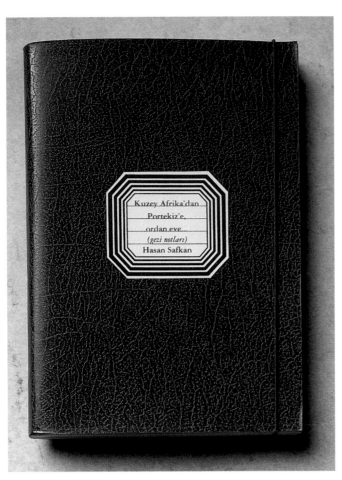

Merit/Turkey

LIMITED EDITION, PRIVATE OR FINE PRESS, OR SPECIAL FORMAT
From North Africa to Portugal then Home
ART DIRECTOR *Bülent Erkmen*
CREATIVE DIRECTOR *Bülent Erkmen*
AUTHOR *Hasan Safkan*
DESIGNER *Bülent Erkmen*
PHOTOGRAPHER *Hasan Safkan*
TYPESETTER *Hasan Özer Uzunboy*
PRODUCER *Sermet Tolan*
PUBLISHER *Ofset Production House*
CLIENT *Ofset Production House*

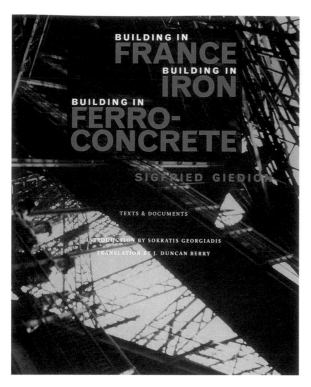

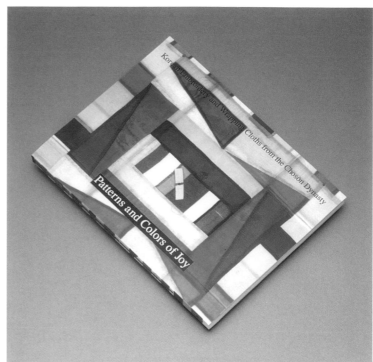

Merit/U.S.A.

**MUSEUM, GALLERY, OR UNIVERSITY PRESS
PUBLICATION**
*Building in France, Building in Iron, Building
in Ferroconcrete*
ART DIRECTOR *Bruce Mau*
DESIGNERS *Bruce Mau, Chris Rowat*
PHOTOGRAPHER *Sigfried Giedion (cover)*
PRINTER *Bowne of Toronto*
STUDIO *Bruce Mau Design*
CLIENT *The Getty Center for the History of Art
and the Humanities*

Merit/Japan

**MUSEUM, GALLERY, OR UNIVERSITY PRESS
PUBLICATION**
Patterns and Colors of Joy
ART DIRECTOR *Kijuro Yahagi*
STUDIO *Kijuro Yahagi Inc.*
CLIENT *Japan Art and Culture Association*

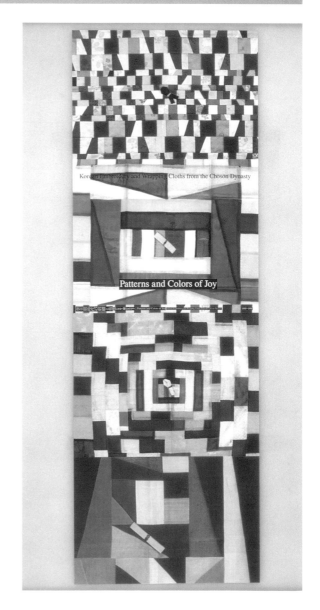

Merit/Germany

**MUSEUM, GALLERY, OR UNIVERSITY PRESS
PUBLICATION**
Voko: Office View 1
ART DIRECTOR *Urs V. Schwerzmann*
COPYWRITER *Otto Riewoldt*
PHOTOGRAPHERS *Dieter Blum, Gottfried Helnwein,
Dietmar Henneka, Gunter Sachs, Karin Székessy,
Gerhard Vormwald*
PRINTER *H. Schmidt*
STUDIO *Urs V. Schwerzmann*
CLIENT *Voko*

Merit/U.S.A.

CHILDREN'S
If...
DESIGNER *Vickie Sawyer Karten*
ILLUSTRATOR *Sarah Perry*
PRINTER *Tien Wah Press, Singapore*
STUDIO *The J. Paul Getty Trust, Publication Services*
CLIENT *The J. Paul Getty Museum*

Merit/U.S.A.

REFERENCE
A Brief on the Agency Brief (In Brief)
ART DIRECTOR *Todd Waterbury*
CREATIVE DIRECTORS *Todd Waterbury,*
Peter Wegner
COPYWRITER *Peter Wegner*
DESIGNER *Todd Waterbury*
PRINTER *Schultz, Wack, Weir*
AGENCY *Wieden & Kennedy*
CLIENT *The Coca-Cola Company*

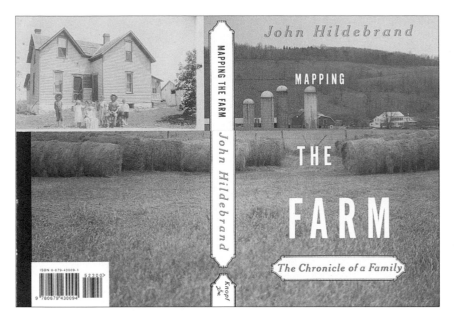

Merit/U.S.A.

JACKET
Mapping the Farm
ART DIRECTOR *Carol Carson*
CREATIVE DIRECTOR *Carol Carson*
DESIGNER *Barbara de Wilde*
PHOTOGRAPHER *Victor Schrager*
PUBLISHER *Alfred A. Knopf*
STUDIO *Barbara de Wilde Design*
CLIENT *Alfred A. Knopf*

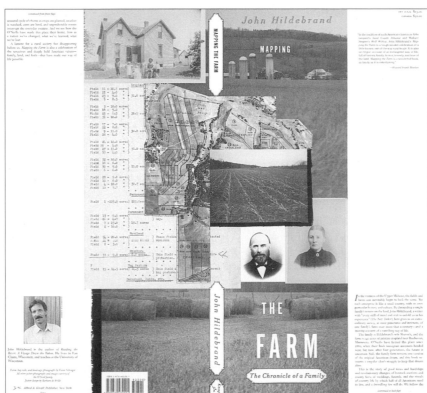

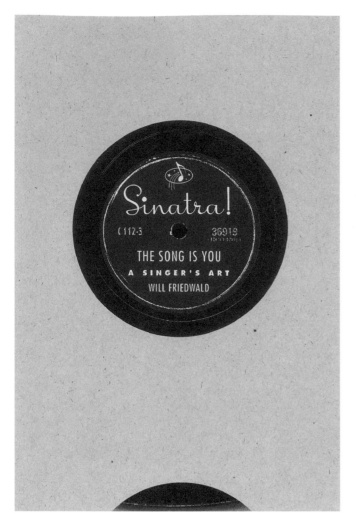

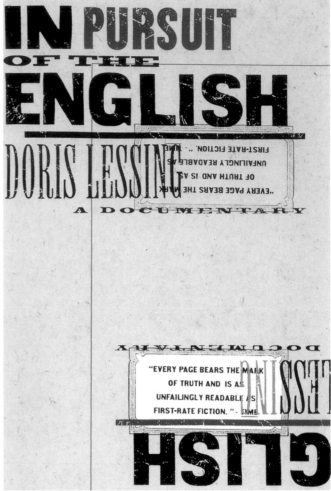

Merit/U.S.A.

JACKET
Sinatra!
ART DIRECTOR *John Fontana*
DESIGNER *Carin Goldberg*
STUDIO *Carin Goldberg Design*
CLIENT *Scribner*

(facing page)
Merit/U.S.A.

JACKET
The Music Box Project
ART DIRECTOR *Takaaki Matsumoto*
AUTHOR *Claudia Gould*
DESIGNER *Takaaki Matsumoto*
PRINTER *Hull Printing Co., Inc.*
STUDIO *Matsumoto Incorporated, NY*
CLIENT *on the table inc.*

Merit/U.S.A.

JACKET
Bases Loaded with History
ART DIRECTOR *Marion English*
CREATIVE DIRECTOR *Marion English*
COPYWRITERS *Coke Matthews, Laura Holmes*
DESIGNER *Marion English*
PHOTOGRAPHERS *Don Harbor, John Huet,*
Glynn West
AGENCY *Slaughter Hanson*
CLIENT *Friends of Rickwood Field*

Merit/U.S.A.

JACKET
In Pursuit of the English
ART DIRECTOR *Suzanne Noli*
DESIGNER *Carin Goldberg*
STUDIO *Carin Goldberg Design*
CLIENT *HarperCollins*

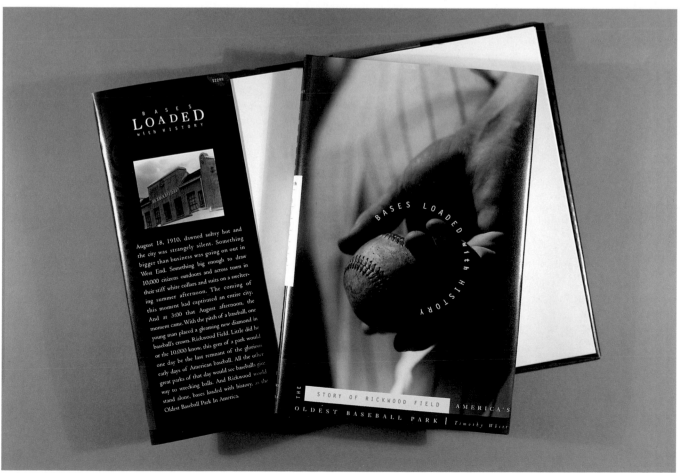

PRAISE FOR

TAKE IT LIKE A MAN

ISBN 0-06-017368-8

90000

9 780060 173685

BOY GEORGE WITH SPENCER BRIGHT TAKE IT LIKE A MAN

HARPER COLLINS

BOY

GEORGE

WITH SPENCER BRIGHT

THE AUTOBIOGRAPHY OF BOY GEORGE

TAKE IT LIKE A

MAN

"*Take It Like a Man* is a vivid, immensely readable trolley tour of the giddy highs and ghastly lows of George's addictions to fame, cross-dressing, drugs, and sex."
—Michael Musto, *Village Voice*

"Whatever I think of Boy George, I have to praise this book for its candour. . . . A definitive portrait of a modern young pop star."
—Quentin Crisp

"An amazingly candid confession about the world of pop music, passionately profound, written with unflinching honesty." —Leila Hadley Luce

"A fascinating insight into the intolerable pressures and temptations of stardom." —*Daily Mail*

"Candid and entertaining. . . . His public image was wildly at odds with his private self, the self that was living fabulously and wildly, gorging on drugs, food and sex, trashing hotel rooms and brawling with friends."
—*Times* (London)

"If there's another book that can top it for bitchiness, sex, glamour, fame, and heartache, then Jackie Collins must be the author." —*Q*

"Touchingly, at the center of this creation, you find an insecure bruiser of a guy, built like a bricklayer and yet cooler than any royal blue-blood. You'll not read a more astonishing music biog this year."
—*NME* (New Musical Express)

GEORGE WITH SPENCER BRIGHT TAKE IT LIKE A

HARPER COLLINS

Merit/U.S.A.

JACKET
Boy George: Take It Like a Man
ART DIRECTOR *Joseph Montebello*
DESIGNER *Chip Kidd*
PHOTOGRAPHER *Uli Weber*
STUDIO *Chipkiddesign*
CLIENT *HarperCollins*

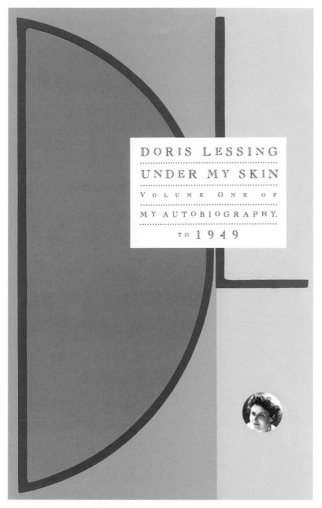

Merit/U.S.A.

JACKET
Doris Lessing: Under My Skin
ART DIRECTOR *Suzanne Noli*
DESIGNER *Carin Goldberg*
STUDIO *Carin Goldberg Design*
CLIENT *HarperCollins*

Merit/U.S.A.

JACKET
I'd Rather Die than Give a Speech
ART DIRECTOR *Steven Brower*
DESIGNER *Steven Brower*
PHOTOGRAPHER *Richard Fahey*
PUBLISHER *Carol Publishing Group*
CLIENT *Carol Publishing Group*

Merit/U.S.A.

JACKET
The History of the Blues
ART DIRECTOR *Victor Weaver*
DESIGNER *Carin Goldberg*
STUDIO *Carin Goldberg Design*
CLIENT *Hyperion Books*

Merit/Finland

JACKET
Leena Krohn
ART DIRECTOR *Marjaana Virta*
WRITER *Leena Krohn*
GRAPHIC ASSISTANT *Sari Marttiini*
PHOTOGRAPHER *Pentti Sammallahti*
PUBLISHER *WSOY*
CLIENT *WSOY*

Merit/Finland

JACKET
Kaksi Vaimoa
ART DIRECTOR *Kirsikka Mänty*
WRITER *Matti Mäkelä*
GRAPHIC ASSISTANT *Jari Nykänen*
PHOTOGRAPHER *Paavo Heikkinen*
PUBLISHER *WSOY*
CLIENT *WSOY*

Merit/The Netherlands

JACKET, SERIES
AP Crime Paperbacks
CREATIVE DIRECTOR *Hans Bockting*
DESIGNERS *Hans Bockting, Pauline Hooweg,*
Clarissa Biolchini
PHOTOGRAPHERS *Lex van Pieterson, Erik van Gurp*
STUDIO *UNA*
CLIENT *De Arbeiderspers*

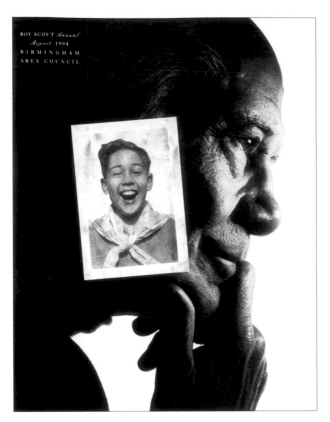

Merit/U.S.A.

ANNUAL REPORT
Birmingham Boy Scout Area Council
1994 Annual Report
ART DIRECTOR *Marion English*
CREATIVE DIRECTOR *Terry Slaughter*
COPYWRITER *Laura Holmes*
DESIGNER *Marion English*
PHOTOGRAPHER *Geoff Knight*
ILLUSTRATOR *David Webb*
AGENCY *Slaughter Hanson*
CLIENT *Birmingham Boy Scout Area Council*

Merit/U.S.A.

ANNUAL REPORT
Cracker Barrel Old Country Store 1995 Annual Report
ART DIRECTOR *Thomas Ryan*
CREATIVE DIRECTOR *Thomas Ryan*
COPYWRITER *John Baeder*
DESIGNER *Thomas Ryan*
PHOTOGRAPHER *McGuire*
ILLUSTRATOR *Paul Ritscher*
FILM *Graphic Process Inc.*
PRINTER *Lithographics*
STUDIO *Thomas Ryan Design*
AGENCY *Corporate Communication Inc.*
CLIENT *Cracker Barrel Old Country Store, Inc.*

Merit/U.S.A.

ANNUAL REPORT
Public Securities Association 1994–1995 Annual Report
CREATIVE DIRECTORS *Kent Hunter, Audrey Balkind*
DESIGNER *Yu Mei Tam*
PHOTOGRAPHER *John Casado*
PRINTER *Innovation Printing*
AGENCY *Frankfurt Balkind Partners*

Merit/U.S.A.

ANNUAL REPORT
BC Telecom 1994 Annual Report
ART DIRECTORS *John Van Dyke, Dave Mason*
COPYWRITERS *Tom McCarthy, Dave Crowe*
DESIGNERS *John Van Dyke, Dave Mason*
PHOTOGRAPHER *Victor Penner*
STUDIO *A Design Collaborative*
CLIENT *BC Telecom*

Merit/U.S.A.

ANNUAL REPORT
Zürich Reinsurance Center 1994 Annual Report
ART DIRECTOR *James Pettus*
CREATIVE DIRECTORS *Frank Oswald,*
David Dunkleberger
COPYWRITER *Frank Oswald*
DESIGNER *James Pettus*
PHOTOGRAPHERS *F. Scott Shaffer,*
Christopher Hawker
ILLUSTRATOR *James Pettus*
PRINTER *Allied Printing Services, Inc.*
STUDIO *WYD Design, Inc.*
CLIENT *Zürich Reinsurance Center*

Merit/U.S.A.

ANNUAL REPORT
ICOS Corporation 1994 Annual Report
ART DIRECTOR *John Van Dyke*
COPYWRITER *Tom McCarthy*
DESIGNERS *John Van Dyke, Ann Kumasaka*
PHOTOGRAPHER *Jeff Corwin*
STUDIO *Van Dyke Company*
CLIENT *ICOS Corporation*

(facing page)
Merit/U.S.A.

ANNUAL REPORT
Oak Technology 1995 Annual Report
ART DIRECTOR *Bill Cahan*
CREATIVE DIRECTOR *Bill Cahan*
COPYWRITER *Tim Peters*
DESIGNER *Craig Clark*
PHOTOGRAPHERS *Various*
ILLUSTRATORS *Various*
PRINTER *Watt/Peterson*
STUDIO *Cahan & Associates*
CLIENT *Oak Technology*

Merit/U.S.A.

ANNUAL REPORT
Shaman Pharmaceuticals 1994 Annual Report
ART DIRECTOR *Bill Cahan*
CREATIVE DIRECTOR *Bill Cahan*
COPYWRITER *Shari Annes*
DESIGNER *Sharrie Brooks*
PHOTOGRAPHERS *Bill McLeod, Various*
PRINTER *Alan Lithograph*
STUDIO *Cahan & Associates*
CLIENT *Shaman Pharmaceuticals, Inc.*

Merit/U.S.A.

ANNUAL REPORT
Rational Software Corporation 1995 Annual Report
ART DIRECTOR *Bill Cahan*
CREATIVE DIRECTOR *Bill Cahan*
COPYWRITER *Tim Peters*
DESIGNER *Bob Dinetz*
ILLUSTRATOR *Jeffrey Fisher*
PRINTER *Watt/Peterson*
STUDIO *Cahan & Associates*
CLIENT *Rational Software Corporation*

Merit/U.S.A.

ANNUAL REPORT
Urban Outfitters 1995 Annual Report
ART DIRECTOR *Howard Brown*
DESIGNERS *Mike Calkins, Howard Brown,*
Anthony Arnold
PHOTOGRAPHERS *Michael D. McLaughlin,*
Tom Crane, Anthony Arnold
STUDIO *Urban Outfitters In-House*
CLIENT *Urban Outfitters*

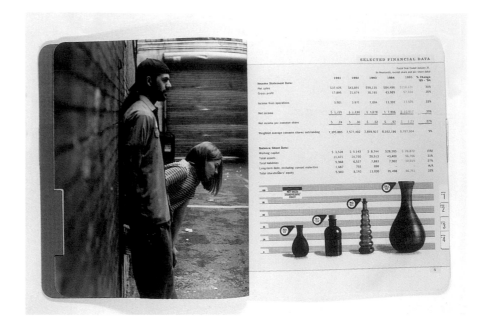

Merit/U.S.A.

ANNUAL REPORT
Gilead Sciences 1995 Annual Report
ART DIRECTOR *Bill Cahan*
CREATIVE DIRECTOR *Bill Cahan*
COPYWRITER *Norma Hayes*
DESIGNER *Kevin Roberson*
PHOTOGRAPHER *Christine Alicino*
PRINTER *Alan Lithograph*
STUDIO *Cahan & Associates*
CLIENT *Gilead Sciences*

Merit/U.S.A.

ANNUAL REPORT
S.E.A.R.C.H. 1994 Annual Report
ART DIRECTOR *Diane Butler*
COPYWRITER *JoAnn Stone*
DESIGNER *Michael Muhlherr*
PHOTOGRAPHER *Terry Vine*
STUDIO *Butler Design*
CLIENT *S.E.A.R.C.H.*

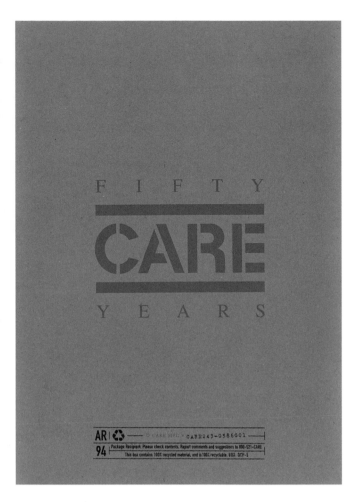

Merit/U.S.A.

ANNUAL REPORT
American Arbitration Association 1994 Annual Report
ART DIRECTOR *Cindy Goldstein*
CREATIVE DIRECTOR *Victor Rivera*
DESIGNER *Cindy Goldstein*
PROJECT MANAGER *Chris Snarey*
ACCOUNT DIRECTOR *Len Fury*
PRINTER *D.C. Terwiliger/Sterling Roman*
STUDIO *Addison Corporate Annual Reports*
CLIENT *American Arbitration Association*

Merit/U.S.A.

ANNUAL REPORT
CARE 1994 Annual Report
CREATIVE DIRECTORS *Bob Wages, Ted Fabella*
COPYWRITERS *Matt Degalan, Erin Blair*
DESIGNERS *Rory Myers, Kevin Kemmerly*
PHOTOGRAPHY *CARE Archive*
PRINTER *Williams Printing*
STUDIO *Wages Design*
CLIENT *CARE*

Merit/U.S.A.

ANNUAL REPORT
Adaptec 1995 Annual Report
ART DIRECTOR *Bill Cahan*
CREATIVE DIRECTOR *Bill Cahan*
COPYWRITER *Lindsay Beaman*
DESIGNER *Craig Clark*
ILLUSTRATOR *Steve Vance*
PRINTER *Alan Lithograph*
CLIENT *Adaptec, Inc.*

Merit/U.S.A.

ANNUAL REPORT
Barnes & Noble 1994 Annual Report
CREATIVE DIRECTOR *Kiku Obata*
COPYWRITER *Sara Harrell*
DESIGNER *Joe Floresca*
PHOTOGRAPHERS *Various*
ILLUSTRATOR *Maira Kalman*
STUDIO *Kiku Obata & Company*
CLIENT *Barnes & Noble, Inc.*

Merit/U.S.A.

ANNUAL REPORT
Earth Tech 1995 Annual Report
ART DIRECTOR *Lana Rigsby*
CREATIVE DIRECTOR *Lana Rigsby*
COPYWRITER *JoAnn Stone*
DESIGNERS *Lana Rigsby, Michael B. Thede,*
Alvin Ho Young
PHOTOGRAPHERS *Chris Shinn, Sebastião Salgado*
PRINTER *H. MacDonald Printing*
STUDIO *Rigsby Design, Inc.*
CLIENT *Earth Tech*

Merit/U.S.A.

ANNUAL REPORT
Trident Microsystems 1995 Annual Report
ART DIRECTOR *Bill Cahan*
CREATIVE DIRECTOR *Bill Cahan*
COPYWRITER *Tim Peters*
DESIGNER *Bob Dinetz*
PHOTOGRAPHERS *Various*
PRINTER *Grossberg Tyler*
STUDIO *Cahan & Associates*
CLIENT *Trident Microsystems*

(facing page)
Merit/U.S.A.

ANNUAL REPORT
Chicago Volunteer Legal Services 1995 Annual Report
ART DIRECTORS *Ted Stoik, Tim Bruce*
CREATIVE DIRECTOR *Tim Bruce*
COPYWRITING *Chicago Volunteer Legal Services*
DESIGNER *Tim Bruce*
PRINTER *Bruce Offset*
STUDIO *VSA Partners, Inc.*
CLIENT *Chicago Volunteer Legal Services*

Merit/Japan

ANNUAL REPORT
Grelan Pharmaceutical of Japan
ART DIRECTOR *Akira Oshima*
CREATIVE DIRECTOR *Akira Oshima*
COPYWRITER *Akira Oshima*
DESIGNER *Akira Oshima*
PHOTOGRAPHER *Hideo Mori*
PRODUCER *Ichiro Sano*
PRINTER *Taiyo Printing*
AGENCY *Recruit*
CLIENT *Grelan Pharmaceutical of Japan*

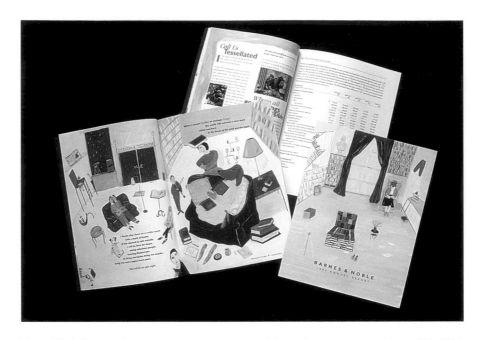

Attorneys and paralegals in Baker & McKenzie's Latin American Practice Group are accustomed to wrestling with complex international law issues for corporate clients. When the Howard Area Community Center, a CVLS client service partner for over 25 years, asked for help with Spanish-speaking clients, the Group offered to conduct a monthly clinic. The lawyers soon learned that international treaties, jurisdictional conflicts, and immigration laws can turn a routine case into a Big Challenge. Victor and Esther surmounted all these hurdles and got Iris Muñoz her divorce. "The satisfaction of helping new arrivals to this country understand and deal with our law is its own reward," reports Victor. This clientele got more help last winter when the Chicago Chapter of the American Immigration Lawyers Association opened a new clinic in our Administrative Office.

(page 14)

Divorce Case
Client. Peruvian woman in IL,
husband married w/ other woman in CA
(bigamy ??)
— 2 kids, 1 in CA w/ husband
1 in Peru w/ grandma
Client lives w/ boyfriend, boyfriend wants to marry,
has 2 daughters w/ him, pregnant w/ 3rd.
Boyfriend threatens to leave her unless she gets DIV
— Immigration Status ??

Strategy
What law applies?
Peru, IL, CA, residence of parties?
Any treaty?
Jurisdiction?
Over Parties
Over kids

— Does CA wife know H is married?
Should we say anything?

Options
— Appearance by counsel
— Agreement.

Volunteers: Victor Marroquin, Attorney, Baker & McKenzie
Esther Aranda, Paralegal, Baker & McKenzie
Baker & McKenzie Latin American Practice Group Legal Clinic
Client: Iris Muñoz

(page 15)

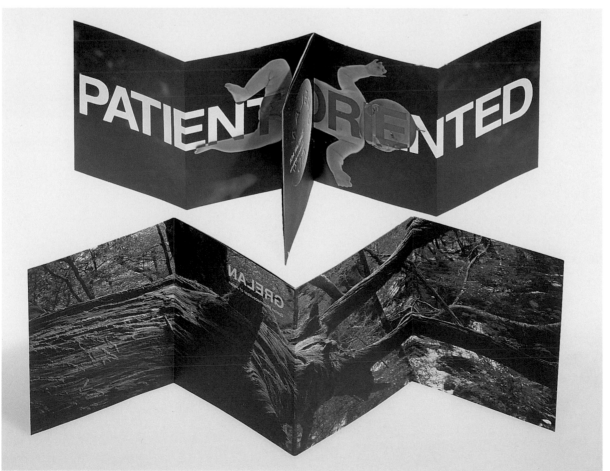

Merit/Singapore

ANNUAL REPORT
SIMEX 1994 Annual Report
CREATIVE DIRECTOR *Craig Hutton*
COPYWRITER *Chik Lynn*
DESIGNER *Craig Hutton*
PHOTOGRAPHER *Jorg Sunderman*
PRODUCER *Cindy Lim*
STUDIO *Equus Design*
CLIENT *SIMEX (Singapore International
Monetary Exchange)*

(facing page)
Merit/U.S.A.

BOOKLET OR BROCHURE
Mohawk: Chair
ART DIRECTOR *Michael Bierut*
COPYWRITER *Sam Angeloff*
DESIGNER *Esther Bridavsky*
PHOTOGRAPHERS *Various*
ILLUSTRATORS *Various*
STUDIO *Pentagram Design*
CLIENT *Mohawk Paper Mills*

Merit/U.S.A.

BOOKLET OR BROCHURE
Response 10 Program
ART DIRECTOR *Kevin Dean Budelmann*
CREATIVE DIRECTOR *Kevin Dean Budelmann*
COPYWRITERS *Nancy Nordstrom, Julie Ridl*
DESIGNER *Kevin Dean Budelmann*
PHOTOGRAPHY *Nick Merrick, James Terkeurst,
Herman Miller Archives*
ILLUSTRATION *Gould Design*
CLIENT *Herman Miller, Inc.*

Merit/U.S.A.

BOOKLET OR BROCHURE
Pottery Barn Gift Registry
ART DIRECTOR *Mauricio Arias*
CREATIVE DIRECTOR *Mauricio Arias*
COPYWRITER *Laura Martin*
DESIGNERS *Mauricio Arias, Karin Bryant*
PHOTOGRAPHER *Joyce Oudkerk Pool*
ILLUSTRATOR *Mike Halbert*
PRINTER *H. MacDonald Printing*
STUDIO *Arias Studio*
CLIENT *Pottery Barn*

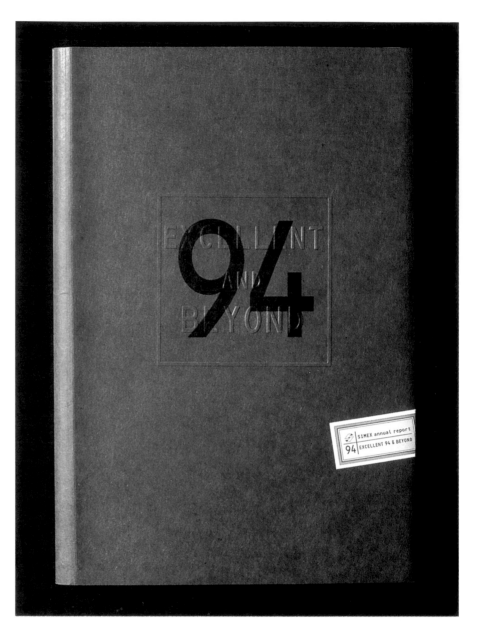

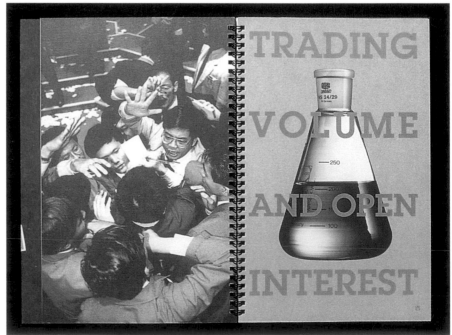

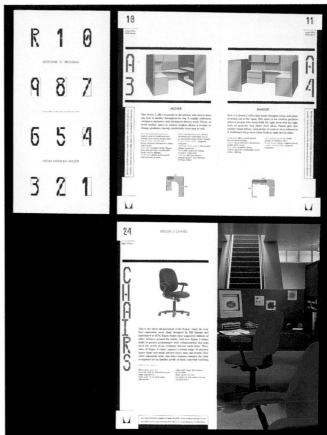

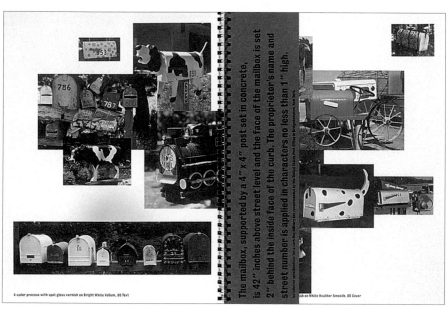

Merit/U.S.A.

BOOKLET OR BROCHURE
Mohawk: Options
ART DIRECTOR *Michael Bierut*
COPYWRITERS *Michael Bierut, Emily Hayes*
DESIGNER *Emily Hayes*
PHOTOGRAPHERS *Various*
ILLUSTRATORS *Various*
STUDIO *Pentagram Design*
CLIENT *Mohawk Paper Mills*

(facing page)
Merit/U.S.A.

BOOKLET OR BROCHURE
Rusk Source Book
ART DIRECTOR *Rick Stermole*
CREATIVE DIRECTOR *Rick Stermole*
COPYWRITER *MaryEllen Flynn*
DESIGNER *Rick Stermole*
PHOTOGRAPHERS *Troy Word, Jodi Brown*
PRINTER *Sayers Communications, Inc.*
STUDIO *StermoleStudio, Inc.*
CLIENT *Rusk Inc.*

Merit/U.S.A.

BOOKLET OR BROCHURE
South Texas College of Law 95/96 Admissions Bulletin
ART DIRECTOR *Mark Geer*
COPYWRITER *Richelle Perrone*
DESIGNERS *Mark Geer, Mandy Stewart*
PHOTOGRAPHER *Chris Shinn*
ILLUSTRATOR *Regan Dunnick*
STUDIO *Geer Design*
CLIENT *South Texas College of Law*

Merit/U.S.A.

BOOKLET OR BROCHURE
Prescriptives Fall 95
ART DIRECTOR *Kirsti Kroener*
CREATIVE DIRECTOR *James Gager*
COPYWRITER *Sally Amick*
PHOTOGRAPHER *Carlton Davis*
STUDIO *Prescriptives In-House*
CLIENT *Prescriptives*

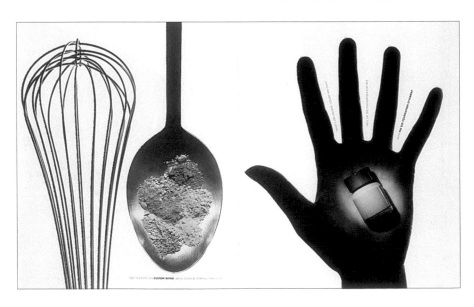

Merit/U.S.A.

BOOKLET OR BROCHURE
JBL Home Media Systems
ART DIRECTOR *Ann Gildea*
COPYWRITER *Michael Mooney*
DESIGNERS *Fred Weaver, David Warren*
PHOTOGRAPHERS *Peter Medilek, Tim Lee*
PRODUCERS *Sarah DeLeon, Jennifer Boyle*
STUDIO *Fitch Inc.*
CLIENT *JBL Consumer Products, Inc.*

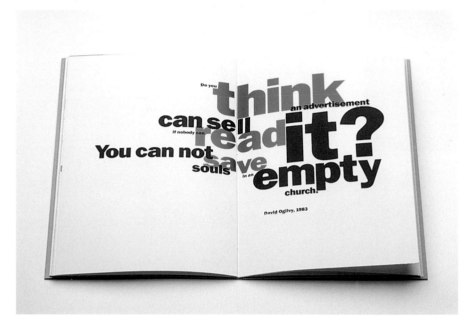

Merit/U.S.A.

BOOKLET OR BROCHURE
I Can't Read This
CREATIVE DIRECTOR *Michael Skjei*
DESIGNER *Michael Skjei*
PRINTER *Custom Color Printing*
STUDIO *M. Skjei Design Co.*
CLIENT *Shay, Shea, Hsieh & Skjei Publishers*

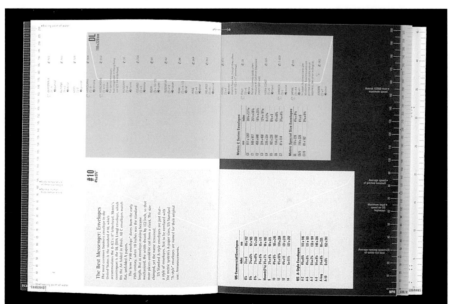

Merit/U.S.A.

BOOKLET OR BROCHURE
Crane Global Guide
ART DIRECTOR *Steff Geissbuhler*
COPYWRITER *Lisa Friedman*
DESIGNER *James D. McKibben*
STUDIO *Chermayeff & Geismar Inc.*
CLIENT *Crane*

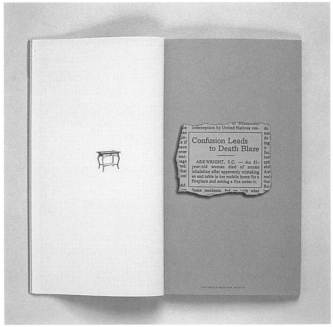

Merit/U.S.A.

BOOKLET OR BROCHURE
What the Hell Is Going on Here?
ART DIRECTOR *Sharon Werner*
CREATIVE DIRECTOR *Saul Torres*
COPYWRITING *Comedy Central*
DESIGNERS *Sharon Werner, Todd Bartz*
PHOTOGRAPHY *Comedy Central, Paul Irmiter*
ILLUSTRATOR *Sharon Werner*
PRINTER *Heartland Graphics*
STUDIO *Werner Design Werks Inc.*
AGENCY *Comedy Central*
CLIENT *Comedy Central*

Merit/U.S.A.

BOOKLET OR BROCHURE
Strange But True
ART DIRECTOR *Eric Baker*
DESIGNER *Greg Simpson*
STUDIO *Eric Baker Design Associates*
CLIENT *Gilbert Paper*

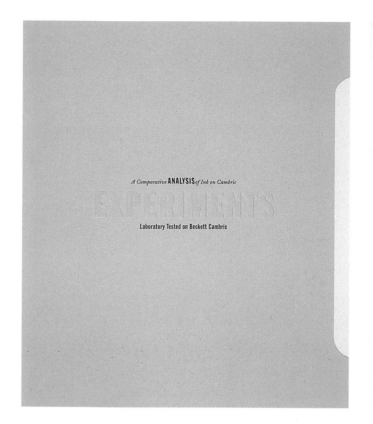

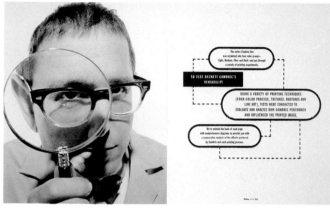

Merit/U.S.A.

BOOKLET OR BROCHURE
Experiments
ART DIRECTOR *James Koval*
COPYWRITER *Mike Noble*
DESIGNER *Steven Ryan*
ILLUSTRATORS *Jo Ann Boutin, Joy Panos Stauber*
STUDIO *VSA Partners, Inc.*
CLIENT *Northlich Stolley Lawarre*

Merit/U.S.A.

BOOKLET OR BROCHURE
Work in Progress
ART DIRECTORS *Diti Katona, John Pylypczak*
DESIGNERS *Diti Katona, John Pylypczak*
PHOTOGRAPHER *Ron Baxter Smith*
ILLUSTRATOR *John Pylypczak*
PRINTER *C.J. Graphics Inc.*
STUDIO *Concrete Design Communications Inc.*
CLIENT *C.J. Graphics Inc.*

Merit/U.S.A.

BOOKLET OR BROCHURE
Crane A6 Brochure
ART DIRECTOR *Eric Madsen*
CREATIVE DIRECTOR *Eric Madsen*
COPYWRITING *Words At Work*
DESIGNER *Eric Madsen*
ILLUSTRATORS *Lynn Schulte, Kim Feldman*
PRINTER *Fine Arts Engraving Company*
STUDIO *The Office of Eric Madsen*
CLIENT *Crane*

Merit/U.S.A.

BOOKLET OR BROCHURE
Scandia Down
ART DIRECTORS *Allison Muench, J. P. Williams*
COPYWRITER *Laura Silverman*
DESIGNERS *Allison Muench, Mats Hakansson*
PHOTOGRAPHER *William Abranowicz*
STUDIO *Design: M/W*
CLIENT *Scandia Down*

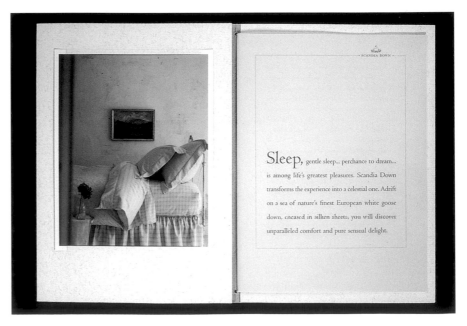

Merit/U.S.A.

BOOKLET OR BROCHURE
The Essential Nature of Things
ART DIRECTORS *Kevin Kuester, Stefan Hartung*
CREATIVE DIRECTOR *Kevin Kuester*
COPYWRITERS *Vicki Niemic, David Forney*
DESIGNER *Stefan Hartung*
PHOTOGRAPHERS *Various*
AGENCY *The Kuester Group*
CLIENT *Potlatch Corporation*

Merit/Japan

BOOKLET OR BROCHURE
Everybody Knows That
ART DIRECTOR *Satoji Kashimoto*
CREATIVE DIRECTOR *Toshio Hoshino*
COPYWRITERS *Nozomi Chiba, Toshio Hoshino*
DESIGNER *Yuji Nagai*
PHOTOGRAPHERS *Seichi Hatakeyama,*
Hideto Machikawa
CLIENT *Recruit Co., Ltd.*

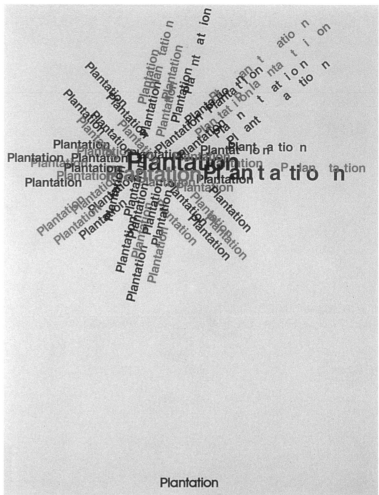

Merit/Japan

BOOKLET OR BROCHURE
Hikomizuno College of Jewelry Brochure
ART DIRECTOR *Zempaku Suzuki*
CREATIVE DIRECTOR *Kohji Yamada*
COPYWRITER *Kohji Yamada*
DESIGNER *Aritomo Ueno*
PHOTOGRAPHY *World Photo Press*
STUDIO *B·BI Studio Inc.*
CLIENT *Hikomizuno College of Jewelry*

Merit/Japan

BOOKLET OR BROCHURE
Plantation
ART DIRECTOR *Kan Akita*
DESIGNER *Masayoshi Kodaira*
PHOTOGRAPHER *NAKA*
STUDIO *Akita Design Kan Inc.*
CLIENT *Issey Miyake Inc.*

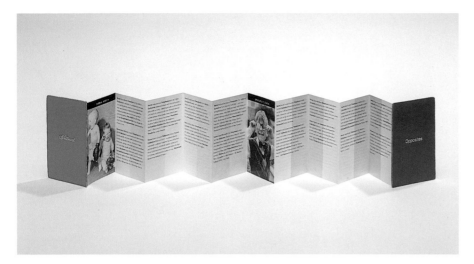

Merit/England

BOOKLET OR BROCHURE
Opposites Attract
ART DIRECTOR *Ben Casey*
CREATIVE DIRECTOR *Ben Casey*
DESIGNER *Lise Warburton*
PHOTOGRAPHY *Robert Walker, Stock*
PRINTER *West Yorkshire Print Co.*
STUDIO *The Chase Creative Consultants*
CLIENT *The University of Central Lancashire*

Merit/Germany

BOOKLET OR BROCHURE
Eine Straße zwischen
ART DIRECTOR *Sibylle Haase*
COPYWRITER *Johannes Jeltsch*
DESIGNERS *Regina Spiekerman, Katja Hirschfelder*
PHOTOGRAPHERS *Fritz Haase, Jochen Mönch,*
Jürgen Nogai, Klaus Rohmeyer, Alfred Rostek,
Stefanie Schieber
AGENCY *Atelier Haase & Knels*
CLIENT *Böttcherstraße GmbH*

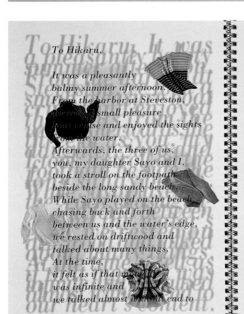

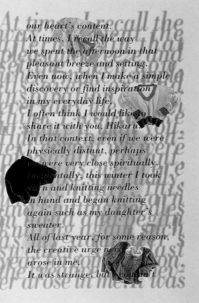

Merit/Japan

BOOKLET OR BROCHURE
Hikaru Tase Works Permanent Knit
ART DIRECTOR *Zempaku Suzuki*
CREATIVE DIRECTOR *Hideyasu Tase*
COPYWRITER *Nob Ogasawara*
DESIGNERS *Naomi Taguchi, Masahiro Naito,*
Aritomo Ueno
PHOTOGRAPHER *Tamotsu Ikeda*
STUDIO *B·BI Studio Inc.*
CLIENT *Hideyasu Tase*

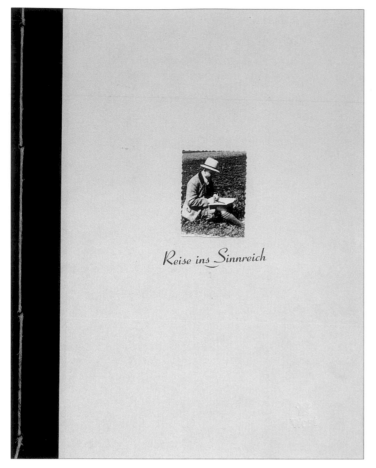

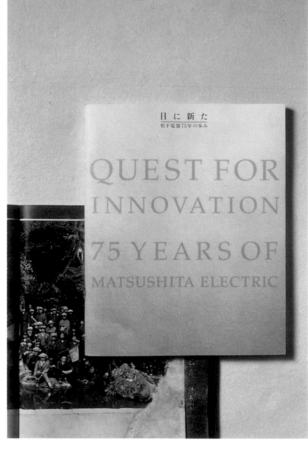

Merit/Germany

BOOKLET OR BROCHURE
Kaufhaus der Sinne
ART DIRECTOR *Helmut Himmler*
CREATIVE DIRECTOR *Rolf Greulich*
COPYWRITER *Dirk Galia*
AGENCY *Lowe & Partners / SMS*
CLIENT *Hamburger Freiheit*

Merit/Japan

BOOKLET OR BROCHURE
Quest for Innovation
ART DIRECTOR *Shinnoske Sugisaki*
CREATIVE DIRECTOR *Katsuhiko Nakamura*
DESIGNER *Shinnoske Sugisaki*
PHOTOGRAPHER *Yasunori Saito*
PRINTER *Nissha Printing Co., Ltd.*
STUDIO *Shinnoske Inc.*
AGENCY *NCP*
CLIENT *Matsushita Electric Industrial Co. Ltd.*

Merit/Canada

BOOKLET OR BROCHURE
In Sight: Media Art from the Middle of Europe
ART DIRECTORS *Diti Katona, John Pylypczak*
DESIGNERS *Diti Katona, Susan McIntee*
PRINTER *C.J. Graphics Inc.*
STUDIO *Concrete Design Communications Inc.*
CLIENT *YYZ Artists' Outlet*

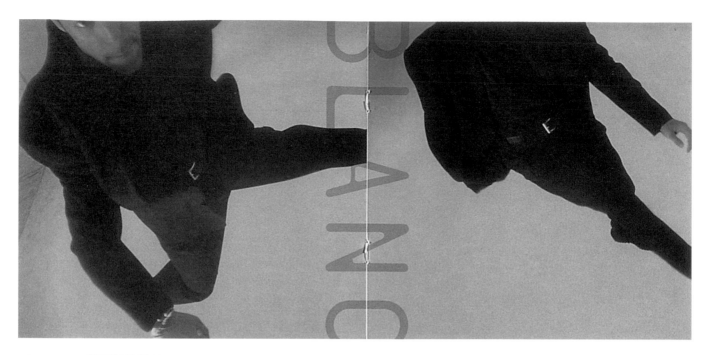

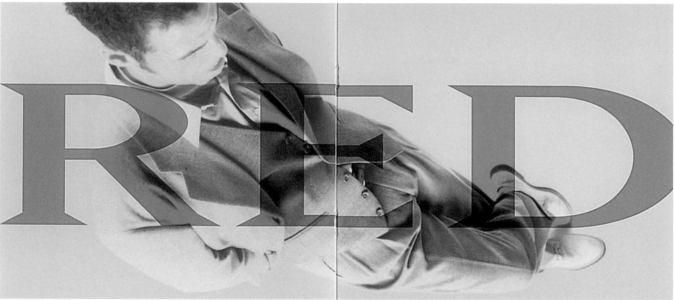

Merit/Canada

BOOKLET OR BROCHURE
Caldo: Matteo Maas Spring/Summer '96
ART DIRECTOR *Del Terrelonge*
COPYWRITER *Robin Lewis*
DESIGNERS *Del Terrelonge, Karen Oikonen*
PHOTOGRAPHER *Shin Sugino*
PRINTER *C. J. Graphics Inc.*
STUDIO *Terrelonge*
CLIENT *Matteo Maas*

Merit/U.S.A.

BOOKLET OR BROCHURE, SERIES
Gilbert Paper Letterhead Collection Series
ART DIRECTOR *Eric Baker*
COPYWRITER *Todd Lief*
DESIGNERS *Eric Baker, Greg Simpson*
STUDIO *Eric Baker Design Associates*
CLIENT *Gilbert Paper*

Merit/Japan

BOOKLET OR BROCHURE
Billionaire
ART DIRECTOR *Yuji Nagai*
CREATIVE DIRECTOR *Hitoshi Itagaki*
COPYWRITER *Katsuhiko Iida*
DESIGNER *Watch*
PHOTOGRAPHER *Jyuro Hayashi*
STUDIO *Creative Max*
CLIENT *Avex D.D. Inc.*

Merit/U.S.A.

CATALOGUE
Nylint 1996 Toy Catalog
ART DIRECTOR *Jeff Larson*
DESIGNER *Jeff Larson*
PHOTOGRAPHER *Bob Cholke*
PRINTER *Litho Productions*
STUDIO *The Larson Group*
CLIENT *Nylint Corporation*

Merit/U.S.A.

CATALOGUE
Cleveland Institute of Art 1995–96 Catalogue
ART DIRECTORS *Joyce Nesnadny, Mark Schwartz*
CREATIVE DIRECTORS *Joyce Nesnadny,*
Mark Schwartz
COPYWRITER *Anne Brooks Ranallo*
DESIGNERS *Joyce Nesnadny, Brian Lavy*
PHOTOGRAPHERS *Robert A. Muller,*
Mark Schwartz
PRINTER *Fortran Printing, Inc.*
STUDIO *Nesnadny + Schwartz*
CLIENT *Cleveland Institute of Art*

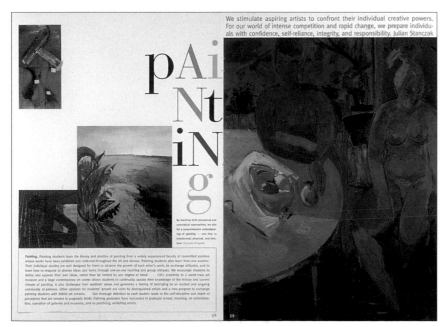

treasures dreamt of, wishes answered

Takashimaya
NEW YORK

Holidays are a time for dramatic dining rooms, elegant parties and extravagant adornments. Unique arrangements by renowned Parisian florist Christian Tortu are available through Takashimaya's in-house boutique.

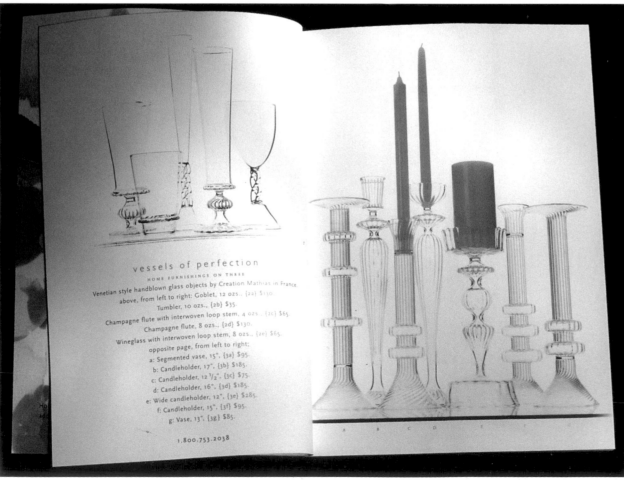

vessels of perfection

HOME FURNISHINGS ON THREE

Venetian style handblown glass objects by Creation Mathias in France.
above, from left to right: Goblet, 12 ozs., {2a} $130.
Tumbler, 10 ozs., {2b} $35.
Champagne flute with interwoven loop stem, 4 ozs., {2c} $65.
Champagne flute, 8 ozs., {2d} $130.
Wineglass with interwoven loop stem, 8 ozs., {2e} $65.
opposite page, from left to right:
a: Segmented vase, 15", {3a} $95.
b: Candleholder, 17", {3b} $185.
c: Candleholder, 12 ½", {3c} $75.
d: Candleholder, 16", {3d} $185.
e: Wide candleholder, 12", {3e} $285.
f: Candleholder, 15", {3f} $95.
g: Vase, 13", {3g} $85.

1.800.753.2038

'Fraught'

Merit/England

CATALOGUE
Diesel: We Meet
ART DIRECTOR *Brian Baderman*
CREATIVE DIRECTOR *Brian Baderman, assisted by*
Nick Oates
COPYWRITER *Brian Baderman*
DESIGNERS *Brian Baderman, Nick Oates,*
Joe Wright
PHOTOGRAPHER *Peter Gehrke*
ILLUSTRATOR *Brian Baderman*
STUDIO *Brian Baderman Design*
CLIENT *Diesel*

(facing page)
Merit/U.S.A.

CATALOGUE
Treasures Dreamt of, Wishes Answered
ART DIRECTORS *Allison Muench, J. P. Williams*
COPYWRITER *Laura Silverman*
PHOTOGRAPHER *Carlton Davis*
STUDIO *Design: M/W*
CLIENT *Takashimaya New York*

Merit/England

CATALOGUE
Robert Welch: Cutlery Direct
ART DIRECTOR *David Hillman*
COPYWRITER *David Gibbs*
DESIGNERS *David Hillman, Emily Chow*
PHOTOGRAPHER *Steve Rees*
STUDIO *Pentagram Design Ltd.*
CLIENT *Robert Welch Designs Ltd.*

Ammonite Hollow

Ammonite is a contemporary version of the traditional pistol-grip handle design which has been popular ever since the mid-eighteenth century. The cutlery is one of Robert Welch's latest designs and has bold, rounded handle ends with the decorative emphasis inspired by the spiral of the ammonite fossil. The range is unusual in that all items (except for the coffee and tea spoons) are available with hollow handles.

Spoons, forks and the hollow handles of knives are made from 18/8 stainless steel; the knife blades are made from a specially hardened stainless steel that maintains a sharp cutting edge.

SERVING SPOON
COFFEE SPOON
MEAT FORK
SLOTTED SERVING SPOON
BUTTER KNIFE

Ammonite Flat

An economical variation of Ammonite design has also been introduced, forged from thick stainless steel sheet. Each piece has the Ammonite motif stamped on its handle. Spoons and forks are made from 18/8 stainless steel and the knives are forged from a single ingot of specially hardened stainless steel that maintains a cutting edge.

Both versions of the Ammonite design are available in bright finish only, and are fully guaranteed and dishwasher-safe.

The place settings shown overleaf are actual size.

SERVING SPOON
COFFEE SPOON
MEAT FORK

Ammonite Flat

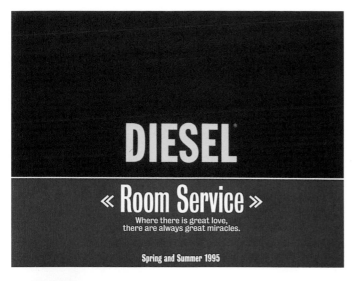

Merit/England

CATALOGUE
Diesel: Room Service
ART DIRECTOR *Brian Baderman, assisted by*
Adam Whitaker
CREATIVE DIRECTOR *Brian Baderman*
COPYWRITER *Brian Baderman*
DESIGNERS *Brian Baderman, Adam Whitaker*
PHOTOGRAPHER *Henrik Halvarsson*
PRODUCER *Brian Baderman*
STUDIO *Brian Baderman Design*
CLIENT *Diesel*

Merit/Switzerland

CATALOGUE
Lida Baday Fall '95 Collection
ART DIRECTOR *Diti Katona*
DESIGNERS *Diti Katona, Renata Chubb*
PHOTOGRAPHER *Chris Nicholls*
STUDIO *Concrete Design Communications Inc.*
AGENCY *Baker Gurney McClaren*
CLIENT *Lida Baday*

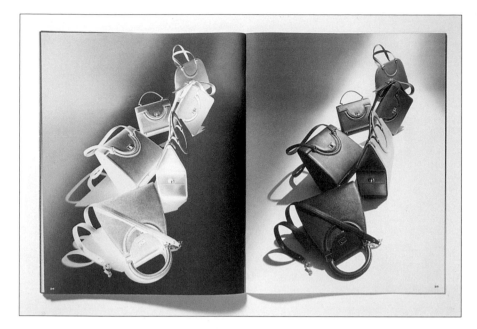

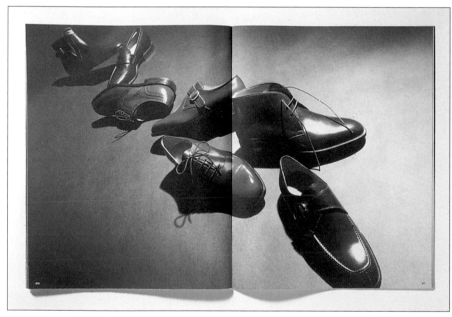

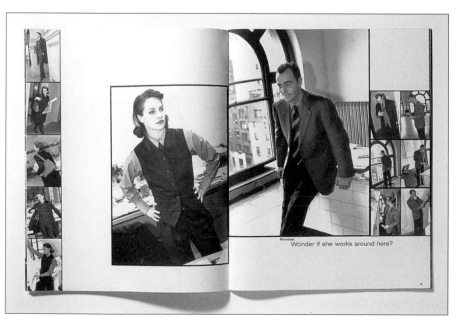

Merit/Switzerland

CATALOGUE
Bally
ART DIRECTOR *Antonie Reinhard*
CREATIVE DIRECTOR *Antonie Reinhard*
COPYWRITER *Claudia Mauner*
PHOTOGRAPHERS *Hanspeter Schneider,*
Adriano Biondo
PRINTER *Benteli Druck & Verlag, Berne*
AGENCY *Seiler DDB, Berne*
CLIENT *Bally Management AG*

Merit/England

NEWSLETTER, JOURNAL, OR HOUSE PUBLICATION
Pork No. 1
ART DIRECTORS *Alan Herron, Martyn Hey,*
Neil Smith, Mark Rollinson
CREATIVE DIRECTORS *Alan Herron, Martyn Hey,*
Neil Smith, Mark Rollinson
COPYWRITER *Neil Smith*
DESIGNERS *Alan Herron, Martyn Hey, Neil Smith,*
Mark Rollinson
PHOTOGRAPHERS *Ian Skelton, Brian Nessam*
PRINTER *Fairprint*
AGENCY *Giant Limited*
CLIENT *Giant Limited*

Council of Fashion
Designers of America

1994

Merit/U.S.A.

ENTERTAINMENT PROGRAM
CFDA 1994 Awards Program
ART DIRECTOR *Michael Bierut*
DESIGNER *Esther Bridavsky*
PHOTOGRAPHERS *Various*
ILLUSTRATORS *Various*
STUDIO *Pentagram Design*
CLIENT *Council of Fashion Designers of America*

Merit/U.S.A.

ENTERTAINMENT PROGRAM
CFDA 1994 Awards Program
ART DIRECTOR *Michael Bierut*
DESIGNER *Esther Bridavsky*

Merit/U.S.A.

TECHNICAL OR INSTRUCTION MANUAL
Fusion
CREATIVE DIRECTOR *Bill Thorburn*
COPYWRITER *Matt Elhardt*
DESIGNER *Chad Hagen*
PHOTOGRAPHER *Chuck Smith*
STUDIO *Thorburn Design*
CLIENT *Domtar*

(facing page)
Merit/U.S.A.

CORPORATE IDENTITY PROGRAM
The Little Book of Burton Fun
ART DIRECTOR *David Covell*
CREATIVE DIRECTOR *Michael Jager*
DESIGNER *John Phemister*
PRINTER *DePalma Printing*
STUDIO *Jager Di Paola Kemp Design*
CLIENT *Burton Snowboards*

Merit/Switzerland

CORPORATE IDENTITY PROGRAM
2500 Kultur/Culture
ART DIRECTORS *Andréas Netthoevel,*
Martin Gaberthüel
CREATIVE DIRECTORS *Andréas Netthoevel,*
Martin Gaberthüel
DESIGNERS *Andréas Netthoevel, Martin Gaberthüel*
PRINTER *Witschi & Co., Nidau*
AGENCY *second floor south*
CLIENT *2500 Kultur/Culture*

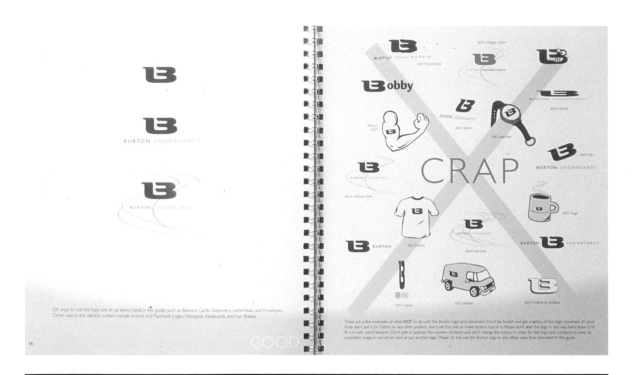

Merit/U.S.A.

STATIONERY
The Chinese Gourmet Society
ART DIRECTORS *Robert Reitzfeld, Allan Beaver*
CREATIVE DIRECTORS *Robert Reitzfeld,*
Allan Beaver
COPYWRITERS *Robert Reitzfeld, Allan Beaver*
DESIGNERS *Robert Reitzfeld, Allan Beaver*
ILLUSTRATOR *Robert Reitzfeld*
PRINTER *A & M Litho*
AGENCY *Beaver Reitzfeld*
CLIENT *The Chinese Gourmet Society*

Merit/U.S.A.

STATIONERY
Michael Patrick Partners
ART DIRECTORS *Duane Maidens, Daniel O'Brien*
DESIGNERS *Roy Tazuma, Michael Mescal*
STUDIO *Michael Patrick Partners*
CLIENT *Michael Patrick Partners*

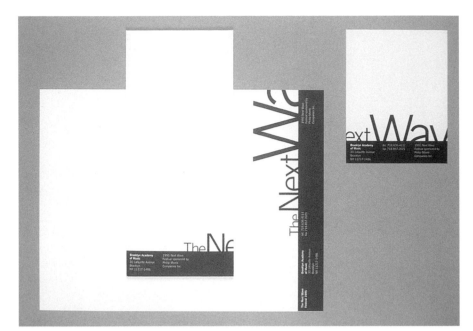

Merit/U.S.A.

STATIONERY
Next Wave Festival Stationery
ART DIRECTOR *Michael Bierut*
DESIGNERS *Michael Bierut, Emily Hayes*
STUDIO *Pentagram Design*
CLIENT *Brooklyn Academy of Music*

Merit/U.S.A.

STATIONERY
GoodNet
ART DIRECTION *After Hours Creative*
CREATIVE DIRECTION *After Hours Creative*
DESIGN *After Hours Creative*
STUDIO *After Hours Creative*
CLIENT *GoodNet*

Lakeland Elementary School

Lewisville I.S.D.

800 Fox Avenue

School (214) 436-2712

Lewisville, Texas 75067

Home (214) 394-1397

Jim Ayres

Educator

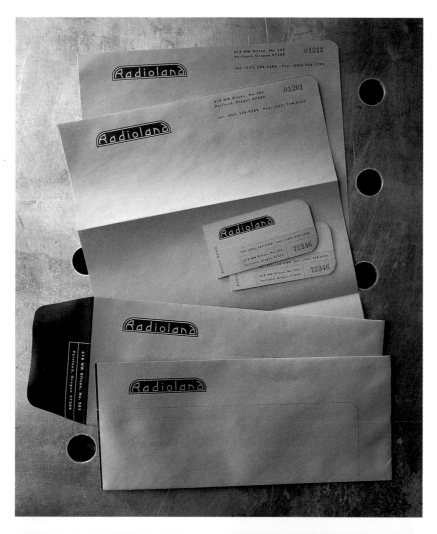

Merit/U.S.A.

STATIONERY
Radioland
ART DIRECTOR *Steve Sandstrom*
CREATIVE DIRECTOR *Steve Sandstrom*
DESIGNER *Steve Sandstrom*
STUDIO *Sandstrom Design*
CLIENT *Radioland*

Merit/U.S.A.

STATIONERY
Big Flower Press Stationery
ART DIRECTOR *Susan Hochbaum*
CREATIVE DIRECTOR *Generosa Ammon*
DESIGNER *Susan Hochbaum*
PHOTOGRAPHERS *John Endress, Kathy Grove*
STUDIO *Susan Hochbaum Design*
CLIENT *Big Flower Press*

(facing page)
Merit/U.S.A.

STATIONERY
Jim Ayres Business Card
ART DIRECTOR *Robin Ayres*
DESIGNER *Robin Ayres*
PRINTER *Image Express, Williamson Printing*
STUDIO *RBMM/The Richards Group*
CLIENT *Jim Ayres*

Merit/U.S.A.

STATIONERY
Michael Reiff & Associates
ART DIRECTORS *Nora Vaivads, Dean Hacohen*
CREATIVE DIRECTOR *Gary Goldsmith*
PHOTOGRAPHER *Ilan Rubin*
AGENCY *Goldsmith/Jeffrey*
CLIENT *Michael Reiff & Associates*

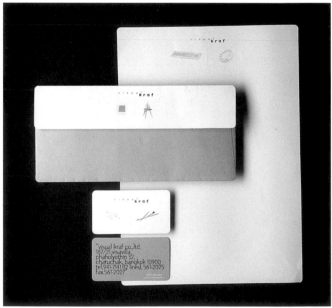

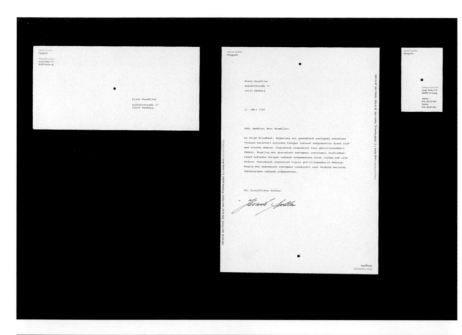

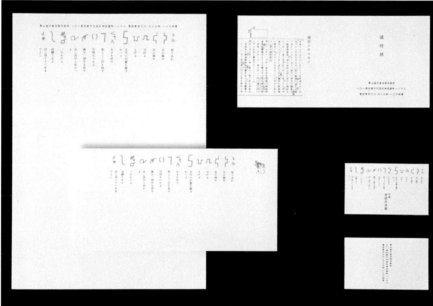

Merit/Germany

STATIONERY
Fotografenkontor
ART DIRECTOR *Hans Günter Schmitz*
DESIGNER *Hans Günter Schmitz*
STUDIO *Hans Günter Schmitz,*
Gruppe für Visuelle Kommunikation
CLIENT *Fotografenkontor*

Merit/Japan

STATIONERY
AOYAMA-Shinkodo Letterpress Co., Ltd. Stationery
ART DIRECTOR *Akihiko Tsukamoto*
DESIGNER *Akihiko Tsukamoto*
PRINTER *TRI Company Limited*
STUDIO *Design Club*
CLIENT *Yamato Inc.*

(facing page)
Merit/Japan

STATIONERY
Osaka University Medical School
ART DIRECTOR *Shinnoske Sugisaki*
CREATIVE DIRECTOR *Toru Hayakawa, M.D.*
DESIGNER *Shinnoske Sugisaki*
STUDIO *Shinnoske Inc.*
CLIENT *Osaka University Medical School,*
Department of Neurosurgery

Merit/England

STATIONERY
September Stationery
CREATIVE DIRECTOR *Richard Scholey*
DESIGNER *Richard Scholey*
PHOTOGRAPHER *Robert Walker*
TYPOGRAPHER *Andrew Harkcom*
STUDIO *The Chase Creative Consultants*
CLIENT *September Brasserie & Hair Studio*

Merit/Thailand

STATIONERY
How
ART DIRECTORS *Chatchaval Khonkajee,*
Nakoon Tachaputthapong
CREATIVE DIRECTORS *Chatchaval Khonkajee,*
Nakoon Tachaputthapong
COPYWRITER *Chanin Chiwasriprugta*
DESIGNERS *Chatchaval Khonkajee,*
Nakoon Tachaputthapong
STUDIO *Blind Co. Ltd.*
CLIENT *How Company Limited*

Merit/Thailand

STATIONERY
Visual Kraf
ART DIRECTORS *Chatchaval Khonkajee,*
Nakoon Tachaputthapong
CREATIVE DIRECTORS *Chatchaval Khonkajee,*
Nakoon Tachaputthapong
DESIGNERS *Chatchaval Khonkajee,*
Nakoon Tachaputthapong
ILLUSTRATOR *Saharut Sirichai*
STUDIO *Blind Co. Ltd.*
CLIENT *Visual Kraf Co., Ltd.*

Merit/U.S.A.

LOGO OR TRADEMARK
Columbus Bakery
ART DIRECTOR *Mark Randall*
COPYWRITER *Mark Randall*
ILLUSTRATOR *Ward Schumaker*
STUDIO *World Studio*
CLIENT *Columbus Bakery*

Merit/U.S.A.

LOGO OR TRADEMARK
Local Commotion
ART DIRECTOR *Steven Brower*
DESIGNER *Steven Brower*
ILLUSTRATOR *Steven Brower*
AGENCY *Steven Brower Design*
CLIENT *Local Commotion Repertory*

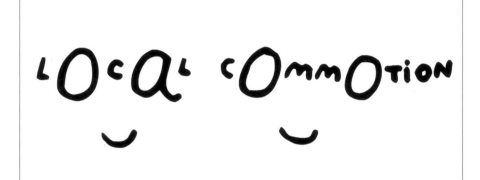

Merit/U.S.A.

LOGO OR TRADEMARK
Typhoon Restaurant
ART DIRECTOR *Barbara Lee*
DESIGNER *Rodney Davidson*
STUDIO *DogStar*
AGENCY *Suka & Friends Design*
CLIENT *Typhoon Restaurant*

Merit/U.S.A.

LOGO OR TRADEMARK
Go Spot Go Car Wash
ART DIRECTOR *Steve Sandstrom*
CREATIVE DIRECTOR *Steve Sandstrom*
DESIGNER *Steve Sandstrom*
ILLUSTRATORS *Steve Sandstrom, Donjiro Ban*
STUDIO *Sandstrom Design*
CLIENT *Go Spot Go Car Wash*

Merit/U.S.A.

LOGO OR TRADEMARK
Think
DESIGNER *Tasso Stathopulos*
ILLUSTRATOR *Tasso Stathopulos*
AGENCY *Populos Inc.*
CLIENT *Think Advertising Agency*

Merit/U.S.A.

LOGO OR TRADEMARK
The Dallas Symphony Orchestra
ART DIRECTOR *Horacio Cobos*
CREATIVE DIRECTOR *Horacio Cobos*
DESIGNER *Horacio Cobos*
ILLUSTRATOR *Horacio Cobos*
STUDIO *RBMM/The Richards Group*
CLIENT *The Dallas Symphony Orchestra*

Merit/Australia

LOGO OR TRADEMARK
Café Racer
ART DIRECTOR *Andrew Hoyne*
DESIGNERS *Andrew Hoyne, Amanda McPherson*
ILLUSTRATORS *Andrew Hoyne, Amanda McPherson*
STUDIO *Andrew Hoyne Design*
CLIENT *Café Racer*

(facing page)
Merit/U.S.A.

PUBLIC SERVICE
*The Robin Hood Foundation Guerrilla Philanthropists
Brochure*
ART DIRECTOR *Jason Gaboriau*
CREATIVE DIRECTOR *Gary Goldsmith*
COPYWRITER *Justin Rohrlich*
ILLUSTRATOR *Christian Northeast*
PRINTER *Trejon*
AGENCY *Goldsmith/Jeffrey*
CLIENT *The Robin Hood Foundation*

Merit/Austria

PRESS OR PROMOTIONAL KIT
ORF Programm 96
ART DIRECTOR *Gustav Lohrmann*
CREATIVE DIRECTOR *Michael Hajek*
COPYWRITING *ORF Public Relations*
DESIGNER *Peter Ujfalusi*
PHOTOGRAPHY *ORF*
PRODUCTION *ORF*
PRINTER *Sares Verlag GmbH/Pindur Displays*
CLIENT *ORF (Austrian Broadcasting Corporation)*

(facing page)
Merit/U.S.A.

SELF-PROMOTION
Peanuts
ART DIRECTOR *Rodney Davidson*
COPYWRITER *Rodney Davidson*
ILLUSTRATOR *Rodney Davidson*
STUDIO *DogStar*
CLIENT *DogStar*

Merit/U.S.A.

SELF-PROMOTION
Deck of Cards
ART DIRECTORS *Steve Gibbs, Willie Baronet*
CREATIVE DIRECTORS *Willie Baronet, Steve Gibbs*
COPYWRITER *Willie Baronet*
DESIGNERS *Willie Baronet, Steve Gibbs,*
Kellye Kimball
PHOTOGRAPHER *Eric Pearle*
PRINTER *Padgett Printing*
STUDIO *Gibbs Baronet*
CLIENT *Gibbs Baronet*

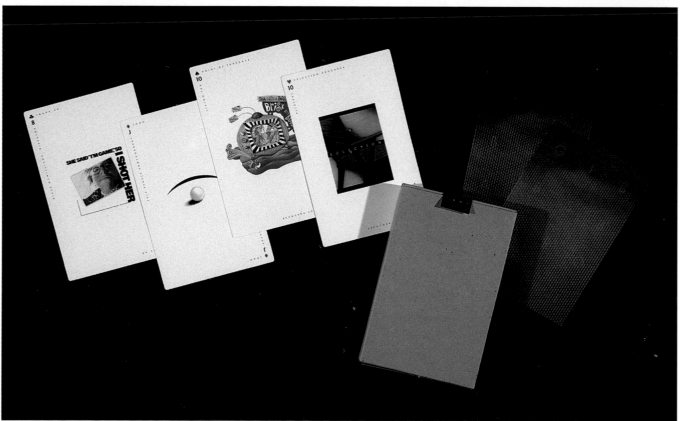

Merit/U.S.A.

SELF-PROMOTION
Jack Macholl
ART DIRECTORS *Ted Stoik, Tim Bruce*
CREATIVE DIRECTOR *Tim Bruce*
COPYWRITERS *Jack Macholl, Ted Stoik*
DESIGNER *Tim Bruce*
PRINTER *Dupligraphics*
STUDIO *VSA Partners, Inc.*
CLIENT *Jack Macholl*

Merit/U.S.A.

SELF-PROMOTION
Seeing
ART DIRECTOR *Jeff Lin*
CREATIVE DIRECTOR *Mike Scricco*
COPYWRITER *Mel Maffei*
DESIGNER *Jeff Lin*
PHOTOGRAPHER *Nick Pavloff*
STUDIO *Keiler Design Group*
CLIENT *Lithographics, Inc.*

(facing page)
Merit/U.S.A.

SELF-PROMOTION
Gizmo
ART DIRECTOR *Rick Vaughn*
CREATIVE DIRECTOR *Rick Vaughn*
COPYWRITING *Vaughn Wedeen Creative*
DESIGNER *Rick Vaughn*
PRINTER *Albuquerque Printing*
STUDIO *Vaughn Wedeen Creative*
CLIENT *Vaughn Wedeen Creative*

Merit/Canada

SELF-PROMOTION
Fire Flip Book
ART DIRECTORS *Christine Lajeunesse,*
Orazio Fantini
CREATIVE DIRECTOR *Christine Lajeunesse*
DESIGNER *Orazio Fantini*
ILLUSTRATOR *Diane O'Bomsawin*
PRODUCER *Sophie Simonnet*
PRINTER *Paul Paradis*
PUBLISHER *Diana Shearwood*
STUDIO *Discreet Logic Design Group*
CLIENT *Discreet Logic Design Group*

Merit/Scotland

SELF-PROMOTION
EH6 New Year's Card
CREATIVE DIRECTORS *Graham Walker, Ian McIlroy*
DESIGNER *Graham Walker*
STUDIO *EH6 Design Consultants*
CLIENT *EH6 Design Consultants*

[JACK MACHOLL]

I'm looking for a position in which I can contribute to business success – a place to hang my hat long-term.

I'm eager to meet face-to-face to discuss my background and opportunities to make a difference for a dynamic organization.

Thank you for your consideration.

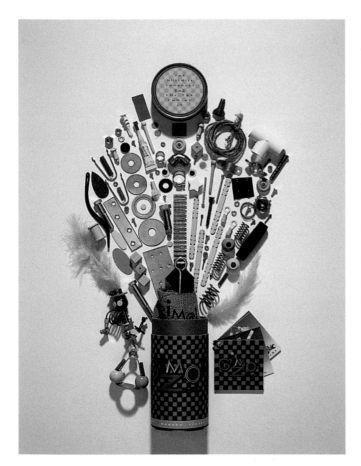

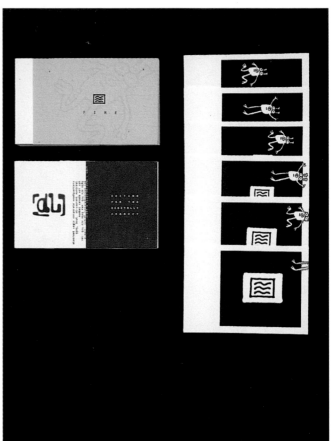

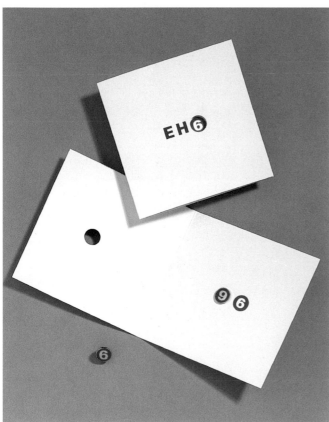

Merit/England

SELF-PROMOTION
Cigar Papers
ART DIRECTOR *John McConnell*
COPYWRITER *Juliet Barclay*
DESIGNERS *John McConnell, Justus Oehler,*
Kristina Langhein
PHOTOGRAPHERS *Nick Turner, Amanda Clement*
STUDIO *Pentagram Design Ltd.*
CLIENT *Pentagram Design Ltd.*

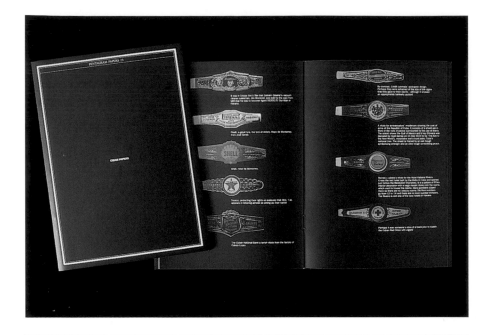

Merit/England

SELF-PROMOTION
The Pressman's Hat
ART DIRECTOR *John McConnell*
DESIGNERS *John McConnell, Alan Dye*
PHOTOGRAPHER *Nick Turner*
STUDIO *Pentagram Design Ltd.*
CLIENT *Pentagram Design Ltd.*

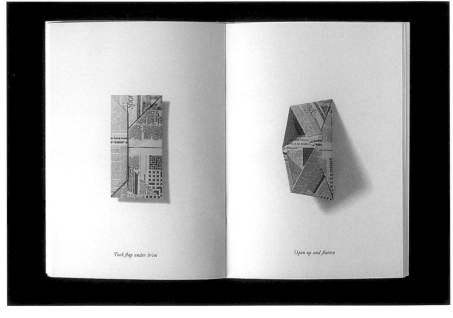

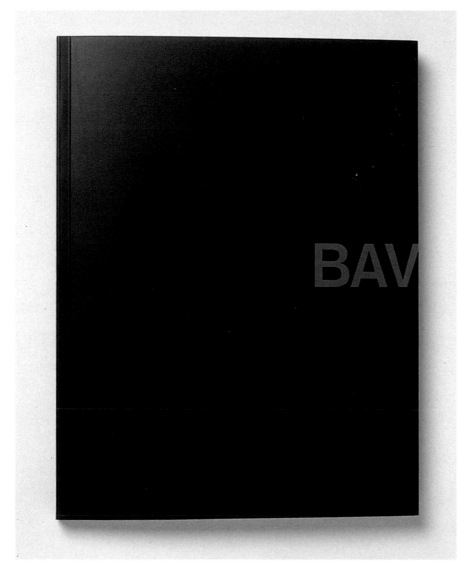

Merit/Switzerland

SELF-PROMOTION
Baviera P.K.W.
ART DIRECTOR *Michael Baviera*
CREATIVE DIRECTOR *Siegrun Nuber*
COPYWRITER *Michael Baviera*
DESIGNER *Michael Baviera*
STUDIO *BBV*
CLIENT *Michael Baviera*

Merit/Switzerland

SELF-PROMOTION
Baviera P.K.W.
ART DIRECTOR *Michael Baviera*
CREATIVE DIRECTOR *Siegrun Nuber*
COPYWRITER *Michael Baviera*
DESIGNER *Michael Baviera*
STUDIO *BBV*
CLIENT *Michael Baviera*

Merit/Finland

SELF-PROMOTION
1945 Kirjapaino Koteva 1995
ART DIRECTOR *Erkki Ruuhinen*
CREATIVE DIRECTOR *Erkki Ruuhinen*
COPYWRITERS *Reijo Mäki, Erkki Ruuhinen*
DESIGNERS *Erkki Ruuhinen, Pia Pirhonen*
PRINTER *Koteva Printing House*
STUDIO *Erkki Ruuhinen Design*
CLIENT *Koteva Printing House*

Merit/England

SELF-PROMOTION
ISTD Fine Paper
ART DIRECTOR *Aziz Cami*
CREATIVE DIRECTOR *Aziz Cami*
COPYWRITER *Beryl McAlhone*
DESIGNERS *Marita Lashro, Andrew Howell*
PHOTOGRAPHER *John Swannell*
PRINTER *CTD*
STUDIO *The Partners*
CLIENT *ISTD Fine Paper Ltd.*

Merit/Thailand

SELF-PROMOTION
Thongchai McIntyre, "Feather and Flowers"
ART DIRECTOR *Lee Wattana Worawut*
CREATIVE DIRECTOR *Lee Wattana Worawut*
DESIGNER *Lee Wattana Worawut*
PHOTOGRAPHER *Pernpanich Phapra*
ILLUSTRATORS *Lee Wattana Worawut,*
Kamonsiripichiphorn Atthaphorn
PRINTER *Plus Press Co. Ltd.*
AGENCY *Grammy Entertainment Public Co. Ltd.*
(Thailand)
CLIENT *Grammy Entertainment Public Co. Ltd.*
(Thailand)

Merit/U.S.A.

SELF-PROMOTION, SERIES
Les Art Florissants Fundraising/Promotional Brochures
ART DIRECTOR *Dan Koh*
CREATIVE DIRECTOR *Dan Koh*
PROJECT MANAGER *Lyn Clerget*
ACCOUNT DIRECTOR *David Stewart*
PHOTOGRAPHER *Doug Rosa*
PRINTER *Dolan Wohlers*
STUDIO *Addison Design Company*
CLIENT *The American Friends of Les Arts Florissants*

Merit/U.S.A.

SELF-PROMOTION, SERIES
Jager Di Paola Kemp Design Postcards
ART DIRECTORS *Michael Jager, Janet Johnson,*
Christopher Vice
CREATIVE DIRECTOR *Michael Jager*
DESIGNERS *Keith Brown, David Covell,*
Richard Curren, Steve Farrar, Kirk James,
George Mench, Steve Redmond, Karin Johnson,
Dan Sharp, Michael Shea, Mark Sylvester,
Andrew Szurley, Christopher Vice
PHOTOGRAPHERS *Geoff Fosbrook, Michael Jager,*
Kirk James
ILLUSTRATORS *Keith Brown, David Covell,*
Cam DeLeon
STUDIO *Jager Di Paola Kemp Design*
CLIENT *Jager Di Paola Kemp Design*

Merit/U.S.A.

SELF-PROMOTION, SERIES
Baker Design Associates Self-Promotion
ART DIRECTOR *Gary Robert Baker*
CREATIVE DIRECTORS *Gary Robert Baker,*
Roxanne White
COPYWRITER *Robert Bailey*
DESIGNER *Yee-Ping Cho*
PHOTOGRAPHY *Vintage*
PRINTER *Costello Brothers Lithographers, Inc.*
STUDIO *Baker Design Associates*
CLIENT *Baker Design Associates*

Merit/U.S.A.

SELF-PROMOTION, SERIES
Joanie Bernstein's Illustrators
ART DIRECTOR *Sharon Werner*
DESIGNERS *Sharon Werner, Sarah Nelson*
ILLUSTRATORS *Dan Picasso, Eric Hanson,*
Jack Molloy
STUDIO *Werner Design Werks Inc.*
CLIENT *Joanie Bernstein*

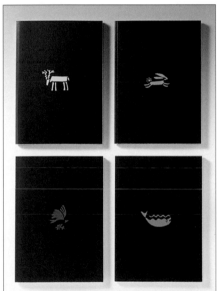

Merit/Germany

SELF-PROMOTION, SERIES
1996 Calendars
ART DIRECTORS *Bene von Schorlemer, Claus Koch*
CREATIVE DIRECTOR *Claus Koch*
DESIGNERS *Claus Koch, Heiner Nitsch,*
Bene von Schorlemer
ILLUSTRATOR *Josephine Prokop*
AGENCY *Claus Koch Corporate Communications*
CLIENT *Claus Koch Corporate Communications*

ADDITIONAL AWARD

Merit
CORPORATE AND PROMOTIONAL
COMMUNICATIONS, CALENDAR

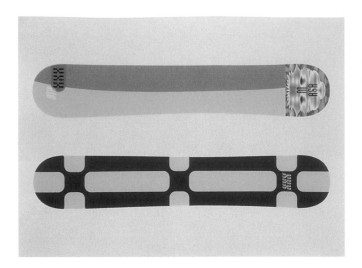

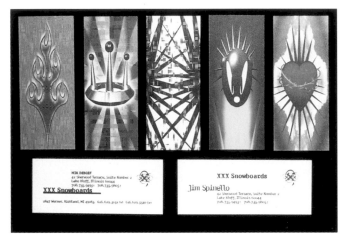

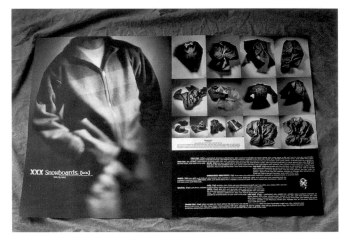

Merit/U.S.A.

MIXED-MEDIA OR SPECIALTY PROMOTION
XXX Snowboards
ART DIRECTOR *Carlos Segura*
CREATIVE DIRECTOR *Carlos Segura*
COPYWRITING *XXX Snowboards*
DESIGNER *Carlos Segura*
PHOTOGRAPHER *Jeff Sciortino*
ILLUSTRATORS *Tony Klassen, Carlos Segura*
PRINTER *Bradley*
STUDIO *Segura Inc.*
CLIENT *XXX Snowboards*

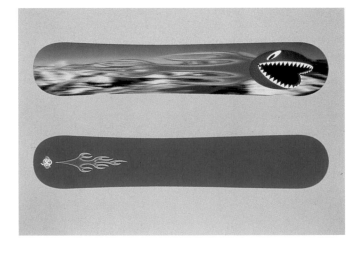

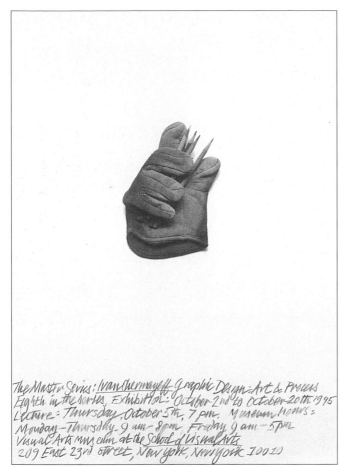

Merit/U.S.A.

MIXED-MEDIA OR SPECIALTY PROMOTION, SERIES
The Master Series: Ivan Chermayeff
ART DIRECTOR *Ivan Chermayeff*
COPYWRITERS *Ikko Tanaka, Ivan Chermayeff*
DESIGNER *Ivan Chermayeff*
PHOTOGRAPHY *Gamma One Conversions, Various*
ILLUSTRATOR *Ivan Chermayeff*
PRINTERS *Canfield Printing Co.,*
Kenner Printing Co.
STUDIO *Chermayeff & Geismar Inc.*
CLIENT *Visual Arts Museum at the School of*
Visual Arts

Merit/U.S.A.

MIXED-MEDIA OR SPECIALTY PROMOTION, SERIES
Howard Bjornson: Color, Elements
ART DIRECTOR *James Koval*
DESIGNERS *James Koval, Steve Ryan*
PHOTOGRAPHER *Howard Bjornson*
STUDIO *VSA Partners, Inc.*
CLIENT *Howard Bjornson Photography*

Merit/U.S.A.

ANNOUNCEMENT OR INVITATION

Envisioning Change

ART DIRECTOR *Robert Vogele*

CREATIVE DIRECTORS *Curt Schreiber, Adam Smith,*
Jeff Breazeale

COPYWRITERS *Mike Noble, Robert Vogele*

DESIGNERS *Curt Schreiber, Adam Smith*

PRINTER *Dupligraphics*

STUDIO *VSA Partners, Inc.*

CLIENT *VSA Partners, Inc.*

Merit/U.S.A.

ANNOUNCEMENT OR INVITATION

Elite Model Management Invitation

ART DIRECTOR *Del Terrelonge*

COPYWRITER *Robin Lewis*

DESIGNERS *Del Terrelonge, Karen Oikonen*

PHOTOGRAPHER *Shin Sugino*

PRINTER *C.J. Graphics Inc.*

STUDIO *Terrelonge*

CLIENT *Elite Toronto Ltd.*

Merit/U.S.A.

ANNOUNCEMENT OR INVITATION

World Financial Center Invitation

ART DIRECTOR *Daniel Miyahara*

CREATIVE DIRECTORS *Simon Doonan,*
Bonnie Solomon

COPYWRITER *Daniel Miyahara*

DESIGNER *Daniel Miyahara*

AGENCY *Barneys New York Advertising*

CLIENT *Barneys New York*

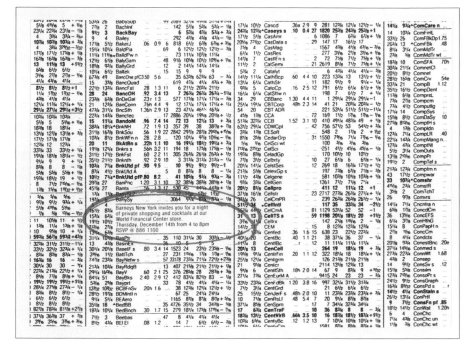

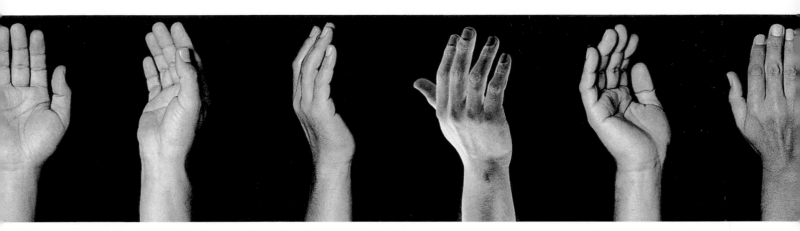

Merit/Japan

ANNOUNCEMENT OR INVITATION
Matsuda Spring/Summer 1996 Collection Invitation
ART DIRECTOR *Hideki Nakajima*
DESIGNER *Hideki Nakajima*
PHOTOGRAPHER *NAKA*
ARTIST *Yukio Kobayashi*
STUDIO *Nakajima Design*
CLIENT *Nicole Co., Ltd.*

Merit/U.S.A.

GREETING CARD OR NOTECARD, SERIES
The J. Paul Getty Museum Postcards
DESIGNER *Vickie Sawyer Karten*
PHOTOGRAPHER *Alexander Vertikoff*
PRINTER *Anderson Lithograph*
STUDIO *The J. Paul Getty Trust, Publication Services*
CLIENT *The J. Paul Getty Trust*

Merit/U.S.A.

CALENDAR OR APPOINTMENT BOOK
1996 Calendar
ART DIRECTOR *Peter King Robbins*
CREATIVE DIRECTOR *Peter King Robbins*
COPYWRITER *Tabitha De La Torre*
DESIGNER *Peter King Robbins*
PHOTOGRAPHERS *Amedeo, Glen Erler*
PRINTER *Foundation Press*
STUDIO *BRD Design*
CLIENT *BRD Design*

Merit/U.S.A.

CALENDAR OR APPOINTMENT BOOK
ASMP 1996 Calendar
ART DIRECTOR *Steve Sandstrom*
CREATIVE DIRECTOR *Steve Sandstrom*
DESIGNER *Steve Sandstrom*
PHOTOGRAPHY *ASMP Oregon Members*
STUDIO *Sandstrom Design*
CLIENT *ASMP Oregon*

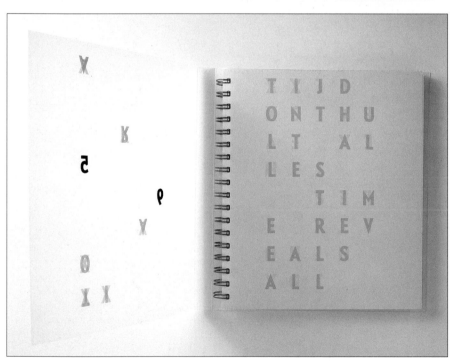

Merit/The Netherlands

CALENDAR OR APPOINTMENT BOOK
1995 Calendar
CREATIVE DIRECTOR *Hans Bockting*
COPYWRITER *Meghan Ferrill*
DESIGNERS *Hans Bockting, Will de l'Eluse*
PHOTOGRAPHER *Reinier Gerritsen*
PRINTER *Koopmans' Drukkerij*
STUDIO *UNA*
CLIENTS *UNA, Bij-voorbeeld, Koopmans' Drukkerij*

 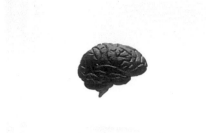 

 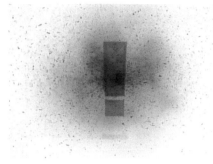 

Merit/U.S.A.

STATION ID OR BROADCAST GRAPHICS
E! Fly ID
ART DIRECTOR *Reuben Lee*
CREATIVE DIRECTOR *Andy Hann*
DESIGNER *Reuben Lee*
ILLUSTRATOR *Reuben Lee*
PRODUCER *Karin Rainey*
AGENCY *E! Entertainment Television*
CLIENT *E! Entertainment Television*

Merit/U.S.A.

STATION ID OR BROADCAST GRAPHICS
E! Relief ID
ART DIRECTOR *Reuben Lee*
CREATIVE DIRECTOR *Andy Hann*
DESIGNER *Reuben Lee*
PRODUCER *Karin Rainey*
AGENCY *E! Entertainment Television*
CLIENT *E! Entertainment Television*

ADDITIONAL AWARD

Merit
TELEVISION, FILM, AND VIDEO, SPECIAL EFFECTS

Merit/U.S.A.

STATION ID OR BROADCAST GRAPHICS
Black List: Hollywood on Trial
ART DIRECTOR *Ada Whitney*
CREATIVE DIRECTOR *Ada Whitney*
DESIGNER *Roberto Gonzalez*
PHOTOGRAPHER *Ralph Petrie*
PRODUCER *Marion Rosenfeld*
EDITOR *Jon Vesey*
AGENCY *Beehive*
CLIENT *American Movie Classics*

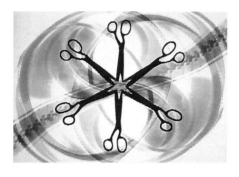  

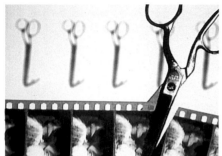  

Merit/U.S.A.

STATION ID OR BROADCAST GRAPHICS
Cut to the Chase
ART DIRECTOR *Ulrike Kerber*
CREATIVE DIRECTOR *Andy Hann*
DESIGNER *Ulrike Kerber*
PRODUCER *Karin Rainey*
COMPOSER *Elyse Schiller*
AGENCY *E! Entertainment Television*
CLIENT *E! Entertainment Television*

Merit/Argentina

STATION ID OR BROADCAST GRAPHICS
Fiber Optics
ART DIRECTOR *Guillermo Stein*
CREATIVE DIRECTOR *Guillermo Stein*
COPYWRITER *Hugo Raffinetti*
DESIGNER *Federico Martini*
PRODUCER *Federico Martini*
DIRECTOR *Federico Martini*
STUDIO *Multimedios America*
CLIENT *CableVisión TCI²*

Merit/Argentina

STATION ID OR BROADCAST GRAPHICS
Suspenso Sin Cortes
ART DIRECTOR *Guillermo Stein*
CREATIVE DIRECTOR *Guillermo Stein*
PRODUCERS *Federico Martini, Fernando Boscolo*
DIRECTOR *Federico Martini*
MUSIC *Daniel Goldberg*
STUDIO *Multimedios America*
CLIENT *America TV Channel*

Merit/U.S.A.

STATION ID OR BROADCAST GRAPHICS, SERIES
VH1 Premiere Videos
ART DIRECTOR *Dan Appel*
CREATIVE DIRECTOR *Lauren Zalaznick*
DESIGNER *Liz Daggar*
PRODUCERS *Rob Grobengieser, Cari Ellen Shields*
COMPOSER *Ed Potakar*
AGENCY *VH1 On-Air Promos*
CLIENT *VH1*

Merit/U.S.A.

STATION ID OR BROADCAST GRAPHICS, SERIES
Feature Presentation Opening, Open All Night,
Inside the Dream Factory
ART DIRECTOR *Shannon Davis Forsyth*
CREATIVE DIRECTOR *Jakob Trollbeck*
DESIGNERS *Jakob Trollbeck, Kyle Cooper,*
Michael Riley
PRODUCER *Glen Kessner*
STUDIO *R/GA Digital Studios*
CLIENT *Turner Classic Movies*

Merit/England

STATION ID OR BROADCAST GRAPHICS, SERIES
The Disney Channel
CREATIVE DIRECTOR *Brian Eley*
DESIGNER *Jason Keeley*
DIRECTOR *Jason Keeley*
ACCOUNT DIRECTOR *Celia Chapman*
AGENCY *Lambie – Nairn*
CLIENT *The Disney Channel*

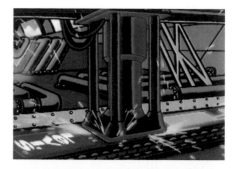

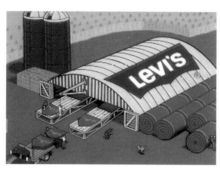

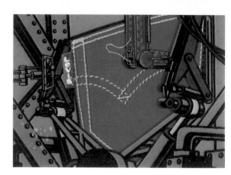

Merit/U.S.A.

SPECIAL EFFECTS
Beach Blanket
ART DIRECTOR *Brook Boley*
CREATIVE DIRECTOR *Mark Erwin*
COPYWRITER *Avery Carroll*
EXECUTIVE PRODUCER *Robin Skirboll*
AGENCY PRODUCERS *Gary Paticoff, Jack Epsteen*
SPECIAL EFFECTS PRODUCER *Susan Davis*
SPECIAL EFFECTS DIRECTOR *Jonathan Keeton*
SPECIAL EFFECTS *Simon Mowbray*
DIRECTOR *Richard Kizu-Blair*
STUDIO *Good Pictures!*
AGENCY *Rubin Postaer & Associates*
CLIENT *American Honda Motor Co., Inc.*

Merit/U.S.A.

ANIMATION
Farm
ART DIRECTOR *Leslie Caldwell*
CREATIVE DIRECTOR *Mike Koelker*
COPYWRITER *Mike Koelker*
DESIGNER *Douglas Fraser*
PRODUCER *Anna Frost*
DIRECTOR *J. J. Sedelmaier*
ANIMATOR *Tony Eastman*
PHOTOGRAPHER *Daniel Esterman*
ILLUSTRATOR *Douglas Fraser*
MUSIC *Elias West*
STUDIO *J. J. Sedelmaier Productions, Inc.*
AGENCY *Foote, Cone & Belding, San Francisco*
CLIENT *Levi Strauss & Co.*

Merit/U.S.A.

ANIMATION
Factory
ART DIRECTOR *Leslie Caldwell*
CREATIVE DIRECTOR *Mike Koelker*
COPYWRITER *Mike Koelker*
DESIGNER *Douglas Fraser*
PRODUCER *Anna Frost*
DIRECTOR *J. J. Sedelmaier*
ANIMATOR *Tony Eastman*
PHOTOGRAPHER *Daniel Esterman*
ILLUSTRATOR *Douglas Fraser*
MUSIC *Elias West*
STUDIO *J. J. Sedelmaier Productions, Inc.*
AGENCY *Foote, Cone & Belding, San Francisco*
CLIENT *Levi Strauss & Co.*

Merit/U.S.A.

PROMOTIONAL
Horsepower
ART DIRECTOR *Howard Brown*
DESIGNER *Howard Brown*
STUDIO *Urban Outfitters In-House*
CLIENT *Urban Outfitters*

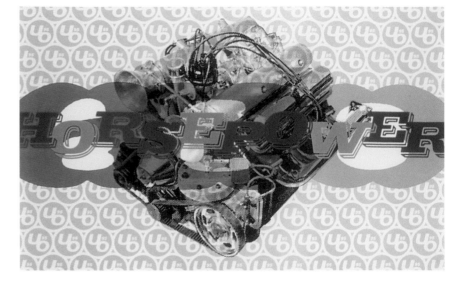

Merit/U.S.A.

PROMOTIONAL
Herron School of Art Visiting Artist Poster
ART DIRECTOR *Liz Charman*
DESIGNERS *Liz Charman, Bradley Trost*
PHOTOGRAPHER *Liz Charman*
STUDIO *Loft 219*
CLIENT *Herron School of Art*

Merit/China

PROMOTIONAL
Output Centre Fortune DTP Compugraphic Ltd.
ART DIRECTOR Wang Xu
DESIGNER Wang Xu
PRINTER Shenzhen Meiguang Color Printing Co., Ltd.
STUDIO Wang Xu & Associates
CLIENT Output Centre Fortune DTP
Compugraphic Ltd.

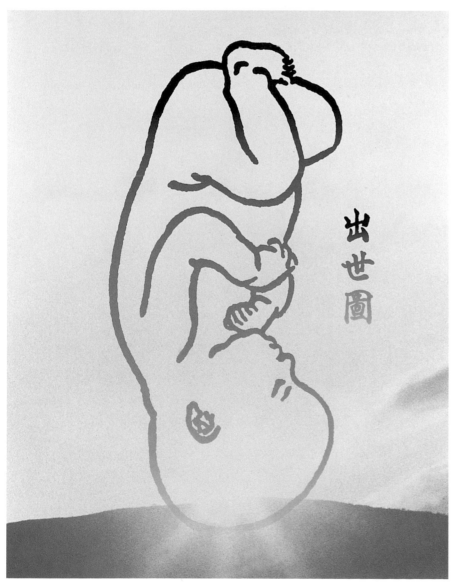

Merit/China

PROMOTIONAL
Shenzhen Graphic Design Association
ART DIRECTOR Wang Xu
DESIGNER Wang Xu
PRINTER Shenzhen Meiguang Color Printing Co., Ltd.
STUDIO Wang Xu & Associates
CLIENT Shenzhen Graphic Design Association

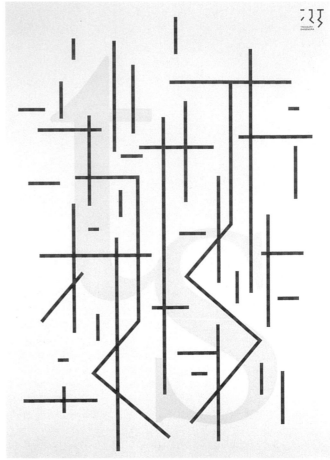

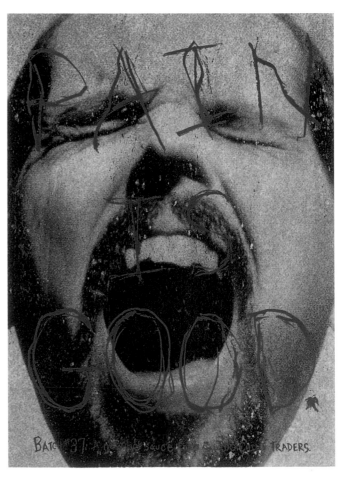

Merit/Japan

PROMOTIONAL, SERIES
Image Posters for Architecture Office
ART DIRECTOR *Toshiyasu Nanbu*
DESIGNER *Toshiyasu Nanbu*
STUDIO *Taste Inc.*
CLIENT *Treasury Shigemura Co., Ltd.*

Merit/U.S.A.

POINT-OF-PURCHASE
Pain Is Good
ART DIRECTOR *Eric Tilford*
CREATIVE DIRECTORS *Eric Tilford, Todd Tilford*
COPYWRITER *Todd Tilford*
PHOTOGRAPHER *Richard Reens*
AGENCY *CORE/R & D/The Richards Group*
CLIENT *Calido Chile Traders*

Merit/Japan

PRODUCT OR SERVICE
1996 Calendar
ART DIRECTOR *Giichi*
CREATIVE DIRECTOR *Hiroshi Tanaka*
DESIGNER *Giichi*
PHOTOGRAPHER *Takashi Iwakiri*
PRINTER *Tanaka Sangyo Co. Ltd.*
CLIENT *Tanaka Sangyo Co. Ltd.*

Merit/Japan

PRODUCT OR SERVICE
Studio Voice
ART DIRECTOR *Koji Mizutani*
CREATIVE DIRECTOR *Koji Mizutani*
DESIGNERS *Hiroshi Ohmizo, Tsutomu Aoyagi*
PHOTOGRAPHER *Kyoji Takahashi*
PRINTER *King Printing Co., Ltd.*
STUDIO *Mizutani Studio*
CLIENT *Studio Voice*

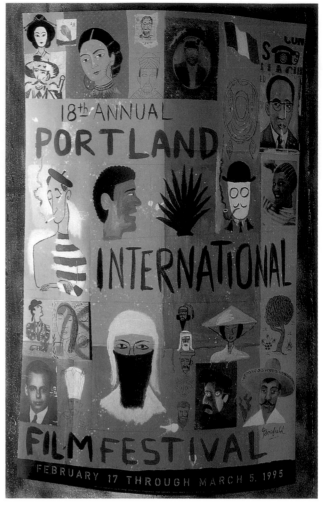

Merit/Japan

PRODUCT OR SERVICE
Kirima Design Office
ART DIRECTOR *Harumi Kirima*
CREATIVE DIRECTOR *Harumi Kirima*
DESIGNERS *Harumi Kirima, Fumitaka Yukawa*
STUDIO *Kirima Design Office*
CLIENT *Kirima Design Office*

Merit/U.S.A.

ENTERTAINMENT OR SPECIAL EVENT
*18th Annual Portland International Film
Festival*
ART DIRECTOR *Steve Sandstrom*
CREATIVE DIRECTORS *Steve Sandstrom,
Steve Sandoz*
DESIGNER *Steve Sandstrom*
ILLUSTRATOR *Josh Gosfield*
STUDIO *Sandstrom Design*
CLIENT *Northwest Film Center*

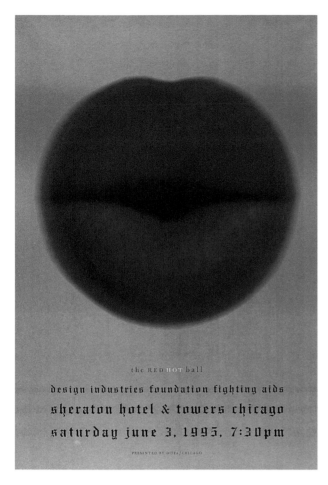

Merit/U.S.A.

ENTERTAINMENT OR SPECIAL EVENT, SERIES
The Red Hot Ball
ART DIRECTORS *Dana Arnett, Ken Fox*
DESIGNER *Ken Fox*
PHOTO IMAGERY *VSA Partners, Inc.*
PRINTER *Bradley Printing Company*
STUDIO *VSA Partners, Inc.*
CLIENT *DIFFA/Chicago*

Merit/U.S.A.

ENTERTAINMENT OR SPECIAL EVENT
HempFest
ART DIRECTORS *Jamie Sheehan, Art Chantry*
CREATIVE DIRECTORS *Jamie Sheehan, Art Chantry*
COPYWRITER *Jamie Sheehan*
DESIGNERS *Jamie Sheehan, Art Chantry*
PRINTER *Windward Press*
STUDIO *Sheehan Design*
CLIENT *Peace Heathens*

Merit/U.S.A.

ENTERTAINMENT OR SPECIAL EVENT
Austin Film Festival
DESIGNER *Kevin Goodbar*
STUDIO *Fuller Dyal & Stamper*
CLIENT *Austin Film Festival*

Merit/U.S.A.

ENTERTAINMENT OR SPECIAL EVENT
Oak Street Fashion Show
ART DIRECTORS *Dana Arnett, Ken Fox*
DESIGNER *Ken Fox*
PHOTOGRAPHER *Howard Bjornson*
PRINTER *Etheridge Printing*
STUDIO *VSA Partners, Inc.*
CLIENT *DIFFA/Chicago*

Merit/U.S.A.

ENTERTAINMENT OR SPECIAL EVENT
The World Exposed
ART DIRECTOR *Heidi Flora*
COPYWRITER *Kevin Jones*
PHOTOGRAPHER *Everard Williams, Jr.*
PRINTER *Heath Printers*
AGENCY *Cole & Weber*
CLIENT *Seattle International Film Festival*

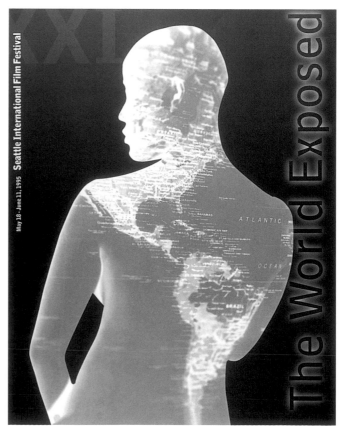

Merit/U.S.A.

ENTERTAINMENT OR SPECIAL EVENT
Him
ART DIRECTOR *Paula Scher*
DESIGNERS *Paula Scher, Ron Louie, Lisa Mazur*
PRINTER *Ambassador Arts, Inc.*
STUDIO *Pentagram Design*
CLIENT *The Public Theater*

Merit/U.S.A.

ENTERTAINMENT OR SPECIAL EVENT
Public Space/Culture Wars
ART DIRECTOR *David Mellen*
DESIGNER *David Mellen*
PHOTOGRAPHER *John Kiffe*
PRINTER *Gardner Lithograph*
STUDIO *David Mellen Design*
CLIENT *The Getty Center for the History of Art
and the Humanities*

Merit/U.S.A.

ENTERTAINMENT OR SPECIAL EVENT
Dance Month
ART DIRECTOR *Fritz Klaetke*
CREATIVE DIRECTOR *Fritz Klaetke*
COPYWRITER *Rozann Kraus*
DESIGNER *Fritz Klaetke*
PHOTOGRAPHER *Charles Barclay Reeves*
PRINTER *Pride Printers*
STUDIO *Visual Dialogue*
CLIENT *The Dance Complex*

Merit/U.S.A.

ENTERTAINMENT OR SPECIAL EVENT
Next Wave Festival
ART DIRECTOR *Michael Bierut*
DESIGNER *Emily Hayes*
PHOTOGRAPHER *Timothy Greenfield-Sanders*
PRINTER *Ambassador Arts, Inc.*
STUDIO *Pentagram Design*
CLIENT *Brooklyn Academy of Music*

Merit/U.S.A.

ENTERTAINMENT OR SPECIAL EVENT
Dog Opera
ART DIRECTOR *Paula Scher*
DESIGNERS *Paula Scher, Liza Mazur*
PRINTER *Ambassador Arts, Inc.*
STUDIO *Pentagram Design*
CLIENT *The Public Theater*

Merit/U.S.A.

ENTERTAINMENT OR SPECIAL EVENT
Phaedra
ART DIRECTOR *Stephen Doyle*
DESIGNER *Katrin Schmitt-Tegge*
STUDIO *Drenttel Doyle Partners*
CLIENT *Creation Production Company*

Merit/U.S.A.

ENTERTAINMENT OR SPECIAL EVENT
Not in My Name
ART DIRECTOR *Luba Lukova*
DESIGNER *Luba Lukova*
ILLUSTRATOR *Luba Lukova*
PRINTER *Rosepoint*
STUDIO *Luba Lukova Studio*
CLIENT *The Living Theatre*

Merit/Hong Kong

ENTERTAINMENT OR SPECIAL EVENT
Out of the Blue
ART DIRECTORS *Jan Lamb, Joel Chu, Wing Shya*
CREATIVE DIRECTORS *Jan Lamb, Joel Chu,*
Wing Shya
DESIGNER *Godfrey Kwan*
PHOTOGRAPHER *Wing Shya*
STUDIO *Double X Workshop*

Merit/Japan

ENTERTAINMENT OR SPECIAL EVENT
Welcome to Tadanori Yokoo
ART DIRECTOR *Katsuhiro Kinoshita*
COPYWRITER *Tadanori Yokoo*
DESIGNER *Katsuhiro Kinoshita*
ARTIST *Tadanori Yokoo*
PRODUCER *Takayo Iida*
STUDIO *Design Club Inc.*
CLIENT *Tokyo Gas Urban Development Co., Ltd.*

Merit/Japan

ENTERTAINMENT OR SPECIAL EVENT
Di Amor
ART DIRECTOR *Akio Okumura*
DESIGNER *Mitsuo Ueno*
STUDIO *Packaging Create Inc.*
AGENCY *Dentsu Inc., Kansai*
CLIENT *Di Amor*

Merit/U.S.A.

ENTERTAINMENT OR SPECIAL EVENT
Unseen
ART DIRECTORS *Gerhard Blättler,*
Martin Gaberthüel, Andréas Netthoevel
CREATIVE DIRECTORS *Gerhard Blättler,*
Martin Gaberthüel, Andréas Netthoevel
COPYWRITERS *Rätus Luck, Peter Edwin Erismann*
DESIGNERS *Gerhard Blättler, Martin Gaberthüel,*
Andréas Netthoevel
PHOTOGRAPHER *Dominique Uldry*
PRINTER *Serigraphie Uldry*
AGENCY *second floor south*
CLIENT *Swiss National Library*

Merit/U.S.A.

ENTERTAINMENT OR SPECIAL EVENT, SERIES
Hunger Crime, Eco Crime, War Crime
ART DIRECTOR *Luba Lukova*
DESIGNER *Luba Lukova*
ILLUSTRATOR *Luba Lukova*
PRINTER *Rosepoint*
STUDIO *Luba Lukova Studio*
CLIENT *The Living Theatre*

(facing page)
Merit/Japan

ENTERTAINMENT OR SPECIAL EVENT
In Japan I
ART DIRECTOR *Masaaki Hiromura*
CREATIVE DIRECTOR *Masaaki Hiromura*
COPYWRITER *Hiroyuki Nakazaki*
DESIGNERS *Masaaki Hiromura,*
Takafumi Kusagaya
PHOTOGRAPHER *Takashi Oyama*
STUDIO *Hiromura Design Office*

Merit/Japan

ENTERTAINMENT OR SPECIAL EVENT
In Japan II
ART DIRECTOR *Masaaki Hiromura*
CREATIVE DIRECTOR *Masaaki Hiromura*
COPYWRITER *Hiroyuki Nakazaki*
DESIGNERS *Masaaki Hiromura,*
Takafumi Kusagaya
PHOTOGRAPHER *Takashi Oyama*
STUDIO *Hiromura Design Office*

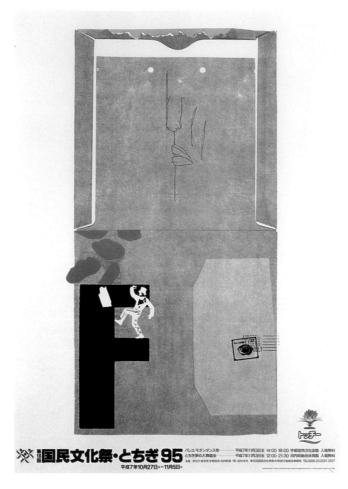

Merit/Japan

ENTERTAINMENT OR SPECIAL EVENT
The 10th National Culture Festival
ART DIRECTOR *Masakazu Tanabe*
DESIGNER *Masakazu Tanabe*
ILLUSTRATOR *Masakazu Tanabe*
STUDIO *Media Co. Ltd.*
CLIENT *Executive Committee for the 10th National Culture Festival*

(facing page)
Merit/Japan

ENTERTAINMENT OR SPECIAL EVENT, SERIES
Sankai Juku
ART DIRECTOR *Toshio Yamagata*
CREATIVE DIRECTOR *Toshio Yamagata*
DESIGNER *Toshio Yamagata*
PHOTOGRAPHER *Yoshihiko Ueda*
PRINTER *Nissha Printing Co., Ltd.*
CLIENT *Sankai Juku*

Merit/Japan

ENTERTAINMENT OR SPECIAL EVENT
Exhibition of the Works
ART DIRECTOR *Akio Okumura*
DESIGNER *Emi Kajihara*
STUDIO *Packaging Create Inc.*
CLIENT *New Oji Paper Co., Ltd.*

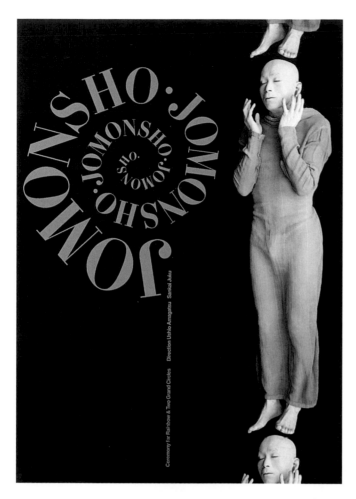

Ceremony for Rainbow & Two Grand Circles   Direction Ushio Amagatsu   Sankai Juku

The Grazed Surface   Direction Ushio Amagatsu   Sankai Juku

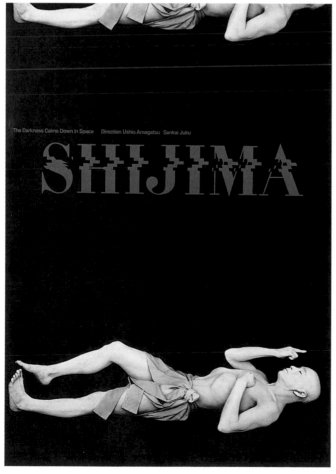

The Darkness Calms Down in Space   Direction Ushio Amagatsu   Sankai Juku

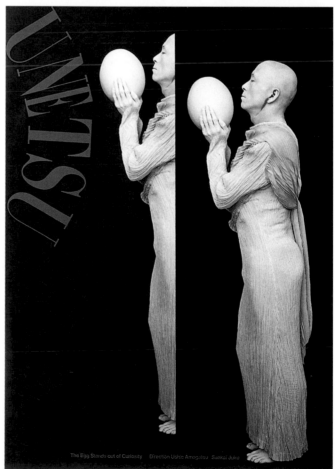

The Egg Stands out of Curiosity   Direction Ushio Amagatsu   Sankai Juku

Merit/U.S.A.

PUBLIC SERVICE
Protect
COPYWRITER *Ness Feliciano*
DESIGNER *Ness Feliciano*
PHOTOGRAPHER *Ness Feliciano*
STUDIO *ness graphic design*
CLIENT *Children Everywhere*

Merit/U.S.A.

PUBLIC SERVICE
If A, Then B
CREATIVE DIRECTOR *Stephen Doyle*
DESIGNER *Stephen Doyle*
PHOTOGRAPHER *Victor Schrager*
STUDIO *Drenttel Doyle Partners*
CLIENT *AIGA, Los Angeles*

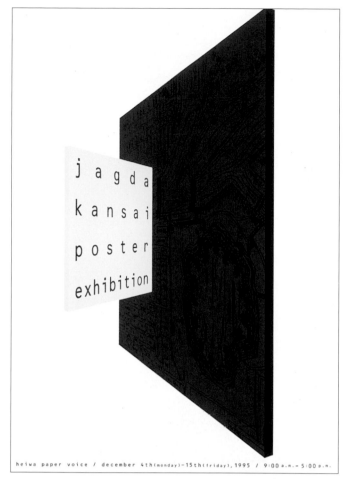

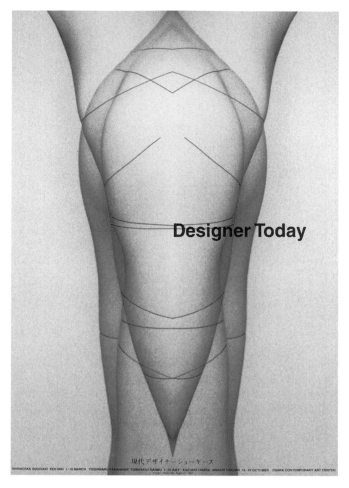

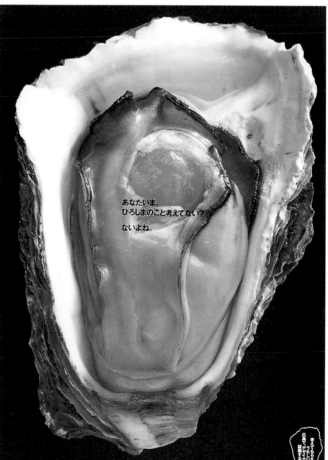

Merit/Japan

PUBLIC SERVICE
JAGDA Kansai Poster Exhibition
ART DIRECTOR *Ken Miki*
DESIGNER *Ken Miki*
CLIENT *JAGDA (Japan Graphic Designers Association Inc.)*

Merit/Japan

PUBLIC SERVICE
Designer Today
ART DIRECTOR *Shinnoske Sugisaki*
DESIGNER *Shinnoske Sugisaki*
PRINTER *Kotobuki Seihan Printing*
STUDIO *Shinnoske Inc.*
CLIENT *Osaka Contemporary Art Center*

Merit/Japan

PUBLIC SERVICE
Are You Thinking About Hiroshima Right Now?
ART DIRECTOR *Satoji Kashimoto*
CREATIVE DIRECTOR *Satoji Kashimoto*
COPYWRITER *Yuhei Nayuki*
DESIGNER *Satomi Izawa*
PHOTOGRAPHER *Kenichi Shimoyana*
CLIENT *Genshoku Art Printing Co., Ltd.*

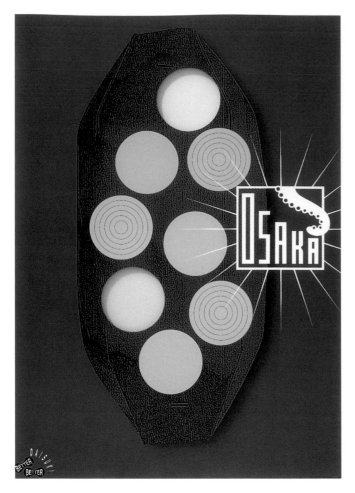

Merit/Japan

PUBLIC SERVICE
Discovery Osaka
ART DIRECTOR *Nobuharu Takanishi*
CREATIVE DIRECTOR *Nobuharu Takanishi*
DESIGNERS *Tomonari Endo, Hidekazu Fujii*
PHOTOGRAPHER *Shigeru Hoshino*
PRINTER *Field Center Inc.*
CLIENT *JAGDA (Japan Graphic Designers Association Inc.)*

(facing page)
Merit/Japan

PUBLIC SERVICE, SERIES
Ideas Want to Have Form
ART DIRECTOR *Seijo Kawaguchi*
CREATIVE DIRECTOR *Seijo Kawaguchi*
COPYWRITER *Norihisa Dohmen*
DESIGNERS *Noritoshi Nishioka, Toshihiro Hyodo*
ILLUSTRATOR *Hideyuki Kawarazaki*
AGENCY *Dentsu Inc., Tokyo*
CLIENT *Dentsu Inc., Tokyo*

Merit/Japan

PUBLIC SERVICE
Help
ART DIRECTOR *Masaru Yoshihara*
COPYWRITER *Masaru Yoshihara*
DESIGNER *Masaru Yoshihara*
PHOTOGRAPHER *Masaru Yoshihara*
CLIENT *Masaru Yoshihara*

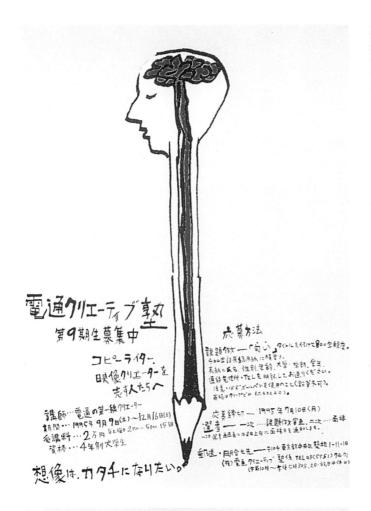

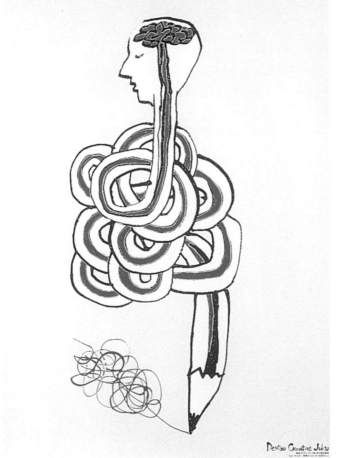

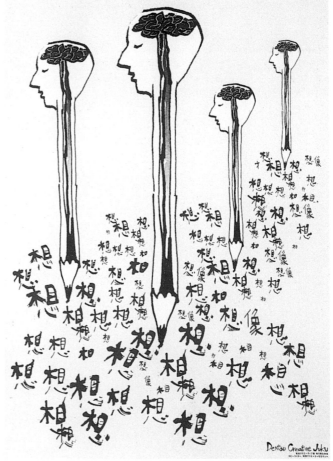

Merit/Japan

PUBLIC SERVICE, SERIES
Come Together for Kobe
ART DIRECTOR *Koji Mizutani*
CREATIVE DIRECTOR *Koji Mizutani*
DESIGNER *Hiroshi Ohmizo*
PHOTOGRAPHER *Arao Yokogi*
PRINTERS *King Printing Co., Ltd., Koyosha Inc.*
STUDIO *Mizutani Studio*
CLIENT *Come Together for Kobe Secretariat*

(facing page)
Merit/Japan

PUBLIC SERVICE, SERIES
Here=There: Wall, Ceiling and Floor, Pillar,
Bridge, Gate, Stairs
ART DIRECTOR *Ken Miki*
DESIGNER *Ken Miki*
CLIENT *Nara City Naramachi*

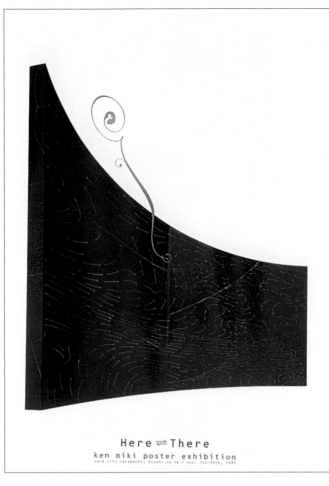

Here ⇌ There
ken miki poster exhibition
nara city naramachi, koushi no ie / nov. 1st-30th, 1995

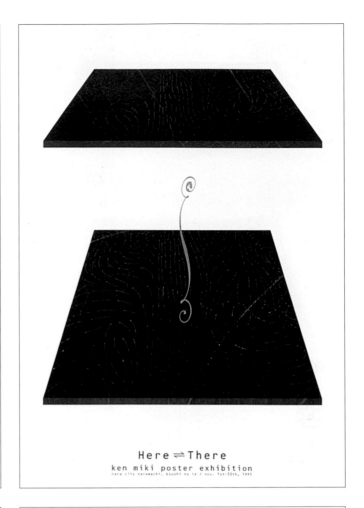

Here ⇌ There
ken miki poster exhibition
nara city naramachi, koushi no ie / nov. 1st-30th, 1995

Here ⇌ There
ken miki poster exhibition
nara city naramachi, koushi no ie / nov. 1st-30th, 1995

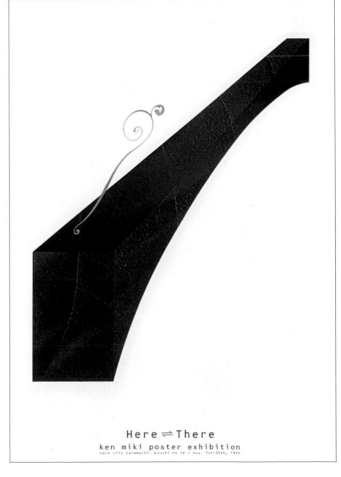

Here ⇌ There
ken miki poster exhibition
nara city naramachi, koushi no ie / nov. 1st-30th, 1995

Merit/U.S.A.

CONSUMER PRODUCT
Inkjet
CREATIVE DIRECTOR *Bill Thorburn*
COPYWRITER *Matt Elhardt*
DESIGNER *Alex Tylevich*
PHOTOGRAPHER *Chuck Smith*
STUDIO *Thorburn Design*
CLIENT *Domtar*

Merit/U.S.A.

CONSUMER PRODUCT
Papier Français
ART DIRECTOR *Louise Fili*
CREATIVE DIRECTOR *Louise Fili*
DESIGNER *Louise Fili*
STUDIO *Louise Fili*
CLIENT *Chronicle Books*

Merit/U.S.A.

CONSUMER PRODUCT
Alanis Morissette, "Jagged Little Pill"
ART DIRECTOR *Tom Recchion*
DESIGNER *Tom Recchion*
PHOTOGRAPHER *John Patrick Salisbury*
STUDIO *Warner Bros. Records*
CLIENT *Maverick Recording Company*

Merit/U.S.A.

CONSUMER PRODUCT
Filter, "Short Bus"
ART DIRECTOR *Deborah Norcross*
DESIGNER *Deborah Norcross*
PHOTOGRAPHER *Chris Beirne*
STUDIO *Warner Bros. Records*
CLIENT *Reprise Records*

Merit/U.S.A.

CONSUMER PRODUCT
H. P. Zinker, "Mountains of Madness"
CREATIVE DIRECTOR *Stefan Sagmeister*
COPYWRITER *Hans Platzgummer*
DESIGNERS *Stefan Sagmeister, Veronica Oh*
PHOTOGRAPHER *Tom Schierlitz*
STUDIO *Sagmeister Inc.*
CLIENT *Energy Records, Inc.*

Merit/U.S.A.

CONSUMER PRODUCT
The Velvet Underground Box Set
ART DIRECTORS *SMAY VISION, Spencer Drate,*
Jutka Salavetz, Sylvia Reed
ARTIST *Andy Warhol*
PHOTOGRAPHY *Mario Anniballi, Ron Campisi,*
Susan Cooper Archives, Nat Finkelstein,
Donald Greenhaus, Lisa Law,
Gerard Malanga Archives,
Sterling Morrison Archives, Billy Name,
Dustin Pittman, Polygram Archives,
Stephen Shore, Hugo
PRINTER *AGI Printer*
STUDIO *A & M Records*
CLIENT *A & M Records*

Merit/U.S.A.

CONSUMER PRODUCT
Anon
ART DIRECTOR *Clifford Stoltze*
DESIGNERS *Clifford Stoltze, Peter Farrell,*
Heather Kramer
STUDIO *Stoltze Design*
CLIENT *Castle von Buhler Records*

Merit/U.S.A.

CONSUMER PRODUCT
Cake Decorating Kit
ART DIRECTORS *Dina Dell'Arciprete, Anne Johnson*
CREATIVE DIRECTOR *Gael Towey*
DESIGNER *Dina Dell'Arciprete*
PHOTOGRAPHER *Carlton Davis*
DIRECTOR *Susan Spungen*
STUDIO *Martha By Mail*
CLIENT *Martha By Mail*

Merit/U.S.A.

CONSUMER PRODUCT
Rohol
ART DIRECTORS *Steve Mitchell, Bill Thorburn*
COPYWRITER *Matt Elhardt*
DESIGNER *Chad Hagen*
STUDIO *Thorburn Design*
CLIENT *Millennium Import Co.*

Merit/U.S.A.

CONSUMER PRODUCT
OXO BBQ Set
ART DIRECTOR *Jack Anderson*
DESIGNERS *Jack Anderson, Heidi Favour,*
John Anicker, Eulah Sheffield, David Bates
PHOTOGRAPHER *Tom Collicott*
PRINTER *Rand-Whitney*
STUDIO *Hornall Anderson Design Works, Inc.*
CLIENT *OXO International*

Merit/U.S.A.

CONSUMER PRODUCT
Smith Sunglasses
ART DIRECTOR *Jack Anderson*
DESIGNERS *Jack Anderson, David Bates*
STUDIO *Hornall Anderson Design Works, Inc.*
CLIENT *Smith Sport Optics, Inc.*

Merit/U.S.A.

CONSUMER PRODUCT
Ruffnexx, "Sound System"
ART DIRECTOR *Deborah Norcross*
DESIGNER *Deborah Norcross*
PHOTOGRAPHERS *Exum, Danny Clich,*
Cati Gonzales
AGENCY *Warner Bros. Records*
CLIENT *Qwest Records*

Merit/U.S.A.

CONSUMER PRODUCT
*Adventures in Afropea, Vol. 3:
"Telling Stories to the Sea"*
DESIGNER *Stefan Sagmeister*
PHOTOGRAPHER *Tom Schierlitz*
ILLUSTRATION *Indigo Arts*
AGENCY *Warner Bros. Records*
CLIENT *Luaka Bop, Inc.*

Merit/U.S.A.

CONSUMER PRODUCT
Armagedden Dildos, "Lost"
ART DIRECTOR *Deborah Norcross*
DESIGNER *Deborah Norcross*
PHOTOGRAPHER *Exum*
LINE ART *Bayrle/Sebastian 1970*
AGENCY *Warner Bros. Records*
CLIENT *Sire Recording Company*

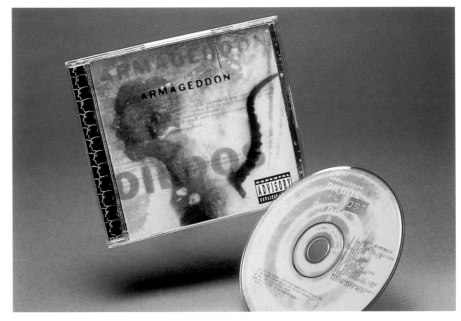

Merit/U.S.A.

CONSUMER PRODUCT
Ciao! Sport
ART DIRECTOR *Jenny W. Ng*
CREATIVE DIRECTOR *Joanne De Luca*
DESIGNER *Jenny W. Ng*
ILLUSTRATOR *Jenny W. Ng*
STUDIO *Sputnik Entertainment, Inc.*
AGENCY *Sputnik Entertainment, Inc.*
CLIENT *Bennett Importing, Inc.*

Merit/U.S.A.

CONSUMER PRODUCT
Zia
ART DIRECTOR *Jeffrey Caldeway*
DESIGNER *Jeffrey Caldeway*
PRINTER *Gordon Graphics*
CLIENT *Zia Cellars*

Merit/Japan

CONSUMER PRODUCT
Self Maintenance System
ART DIRECTOR *Minoru Tabuchi*
CREATIVE DIRECTOR *Minoru Tabuchi*
DESIGNERS *Minoru Tabuchi, Akimori Kawamura,*
Hiroki Miyazono
PHOTOGRAPHER *Akinori Hasegawa*
PRODUCER *Hiroshi Hanbusa*
STUDIO *MCA Inc.*
AGENCY *Daiko Advertising Inc.*
CLIENT *Fujitsu Tokushima System*
Engineering Co., Ltd.

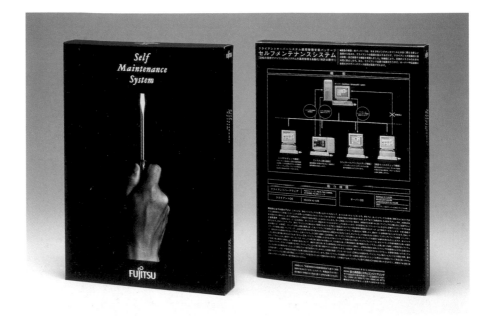

Merit/Australia

CONSUMER PRODUCT
DNA Alcoholic Spring Water
CREATIVE DIRECTOR *Mike Staniford*
DESIGNERS *Paul Drury, Eddie Turley*
DIRECTORS *Andrew Lewis, Simon Williams*
MARKETING MANAGER *Andy Bell*
AGENCY *Lewis Kahn*
CLIENT *Grand Slam Beverage Company*

Merit/Germany

CONSUMER PRODUCT, SERIES
The Mustard Seeds
ART DIRECTORS *S. Bogner, B. Simon*
CREATIVE DIRECTOR *S. Bogner*
DESIGNER *S. Bogner*
PHOTOGRAPHER *Jeffrey Weiss*
STUDIO *Factor Product München*
AGENCY *Factor Product München*
CLIENT *Marlboro Music*

Merit/England

CONSUMER PRODUCT, SERIES
Mio Essential Fragrances
CREATIVE DIRECTOR *Kathy Miller*
PROJECT DIRECTOR *Sian Sutherland*
COPYWRITER *Sian Sutherland*
DESIGNER *Kathy Miller*
AGENCY *Miller Sutherland*
CLIENT *Harris Oils Ltd.*

Merit/U.S.A.

CONSUMER PRODUCT, SERIES
Roses Cards, Weddings Cards
ART DIRECTORS *Dina Dell'Arciprete,*
Claudia Bruno
CREATIVE DIRECTOR *Gael Towey*
DESIGNER *Dina Dell'Arciprete*
PHOTOGRAPHERS *Various*
STUDIO *Martha By Mail*
CLIENT *Martha By Mail*

Merit/U.S.A.

CONSUMER PRODUCT, SERIES
Our Secret Century
ART DIRECTOR *Paula Kelly*
CREATIVE DIRECTOR *Paula Kelly*
COPYWRITER *Kristin Celona*
DESIGNER *Paula Kelly*
PHOTOGRAPHY *Archive Photos*
PUBLISHER *The Voyager Company*
STUDIO *Paula Kelly Design*
CLIENT *The Voyager Company*

Merit/U.S.A.

CONSUMER PRODUCT, SERIES
Fossil Car Tins
ART DIRECTOR *Brian Delaney*
CREATIVE DIRECTOR *Tim Hale*
DESIGNERS *Stuart Cameron, Brian Delaney,*
Glenn Hadsall, Carlos Perez, James Ward
ILLUSTRATOR *James Ward*
PRINTER *Wai Lee, China*
STUDIO *Fossil Watches In-House*
CLIENT *Fossil Watches*

Merit/U.S.A.

CONSUMER PRODUCT, SERIES
Fossil Motor Watches
ART DIRECTOR *Tim Hale*
CREATIVE DIRECTOR *Tim Hale*
COPYWRITER *Tim Hale*
DESIGNER *Tim Hale*
PRINTER *Wai Lee, China*
STUDIO *Fossil Watches In-House*
CLIENT *Fossil Watches*

Merit/U.S.A.

CONSUMER PRODUCT, SERIES
Tropical Source Organic Chocolate Bars
DESIGNER *Haley Johnson*
ILLUSTRATOR *Haley Johnson*
STUDIO *Haley Johnson Design*
CLIENT *Cloud Nine Inc.*

Merit/U.S.A.

CONSUMER PRODUCT, SERIES
Iomega
ART DIRECTOR *Jaimie Alexander*
DESIGNERS *Carolina Senior, Kate Murphy,
Eric Weissinger, Paul Lycett, Sarah Spatt*
PHOTOGRAPHER *Mark Steele*
PRODUCERS *Sheri Worrall, Joanie Hupp,
Sandy McKissick*
STUDIO *Fitch Inc.*
CLIENT *Iomega Corporation*

Merit/U.S.A.

CONSUMER PRODUCT, SERIES
Digital Equipment Corporation
ART DIRECTORS *Robert Wood, Tammie Hunt*
DESIGNERS *Robert Wood, Ellen Hartshorne,*
Carolina Senior, Brooks Beisch, Linda Harriman
PHOTOGRAPHERS *Peter Medilek, Mark Steele*
STUDIO *Fitch Inc.*
CLIENT *Digital Equipment Corporation*

Merit/Japan

CONSUMER PRODUCT, SERIES
We're
ART DIRECTOR *Tetsuo Hiro*
CREATIVE DIRECTOR *Tetsuo Hiro*
DESIGNER *Eriko Misawa*
STUDIO *Shiseido Co. Ltd.*
CLIENT *Shiseido Co. Ltd.*

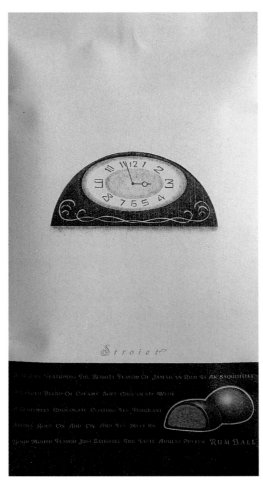

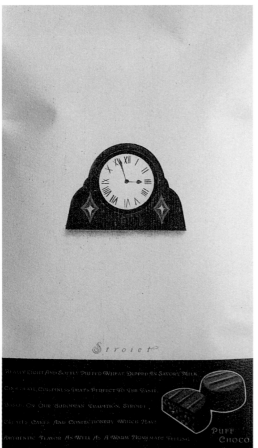

Merit/Japan

CONSUMER PRODUCT, SERIES
Stroiet Chocolates
ART DIRECTOR *Norikazu Machida*
CREATIVE DIRECTOR *Norikazu Machida*
COPYWRITER *Norikazu Machida*
DESIGNER *Norikazu Machida*
ILLUSTRATOR *Keiko Yamaguchi*
STUDIO *GRAPAC Japan Co., Inc.*
AGENCY *Norikazu Machida Design Office*
CLIENT *Stroiet Co., Ltd.*

Merit/Germany

PROMOTIONAL
Haindling, "Weiss"
ART DIRECTOR *Thomas Sassenbach*
DESIGNER *Martin Scharf*
PHOTOGRAPHER *Bernhard Kühmstedt*
STUDIO *BMG Ariola München Advertising Department*
CLIENT *BMG Ariola Media*

Merit/Japan

PROMOTIONAL, SERIES
Opgo Hako
ART DIRECTOR *Akio Okumura*
DESIGNER *Akio Okumura*
STUDIO *Packaging Create Inc.*
CLIENT *New Oji Paper Co., Ltd.*

(facing page)
Merit/Germany

PROMOTIONAL, SERIES
Schmidhauers
ART DIRECTOR *Thomas Sassenbach*
DESIGNER *Christina Krutz*
PHOTOGRAPHER *Alexander Walter*
STUDIO *BMG Ariola München Advertising Department*
CLIENT *Red Rooster*

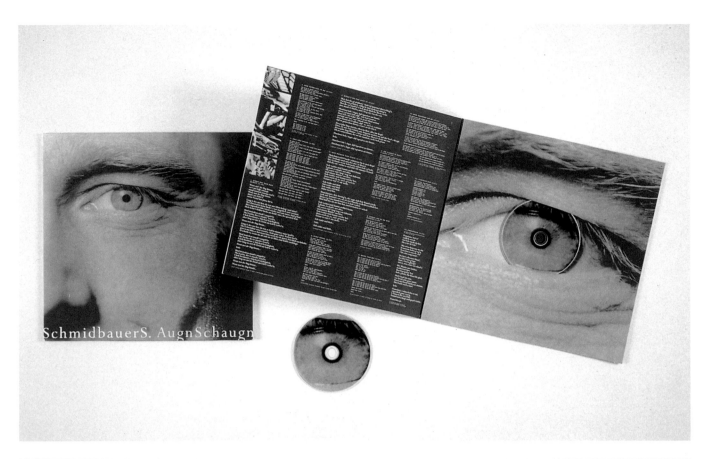

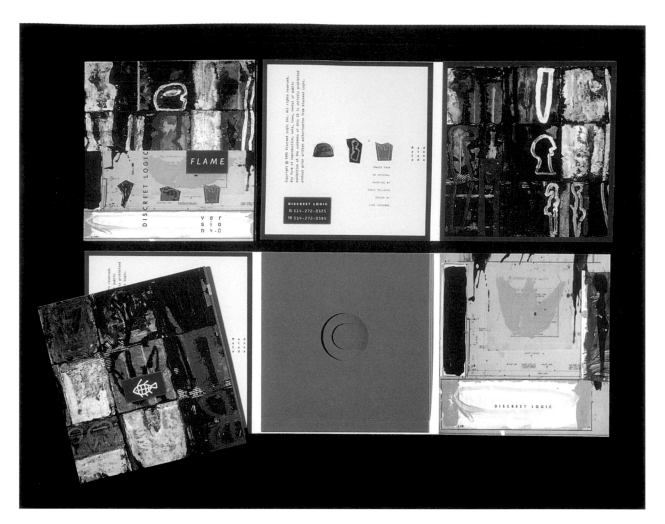

Merit/U.S.A.

LABEL OR HANGTAG
Kathleen Sommers
ART DIRECTORS *Jill Giles, Cindy Greenwood*
CREATIVE DIRECTOR *Jill Giles*
DESIGNERS *Jill Giles, Stephen Arevalos*
PHOTOGRAPHER *Jeffrey Newbury*
STUDIO *Giles Design*
CLIENT *Kathleen Sommers*

(facing page)
Merit/Canada

PRODUCT GRAPHICS
Flame Version 4.0
ART DIRECTOR *Lyne Lefebvre*
CREATIVE DIRECTOR *Lyne Lefebvre*
DESIGNER *Lyne Lefebvre*
PAINTING *Denis Pellerin*
PRODUCTION COORDINATOR *Sophie Simonnet*
PRINTER *Datamark Lithochrome*
PUBLISHER *Diana Shearwood*
STUDIO *Discreet Logic Design Group*
CLIENT *Discreet Logic Design Group*

Merit/U.S.A.

PROMOTIONAL
Holiday Treat Mailer with Lights Out V CD
ART DIRECTOR *Steve Sandstrom*
CREATIVE DIRECTOR *Steve Sandstrom*
DESIGNER *Donjiro Ban*
PHOTOGRAPHER *Steve Bonini*
STUDIO *Sandstrom Design*
CLIENT *KINK 102FM*

Merit/U.S.A.

PROMOTIONAL DISPLAY
JBL Comdex Booth
ART DIRECTORS *Ann Gildea, Jane Brady*
INFORMATION DESIGN *Mike Mooney*
DESIGNERS *Christian Uhl, Ben Segal*
CLIENT *JBL Consumer Products, Inc.*

(facing page)
Merit/U.S.A.

PUBLIC INTERIOR
Comedy Central Viewing Room
ART DIRECTOR *Saul Torres*
DESIGNER *Charlie Lagola*
VIDEO PRODUCER *Chris Claro*
ILLUSTRATOR *Lin Frisino*
CLIENT *Comedy Central*

Merit/U.S.A.

PUBLIC INTERIOR
Nickelodeon Balls
ART DIRECTOR *Stuart Williams*
CREATIVE DIRECTOR *Steve Thomas*
DESIGNER *Stuart Williams*
DIRECTOR *Marva Smalls*
PRODUCTION MANAGER *Christopher McDonald*
CLIENT *Nickelodeon*

(facing page)
Merit/U.S.A.

PUBLIC INTERIOR
Ann Taylor Madison Avenue Flagship Store
CREATIVE DIRECTOR *Wendy Hald*
DESIGNERS *Ray Schick, Werner Franz, Mary Meuer*
PHOTOGRAPHER *Andrew Bordwin*
STUDIO *Desgrippes Gobé & Associates*
CLIENT *Ann Taylor*

Merit/England

MUSEUM OR GALLERY SIGNAGE
Artnow
ART DIRECTOR *David Hillman*
DESIGNERS *David Hillman, Jane Chipchase*
STUDIO *Pentagram Design Ltd.*
CLIENT *Tate Gallery, London*

PHOTOGRAPHY+
ILLUSTRATION

GOLD+SILVER MEDALISTS

JUNE

MARCH

MAY

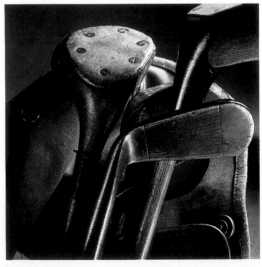

APRIL

Silver Medalist/England

PRODUCT OR SERVICE, SERIES
Real Time Studio 1996 Calender
ART DIRECTOR *Paul Clarke*
CREATIVE DIRECTOR *Trevor Chambers*
COPYWRITER *Patrick Baglee*
DESIGNER *Trevor Chambers*
PHOTOGRAPHER *Gary Hamill*

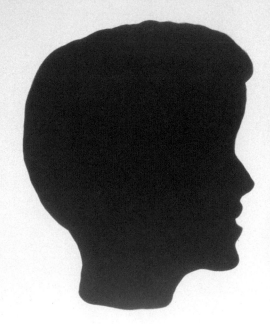

BOB
IS NORMAL

CALVIN
USES A PSYCHIC TO PICK HIS
LOTTERY NUMBERS

PATRICIA
SAYS HER MOM REFUSES TO
GROW UP

MEAGAN
MARRIED TO TWO MEN AT THE SAME
TIME

JESSICA
WAS ADOPTED AS AN
INFANT

LOTHER
NOT READY FOR THE COMPUTER
AGE

MICKY
SAYS HIS GIRLFRIEND DRIVES
HIM CRAZY

BILL
BUY AMERICAN, BUY AMERICAN,
BUY AMERICAN

MYRA
WORKS 60 HOURS A WEEK TO
SUPPORT HER ARTIST HUSBAND

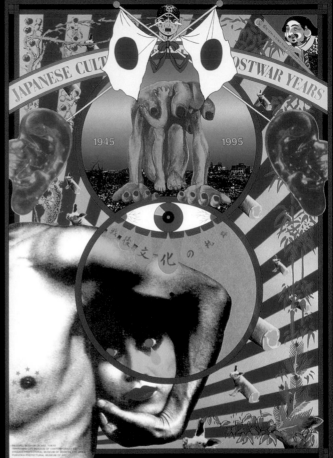

DISTINCTIVE MERIT AWARDS

SOUTH VIETNAM JUNE 8, 1972

t almost didn't run. An Associated Press staffer thought newspaper editors would find the girl's nakedness offensive. But hundreds of papers did print it. People were offended, and ashamed. South Vietnamese aircraft had dropped U.S. napalm near the Buddhist temple where nine-year-old Phan Thi Kim Phuc and her family had been hiding in Trang Bang, a village besieged by the North Vietnamese Army. AP photographer NICK UT took this picture just before Kim Phuc passed out. He remembers: "Her whole back, neck and arm were black like a barbecue." Ut took her to a hospital. "Chu Ut," she calls him—Uncle Ut. He was the first person she phoned after defecting to Canada in 1992.

I see the bombs. I see the fire. I run, run and run. It is lucky my feet are not burned. My clothes burn. I tear them off, but the burning doesn't stop. I rub my arm with my right hand—and spread the napalm onto it. I keep running. I'm told that I yelled *'Nong qua,'* which means 'too hot.' I lost consciousness, and my mom and dad found me in the hospital. I had lost blood. My mom gave me hers in a transfusion. Nurses bathed me each morning to remove the dead skin. It was so painful, month after month. My sister came to see me, and she fainted. Mom said, 'If you are afraid of pain and don't do exercises, you will be ugly. You have to do them to feel better again.' Every time I took a shower and saw the mirror, I cried. My mother said, 'If you love us, don't cry anymore. We love you. We can take care of everything but the pain. You alone have to suffer it.' I love them, so I don't cry anymore. I try, I try.

As a teenager, there was just one thing I wanted: to wear a short-sleeved dress. My friends all looked very beautiful in them. Now it doesn't matter, but then I thought I'd never have a boyfriend. I met my husband, Toan, in Cuba, where I was studying. We were friends for six years because I felt it was not easy to marry—nobody should suffer with me. When I had been in Vietnam, a German journalist wanted to find me, dead or alive. Once he did, a lot of journalists came, and Hanoi wanted me to cooperate. I was asked to travel so often that I couldn't complete my medical studies. I always traveled under their control; that helped me to want a human right—freedom. My picture made me very famous, but it made my life not what I want. I think a lot of people know of me, but I need one, just one, to understand me. Toan does. I know my picture did something to help stop the war. My son's Vietnamese name, Huan, means 'prospects.' I have to show him what happened to his mom, to her country, and that there should never be war again. ▯

44

Distinctive Merit/U.S.A.

EDITORIAL
Phan Thi Kim Phuc with Child
DESIGN DIRECTOR *Tom Bentkowski*
DESIGNER *Mimi Park*
PHOTOGRAPHY DIRECTOR *David Friend*
PHOTOGRAPHER *Joe McNally*
PUBLISHER *Time Inc.*
CLIENT *Life Magazine*

(facing page)
Distinctive Merit/Germany

FASHION, SERIES
Hudson Illustrations
ART DIRECTORS *Gertrud Eisele, Waldemar Meister*
CREATIVE DIRECTORS *Waldemar Meister,*
Dr. Detlef Kulessa
DESIGNER *Karin Bausch*
ILLUSTRATOR *Michel Canetti*
AGENCY *Leonhardt & Kern Beta GmbH*
CLIENT *Hudson International Vetriebs GmbH*

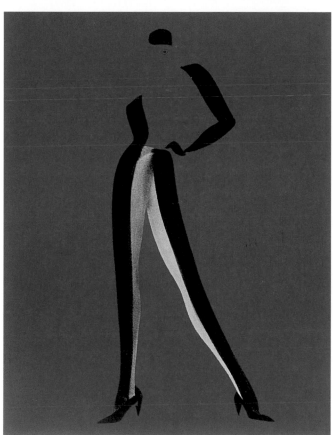

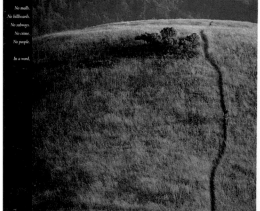

SUCCESS.
IT'S A
MIND
GAME.

Merit/England

PRODUCT OR SERVICE, SERIES
Ein Stück von mir
ART DIRECTOR *Tonguç Baykurt*
CREATIVE DIRECTOR *Erik Heitmann*
COPYWRITERS *Erik Heitmann, Alexander Tramm*
PHOTOGRAPHER *Jerry Oke*
STYLIST *Karin Otte*
STUDIO *Jerry Oke Studios*
AGENCY *Springer & Jacoby, Hamburg*
CLIENT *Burda Moden*

(facing page, left)
Merit/U.S.A.

CORPORATE, SERIES
The American Crew Collection: Volume 01
ART DIRECTOR *Steve Liska*
CREATIVE DIRECTOR *Steve Liska*
DESIGNER *Marcos Chavez*
PHOTOGRAPHER *Mark Havriliak*
PRINTER *MG Prints*
STUDIO *Liska and Associates, Inc.*
CLIENT *American Crew*

(facing page, top right)
Merit/U.S:A.

CORPORATE, SERIES
Penwest, Ltd.
ART DIRECTOR *Kerry Leimer*
DESIGNER *Kerry Leimer*
PHOTOGRAPHER *Jeff Corwin*
STUDIO *Leimer Cross Design*
CLIENT *Penwest, Ltd.*

(facing page, bottom right)
Merit/U.S.A.

CORPORATE, SERIES
The Nature of...
ART DIRECTORS *Karen Kwan, Kenny Chan*
CREATIVE DIRECTOR *Randall Hull*
COPYWRITER *Timothy Cohrs*
DESIGNER *Karen Kwan*
PHOTOGRAPHER *John Huet*
PRODUCTION *L. A. Smith-Dickens*
PRINTER *Woods Lithographics*
AGENCY *Lai Venuti & Lai Advertising*
CLIENT *Lai Venuti & Lai Advertising*

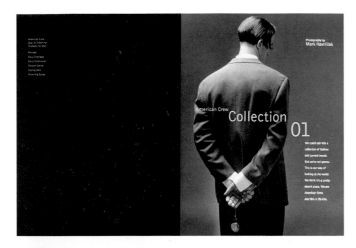

Merit/U.S.A.

EDITORIAL
Refueled & Reborn
ART DIRECTOR *Fred Woodward*
DESIGNER *Geraldine Hessler*
PHOTOGRAPHER *Anton Corbijn*
PHOTO EDITOR *Jodi Peckman*
PUBLISHER *Wenner Media*
CLIENT *Rolling Stone*

Merit/U.S.A.

EDITORIAL
Married to Metal
ART DIRECTOR *Fred Woodward*
DESIGNERS *Fred Woodward, Geraldine Hessler*
PHOTOGRAPHER *Frank W. Ockenfels III*
PHOTO EDITOR *Jodi Peckman*
PUBLISHER *Wenner Media*
CLIENT *Rolling Stone*

Merit/U.S.A.

EDITORIAL
Taj Mahal
DESIGN DIRECTOR *Tom Bentkowski*
DESIGNER *Jean Andreuzzi*
PHOTOGRAPHER *MacDuff Everton*
PHOTO EDITOR *Marie Schumann*
PUBLISHER *Time Inc.*
CLIENT *Life Magazine*

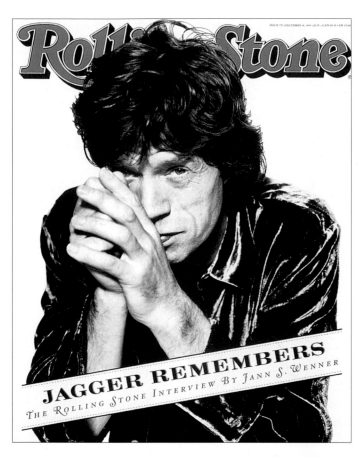

Merit/U.S.A.

EDITORIAL
Mick Jagger Cover
ART DIRECTOR *Fred Woodward*
DESIGNER *Fred Woodward*
PHOTOGRAPHER *Peter Lindbergh*
PHOTO EDITOR *Jodi Peckman*
PUBLISHER *Wenner Media*
CLIENT *Rolling Stone*

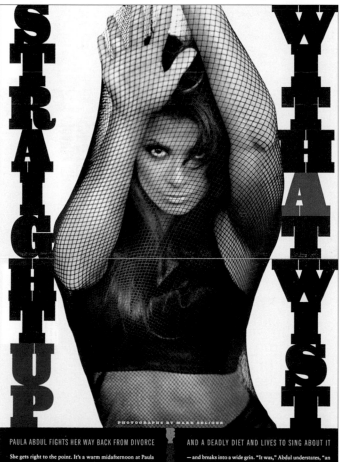

Merit/U.S.A.

EDITORIAL
Paula Abdul
ART DIRECTOR *Richard Baker*
PHOTOGRAPHER *Mark Seliger*
PHOTO EDITOR *Jennifer Crandall*
ASSOCIATE PHOTO EDITOR *Rachel Knepfer*
CLIENT *US Magazine*

Merit/U.S.A.

EDITORIAL, SERIES
Rwanda
DESIGN DIRECTOR *Tom Bentkowski*
DESIGNER *Marti Golon*
PHOTOGRAPHER *Sebastião Salgado*
PHOTO EDITOR *Barbara Baker Burrows*
PUBLISHER *Time Inc.*
CLIENT *Life Magazine*

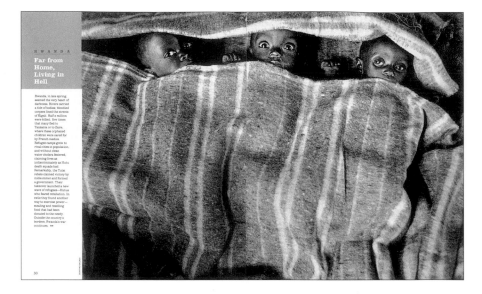

Merit/U.S.A.

EDITORIAL, SERIES
Eye View
DESIGN DIRECTOR *Diana LaGuardia*
PHOTOGRAPHY DIRECTOR *Kathleen Klech*
PHOTOGRAPHER *Yann Arthus-Bertrand*
PUBLISHER *Condé Nast*
CLIENT *Condé Nast Traveler*

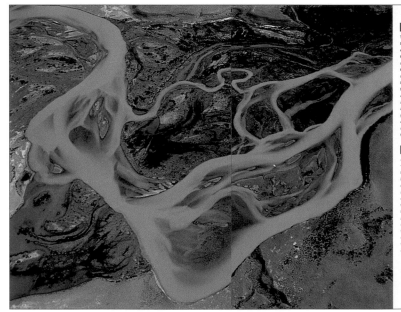

Merit/U.S.A.

EDITORIAL, SERIES
Northern Solitaire
DESIGN DIRECTOR *Diana LaGuardia*
PHOTOGRAPHY DIRECTOR *Kathleen Klech*
PHOTOGRAPHER *Hakan Ludwigson*
PUBLISHER *Condé Nast*
CLIENT *Condé Nast Traveler*

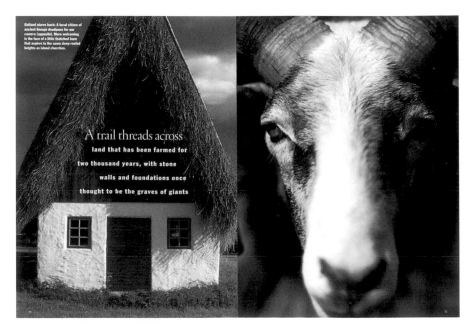

God's sweetest works

Hawaiian novelist SUSANNA MOORE *rediscovers in the Cook Islands the pristine Polynesia of her childhood, islands blessed with ravishing beaches that the outside world nearly forgot*

Basking in Aitutaki lagoon (opposite). The author's daughter (above) wears an ei.

The author on Pa's nature walk through the Rarotongan rain forest.

He taught us how to plait flowers in our hair, to hold water in our cupped hands. Old Garden of Eden tricks

Opposite: Traditional palm-leaf-thatched shelter on a motu. Above: Cook Islands Christian Church in Avarua.

Merit/U.S.A.

EDITORIAL, SERIES
God's Sweetest Works
DESIGN DIRECTOR *Diana LaGuardia*
PHOTOGRAPHY DIRECTOR *Kathleen Klech*
PHOTOGRAPHER *Victoria Pearson*
PUBLISHER *Condé Nast*
CLIENT *Condé Nast Traveler*

Merit/U.S.A.

EDITORIAL, SERIES
Optic Verve
ART DIRECTOR *Janet Froelich*
DESIGNER *Janet Froelich*
PHOTOGRAPHER *David Seidner*
STYLIST *Franciscus Ankoné*
CLIENT *The New York Times Magazine*

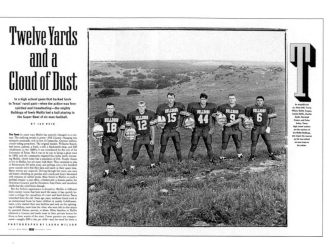

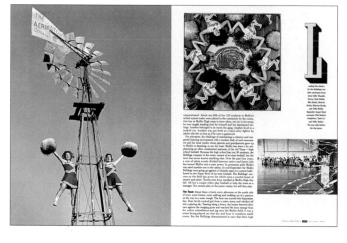

Merit/U.S.A.

EDITORIAL, SERIES
Burning Down the Woods
ART DIRECTOR *D. J. Stout*
CREATIVE DIRECTOR *D. J. Stout*
COPYWRITER *Robert Draper*
DESIGNERS *D. J. Stout, Nancy McMillen*
PHOTOGRAPHER *Shelby Lee Adams*
PUBLISHER *Mediatex*
CLIENT *Texas Monthly*

Merit/U.S.A.

EDITORIAL, SERIES
Twelve Yards and a Cloud of Dust
ART DIRECTOR *D. J. Stout*
CREATIVE DIRECTOR *D. J. Stout*
COPYWRITER *Jan Reid*
DESIGNERS *D. J. Stout, Nancy McMillen*
PHOTOGRAPHER *Laura Wilson*
PUBLISHER *Mediatex*
CLIENT *Texas Monthly*

Merit/U.S.A.

EDITORIAL, SERIES
Red Hot Chili Peppers
ART DIRECTOR *Fred Woodward*
DESIGNER *Geraldine Hessler*
PHOTOGRAPHER *Anton Corbijn*
PHOTO EDITOR *Jodi Peckman*
PUBLISHER *Wenner Media*
CLIENT *Rolling Stone*

Merit/U.S.A.

EDITORIAL, SERIES
Shaken Not Stirred
ART DIRECTOR *Diddo Ramm*
DESIGNER *Diddo Ramm*
PHOTOGRAPHER *Butch Belair*
CLIENT *Vibe Magazine*

CASUALTIES of WAR

Inside the Balkans' Refugee Camps

PHOTOGRAPHS by SEBASTIÃO SALGADO

"TWENTY YEARS AGO, in 1975, there were 2.5 million. Today there are more than 20 million refugees [in the world]. And that's not counting those who can't cross the border into another country. It's a tidal wave!" – SEBASTIÃO SALGADO

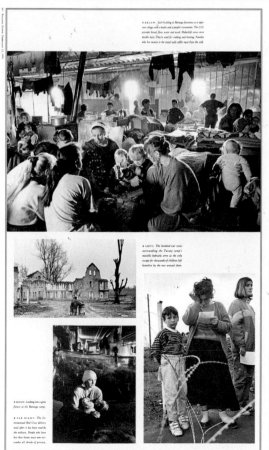

Merit/U.S.A.

EDITORIAL, SERIES
Casualties of War
ART DIRECTOR *Fred Woodward*
DESIGNERS *Fred Woodward, Gail Anderson*
PHOTOGRAPHER *Sebastião Salgado*
PHOTO EDITOR *Jodi Peckman*
PUBLISHER *Wenner Media*
CLIENT *Rolling Stone*

Merit/U.S.A.

EDITORIAL, SERIES
Audubon Magazine: Crossing Borders
PHOTOGRAPHY DIRECTOR *Peter Howe*
PHOTOGRAPHER *Mary Ellen Mark*
CLIENT *National Audubon Society*

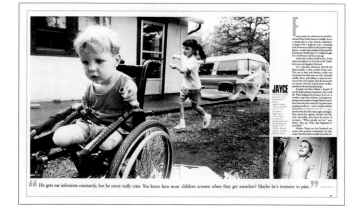

Merit/U.S.A.

EDITORIAL, SERIES
The Tiny Victims of Desert Storm
DESIGN DIRECTOR *Tom Bentkowski*
DESIGNER *Marti Golon*
PHOTOGRAPHY DIRECTOR *David Friend*
PHOTOGRAPHER *Derek Hudson*
CLIENT *Life Magazine*

Merit/U.S.A.

EDITORIAL, SERIES
Grozny's Morning After
ART DIRECTOR *Janet Froelich*
DESIGNER *Joel Cuyler*
PHOTOGRAPHER *Anthony Suau*
PRODUCER *Kathy Ryan*
CLIENT *The New York Times Magazine*

Merit/U.S.A.

EDITORIAL, SERIES
How They See Themselves
ART DIRECTOR *Janet Froelich*
DESIGNER *Joel Cuyler*
PHOTOGRAPHER *Lars Tunbjörk*
PHOTO EDITOR *Kathy Ryan*
CLIENT *The New York Times Magazine*

Merit/U.S.A.

EDITORIAL, SERIES
The Wild Bunch
ART DIRECTOR *Janet Froelich*
DESIGNER *Miriam Campiz*
PHOTOGRAPHER *Christian Witkin*
STYLIST *Elizabeth Stewart*
CLIENT *New York Times Magazine*

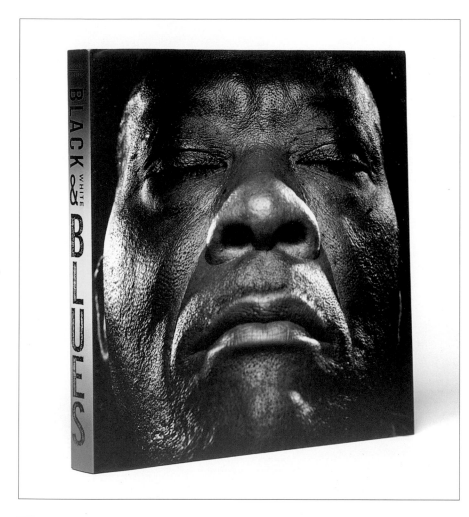

Merit/U.S.A.

BOOK
Black & White Blues
ART DIRECTOR *B. Martin Pedersen*
CREATIVE DIRECTOR *B. Martin Pedersen*
COPYWRITER *Tom Surowicz*
DESIGN *Samata Associates*
PHOTOGRAPHER *Marc Norberg*
PUBLISHER *Graphis U.S., Inc.*
STUDIO *Samata Associates*
CLIENT *Graphis U.S., Inc.*

ADDITIONAL AWARD

Merit
GRAPHIC DESIGN, BOOK, SPECIAL TRADE

Merit/South Africa

FOOD OR STILL LIFE
Fishing for Compliments
ART DIRECTOR *Joanne Thomas*
CREATIVE DIRECTOR *Ross Chowles*
COPYWRITER *Mark Winkler*
ILLUSTRATOR *Tobie Beele*
AGENCY *The Jupiter Drawing Room*
CLIENT *Compass Bakery*

Merit/U.S.A.

CORPORATE, SERIES
Value, Change, Markets, Regulation, Technology
ART DIRECTOR *Michael Gunselman*
DESIGNER *Michael Gunselman*
ILLUSTRATOR *Guy Billout*
CLIENT *New Jersey Resources Corporation*

Merit/U.S.A.

EDITORIAL
The Devil and Anne Rice
ART DIRECTOR *Fred Woodward*
DESIGNER *Geraldine Hessler*
ILLUSTRATOR *Joan Collier*
PUBLISHER *Wenner Media*
CLIENT *Rolling Stone*

Merit/U.S.A.

EDITORIAL
Speak of the Devil
ART DIRECTOR *Sam Shahid*
ILLUSTRATOR *Brad Holland*
CLIENT *Mirabella*

Merit/U.S.A.

EDITORIAL
Envy
ART DIRECTOR *Nancy J. Canfield*
CREATIVE DIRECTOR *Nancy J. Canfield*
EDITOR *Denis Gosselin*
ILLUSTRATOR *Steven Brodner*
CLIENT *Chicago Tribune Magazine*

Merit/U.S.A.

EDITORIAL

Movies Crime Fiction
ART DIRECTOR *Fred Woodward*
ILLUSTRATOR *Gary Kelley*
PUBLISHER *Wenner Media*
CLIENT *Rolling Stone*

Merit/U.S.A.

EDITORIAL

Jerry Garcia, 1942–1995
ART DIRECTOR *Fred Woodward*
ILLUSTRATOR *Milton Glaser*
PUBLISHER *Wenner Media*
CLIENT *Rolling Stone*

Merit/U.S.A.

EDITORIAL

Björk
ART DIRECTOR *Ted Keller*
CREATIVE DIRECTOR *Audrey Shachnow*
ILLUSTRATOR *Hanoch Piven*
CLIENT *The Village Voice*

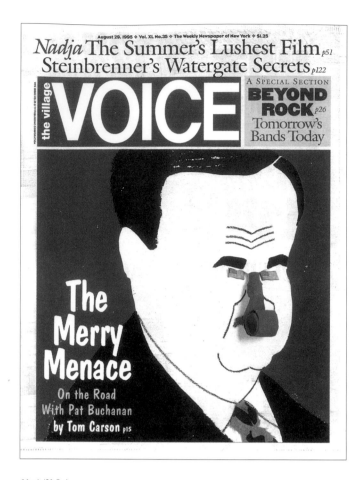

Merit/U.S.A.

EDITORIAL
The Merry Menace
ART DIRECTORS *Audrey Shachnow, Ted Keller*
CREATIVE DIRECTOR *Audrey Shachnow*
ILLUSTRATOR *Hanoch Piven*
CLIENT *The Village Voice*

(facing page)
Merit/U.S.A.

EDITORIAL
Against All Odds
ART DIRECTOR *Arthur Hochstein*
DESIGNER *Jane Frey*
ILLUSTRATOR *Brian Cronin*
PUBLISHER *Time Inc.*
CLIENT *Time Magazine*

Merit/U.S.A.

EDITORIAL
Unsafe
ART DIRECTOR *Ted Keller*
DESIGNER *Audrey Shachnow*
ILLUSTRATOR *Matt Mahurin*
CLIENT *The Village Voice*

Merit/U.S.A.

EDITORIAL
Jiang Steps Forward
ART DIRECTOR *Arthur Hochstein*
DESIGNER *Jane Frey*
ILLUSTRATOR *Robert Andrew Parker*
PUBLISHER *Time Inc.*
CLIENT *Time Magazine*

■ ECONOMIES

AGAINST ALL ODDS

Out of step in every way, the German economy remains the economic engine of the New Europe

By JAY BRANEGAN BRUSSELS

AMERICA, TAKE A BOW. THE REPUBLICANS are in and so is the verdict: the U.S. economic revival is the result of deep and liquid financial markets, low wages and taxes, freedom to hire and fire, weak unions, a booming service sector, a falling currency to boost exports, deregulation to eliminate burdensome red tape, and a quick-payoff stock-market culture that has forced companies to become lean and mean.

So what would you call a nation that didn't have any of these things? A basket case? No, you could call it Germany, one of the world's strongest economies. With a currency that towers over the deflated dollar, the country will experience strong growth this year: 2.9% overall, and a sizzling 9.0% in the former East Germany, Europe's fastest-growing region. Like the proverbial bumblebee that flouts the laws of aerodynamics yet still manages to fly, Germany continues to defy economic logic and keep buzzing along. Despite too much regulation, underdeveloped financial markets, workers with the highest wages and the shortest hours in the world, and faith in the outdated notion that a modern economy can make "things," Germany still delivers rising living standards to most of its citizens.

To be sure, the economy faces plenty of threats, from a too-strong currency to a too-costly welfare system. And there are plenty of experts who think a crash is imminent or inevitable. Even so, the latest edition of the annual world-competitiveness survey by the Switzerland-based International Institute for Management Development put Germany near the top six, second only to Switzerland in Europe. While the report said the two nations may be living off the past, Germany's future looks bright to businessmen polled by IMD; they predict it will still be a top competitor in 2030, along with Japan, the U.S. and China. "If you look at the long-term prospects for economic growth," says Ludolf von Wartenberg, general manager of the Federation of German Industry, "you have no choice but to favor Germany. We are the economic nucleus of the New Europe."

The discrepancy between practice and economic theory, especially the resolute free-market ideas championed by the U.S. and Britain, only highlights the fact that "Germany does not have Anglo-American capitalism," says Christopher Flockton of the University of Surrey in England. Perhaps most remarkable is that the German model of a "social-market economy" has survived, unbowed if a bit battered, the huge cost of absorbing the former East Germany, which sucks up close to $100 billion a year in subsidies and transfer payments. But while growth in the ex-communist economy is still not self-sustaining and unification will extract a high price for years to come, "the eastern German problem has more or less been tackled," says Horst Siebert, president of the Kiel Institute of World Economics, who predicts that the East will catch up to the poorer parts of the West by 2004.

BUMBLEBEE
Like the insect, the overregulated German economy defies rules of logic and just keeps buzzing along

Germany never could have withstood unification so well without tough-minded economic management, led by the central bank, which kept inflation at bay despite heavy spending to help the East. The federal government is reining in the bloated budget deficits of the early unification years with painful taxes, including a special 7.5% "solidarity" income-tax surcharge this year. Germany's household-savings rate is 11% of income—twice the American average—while its national debt, at 58% of gross domestic product, is lower than that of many major Western countries. Such sound macroeconomic policy can make up for many sins. But it has also had a down side: a soaring deutsche mark, which has leaped 20% against the dollar in the past year and a half, forcing up the prices of German exports even as industrial competitors such as the U.S., Italy and Britain are winning orders and drawing investment with weak currencies.

The mark's surge, only partly offset by August's central bank-led drop, has intensified the country's long-raging debate over how to maintain its competitiveness. Last week Daimler-Benz, Germany's largest industrial group, rocked the markets by announcing a $1 billion first-half loss, due largely to roiling currency markets, and repeated its vow made earlier this year to move production of components abroad as rapidly as possible. Although Mercedes car sales are booming, red ink is gushing from the Daimler-Benz Aerospace (DASA) division, which competes in an industry where most products are priced in dollars. Since more than 70% of DASA's costs are paid in marks, chairman Manfred Bischoff said, "we are worse hit by the dollar exchange rate than other industries in Germany." The strong currency is especially vexing because Germany is the world's second-largest exporter (after the U.S.) in absolute terms and far more dependent on exports than the U.S. or Japan.

Yet the historically robust mark is Germany's pride. It dampens inflation; keeps interest rates low; makes imports cheaper, especially oil; and helps German industries buy what they need abroad, be it computer chips or entire companies, as in chemical giant Hoechst's $7.1 billion purchase last May of America's Marion Merrell Dow. The damage from the mark's high value has been blunted because rival Japan suffers equally from a strong yen, and 40% of German exports go to countries whose currencies are formally tied to the mark through the European Monetary System—Holland, Belgium, Luxembourg, France, Austria plus strong-currency Switz-

TIME, SEPTEMBER 25, 1995 27

ILLUSTRATION *by* MATT MAHURIN

VOICE January 31, 1995

unsafe

Why Gay Men Are Having Risky Sex

BY MICHAEL WARNER

IN FLYBLOWN OFFICES near Union Square, men arrive, fill out a questionnaire, and take an HIV test. Then they sit down with a counselor to talk about their sex lives. Have you rimmed another man in the past three months? What were your thoughts when you asked him to fuck you?

These men are part of Project ACHIEVE, a study launched by the New York Blood Center over a year ago. Its main purpose is to identify a population for future vaccine trials. But in the process of interviewing over 450 gay men every three months, Project ACHIEVE is yielding probably the most reliable picture anyone has of risky sex among HIV-negative gay men in New York.

Investigators wanted to know: Have you had anal sex in the last three months, without using a condom, with another man who was either positive or of unknown status? The response was alarming enough: 20 per cent said they'd been fucked unsafely, 25 per cent that they had fucked someone else without a condom. But these figures show why statistics are misleading about sex. The interviewers discovered that many men were having partial or momentary insertions they did not consider to be "anal sex." When these encounters are included, the numbers rise to 30 per cent (fucked) and 38 per cent (fucking).

This is no random sample; the project recruits negative men, and involvement in it implies awareness of AIDS and a conscious gay or bi identity. If even these men are turning to unsafe sex, the numbers may be higher among gays as a whole.

Similar figures are coming in from other studies. One group of researchers, surveying gay men in 16 small cities from upstate New York to West Virginia and Montana, found that about a third of the men reported fucking without condoms in the previous two months. A soon-to-be-released study of young men in San Francisco found rates of new infection nearly four times what they were in 1987.

Researchers at Columbia University focused on younger gay men in New York. They recently projected that the infection rate among gay men is likely to remain stable for a long time, with a slight decline over 40 years. But they add that if the men they interviewed had underreported their unsafe contacts by as little as one per year, the disease will become even more widespread than it already is, with infection rates for some age groups rising to over 60 per cent in the next decade. The epidemic, they conclude, presents one of the classic disaster scenarios of game theory: An increase in unprotected sex may only slightly raise the risk for individuals (since that risk is high already), but if everyone were to take that gamble at once, infection rates would explode.

Studies such as these have led many to speak of a coming "second wave of AIDS." But we may only now be noticing what has been there for a long time: that safer sex is easier to adopt in the short run than to sustain. And we may be noticing this for a simple reason: Since the 1993 Berlin AIDS conference, which doused hopes for an imminent cure and dashed faith in drugs like AZT, it has become increasingly clear that the AIDS epidemic is likely to last for the rest of our lives. Slogans like "Be here for the cure!" are starting to ring hollow. Under these conditions, surrounded by positive friends and lovers, negative gay men face a new kind of challenge, one few outside our milieu can understand.

What makes some men fuck without protection when they know about the dangers, when they have access to condoms, when they have practiced safe sex for years, even when they have long involvement in AIDS activism—in short, when they "know better"? The question is shocking, incomprehensible. I know. When I had an unsafe encounter last winter, I spooked myself blank.

Afterward, I thought: good. Be afraid. Be very afraid. It will keep you safer in the future. I checked the calendar to see when three months would pass. (The body can take that long—some specialists say up to six months—to produce antibodies to HIV.) It seemed, to use America's Favorite Cliché, a wake-up call.

Some men think they're immune, because they're too young, or because they're not bottoms, or because the other guy just looks healthy. But I was not that kind of fool. The city's Department of Health has never bothered to do the studies that San Francisco has, but the best estimates are that about 50 per cent of gay men my age in New York have HIV. If you have only one partner, the chances are pretty good that he has it.

The odds occurred to me at the time, in a kind of instant calculus that was not even recognizable as thinking, much less as making a decision. The quality of consciousness was more like impulse shoplifting. When I talked to my best friends about the episode, I mentioned only how explosive the sex had been; not that it was unsafe. I recalled so much from what I had done that it seemed to be not my choice at all. A mystery, I thought. A monster did it.

The next time I saw the same man, we went back to his apartment again. I thought to myself to take precautions, but I could tell by the heady thrill that my monster was in charge. Even scarier than the risk itself was the realization that shame and fear had not been enough to keep me safe. Suddenly I had to think about why I wanted risky sex, knowing that the danger was part of the attraction. In the vast industry of AIDS education and prevention, I knew of nothing that would help me answer this question.

Safer sex has been around since 1983, and the basic priorities of prevention have changed little since then: Get the information out and make it attractive. But over and over I hear the same thing from prevention workers: information itself is no longer doing the job. "Everybody's grandmother knows about anal sex and latex," one activist said to me. The Minority Task Force on AIDS sends out health educators like Juan Olmedo to cruisy spots. They go to bars and cruising spots in parks to pass out condoms and lube. Their aim is to reach men who aren't immersed in gay culture, who spend little time in information-rich white neighborhoods. But most of the men they find there already know more than the basics of safe sex. Says Olmedo, "People look at the condoms we give them and say, 'Oh, I thought nonoxynol-9 isn't supposed to be good for you any more.' "

Prevention activists have gone back to the drawing board. They convened an HIV-prevention summit in Dallas last June, with federal help. As a follow-up, 16 prevention-related organizations in New York held an open community meeting on November 16. Not surprisingly, it produced more talk than action. Some of the talk is new: "harm reduction," "self-efficacy," "negotiated safety," "stages of change," "maintenance." But everyone seems to be waiting for a much bigger New Idea. "We need a prevention movement," says Mike Isbell, a policy director at Gay Men's Health Crisis. And no one yet knows what that would look like.

There is also plenty of disagreement about how "unsafe" should be defined. The biggest arguments involve oral sex. The San Francisco Young Men's Health Study is typical of much research in concluding that oral sex alone had "no association" with positivity. The Multicenter AIDS Cohort Study (MACS) found that oral transmission was "possible, albeit rare." Other specialists argue that these statistics may understate the risk by attributing some oral transmission to anal sex. At any rate, it has been documented that HIV can be spread through oral sex.

The debate gets very technical, but ultimately reduces to a question on which no one is an expert: How much risk is acceptable? For years the major prevention organizations—including GMHC—and government agencies said none. They classified oral sex without latex, even without ejaculation, as unsafe. By most accounts, a significant number of gay men—like most heterosexuals—have simply ignored the advice, or have set a goal of safer rather than absolutely safe sex.

On top of these disputes, government remains reluctant to fund research into infection trends, risk, and prevention. The now notorious *Sex in America* survey was initially conceived as research to help AIDS prevention; after its funding was gutted by congressional Republicans who feared a new Kinsey Report, the study was so reduced that it finally interviewed fewer than 50 gay or bisexual men. Content restrictions are still in place for some federally funded prevention; even materials for the summit in Dallas had to be vetted for anything that might "promote homosexuality."

In New York, cases among injection-drug users have outnumbered cases among men who have sex with men every year since 1989. Still, the state's AIDS Institute issued 160 prevention contracts for the year ending June 1994; only 16 targeted men who have sex with men. Some local governments, such as San Francisco, have tried to fill the gap. But in New York City, very little has been done to find out what gay men are actually doing or how widespread HIV might be.

Until recently, the future looked a little brighter. The Clinton administration had indicated a willingness to relax content restrictions. The Centers for Disease Control had launched a massive project to give community activists a say in funding priorities. And the New York AIDS Institute had announced a new grant of $2.45 million for preven-

VOICE January 31, 1995

Merit/U.S.A.

EDITORIAL, SERIES
Cyberporn
ART DIRECTOR *Arthur Hochstein*
DESIGNER *Thomas M. Miller*
ILLUSTRATOR *Matt Mahurin*
PRINTER *Time Inc.*
CLIENT *Time Magazine*

Merit/Canada

EDITORIAL
Le Monde
ART DIRECTORS *Teresa Fernandes, Kelly Doe*
DESIGNER *Teresa Fernandes*
ILLUSTRATOR *Frank Viva*
STUDIO *Viva Dolan Communications & Design*
CLIENT *The French Embassy*

Merit/U.S.A.

EDITORIAL, SERIES
VMA Book
ART DIRECTORS *Jeffrey Keyton, Stacy Drummond*
CREATIVE DIRECTORS *Jeffrey Keyton,*
Stacy Drummond
COPYWRITER *David Sandlin*
DESIGNER *David Sandlin*
ILLUSTRATOR *David Sandlin*
STUDIO *MTV Off-Air Creative*
CLIENT *MTV*

Merit/U.S.A.

EDITORIAL, SERIES
1995 A to Z
ART DIRECTOR *Robert Newman*
DESIGNERS *Florian Bachleda, Andrea Dunham*
ILLUSTRATORS *Paul Corio, S. B. Whitehead,
Bob Eckstein, Kaz, J. D. King, Steve Cerio,
Josh Gosfield, Anita Kunz, David Coulsen,
Barry Blitt, Drew Friedman, Ross MacDonald,
Kim Roberson, Calef Brown, Stephen Kroninger,
Hanoch Piven, Lynda Barry, Hungry Dog Studios,
Scott Menchin, Danny Hellman, Sue Coe,
Frances Jetter, David Cowles, Eric Palma,
Gary Panter, Mark Matcho, Michael Dougan*
CLIENT *Entertainment Weekly*

GOLD+SILVER MEDALISTS

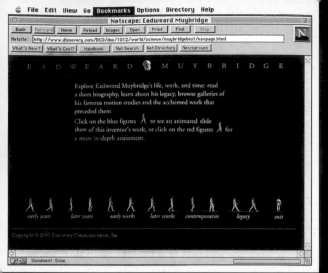

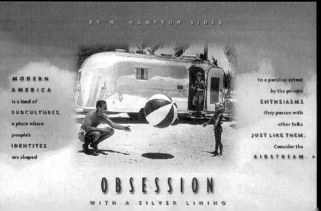

Silver Medalist/U.S.A.

PROMOTION
Throwing Apples at the Sun
ART DIRECTOR *Elliott Peter Earls*
CREATIVE DIRECTOR *Elliott Peter Earls*
COPYWRITER *Elliott Peter Earls*
DESIGNER *Elliott Peter Earls*
PHOTOGRAPHER *Elliott Peter Earls*
ILLUSTRATOR *Elliott Peter Earls*
PUBLISHER *The Apollo Program*
DISTRIBUTER *Emigre Inc.*
STUDIO *The Apollo Program*

CATALOGUE
Collection of Clip Art for Design Use
ART DIRECTORS *Charles S. Anderson,*
Paul Howalt
COPYWRITERS *Renee Valois, Lisa Pemrick*
DESIGNERS *Charles S. Anderson, Brian Smith,*
Darrell Eager, Andy Kingsbury, Tom Eslinger
ILLUSTRATION *CSA Archive*
CLIENT *CSA Archive*

PAINTINGS FROM THE COLLECTION OF JOSEPH H. HAZEN

Guided Tour

The Paintings

The Artists

Joseph H. Hazen

Timeline

Sotheby's

Credits   ? ○

Nature Morte Corbeille de
Fruits et Bouteille
Pablo Picasso

La Pipe
Fernand Léger

Jeune Fille au Bouquet
Fernand Léger

Femme au Costume Turc Dans
un Fauteuil
Pablo Picasso

Das Jüngste Gericht
Wassily Kandinsky

À Grenelle Buveuse
D'Absinthe
Toulouse-Lautrec

Maisons à Cagnes
Pierre-Auguste Renoir

Silver Medalist/U.S.A.

CONSUMER INFORMATION
Paintings from the Collection of Joseph H. Hazen
ART DIRECTION *Tsang Seymour Design*
CREATIVE DIRECTOR *Carley Roney*
COPYWRITER *Augustine Hope*
DESIGNERS *Patrick Seymour, Catarina Tsang*
PRODUCER *Sorel Husbands*
DIRECTOR *David Liu*
MUSIC *Miles Green*
PUBLISHER *Sotheby's*
STUDIO *Runtime*
AGENCY *Margeotes Fertitta & Partners*
CLIENT *Sotheby's*

Wassily Kandinsky
Das Jüngste Gericht, *1910*

Oil on canvas
49¾ x 28¾ in.
126.4 x 73 cm.

zoom in

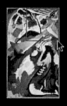

《   ?

1840   1875   1900   1925   1950   1975   1995

Wassily Kandinsky
Das Jüngste Gericht, *1910*

Oil on canvas
49¾ x 28¾ in.
126.4 x 73 cm.

About the Painting
About the Artist

DISTINCTIVE MERIT AWARDS

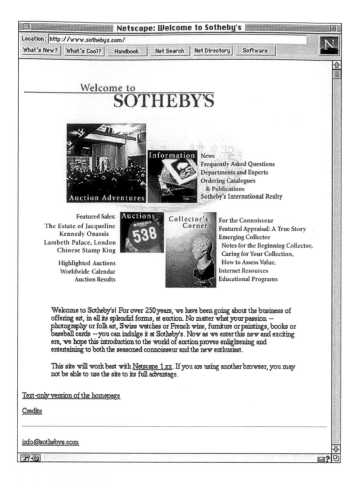

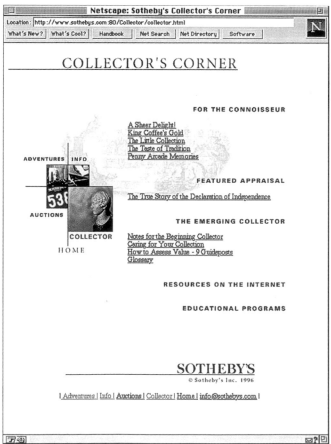

Distinctive Merit/U.S.A.

ADVERTISING

Sotheby's Web Site (http://www.sothebys.com)
ART DIRECTOR *Dindo Magallanes*
COPYWRITER *Augustine Hope*
DESIGNER *Nathalie De La Gorce*
PRODUCER *Sorel Husbands*
STUDIO *I/O 360 Digital Design*
AGENCY *Margeotes Fertitta & Partners*
CLIENT *Sotheby's*

Distinctive Merit/U.S.A.

PROMOTION
Maus Haus Demo
ART DIRECTOR *Bob Slote*
CREATIVE DIRECTOR *Bob Slote*
COPYWRITER *Jeff Davis*
DESIGNER *Bob Slote*
PHOTOGRAPHER *John Greenleigh*
PROGRAMMER *Robert Ramsden*
MUSIC *Greg Jones*
STUDIO *Maus Haus*
CLIENT *Maus Haus*

Distinctive Merit/U.S.A.

INTERNAL OR CORPORATE IMAGE
The Last Seven Years
ART DIRECTOR *John Avery*
CREATIVE DIRECTOR *Lee Clow*
COPYWRITERS *David Butler, Ken Siegel*
DESIGNER *Laurel Burden*
PHOTOGRAPHERS *Various*
ILLUSTRATOR *Hank Hinton*
PRODUCERS *Emma du Boisson, Amy Moorman*
STUDIO *@radical.media*
AGENCY *TBWA Chiat/Day Inc. Advertising*

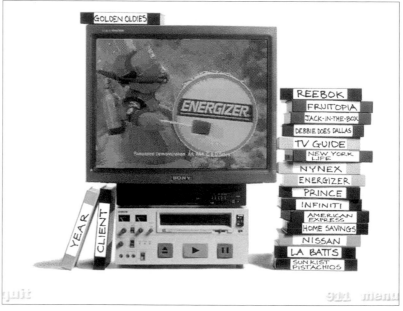

Consumer Product & Service
Apparel/Fashion
Gold

NIKE
Title: The Wall
Advertising Agency: Wieden & Kennedy, Amsterdam
Production Company: PYTKA, Venice
Editing Company: Red Car, Hollywood
Account Executive: Randy Browning
Creative Directors: Bob Moore, Warren Eakins
Copywriter: Bob Moore
Art Director: Warren Eakins
Agency Producers: Derek Ruddy, Jane Brimblecombe
Director: Joe Pytka
Cinematographer: Joe Pytka
Producer: Lilly Weingarten
Editor: Rob Watzke

1 of 113

MCJDF

Distinctive Merit/U.S.A.

PROMOTION
1995 Clio Awards
ART DIRECTOR *Jon Guffey*
CREATIVE DIRECTOR *Ed Price*
DESIGNER *Derek Lerner*
ILLUSTRATOR *Derek Lerner*
PRODUCER *Peter Natale*
DIRECTOR *Peter Natale*
PROGRAMMER *Andy Quay*
STUDIO *Hitachi Multimedia Systems*
CLIENT *Clio Awards*

MERIT AWARDS

Merit/U.S.A.

CATALOGUE
GRP Collection on CD-ROM
ART DIRECTOR *Mary Kay Fletcher*
INTERACTIVE ARCHITECT *Chris Bell*
EXECUTIVE PRODUCER *Larry Rosen*
STUDIO *N2K Inc.*
CLIENT *GRP Records Inc.*

The Art Directors Club is like a vigorous, enduring tree, its roots deeply embedded in advertising and graphic design, its branches, freshly leafed each year with new members and events, reaching around the world. Our mission encompasses the broad spectrum of visual communications—advertising, editorial and graphic design, illustration, photography, film, video, and new media.

During the past year, exhibitions in the ADC Gallery included The Best of "Rolling Stone", Art Center Inside/Out, *the premiere of* Dream Girls: 100 Years of Images of Women in Advertising *from the American Advertising Museum in Portland, Oregon, Wieden & Kennedy's Nike campaign, UNESCO's* The World's Most Memorable Poster, *and a members' art show.*

Outstanding speakers were Paul Capelli, David Carson, Laurel Cutler, Betty Friedan, John. C. Jay, Barbara Lippert, Matt Mahurin, Jay Maisel, Randall Rothenberg, John Waters, and Fred Woodward. Membership grew in every category. Our newsletter, "The ADC International Review," became a regular feature in GRAPHIS *magazine.*

Proceeds from the Annual help make these far-reaching activities and programs possible. To our members, colleagues, and friends, thank you for your continuing support.

—Myrna Davis
Executive Director, The Art Directors Club

Cooper Union
Robert Rindler, Dean

Jeffrey Piazza
Robert Reed
Irene Zborovsky

F.I.T.
Jerry McDaniel, Chairperson

Jamie Arvelo
Wendi Morrissey
Harry Wackett

New York City Technical College
Joel Mason, Department Chairperson

Silliam Heredia
Sean James
Dominique Thomas

Parsons School of Design
William Bevington, Department Chairperson

Cary Murnion
Catherine Tolson
Jany Tran

Pratt Institute
Joseph Roberts, Department Chairperson

Rebecca Krajcir
David Ormes
Richard Welch

Pratt Manhattan
Elliott Gordon, Department Chairperson

Debra Rapoport
Michael Skrzelowski

School of Visual Arts
Richard Wilde, Department Chairperson

Cybill Conklin
Michelle Keller
Chien Hua Lin

The Art Directors Scholarship Foundation, Inc. (formerly the Visual Communicators Education Fund, Inc.) was founded by members of the Art Directors Club to aid and encourage the development of talented students entering the profession of art direction. It awards scholarship funds annually to advertising and design schools, who then designate the students who are to share them. Seven schools in the metropolitan area were invited to participate this year. Department heads from each school selected the most deserving students entering their senior year of studies.

It was heartwarming to see the 20 student recipients gather at the Club for the awards presentation, anticipating their names being called as their families and friends stood proudly by their sides. The evening served as an opportunity for the students and department chairs to interact with each other and with Art Directors Club board members, including ADC President Carl Fischer.

All contributions to the ADSF are tax-deductible. In recent years, sources of funding have been entries in the Annual Exhibition, ticket proceeds from the Hall of Fame dinner, and net proceeds from the Holiday Book Fair. Our goal is to collaborate with ADC members and friends to develop new ideas and implement the ones we can to help aspiring art students fulfill their dreams.

—Richard MacFarlane
President, Art Directors Scholarship Foundation (1995–96)

Board of Directors

Carl Fischer,
Carl Fischer Photography, Inc.
President

Ruth Lubell,
Lubell Brodsky, Inc.
First Vice-President

Leslie Singer,
Singer Design
Second Vice-President

Richard Wilde,
School of Visual Arts
Secretary

Theodore Pettus,
Advertising Consultant
Treasurer

Bill Oberlander,
Kirshenbaum Bond & Partners
Assistant Secretary/Treasurer

Executive Committee

Mary Kay Baumann,
Hopkins Baumann

Robert Cox,
The Cox Group, Inc.

Jeffrey Keyton,
MTV Music Television

Jack Mariucci

Minoru Morita

Donna Weinheim,
BBDO

75th Annual Exhibition Committee

Kirshenbaum Bond & Partners
Designer, 75th Call for Entries

Dean Stefanides, Hampel/Stefanides
Chairperson, Advertising

Stephen Doyle, Drenttel Doyle Partners
Chairperson, Graphic Design

Rochelle Udell
Chairperson, New Media

Awards Presentation Evening

Bill Oberlander,
Kirshenbaum Bond & Partners
Chairperson

Dale & Company
Event Coordination

Kirshenbaum Bond & Partners
Invitation Design

Vera Steiner Design
Winners Book Design

ADC Publications, Inc.

Steven Brower
President

Seymour Chwast
Vice-President

Sara Giovanitti
Secretary/Treasurer

Paul Davis
Maureen Gleason
Andrew Kner
Jackie Merri Meyer
B. Martin Pedersen
Advisors

The Art Directors Club Newsletter

Seymour Chwast
Steven Brower
Sara Giovanitti
Editorial/Design Committee

Sharon Klahr
Editor

Re:Design, Inc.
Layout

Hall of Fame Selection Committee

Ed Brodsky
Chairperson

R. O. Blechman
Lou Dorfsman
Carl Fischer
Milton Glaser
George Lois
Ruth Lubell
Paul Rand
Richard Wilde
Henry Wolf

Art Directors Scholarship Foundation (formerly the Visual Communicators Education Fund)

Meg Crane,
Ponzi & Weil
President

Richard MacFarlane
First Vice-President

Dorothy Wachtenheim
Secretary

Diane Moore
Assistant Secretary

Peter Adler
Assistant Treasurer

Gladys Barton
William Brockmeier
David Davidian
David H. MacInnes
Walter Kaprielian

The Art Directors Club Committee Chairpersons

Robert S. Smith
Constitution

Richard Wilde
Exhibitions

Shinichiro Tora and
David Davidian
Membership

Martin Solomon
Portfolio Review

Ruby Miye Friedland
Speaker Events

Shinichiro Tora
Traveling Exhibition, Japan

Sara Giovanitti
Video Project

Advisory Board of Past Presidents

Allan Beaver
William Brockmeier
Ed Brodsky
William H. Buckley
David Davidian
Lou Dorfsman
Kurt Haiman
Jack Jamison
Walter Kaprielian
Andrew Kner
George Lois
John Peter
Eileen Hedy Schultz
Robert S. Smith
Karl Steinbrenner
William Taubin
Henry Wolf

The Art Directors Club Staff

Myrna Davis
Executive Director

Olga Grisaitis
Associate Director

Luis De Jesus
Director of Exhibitions

Antje Lenthe-Arcia
Competition Coordinator

Autherine Allison
Membership Administration

Rori DuBoff
Marketing and Development

Sharon Klahr
Public Relations

Glenn Kubota
Exhibition Associate

Gwendolyn Sai Leung
Competition Assistant

Romy Maldonado
Assistant Facilities Manager

Ann Schirripa
Receptionist

Margaret Busweiler
Raymond Hill
Waitstaff

Phillips Gold & Co. LLP
Accountants

BAI Group, Inc.
Financial Management

Marion Sroge, CAE
Management Consultant

Chase Bank
Banking

Special Thanks

Anderson Lithograph
Apple Computer
Interport
Matthew Outdoor Advertising
Mohawk Paper
Pentagram Design
Potlatch
Sheila Smith Design

United States

Adamec, Donald
Adamek, Tina
Adams, Gaylord
Adams, Steven
Adelman, Jim
Adler, Peter
Adorney, Charles S.
Ahlgrim, Dennis
Alikhani, Iraj Mirza
Allen, Heidi Flynn
Altschul, Charles
Anderson, Jack
Anderson, Joseph
Andreozzi, Gennaro
Angelo, David
Angotti, Adriana Amanda
Aragaki, Phyllis
Aronson, Herman
Babitz, Jeff
Bach, Robert O.
Baer, Charles H.
Baer, Priscilla
Baker, Eric
Ballance, Georgette F.
Ballister, Ronald
Barber, Ray
Barker, Floyd
Baron, Richard M.
Barrett, Elizabeth A.
Barrios, Juan Jose Tejeda
Barron, Don
Barthelmes, Robert
Barton, Gladys
Bauch, Nancy
Baumann, Mary K.
Beaver, Allan
Beckman, Arthur
Bender, Lois
Bennett, Edward J.
Bennett, George
Benson, Laurence Key
Berenter, Bill
Berg, John
Berger, Danielle
Berman, Matt
Bernard, Walter L.
Bertulis, Frank
Best, Robert
Bevington, William
Beylerian, George
Binzen, Barbara
Blank, Janet
Blank, Peter J.
Blattner, Robert
Blechman, R. O.
Blend, Robert H.
Bloch, Bruce
Bloom, Karen M.
Bluming, Joel
Boches, Edward
Bode, Robert
Bodenschatz, Sharon
Bogle, Susan L.
Bonavita, Donna
Booth, George Warren
Bourges, Jean
Bowman, Harold A.
Boyd, Doug
Braguin, Simeon
Brauer, Fred J.

Braverman, Al
Breslin, Lynn Dreese
Brockmeier, William
Brodsky, Ed
Brody, Ruth
Brody, Sam
Brooks, Adrienne
Brower, Steven
Brown, Beverly
Brown, George
Brown, Mark Delane
Bruce, Robert
Brugnatelli, Bruno E.
Buckley, William
Burkhardt, Ron
Butler, Bonnie
Bynum, Peter
Cadge, Bill
Canniff, Bryan G.
Caporimo, James
Cardillo, James
Carnase, Michael
Carnase, Thomas
Carruthers, Roy
Casado, Ralph
Castelli, Angelo
Catherines, Diana
Ceradini, David
Cernero, Tina
Chambers, Jean
Chang, Andrew
Chaplinsky, Anthony, Jr.
Chen, Jack C.
Chermayeff, Ivan
Cherry, John
Chester, Laurie
Chetter, Shirley E.
Christie, Alan
Chung, Shelly
Church, Stanley
Churchill, Traci
Chwast, Seymour
Clapps, John
Clark, Herbert H.
Clarke, Bud
Clarke, James V.
Clemente, Thomas F.
Cline, Mahlon
Cohen, Joel
Cohen, Peter
Coll, Michael
Conner, Elaine
Connors, Catherine
Cook, M. Deidre
Corey, Lee
Cotler, Sheldon
Cotler-Block, Susan
Cox, Phyllis Richmond
Cox, Robert
Craig, James Edward
Crane, Meg
Crane, Susan J.
Cronan, Michael
Crossley, Gregory
Crozier, Bob
Crysdale, Erin
Curry, Christine
Cutler, Ethel R.
Davidian, David
Davis, Barbara Vaughn
Davis, Herman

Davis, Paul B.
Davis, Philip
Davis, Randi B.
Davis, Theodore M.
De Castro, Victor
Defrin, Bob
DeGregorio, Tony
Del Sorbo, Joe
Demoney, Jerry
Deutsch, David
DeVito, Frank
DiComo, Charles
Dietrich, Carol
DiFate, Vincent
Dignam, John
Divincenzo, Dennis
Dorfsman, Louis
Dorian, Marc
Douglas, Kay Elizabeth
Drenttel, William
D'Rozario, Chris
Drucker, Rina
Drucks, Alisha
Dubiel, Ann
Duffy, Donald H.
Dunn, Faith
Eckman Silverstein, Heidi
Eckstein, Bernard
Edgar, Peter
Edwards, Geoffrey T.
Egner, May S.
Eidel, Zeneth
Eisenman, Nina
Eisenman, Stanley
Eisner, Robert
Ellis, Judith
Endewelt, Jack
Epstein, David
Epstein, Lee
Ericson, Shirley
Ermoyen, Suren
Fable, Kathleen Quinn
Fama, Joseph
Fanno, George
Faucher, Mari
Fedele, Gene
Federico, Gene
Fenga, Michael
Ferrell, John
Ferrell, Megan
Fery, Guy
Filson, Kristin
Finelli, Douglas
Fink, Len
Fiorentino, Lou
Fiorenza, Blanche
Fischer, Carl
Flock, Donald P.
Fraioli, John
Frankfurt, Stephen O.
Franklin, Richard
Freeland, Bill
Freyss, Christina
Friedland, Ruby Miye
Frith, Michael K.
Frost, Oren
Fuchs, Aaron
Fujita, Neil
Fury, Leonard W.
Gabrich, Michelle
Gage, Robert

Galioto, Rosemarie
Gallo, Danielle
Galowitz, Cara
Gardner, Bert
Gardner, Hope
Garlanda, Gino
Gavasci, Alberto Paolo
Geissbuhler, Steff
Gennarelli, Charles
George, Jeffrey E.
George, Robert J.
Geranmayeh, Vida
Germakian, Michael
Gialleonardo, Victor
Gibson, Kurt
Ginsberg, Frank C.
Giovanitti, Sara
Giraldi, Bob
Glaser, Milton
Gleason, Maureen R.
Gliserman, Tom
Gluckman, Eric
Gobe, Marc
Goen, Tama Alexandrine
Goettel, Manfred
Gold, Bill
Goldberg, Irwin
Goldfarb, Roz
Goldsmith, Gary
Goodfellow, Joanne
Goodman, Lee
Goss, Jeff
Govoni, Jean
Grace, Roy
Greenberg, Karen L.
Greiss, Abe S.
Greiss, Adam
Gribben, Chip
Griffin, Jack
Grisaitis, Olga
Groglio, Glen P.
Growick, Phillip
Grubshteyn, Raisa
Grunther, Ira Alan
Gruppo, Nelson
Guild, S. Rollins
Guzman, George
Guzman, John
Hack, Robert
Hagel, Bob
Haiman, Kurt
Halter, Lisa
Halvorsen, Everett
Hama, Sho
Hamilton, Edward
Hamilton, Frances M.
Haney, David
Hartwell, Alan
Hassel, Barry
Hasselbach, Suzan
Hayes, Connie
Heit, Amy
Heller, Steven
Hensley, Randall
Herche, Maureen
Herman, Joshua David
Hess, Jannike
Hill, Chris
Hillsman, William G.
Hirsch, Peter
Hively, Charles

Hoashi, Jitsuo
Hochhalter, Gordon
Hoffenberg, Harvey
Hoffmann, Nancy
Hoffner, Marilyn
Holland, Barry K.
Holtz, Jennifer
Horn, Steve
Horowitz, Julia L.
Houser, William David
Howard, Paul
Hoyt, Debra Morton
Hutter, Brian
Igarashi, Takenobu
Incorvaia, Vito
Ishii, Skip K.
Jablonski, Andrew
Jacobs, Harry
Jaffee, Lee Ann
Jalbert, Ted
Jamison, John E.
Janerka, Andrzej
Jerina, Patricia
Jervis, Karen C.
Jones, Karen C.
Jubert, Joanne
Kalayjian, Vasken
Kalish, Nicki
Kanai, Kiyoshi
Kaprielian, Walter
Kay, Leslie
Kay, Norman S.
Kay, Woody
Keane, Ronan J.
Keller, Ted
Kelly, Brian M.
Kenny, Alice
Kent, Nancy
Kenzer, Myron W.
Kessler, Linda
Keyton, Jeffrey
Kiel, Ronald
Kier, Ellen Sue
Kim, Bok-Young
Klein, Hedy
Klein, Judith
Klyde, Hilda Stanger
Kner, Andrew
Knier, Maria
Knoepfler, Henry O.
Koepke, Gary
Kohler, Denis
Komai, Ray
Korpijaakko, Kati
Krauss, Oscar
Kurtz, Mara
Kurz, Anna
La Barge, Robert
Lafferty-Dimmick, Christine
La Marca, Howard
Lamarque, Abril
Lanotte, Michael
La Petri, Anthony
La Rochelle, Lisa A.
Larstanna, Lawrence
Lassi, Mark
Lau, Pearl
Lawrence, Marie Christine
Lazzarotti, Sal
Lebeck, Steven W.
Lebron, Michael A.

Lee, Ching
Lee, David
Lee, Edwin
Leeds, Gregory B.
Leon, Maru
LeVesque, Shawn
Levine, Peter
Levine, Rick
Liberman, Alexander
Lindeberg, Johan
Lloyd, Douglas
LoGuzzo, Diana
Lois, George
Lo Monaco, Jon Paul
Lopez, Antonio
Lopez Luna, Dennis
Lott, George
Lubell, Ruth
Lucci, John
Luger, Diane
Luria, Robert A.
Lurin, Larry
Lyon, Robert W., Jr.
Lyons, Michael J.
MacFarlane, Richard
MacInnes, David H.
Magdoff, Samuel
Magnani, Lou
Maloney, Margaret F.
Mancino, Anthony
Mann, Edward Marc
Marcellino, Jean
Marcus, Eric
Marcus, Helen
Margolis, David R.
Mariucci, Jack
Marquez, Andrea
Mason, Joel
Mayer, Susan
Mayhew, Marce
Mazzeo, Joan
Mazzeo, Michael
McCaffery, Bill
McErlain, Stephen J.
McGreevy, Nick
Mednick, Scott A.
Meher, Karen L.
Meher, Nancy A.
Merkley, Parry
Messier, Nadine G.
Metzdorf, Lyle
Metzner, Jeffrey
Meyer, Jackie Merri
Meyn, Robbie
Miano, Thomas A.
Middendorf, Frances
Milbauer, Eugene
Miller, Larry
Milligan, John
Minor, Wendell
Miranda, Michael
Mitsch, Steven
Mizerek, Leonard
Mizrahi, Marise
Modenstein, Sam
Mok, Clement
Montebello, Joseph
Montone, Ken
Moore, Diane
Moore, Richard
Moore, Robert

Moran, Paul
Morita, Minoru
Morooka, Mami
Morris, Ann
Morris, Leonard
Morrison, William R.
Morton, Amy
Morton, Thomas
Moses, Louie
Moshier, David
Moss, Tobias
Moyer, Dale
Mueller, Robert
Muench, Allison
Myrka, Mariaelena
Needleman, Robert S.
Nelson, Daniel
Nessim, Barbara
Newman, Robert
Newman, Susan
Ng, William
Nichols, Mary Ann
Nichols, Raymond
Nissen, Joseph
Nix, Michael
Noether, Evelyn C.
Norman, Barbara J.
Noszagh, George
November, David
Oberlander, Bill
O'Connor, Sandra
O'Donnell, Lisa
Okladek, John
Olson, Stephen Scott
Onatra, Ivan
Ortiz, Jose Luis
Osuna, Susan
Oswald, Mindy
Ovryn, Nina
Owett, Bernard S.
Paccione, Onofrio
Paganucci, Robert
Palancio, John A.
Palecek, Jane
Pallas, Brad
Palleja, Marlow
Panetta, Susan
Pascoe Fischbein, Kathleen
Paul, Art
Pedersen, B. Martin
Peduto, Patrick
Peeri, Ariel
Perone, Christopher C.
Perrotti, Tony
Perry, Harold A.
Peslak, Victoria I.
Peter, John
Peterson, Christos
Petrocelli, Robert
Petrone, Chris
Petrucelli, Daniel
Pettus, Theodore D.
Phelps, Steward
Philiba, Allan
Phipps, Alma
Pioppo, Ernest
Pliskin, Robert
Quackenbush, Michael
Queener, Charles W.
Querze, Elissa
Raboy, Dick

Ramm, Diddo
Rand, Paul
Raphan, Benita
Razaei, Ladan
Reed, Samuel
Reid, Kendrick
Reinke, Herbert
Reitzfeld, Robert
Renaud, Joseph Leslie
Reshen, Amber
Reshen, Patricia J.
Rhodes, David
Richards, Stan
Richert, Ruthann
Rietschel, Barbara
Rigelhaupt, Gail
Riley, Elizabeth T.
Ritter, Arthur
Robbins, Nadine
Roberts, Barbara B.
Roberts, Kenneth
Robinson, Bennett
Rockwell, Harlow
Rodney, Drew Ann
Rohall, Susan
Romano, Andy
Romero, Javier
Rosenthal, Bobbi
Rosner, Charlie
Rosner, Eric
Ross, Andrew
Ross, Mark
Ross, Richard J.
Rossiello, Suzanna M.
Roston, Arnold
Roth, Tom
Rothrock, Salleigh
Rottenberg, Eta
Rousseau, Ann Marie
Rowe, Alan
Rubenstein, Mort
Rubin, Randee
Rubinsky, Shelley
Ruis, Thomas P.
Russell, Henry N.
Russo, Albert
Russo, Deborah
Russo, John
Ruther, Don
Ruzicka, Thomas
Sachs, Joseph C.
Sacklow, Stewart
Saido, Tatsuhiro
Saito, Moriyoshi
Saks, Robert
Sala, Loretta M.
Saladino, Peter
Salpeter, Robert
Salser, James
Saltz, Ina
Salzburg, Diana
Samerjan, George
Sauer, Hans
Sayles, John
Saylor, David J.
Scali, Sam
Scarfone, Ernest
Schaefer, Peter J.
Schaffner, Sue
Schenk, Roland
Scher, Paula

Schermer, Susan
Scheuer, Glenn
Schmalz, Paul
Schmidt, Klaus F.
Schnaufer, Joyce
Schrager-Laise, Beverly
Schrijver, Robert W.
Schultz, Eileen Hedy
Schwartzman, Julie
Scott, Robert A.
Sculco, Georgina
Seabrook, Alexis
Seabrook, William, III
Seagram, Blair
Sears, Amy
Segal, Leslie
Segerstrom-Sato, Rebecca
Seidler, Sheldon
Sellers, John L.
Serres-Cousine, Nicolas
Shachnow, Audrey
Sheehan, John
Silverstein, Louis
Simmons, Robert
Simpson, Milton
Singer, Leslie
Sirowitz, Leonard
Sisman, Lucy
Skolnik, Jack
Smith, Bronson
Smith, Carol Lynn
Smith, Robert S.
Smith, Sheila
Smith, Virginia
Sobel, Edward
Solomon, Martin
Solomon, Russell L.
Solsburg, Mark
Sosnow, Harold
Spangler, Lee
Spears, Harvey
Spegman, Jim
Stackell, Isaac
Stamatopoulos, Nancy
Stansfield, Shelly Laroche
Stanton, Mindy Phelps
Stapelfeldt, Karsten
Starzec, David M.
Steck, Lynn
Stefanides, Dean
Steigelman, Robert
Steinberg, Jane
Steinbrenner, Karl
Steiner, Vera
Stern, Barrie
Stewart, Daniel E.
Stewart, Gerald
Stone, Bernard
Storch, Otto
Storrs, Lizabeth
Strauss, Hilary
Strizver, Ilene
Strosahl, William
Sullivan, Bob
Sullivan, Pamela
Sullivan, Sharon
Swatek, Randall
Sweeny, Ken
Tansman, Jo Ann
Tartaglia, Frank
Tasch, Alex

Taschetti, Vincent
Tashian, Melcon
Taubin, William
Tauss, Jack G.
Tekushan, Mark
Tenne, George
Tessler, Jonathan
Tharp, Louis
Thomas, Steve
Throckmorton, Paula
Todd, Robert
Toland, Toni
Tora, Shinichiro
Torzecua, Marlena
Towners, John C.
Traina, Jean
Trasoff, Victor
Trombley, Michele
Trowbridge, Susan B.
Tsiavos, Anastasios
Tully, Joseph P.
Twomey, John D.
Udell, Rochelle
Ultimo, Clare
Urrutia, Frank
Velsor, James
Verdia, Haydee N.
Vischo-Gallagher, Amy
Vitale, Frank A.
Vogler, David L.
Von Collande, Constance
Von Schreiber, Barbara
Vuong, Thuy
Wachtenheim, Dorothy
Wajdowicz, Jurek
Wallace, Joseph O.
Walsh, Linda
Warren, Allison
Waxberg, Larry
Weber, Denise A.
Weber, Jessica
Weber, John
Weinheim, Donna
Weisel, Mimi
Weiss, Marty
Weithas, Art
West, Robert Shaw
Wilde, Richard
Williams, Rodney C.
Witalis, Rupert
Wittenburg, Ross
Wolf, Henry
Wolf, Jay Michael
Wollner, Michael Kjell
Wong, Nelson
Wong, Robert H.
Wood, Paula
Woods, Laura
Woodward, Fred
Wouters, Bert C.
Yeap, Min Ping
Yoffe, Ira
Yonkovig, Zen
Young, Frank
Young, Shawn
Zabowski, Bill
Zaino, Carmile S.
Zanis, Leo
Zator, Lynette Marie
Zeitsoff, Elaine
Zhukov, Maxim

Zielinski, Mikael T.
Zlotnick, Bernie
Zollinger, Lisa A.
Zwiebel, Alan

Argentina
Rymberg, Gustavo Demian
Stein, Guillermo

Australia
Dilanchian,
   Katheryn Davidian
Lee, Lisa

Austria
Demner, Mariusz Jan
Klein, Helmut
Lammerhuber, Lois
Merlicek, Franz

Belgium
Lemaitre, Pascal

Bermuda
Smith, Paul

Brazil
Miranda, Oswaldo
Petit, Francesc
Vanzo, Ronaldo Predebon

Canada
Davidson, Rob
Lacroix, Jean-Pierre
Tolpin, Larry
Power, Stephanie

Czech Republic
Jasanska, Lenka

Denmark
Simonsson, Dres

Finland
Bergqvist, Harald
Manty, Kirsikka

Germany
Arke, Rainer
Ernsting, Thomas
Hebe, Reiner
Koch, Claus
Kohl, Chris
Leu, Olaf
Meier, Erwin
Mojen, Friederike
Mojen, Ingo
Nebl, Lothar
Pham-Phu, Oanh
Prommer, Helga
Schneider, Frank
Spiekerman, Erik
Todd, Samy J.

Greece
Konstantinidis, Vangelis

Hong Kong
Chan, Elman
Cheung, Eddy
Chuen, Tommy Li Wing
Jacobs, Byron
McCudden, Colleen

India
Pereira, Brendan

Ireland
Helme, Donald

Israel
Reisinger, Dan

Italy
Fabiani, Titti
Guidone, Silvano
Stoppini, Luca

Japan
Akiyama, Takashi
Aoba, Masuteru
Aotani, Hiroyuki
Asaba, Katsumi
Baba, Yuji
Brenoe, Peter
Fukushima, Takenobu
Furumura, Osamu
Hirai, Akio
Ichihashi, Ken
Ito, Yasuyuki
Iwaki, Michio
Iwata, Toshio
Izumiya, Masaaki
Kamijyo, Takahisa
Kaneko, Hideyuki
Kashimoto, Satoji
Katsui, Mitsuo
Kawamoto, Fumio
Kida, Yasuhiko
Kitazawa, Takashi
Kiyomura, Kunio
Kobayashi, Pete
Kojima, Ryohei
Kotani, Mitsuhiko
Krakower, Pepie
Maeda, Kazuki
Matsui, Keizo
Matsumoto, Arata
Matsumoto, Takaharu
Matsumoto, Takao
Matsunaga, Shin
Matsuura, Iwao
Miyasaka, Kuniaki
Mizutani, Koji
Morimoto, Junichi
Nagatomo, Keisuke
Nakahara, Michio
Nakahara, Yasuharu
Nakamura, Makoto
Nakazawa, Jun
Nomura, Sadanari
Nozue, Toshiaki
Oba, Yoshimi
Ohama, Yoshitomo
Ohashi, Toshiyuki
Ohtaka, Takeshi
Okada, Syuji
Okamoto, Shigeo

Okuizumi, Motoaki
Okumura, Akio
Okura, Kyoji
Omori, Shigeshi
Oseko, Nobumitsu
Saito, Toshiki
Sakamoto, Hiroki
Sakamoto, Ken
Sakane, Susumu
Shiraiwa, Tomiyasu
Suzuki, Yasuo
Suzuki, Zempaku
Takahama, Yutaka
Takanokura, Yoshinori
Takeo, Shigeru
Tanabe, Masakazu
Tanaka, Ikko
Tanaka, Soji George
Tomita, Ben
Tomoeda, Yusaku
Uejo, Norio
Usami, Michihiro
Watanabe, Masato
Watanabe, Yoshiko
Yamamoto, Akihiro H.
Yamamoto, Yoji
Yoshida, Masayuki

Korea
Ahn, Dan
Chae, Ki Young
Chang, Don Ryun
Chung, Joon
Chung, Joy
Han, Kwang Soo
Hwang, Jung-Suk
Jang, Jung Hak
Kang, Yeong-Joon
Kim, Chul Han
Kim, Doo Hwang
Kim, Duk Kyu
Kim, Een Seok
Kim, Hae Kyung
Kim, Hyun
Kim, Kwang Kyu
Kwon, Hyun Chang
Lee, Jae Chul
Paik, Nack Mi
Park, Dong Hee
Park, Seung Soon
Park , Woo Duk
Rhee, Sang-Chol
Seo, Woon-Suk
Sohn, Hye-Won
Yoon, Woong-Jin

Malaysia
Ho, Veronica
Hoi, Tatsun
Lee, Yee Ser Angie

Mexico
Beltran, Felix
Flores, Luis Efren Ramirez

Monaco
Turello, Amedeo M.

The Netherlands
Brattinga, Pieter
Dovianus, Joep
Van Lotringen, Walter

Philippines
Abrera, Emily A.

Portugal
Aires, Eduardo

Singapore
Aitchison, Jim
Eng, Chiet-Hsuen

Spain
Trias Folch, Jose M.

Sweden
Yngrodottir, Sigrum

Switzerland
Bundi, Stephan
Dallenbach, Bilal
Jaggi, Moritz
Küste, Helmut
Schuetz, Dominique Anne
Syz, Hans G.
Welti, Philipp

United Kingdom
Baker, Jim
Stothard, Celia
Weidema, Karin

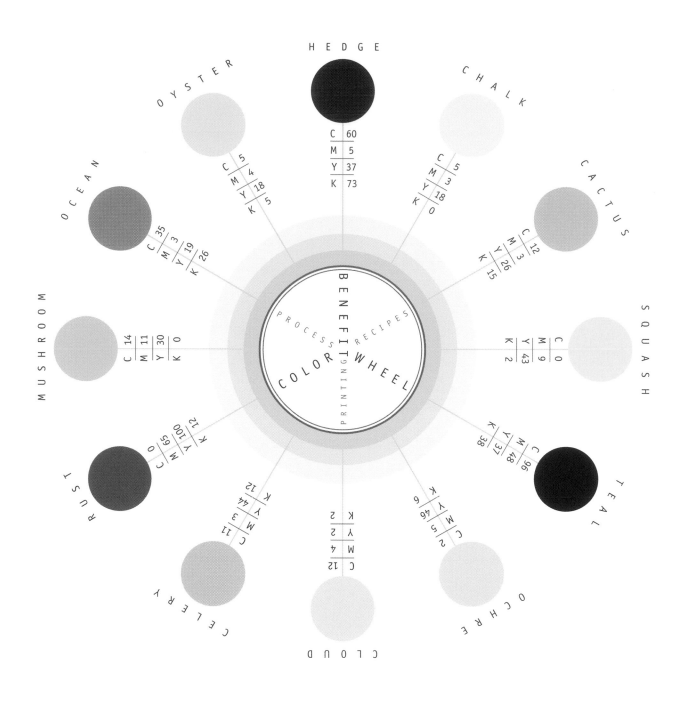

HEDGE

C 60
M 5
Y 37
K 73

OYSTER

C 5
M 4
Y 18
K 5

CHALK

C 5
M 3
Y 18
K 0

OCEAN

C 35
M 3
Y 19
K 26

CACTUS

C 12
M 3
Y 26
K 15

MUSHROOM

C 14
M 11
Y 30
K 0

SQUASH

C 0
M 9
Y 43
K 2

RUST

C 0
M 65
Y 100
K 12

TEAL

C 96
M 48
Y 37
K 38

CELERY

C 11
M 3
Y 44
K 12

OCHRE

C 2
M 5
Y 46
K 6

CLOUD

C 12
M 4
Y 2
K 2

BENEFIT
PROCESS / RECIPES
COLOR WHEEL
PRINTING

TO READ, PLACE LOUPE HERE

PLATINUM

PLATINUM DESIGN, INC.

14 West 23rd St., New York, NY 10010   tel: 212-366-4000   fax: 212-366-4046   http://www.interport.net/~platinum

Key design element.

Lindenmeyr Munroe
Paper Merchants · Division of Central National-Gottesman Inc.

Corporate Office

Three Manhattanville Road
Purchase, NY 10577-2110
914 696 9000   Fax 914 696 9352

Mid-Atlantic

301 Veterans Boulevard
Rutherford, NJ 07070-2564
201 935 2900   212 752 3200
800 631 0193   Fax 201 935 5264
Sales Fax 800 637 4597

1845 New Highway, P.O. Box 6033
Farmingdale, NY 11735-0764
516 293 0505   718 520 1586
Fax 516 293 2108

3300 Horizon Drive
King of Prussia, PA 19406-2650
610 239 9100   800 232 8333
Fax 610 239 9334

3041 Industry Drive
Lancaster, PA 17603-4025
717 393 2111   800 222 4908
Fax 717 393 0948

9630 Gerwig Lane
P.O. Box 2009
Columbia, MD 21046-1519
410 312 7477   800 494 3433
Fax 410 312 7420

New England

14 Research Parkway
P.O. Box 5011
Wallingford, CT 06492-7511
203 294 1141   800 842 8480
Fax 203 294 1023
Sales Fax 800 890 3115

240 Forbes Boulevard
Mansfield, MA 02048
508 339 6161   800 343 7782
Fax 508 339 1996
Sales Fax 800 670 0037

One Second Street, Box 3637
Peabody, MA 01961-3637
617 595 4006   800 237 2737
Fax 508 531 4478
Sales Fax 508 977 9713
or 800 409 1506

468 Pepsi Road
Manchester, NH 03109-5303
603 627 1320   800 462 1911
Fax 603 627 4816

510 County Road
Westbrook, ME 04092
207 874 9000   800 442 1390
Fax 207 874 0653

neth Willardt ph:212 242 2223 fx:212 242 2224 www.i3i.com/kwp/kwhome.html

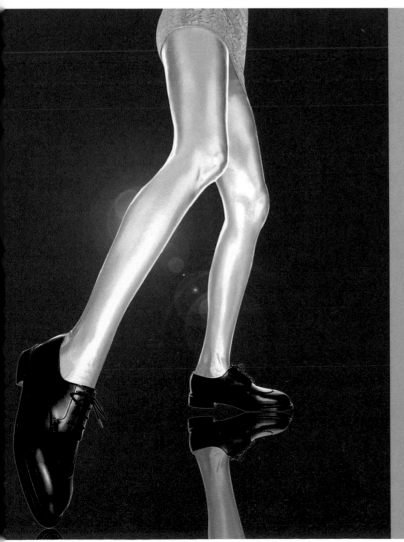

brodock

THE BEST PLACE TO GO FOR *waterless* PRINTING.

800-765-3536

Great idea made better.

MANHATTAN MODEL SHOP

Miniatures • Full Scale Sets • Special Effects • Product Comps and Prototypes
40 Great Jones St., NY, NY 10012, 212-473-6312, Fax 212-979-9841

HAVE YOU SEEN OUR YEARBOOK?

PORTFOLIO CENTER

The School for Art Direction, Copywriting, Graphic Design,
Illustration, & Photography

1-800-255-3169

ATLANTA
PORTFOLIOC@AOL.COM

GREAT PRINTING?
GREAT PRE-PRESS?
IN MIDTOWN NYC?
CHECK IT OUT!

WALBERN PRESS

406 WEST 31ST STREET, NEW YORK CITY 10001   564.0444   FAX 629.4386